Praise for *Beyond the National Interest*

"A thoughtful and wide-ranging survey of the UN's contribution to peace-keeping and world politics after the Cold War. Jean-Marc Coicaud's study effectively combines the nuanced perspective of a former UN insider with the philosophic analysis of a disciplined scholar. I recommend it whole-heartedly to both UN practitioners and the students and professors who follow UN affairs."

—Michael W. Doyle, Columbia University, and
former assistant secretary-general, United Nations

"UN peacekeeping has become one of the central weapons for dealing with complex post-conflict situations in the international community's arsenal. UN peacekeeping is not the right tool for every job, but when our key prin-ciples are observed—not trying to keep peace where there's no peace to keep, ensuring that the peacekeepers accompany a political process, not substitute for one—the blue helmets have proved time and again that they are an effective, flexible and cost efficient mechanism for addressing some of the worlds most difficult crises. Coicaud's Beyond the National Interest *rep-resents a valuable contribution to the important debate on the future of UN peacekeeping."*

—Jean-Marie Guéhenno, UN Under-Secretary-General
for Peacekeeping Operations

"Coicaud's rare combination of theoretical insight and practical experience sheds much light on one of the most crucial problems of world order: the legitimacy of international institutions."

—Pierre Hassner, Centre d'Etudes et
de Recherches Internationales, Sciences Po

"In Beyond the National Interest, *Jean-Marie Coicaud cogently analyzes the weak position of the United Nations Secretary-General, faced with divisive great power interests and the enormous power of the United States. He appeals passionately for multilateralism as a system of legitimacy that could help to create a growing practice of what he calls international soli-darity. His voice is one that America should hear."*

—Robert O. Keohane, Woodrow Wilson School of Public
and International Affairs, Princeton University

BEYOND THE NATIONAL INTEREST

BEYOND THE NATIONAL INTEREST

THE FUTURE OF UN PEACEKEEPING AND MULTILATERALISM IN AN ERA OF U.S. PRIMACY

JEAN-MARC COICAUD

UNITED STATES INSTITUTE OF PEACE PRESS
Washington, D.C.

United States Institute of Peace
1200 17th Street NW
Washington, DC 20036

First published 2007

Printed in the United States of America

The paper used in this publication meets the minimum requirements of American National Standard for Information Sciences—Permanence of Paper for Printed Library Materials, ANSI Z39.48-1984.

Library of Congress Cataloging-in-Publication Data

Coicaud, Jean-Marc.
    Beyond the national interest : the future of UN peacekeeping and multilateralism in an era of U.S. primacy / Jean-Marc Coicaud.
      p. cm.
    Includes bibliographical references and index.
    ISBN-13: 978-1-60127-007-8 (pbk. : alk. paper)
    ISBN-10: 1-60127-007-0 (pbk. : alk. paper)
    ISBN-13: 978-1-60127-008-5 (hardcover : alk. paper)
    ISBN-10: 1-60127-008-9 (hardcover : alk. paper)
    1. Security, International. 2. United Nations. 3. Peace-building. 4. National security—International cooperation. 5. United Nations—United States. I. Title.
    JZ4971.C65 2007
    341.23—dc22
                              2007020376

To Susie and my parents

CONTENTS

CONTENTS

Foreword

S peaking before the forty-second session of the United Nations General Assembly on September 21, 1987, Ronald Reagan put forth his vision of the world's future, laying out what he character-ized as his "fantasy": "In our obsession with antagonisms of the moment, we often forget how much unites all the members of humanity....I occa-sionally think how quickly our differences worldwide would vanish if we were facing an alien threat from outside this world." Although the inter-national scene has changed markedly since Reagan made this remark, he expresses a simple truth about the human condition: man is often so focused on his own self-interests he forgets mankind's common interests. This truth informs the core of this illuminating volume, *Beyond the National Interest: The Future of UN Peacekeeping and Multilateralism in an Era of U.S. Primacy.*

Author and scholar Jean-Marc Coicaud broadly examines a singu-larly pressing question about the state of global affairs that is inextricably connected to this truth: what happened to international peacekeeping and humanitarian interventions? More specifically, how does one explain the continued adherence to narrow national interests among democratic countries in the face of compelling needs to intervene in and manage the profusion of international crises? Such questions are particularly vexing today when considering the growing number of conflicts and looming humanitarian disasters around the world. Although local communities and strong nations shape a response to a domestic crisis—based on bonds emanating from civil society, governmental agencies, and a common sense of identity—the international community's bonds are far more tenuous. Indeed, the established democracies of the West have found it difficult to live up to a central tenet of modern democratic culture: the extension and promotion of progress and human rights through interna-tionalism and moral activism.

Coicaud provides a robust exploration of these and related issues, offering original and keen insights into the limitations of the United Nations as a peacekeeping organization and the mixed results of the West's peacekeeping activities in the immediate post–Cold War period. He states, for example, that the multilateralism witnessed during this period, such as in the form of UN and NATO peacekeeping operations, was à la carte and selective. This multilateralism was based more often on the national interests of Security Council members than on any real sense of internationalism or moral activism.

Perhaps the volume's most significant and relevant findings lie in response to the prescriptive question he asks in its concluding chapter: how can the international community enhance its sense of solidarity and responsibility—and amplify the international rule of law—so that early and effective multilateral peacekeeping and humanitarian interventions might be encouraged in the future? In response to this question, Coicaud makes a number of highly informed recommendations, many of which relate directly to the United States. As he argues, "The difficulty for U.S. multilateral relations is that the superpower status of America generates a disequilibrium that encourages the United States to focus on national interest at the expense of the socially principled dimension of multilateralism." With this understanding—and with the understanding that morality has never trumped the national interest as the animating force of any Western democracy's foreign policy—he appeals for a reframing and reformulating of the U.S. national interest to make it more inclusive.

While such an appeal may have the veneer of utopianism, it is an imminently pragmatic one that should resonate with realists and liberal institutionalists. After all, when accounting for the world's new threats and challenges—the proliferation of weapons of mass destruction, the growing spread of deadly pathogens, and the rising number of virulent societies—the United States has a vested national interest in the internal affairs of most every country, however remote from its borders or traditional spheres of influence. These factors provide ample motivation for the development of positive international bonds. Indeed, given the many troubled societies around the globe, the United States' response to them in concert with other Western countries would go beyond a sense of noblesse oblige to a recognition of national interest. Its effort to right these societies would be an effort to protect itself—the defining element of all national interests—in an increasingly globalized and dangerous world.

With its unsparing account of UN Security Council decision making in multilateral peace operations and its astute lessons and recommendations for projecting international solidarity and responsibility, *Beyond the National Interest* will be read and debated by students, scholars, and policymakers alike. Recent USIP volumes that explore related themes include Michael J. Matheson's *Council Unbound: The Growth of UN Decision Making on Conflict and Postconflict Issues after the Cold War,* Teresa Whitfield's *Friends Indeed? The United Nations, Groups of Friends, and the Resolution of Conflict,* and the Institute's congressionally mandated United Nations Task Force report, *American Interests and UN Reform.* As *Beyond the National Interest* and these volumes attest, today the greatest hope for moral leadership and multilateral action in the international realm—that is, for uniting all of humanity behind a shared conception of global interest, as Reagan's "fantasy" would have it—resides with the democratic power of the United States and with the world's broader community of democracies.

RICHARD H. SOLOMON, PRESIDENT
UNITED STATES INSTITUTE OF PEACE

Acknowledgments

Two institutions have played a critical role in making this book possible: the United States Institute of Peace in Washington, D.C., and the United Nations University (UNU) in Tokyo.

A great deal of the work that led to this manuscript was undertaken during the time I spent as a senior fellow in the Jennings Randolph Program for International Peace at the United States Institute of Peace. At the Institute, a whole team of people contributed to making my stay a useful experience. First and foremost, I would like to thank Joseph Klaits, the director of the Jennings Randolph Program for International Peace at the time, for his kindness and support. Timothy W. Docking and Peter Pavilionis played an important role in helping shape the book. Tim, who was assigned to my project as a program officer, helped me to focus on the questions at the center of my research and provided me with encouragement throughout my twelve-month fellowship. Peter, an editor at the Institute's Press, took an interest in the enterprise from the outset; the conscientiousness with which he read the various drafts of the chapters and the critical but generous eye that he applied to my ideas and ways of presenting them contributed in no small measure to improving my thinking and writing. Other people at the Institute were instrumental in making it an ideal place for research, including Pamela Aall, John T. Crist, Chester Crocker, Ann Driscoll, Harriet Hentges, and Daniel P. Serwer. In addition, the Institute's Library staff—particularly Jim Cornelius and Ellen Ensel—and the Information Services staff were always there when I needed their help.

Other senior fellows in the Jennings Randolph Program proved to be good research companions. The conversations that I had with Daniel Benjamin, Sonja Biserko, Donna Boltz, Graham Day, Shmuel Eisenstadt, Ching Whi Kim, Neil Hicks, David H. P. Maybury-Lewis, Dana Priest, and Henryk Sokalski played a significant role in sharpening my views on what the book should and could be.

Also at the Institute, Molly de Maret served as a stellar work partner, offering the best professional assistance that anyone could hope for. Molly provided tremendous help in making sure that the information on which the book is based was factually accurate. She also served as a first reader of the manuscript. Her comments and criticisms helped to improve the book.

The United Nations University—the UN think tank headquartered in Tokyo—and its staff also played an important role in making this book possible. I am particularly grateful to Hans Van Ginkel, the university's rector, and Ramesh Thakur, senior vice-rector of the university and head of its Peace and Governance Program, for allowing me to take a sabbatical from my professional duties in 2000–2001. Ramesh Thakur took an interest in the issues addressed in the book, shared his views on them, and read the draft manuscript and provided me with comments. In addition, UNU's Peace and Governance Program (in which I served as a senior academic officer from 1996 to 2003), with its focus on global issues at the crossroads of the world organization, international security, human rights, and global governance, served as the perfect setting in which to intellectually explore the ideas at the center of the book. The observations of my Peace and Governance Program colleagues helped me to keep the book intellectually on track. Soisik Habert, Lysette Rutgers, and Gareth Johnston made editorial and substantive suggestions that improved the text. The UNU Library and its rich collection on multilateral and UN issues provided precious research support. Its good-natured librarian at the time, Yoshie Hasehira, ensured that I was able to consult various documents and books in Tokyo and elsewhere in Japan. At UNU's New York office, where I currently serve, Jibecke Jönsson's feedback on the overall argument of the book was very useful. I am very grateful to her.

Some parts of the book are based on insights that I gained while working in the executive office of the UN secretary-general from 1992 to 1996. During this time, I benefited immensely from working under UN secretary-general Boutros Boutros-Ghali; his chief of staff, Jean-Claude Aimé; and the entire team of the executive office of the secretary-general. Working on speechwriting at the side of Paul-Marie Coûteaux and Hervé Cassan proved to be a real learning experience.

I also wish to thank particularly some of the friends and colleagues who, at various stages of the book, took the time to exchange ideas and read various drafts. Charles A. Kupchan, a constant source of friendship, ideas, and advice on international politics and more mundane matters, and Peter Marcotullio, an urban planner with an interest in international politics, challenged my ideas whenever they thought those ideas off target. Nicholas J. Wheeler was also kind enough to take the time to read the manuscript. His comments and suggestions helped to improve the overall thesis of the book.

The comments of two anonymous reviewers commissioned by the Institute of Peace were extremely useful. They helped to strengthen the book, and I thank them for this.

Writing a book is a celebration of life and a form of neurosis. Sometimes, the neurosis takes over the celebratory part of writing and can become more of a burden than an enjoyment to share. I am therefore grateful for my family's support and patience while I was working on the manuscript. Without Susie, in particular, to whom the book is dedicated, as well as to my parents, even the idea of this study would not have been possible.

Preface

On December 3, 1991, I was in Vendée, in the west of France, preparing a book on political legitimacy. Harvard University, with which I was affiliated at the time, had been flexible enough to allow me to spend an academic year in the French countryside to write the manuscript. Boutros Boutros-Ghali, elected secretary-general of the United Nations the previous day, appeared on television during the lunchtime news. The journalist congratulated him on his new appointment and asked him a variety of questions on how he felt about the United Nations, the state of the world, and the issues on which he intended to focus during his tenure. Discovering for the first time the name and face of Boutros Boutros-Ghali, I found him to be a person decidedly from the Old World—courtly, classy, and intellectually sharp. I thought he would certainly be a very interesting person for whom to work.

For a few months after that first "encounter," I did not give more thought to Boutros-Ghali and the United Nations; I was too busy trying to progress with my work. Moreover, I had never really thought about working for the United Nations, let alone its secretary-general. Since my early years as a student in France and then as a young scholar at Harvard, I had set my sights on a regular academic career.

Then, in the early spring of 1992, I received a phone call from the French Ministry of Foreign Affairs. A few years earlier, I had served as a junior officer with the cultural and scientific service of the French consulate in Houston, Texas, and I had kept in touch with some of my former colleagues from the ministry. I was now being contacted in regard to a position in the executive office of the UN secretary-general. Boutros-Ghali was in the process of staffing his cabinet and was looking for someone to join the French speechwriting unit. At the time, my knowledge of the United Nations was fairly limited, but I knew enough to realize the value of the job and that there was probably no shortage of candidates more qualified and more eager than myself. To my surprise, and perhaps because I approached the selection process in a relaxed manner, I was offered the position a few weeks after the interview. I was now forced to make a choice: Would I stick to my initial desire for an academic career or would I take this opportunity to work for the UN secretary-general? Mainly upon the advice of my father, to whom the United Nations meant a lot, I decided to give the latter a try.

I began working in the secretary-general's executive office in mid-July 1992, just a few days after completing a solid draft of my book on political legitimacy. It was the beginning of four extremely hectic years, during which I learned a tremendous amount, not only about the United Nations and international relations, but also about the obscure workings of international politics. My position was not a senior one; I was more of a foot soldier, if not a fly on the wall, trying to as much as possible learn the job on the job, so to speak. As a junior member of the French speechwriting unit, my job entailed three main responsibilities: helping to draft speeches (in French, of course) for the secretary-general on any given topic of the day, as well as on recurrent issues on the UN agenda (mainly European and African issues); note taking during some of the secretary-general's meetings with heads of state, foreign affairs ministers, ambassadors, UN special representatives, and others, and drafting the minutes of the meetings; and taking care of the secretary-general's correspondence.

Typically, a day would begin with reading the confidential cables. Circulated every morning to the professionals in the executive office, the cables came from the field, where the United Nations was deployed mainly in the context of peacekeeping operations, and gave the latest updates on the security, political, social, and economic situation "on the ground." The day would then unfold, filled up with preparing upcoming speeches (doing research, consulting in-house experts, and drafting), attending the secretary-general's meetings, or writing up the minutes of previous meetings. The weeks and days preceding a trip by the secretary-general were particularly busy, ensuring that all the speeches for the trip were ready and approved well before departure. Driven, demanding, and attentive to detail as Boutros Boutros-Ghali was, it was out of the question to leave things to the last minute.

Autumn was a time of especially intense activity. With the UN General Assembly in session and officials attending from around the world, the daily schedules of the secretary-general and his cabinet were filled for weeks at a time with meetings from morning to evening. After the opening of the General Assembly, the second half of September was generally dedicated to meetings between the secretary-general and heads of state and foreign affairs ministers at the United Nations to deliver their yearly addresses to the General Assembly—speeches that traditionally outline the position of the respective governments on perennial items as well as current issues on the UN agenda. The meetings took place either in the secretary-general's office, in the conference room on the thirty-eighth floor of the New York headquarters building, or in the small consultation rooms located just behind the General Assembly hall. October and November were dedicated to following the work of the various committees associated with the work of the General Assembly in session.

The frantic schedule of the UN Security Council and the Department of Peacekeeping Operations (DPKO) during my years in the office of the secretary-general made the daily work all the more intense. With the multiplication and increased complexity of peacekeeping operations, the Security Council and DPKO—whose mission is to monitor the UN operations deployed in areas of conflict—had become the busiest entities of the entire UN Secretariat. Both were round-the-clock operations, with the Council having informal consultations almost every day, and the DPKO linked with field missions twenty-four hours a day through its crisis management situation center (this was before the use of e-mail between headquarters and the field). The pressure under which the Security Council and the DPKO found themselves trickled down to the secretary-general's cabinet, including the speechwriting units. As the Council deliberated and decided on a multiplicity of peace operations involving not only interposition and the search for solutions to conflicts but also humanitarian aid and at times the use of force, it fell to the DPKO and, to a certain extent, the executive office to feed the decision makers in the Council with the secretary-general's reports assessing the situation on the ground and making recommendations.

The speechwriting unit had to deal with questions that had been the staples of the United Nations' work for decades, such as disarmament, poverty and development, and human rights. But it also had to address the specific crises of the period—humanitarian tragedies that came to define the 1990s and the role of the United Nations and multilateralism at the time. In one way or another, the Balkans, Somalia, and Rwanda became constant features of the work. As these crises and their multilateral handling unfolded, the goal was to give as honest and clear a voice as possible to the secretary-general—one that would factor in the various aspects of the situation without losing sight of the need to take a stance on the right course of action. Placing humanitarian crises onto the agenda of the Security Council was a novelty in the United Nations then, and considering the misgivings of key member states about the extent to which they and the United Nations should get involved in these crises, the support role for Secretary-General Boutros-Ghali was more than a bit of a challenge.

At the same time, with perhaps the exception of the Department of Peacekeeping Operations, for most of the UN Secretariat the crises of the period appeared astonishingly distant. That was certainly the case for the executive office of the secretary-general. I remember quite well the spring of 1994, when the genocide was in full swing in Rwanda, how the mass killing of Tutsis and moderate Hutus seemed a rather abstract phenomenon from the thirty-eighth floor of UN headquarters in Manhattan. The same sense of detachment was more or less on display in July 1995, during the siege and takeover of Srebrenica. On both occasions, judging by the atmosphere of quiet concentration prevailing in the corridor of the thirty-eighth floor, one would not have guessed that people were being slaughtered by the tens of thousands on the United Nations' watch.

When I left the executive office of the secretary-general in the early summer of 1996 and, a few weeks later, moved to Tokyo to take a new job with the United Nations University (UNU), I had learned a vast amount about the United Nations, multilateralism, international politics, and the issues of the period. Among other things, I learned how precious it can be to see how international organizations work from within. To witness the decision-making process in a politically and normatively complex environment such as the United Nations' was both a humanly humbling and intellectually enriching experience. Books are certainly an essential medium for learning how the world and its institutions function, but they cannot substitute for firsthand experience. Any analyst-scholar who is eager to understand the constraints and possibilities of political decision making, who is committed to comprehending the institutional and political constraints at play—let alone to go beyond them and try to advance a progressive and hopeful international agenda—will be well advised to get this kind of exposure. In particular, this experience led me to believe that, when the possibility exists of studying an institution from within, doing so and eventually combining that perspective with a view from afar is essential.

This does not mean that I knew all that much when I left Boutros-Ghali's cabinet. In fact, while working in the executive office, caught up in daily tasks, it was difficult to reflect on the crises that seemed to unfold with a disturbing regularity and the ways the international community handled them. This state of affairs, both challenging and frustrating, was not conducive to thinking through the role of the United Nations in international affairs, particularly regarding a theme that had caught my interest while working on the thirty-eighth floor—the extent and limits of the sense of international solidarity and responsibility for this new kind of mass violence in the immediate post–Cold War period.

My position with the United Nations University, geared more toward policy research, gave me the opportunity to revisit the issues to which I had been introduced in speechwriting for Boutros-Ghali. In the various research projects that I was responsible for in UNU's Peace and Governance Program, I made a point of trying to elucidate some of the intellectual and political puzzles that I had been exposed to in the previous years. A senior fellowship with the United States Institute of Peace in 2000–2001 gave me the opportunity to turn what had up to then been insights and analyses dispersed in various publications into a more systematic and comprehensive approach. As I was writing the draft of the current work, the international changes that began to take place in the 2000s, far from relegating the questions at the center of my research into the past, made it all the more important to explore further the global role of multilateralism and the United Nations. September 11, 2001, the Bush administration's unilateralist foreign policy and its War on Terror, the war in Iraq, and their still unforeseeable long-term consequences gave a renewed sense of relevance and urgency to the project.

This book is the product of a personal, professional, and intellectual journey with the United Nations. As such, it has to be seen as an exercise of clarification, as a modest attempt to better understand the world and the way it has been managed since the 1990s.

BEYOND THE NATIONAL INTEREST

"Though men, therefore, generally direct everything according to their own lust, nevertheless, more advantages than disadvantages follow from their forming a common society. So it is better to bear men's wrongs calmly, and apply one's zeal to those things which help to bring men together in harmony and friendship."

Spinoza, *Ethics*, Part IV, Appendix XIV

"The price of greatness is responsibility. . . . [O]ne cannot rise to be . . . the leading community in the . . . world without being involved in its problems, without being convulsed by its agonies and inspired by its causes. If this has been proved in the past, as it has been, it will become indisputable in the future."

Winston Churchill
Address delivered at Harvard University,
September 6, 1943

INTRODUCTION

THE PARADOX OF INTERNATIONAL SOLIDARITY

WHAT HAS BECOME OF MULTILATERALISM? For that matter, what has become of peacekeeping and humanitarian interventions? What has become of the ethics of international solidarity that they came to represent in the 1990s? And what chance do they have to obtain a significant role in the future? These are some of the questions around which this study revolves.

Obviously, part of the answer resides in the Bush administration's unabashed embrace of a unilateralist foreign policy and its focus on fighting terrorism. Quite apart from the kind of normative, gradual restoration of public security and representative government characteristic of so many peacekeeping operations launched in the 1990s, the current emphasis in international interventions is on direct threats to national security. In its preoccupation with "rogue" states, especially after 9/11, the Bush administration's preferred course has been pre-emption—to intervene before the state's actions become a "threat to the peace" and subject to drawn-out deliberations in the UN Security Council to get a murky mandate for intervention.[1] Iraq is the exemplar of this modality, and time will tell if it can be declared a "success."

As the United States has more or less retreated—or, perhaps, shifted priorities—from the multilateral management of "failed" states and humanitarian crises, where does this leave international politics and multilateral interventions in humanitarian crises and ethnic conflict? Do the changes in international affairs and of attitudes in the United States—the most powerful member of the UN Security Council—witness the eclipse of the kind of multilateral management of humanitarian crises and ethnic conflict that was characteristic of the immediate post–Cold War era? In other words, have the years of "robust" United Nations–mandated peacekeeping operations become a distant memory? Or can the management of intra- and interstate conflicts stemming from "failed" states and their attendant pathologies in governance ever again enter the realm of UN-mandated multilateral peacekeeping?

To be sure, the Bush "revolution" in U.S. foreign policy and its underlying assumption that the kind of comprehensive peacekeeping pursued during the 1990s was a long, arduous, and complicated affair well outside the U.S. national interest militate to make multilateral peace operations a thing of the past. Yet there is another side to the story that points to the fact that "failed" states and the ethnic tensions often associated with them will continue to sprout across the globe.[2] Between 1991 and 2000, fifty-two armed conflicts broke out worldwide, of which thirty-five were internal and seventeen interstate in nature. By the mid-2000s, although the total number of conflicts had declined, the number of internal conflicts had increased to represent 95 percent of all conflicts worldwide.[3] There is no reason to believe that this trend is likely to reverse in the years to come.

Thus the international community now stands at an ominous crossroads. Unless the international community and its principal powers are to ignore failing and failed states altogether, inevitably they will have to handle conflicts and humanitarian crises stemming from them. Future U.S. administrations and the international community at large may never return to the exact modalities of the 1990s, in which a UN mandate, at times in coordination with the North Atlantic Treaty Organization (NATO) or other regional organizations, seemed to be the order of the day in so many global hot spots—if only because the mixed results of the peacekeeping operations and missed opportunities of that era still resonate with many current and potential officials in the U.S. foreign policymaking establishment. But neither the United States nor the international community will be able to escape the need for peace operations. Costly they are, but not nearly as costly as unsuccessful unilateral interventions are to the international legitimacy of the United States and other relevant actors, be they states or international organizations. Peace operations are a necessity and a resource that should be used—now and in the future. Hence the imperative to assess the effectiveness of peace operations in light of past experiences and to learn what we can from them, so that understanding and clarity help prevent future mistakes; and there are no better case studies to analyze and learn from than the robust peace operations of the 1990s. Therein lies one of the main purposes of this work.

During the 1990s, the United Nations made significant efforts to respond to humanitarian crises and mass human rights violations. The number of peace operations and troops deployed; the amount of energy, time, and money spent; and the scope of initiatives taken, from prevention to peace enforcement to peacebuilding, were the largest ever in the area of peacekeeping. Still, the end results were mixed. Peace operations certainly helped to protect the civilian populations in a number of instances and to alleviate their suffering. However, they neither prevented major humanitarian catastrophes from occurring nor kept wars from going almost unchecked for years. In this regard, the international community acting through the United Nations probably could have performed better and achieved more in Somalia and the Balkans, let alone in Rwanda and other parts of Africa.

How does one explain this paradox? Answering this question leads to more questions. How can we assess the role of the United Nations regarding humanitarian crises? What has been the impact of the structure of international politics—especially of the normative structure of international politics as epitomized in established principles of international law—on the ways the international community responded to humanitarian emergencies? How are we to understand the attitude of the key member states of the United Nations—the United States foremost among them—vis-à-vis multilateralism and the quest for a just international order?

Also, as mentioned earlier, considering the focus in recent years on terrorism and national security concerns, as well as the rift between the United Nations and the United States, a much more tangible and equally complex question arises: How can the lessons of the 1990s, in operational, political, and normative terms, contribute to making the peace operations of the future more efficient, not only to stop the mass carnage and dislocations in a "complex emergency" but also to ensure that the conditions contributing to the conflict-ridden humanitarian crisis do not return?

To unravel these vexing questions, this study takes three paths: descriptive, analytical, and prescriptive. It is descriptive in that it details the main peace operations launched throughout the 1990s, with special attention to the question of the use of force. Furthermore, the study depicts the role played by some of the key actors of the peace operations, accounting for the perspectives of the UN Secretariat, the UN secretary-general, and the permanent members of the Security Council—in particular, the United Kingdom, France, and, most important, the United States. Along the analytical path, this study searches for explanations that attempt to make sense of the "minimalist activism"—the combination of engagement and restraint—and of the ensuing mixed outcomes of the international community's interventions. The study is prescriptive as it ultimately pursues ways to enhance a sense of international justice geared toward benefiting individuals and the respect of their human rights as well as to achieve a genuine framework of collective security in the international realm.

With this descriptive, analytical, and prescriptive approach in mind, the study calls upon a number of ideas and notions that are used to draw an intellectual road map, including national interest, international legitimacy, international solidarity and its dilemmas, and international democratic culture.

National interest refers to the self-interest of nations, how states envision their defense and projection beyond their borders. Classically, national interest has been divided into those interests that states consider vital and those that relate to the promotion of subsidiary interests. Also, the notion of national interest has historically been associated with a geopolitical understanding of international relations because the pursuit of the national interest has been closely linked to geography: the locations where acts unfold (for economic, military, or other reasons) and that constitute potential fault lines that must be closely surveilled.[4] Although this geographical anchoring remains significant, it is balanced by the changes brought about by the "de-territorialization" of politics at the national and international levels.[5] Such de-territorialization (or, to use an equally nebulous term, globalization) includes normative factors such as the identification with human rights imperatives and the influence that it has on individual and collective interests and values and their interactions, as well as on policies at home and abroad.

International legitimacy is another theme of this work, and it is used in connection with the notion of the socialization of the international realm. At the most general level, the idea of legitimacy concerns first and foremost the authority to govern. As such, it tries to offer a solution to the fundamental problem of justifying power and obedience simultaneously.[6] At the international level, legitimacy amounts to justifying the way international order is organized, including the ways power is projected beyond borders. Unless the norms called upon to justify international order and the projection of power beyond borders are perceived as good, the international system is likely to be seen as illegitimate. In contemporary terms, international legitimacy refers to the international rights and duties that actors (particularly states) have to factor in, not only to project acceptable foreign policies, but also to contribute to an international life that aims for the rule of law. As will be seen later in this study, in order to give a sense of overall legitimacy to their decisions and actions, as well as to the international system and its institutions (including the United Nations), decision makers in the international community (the UN Security Council members in particular) must balance the values and rights expressed by various international norms and legal principles.

The criteria by which assessments are made of what is right and what is wrong internationally are largely a product of history. For example, the norms of legitimacy that are central to collective security are the result of a long but staggered cognitive evolution, most of which has occurred in the past fifty years and is destined to continue through unfolding events and the demands for UN action and multilateral responses to monitor and cope with them. This cognitive evolution is also influenced by the expectations—and thus the push for transformation—that the norms of legitimacy bring to the social reality of the international realm. The historical nature of norms and legitimacy at the international level must be kept in mind as we witness the unfolding of international events that challenge the conventional wisdom about collective security, as we wonder whether or not the established criteria of interpretation and judgment of what is right internationally should adjust to them, and as we wonder how and where to draw the line between what needs to remain the same and what needs to change in the analytical tools of evaluating international reality and in international reality itself.

"International solidarity" is an expression that conveys the need to help people beyond a nation's own borders. Based on the internationalization of the democratic idea of human rights, it has a universalist character.[7] The idea is that although human beings live in a plurality of cultures that exhibit a range of particular moral practices, all have basic needs and rights that must be respected. These basic needs and rights, which constitute the core commonality of individuals across the world, are also what bring these individuals together and impel them to identify with, and care about, the sufferings of others. At the international level, violations of these needs and rights call for a sense of solidarity beyond borders. Failing to respond to the plight of the other, failing to show solidarity, diminishes the humanity of all. As such, international solidarity points to the international community's responsibility and obligation toward victims of conflict regardless of their personal circumstances and geographical location. And if an international humanitarian intervention in the form of a multilateral peace operation is the expression of an ethics of international solidarity, it must be primarily (although not exclusively) motivated by humanitarian reasons.

The notion of dilemmas of international solidarity helps to demonstrate that the international community's handling of the crises in the 1990s, while responding to humanitarian impulses, did not amount to an idyllic picture of international solidarity. Particularly, the central place that dilemmas occupied in the deliberations, decisions, and actions of the United Nations and its key members contributes to a contrasting account of the projection of solidarity at the international level. The dilemmas of ends and means, the weighing process, and the trade-offs that confronted the Security Council in the aftermath of the Cold War show dramatically the constraints that the "us-versus-them" divide imposes upon international solidarity. In the context of this study, this notion has to be understood in relation to the hybrid character of international life—the intertwined pulls of national interest and international solidarity—and its impact on international decision making and action.

The nature and relations of national interest, international solidarity, dilemmas of international solidarity, and international legitimacy lead to an unveiling of some of the critical aspects of contemporary "international democratic culture." At first glance, it may appear incongruous for a study focusing on peace operations and humanitarian crises to make room for the idea of international democratic culture. Nonetheless, peace operations, especially those with a humanitarian-intervention motif, are a perfect venue for reviewing the extent and limits of contemporary international democratic culture in the aftermath of the Cold War. As peace operations were initiated primarily to re-establish order in a failed or failing state with special concern for the defense of the key tenets of democratic culture—universal human rights—they help assess how far international life is moving from a mainly Hobbesian vision of international relations, and how close it is getting to the notion of community and democratic empowerment.

The chapters of the study are organized along the following lines.

Chapter 1 analyzes the most salient initiatives taken by the United Nations to address humanitarian emergencies in the 1990s. It shows how UN peace operations embarked on daunting tasks, both quantitatively and qualitatively, in the ten years or so following the Cold War. Also, while acknowledging that the spectrum of measures encompassed in peace operations could not, immediately or in the long run, solve all problems, the chapter argues that their end results were disappointing.

The next three chapters explain the extent and limits—especially the limits—of international solidarity in the context of UN peace operations. They examine three factors that must be seen as having a *cumulative* effect in the shortcomings of the international community's interventions.

Chapter 2 explores the limitations of the United Nations as an international organization, accounting for the difficulties of peace operations. Concentrating on some of the key operations—mainly Somalia, Bosnia, and Rwanda—it looks into the negative impact of the political disagreement, on the one hand, between the UN secretary-general and the Security Council, and, on the other hand, among the members of the Security Council. In addition, the chapter analyzes the operational shortcomings of the United Nations when it comes to peacekeeping operations from the point of view of the UN Secretariat and the field.

Chapter 3 examines the political and normative structure of international life and how it opens possibilities but also creates constraints in the exercise and projection of international solidarity and responsibility. It argues that the norms of democratic solidarity that inhabit the United Nations and multilateralism embody a sense of international responsibility vis-à-vis the victims of massive human rights violations. Nevertheless, as international life is still structured around a national bias, the sense of international responsibility is hampered by an "us-versus-them" divide and its consequence (i.e., the primacy of national interest considerations over internationalist human rights concerns). This dual characteristic had a great impact in the context of humanitarian interventions and the use of force.

Chapter 4 analyzes the role of President Bill Clinton's foreign policy in the multilateral handling of humanitarian emergencies. It stresses that the initial commitment of the Clinton administration to assertive multilateralism was short-lived and was quickly replaced by a rather erratic internationalist stance. In defense of Clinton's foreign policy, one has to say that the weight of domestic politics, including congressional politics, and the reluctance of the U.S. military establishment to get involved in conflicts without a clear national interest context tempered the ways America took part—diplomatically, politically, and militarily—in peace operations.

The imperative of responding better to an ethics of international solidarity in light of the need for legitimacy in the international system could not have been challenged more dramatically than it has been since 2001, with the arrival of the Bush administration and its foreign policy mixture of selective multilateralism and unilateralism. September 11, 2001, deepened the conservative turn in U.S. foreign policy, particularly with the launch of Operation Iraqi Freedom in March 2003. What did these changes signify? Did they remove the experience with peace operations in the 1990s, the central issues and the lessons that can be drawn from that period, to a past disconnected from the post–9/11 world? To what extent is there continuity between the 1990s and the present in terms of multilateral interventions?

In truth, despite the difference between 1990s and now, current international life and the debates surrounding it are not entirely foreign to the

1990s. In fact, 9/11 and the Bush "revolution" in foreign policy gave a new centrality to one of the issues that had been at the center of peace operations in the 1990s—the use of force—its reasons and ways of implementing it. Starting in the middle of 2003, the Iraqi insurgency also served as a reminder of the familiar difficulty of achieving peace and security, let alone reconciliation and democracy, in a postconflict situation. More generally, the need to balance national and international interests, the tense relationship between the United States and the United Nations, the role of multilateralism as a conduit for international legitimacy, and the importance of the Atlantic Alliance have proved to be as important now as in the 1990s.

Chapter 5 addresses these issues and emphasizes that the Bush administration's impact on multilateralism, peacekeeping, and humanitarian intervention was not a radical departure from mainstream U.S. foreign policy but, rather, pushed some of its core aspects to the edge. A disregard of multilateralism—its principles, institutions, and actions—led to the near collapse of the Atlantic Alliance and created a deep rift between the United States and the international community as a whole. In the process, the Bush administration also learned firsthand that it was not as easy as its most conservative elements had initially assumed to succeed on the ground and, more generally, to unilaterally define what constitutes a legitimate U.S. foreign policy, let alone international legitimacy.

The final chapter of this work argues that enhancing the sense of international solidarity, particularly as expressed in the context of peace operations and humanitarian interventions, calls for improving the United Nations as an institution. It also calls for normative and policy adjustments among national leaders—an important appeal, considering that international solidarity has a direct bearing on the establishment and preservation of international security. The chapter goes on to argue that the progressive dimension of international norms needs to be enhanced, especially by bringing to the fore the empowerment qualities (including the democratic empowerment qualities) of multilateralism. The connection between the inclusive aspects of multilateral politics and the United Nations, member states, regional organizations, and nongovernmental organizations has to be strengthened.

Even if significant progress is achieved in the area of international solidarity, it is unlikely that it will allow a complete break from the constraints identified in this study. At best, the tensions will be brought down to a more tolerable level. As alluded to in the afterword, the unresolved crisis in Darfur is only one indication of how the sense of international solidarity still has a long way to go to become more of a tangible reality. Nevertheless, the attempt to encourage internationalist values as much as possible, and thereby enhance an ethics of international solidarity, is essential for the legitimacy of the international system, as well as for any claim it may have to express and serve an international order inhabited and structured by concerns for justice.

CHAPTER 1

THE EXTENT AND LIMITS OF PEACE OPERATIONS IN THE 1990s

P EACE OPERATIONS ARE AMONG THE MOST PUBLICIZED type of action of the United Nations; this was especially the case in the 1990s, a decade in which they came to be a major international innovation to address local conflicts, humanitarian crises, and the massive human rights violations associated with them. The multiplicity of peace operations launched in the aftermath of the Cold War and the wide and complex range of measures they encompassed caught the public eye the world over. However, no matter how substantial the quantitative and qualitative changes of peace operations in the 1990s, there are two main reasons to remain somewhat unimpressed by their numbers and scale: First, the resources allocated by major powers to peace operations were relatively small compared to those allocated to their own national needs. Second, the peace operations had a decidedly mixed outcome.

INTERNATIONAL SECURITY AND PEACE OPERATIONS

Maintaining and restoring international peace and security have been the key responsibilities of the United Nations since its inception, with the twin objectives of promoting development and democratization, if not democracy itself. The fulfillment of these responsibilities represents a critical test of the United Nations' authority, credibility, and, ultimately, legitimacy. The fact that peace operations have become a significant part of supporting peace and security is rather surprising, considering that they are not mentioned in the United Nations Charter.

COLLECTIVE MEASURES TO DEAL WITH THREATS TO PEACE

According to the United Nations Charter, the UN secretary-general can call emerging or existing crises to the attention of the Security Council and offer suggestions to solve them. But deciding when and how to maintain international peace is the foremost responsibility of the Security Council. In this regard, the Council enjoys two types of authority: the power of interpretation and qualification, and the power of decision and action. The power of interpretation and qualification arises from the Council's authority to assess a situation as "a threat to peace." The power of decision and action deals with the measures called upon to tackle a crisis. These two functions are addressed in the Charter under Chapter VI ("Pacific Settlement of Disputes") and Chapter VII ("Action with Respect to Threats to the Peace").

What the Charter calls "pacific settlement" in Chapter VI is the process by which the Security Council is to resolve any dispute likely to endanger international security.[1] In pursuit of pacific settlement, the Council has a number of options. It may call upon the parties to seek a solution by negotiation, enquiry, mediation, conciliation, arbitration, judicial settlement, resort to regional agencies or arrangements, or other peaceful means.[2] Chapter VII gives the Security Council the function of organizing collective resistance to aggression via enforcement measures, including complete or partial interruption of economic relations and of rail, sea, air, postal, telegraphic, radio, and other means of communication, as well as the severance of diplomatic relations.[3] Chapter VII further indicates that the Security Council can decide to use force if necessary.[4]

Chapter VIII completes Chapters VI and VII by envisioning the possibility of cooperation between the United Nations and regional organizations for the pacific settlement of disputes and collective enforcement. On the use of force, Article 53 of Chapter VIII specifies that regional arrangements require the Security Council's authorization to take enforcement action.[5]

Although pacific settlement of disputes and collective enforcement measures are at the core of the United Nations' mandate, they did not show a high level of activity and success during the Cold War.[6] Superpower competition and the North-South divide, giving local tensions and conflicts a global dimension, hampered the Security Council from using its dispute-settlement methods fully. As a result, the United Nations had to be innovative. This led to the creation of peace operations.

PEACE OPERATIONS AT THE SERVICE OF INTERNATIONAL SECURITY

Peace operations should have logically included the whole range of diplomatic and coercive measures made available by the Charter to the Security

Council against violators of global peace and security. Nevertheless, what made it hard for the Council until the early 1990s to use these measures completely accounts also for the three main principles on which peace operations were established: the need for disputants to consent to the deployment of UN missions, the imperative for the United Nations to remain impartial and not favor any of the disputants, and the rejection of the use of force. Hence, as well, the form adopted by peace operations during the Cold War: peaceful interpositioning of UN personnel in response to an invitation by the disputants to oversee an agreed-upon cease-fire.[7] On these terms, the United Nations could intercede to ensure that combatants would not re-engage on the ground and to encourage negotiations geared toward finding a diplomatic solution.

As a vehicle for interpositioning peacekeeping troops along lines of conflict, peace operations presented a threefold advantage. They did not disrupt (at least not greatly) the culture of strategic competition among the leading global powers, they made it possible to tackle crises whose relative importance or lack thereof required or permitted action, and they gave a sense of purpose to the United Nations. Consequently, peace operations became an important part of the world organization's portfolio—one of its trademarks, as it were.

Between 1948 and 1987, thirteen interpositional peacekeeping missions were initiated in Palestine, Kashmir, Egypt/Israel (twice, in November 1956 and October 1973), Lebanon/Syria, the Congo (currently the Republic of the Congo, also referred to as Congo-Brazzaville), West New Guinea, Cyprus, the Dominican Republic, India/Pakistan, Yemen, the Golan Heights, and Lebanon/Israel. A number of the missions played a positive role. Others did not succeed or were not even completed. To this day, five of the missions initiated decades ago are still active, and it is unlikely that the problems they seek to address will be solved any time soon. Cyprus remains divided between the Greek Cypriot and Turkish Cypriot communities. In Israel, the United Nations Truce Supervision Organization (UNTSO), which began in 1948, goes on. The same applies to the UN missions in Lebanon and the Golan Heights. There is also little prospect that the conflict that necessitates the continued UN presence in Kashmir will be resolved in the near future.

The immediate aftermath of the Cold War brought an expectation of a greater sense of security and stability, but it did not take long to realize how misguided this expectation was. Local conflicts that had previously been kept in check by the demands of global competition multiplied, boosting the need for peace operations.

FROM QUANTITATIVE TO QUALITATIVE CHANGES IN PEACE OPERATIONS

When compared to the past, the peace operations of the 1990s appear strikingly different on two accounts: quantitative and qualitative. As such, they proved to be very demanding operations for the international community.

QUANTITATIVE CHANGES IN PEACE OPERATIONS

The quantitative evolution of peace operations in the 1990s is best captured in two sets of figures: the number of peace operations and the resources (financial and human resources in particular) that they mobilized.

More than thirty peace operations were initiated between 1991 and 2002. It is a striking number compared to the thirteen missions established between 1948 and 1987. The worldwide scope of their deployment is also impressive: fourteen of these missions were in Africa, nine in Europe, six in the Americas, and four in Asia.[8] The most intensive period of activity was probably the one from 1991 to late 1995. During this period, sixteen peace operations—many of the most complex ones—were launched. Although fewer missions were created between 1995 and 1998, peacekeeping remained an active part of the UN portfolio. Eleven operations were established during this period. After 1999, the number of peace operations soared again, with the deployment of large missions in Kosovo, East Timor, Sierra Leone, and the Democratic Republic of the Congo (DRC, also referred to as Congo-Kinshasa).

Not surprisingly, the financial and human resources committed to peace operations by the international community grew with the number of missions. In the case of financial resources, member states (especially the most powerful) covered the mounting expenses through their contributions to the UN system. From 1991 to 2000, peace operation expenses represented a sum close to ten times what was spent on peacekeeping between 1948 and 1990, reaching a total of $19.9 billion.[9] These costs exceeded the regular budget of the United Nations, yet they constituted only a fraction of the full amount spent by the UN system as a whole on peace operations throughout the 1990s.[10] To these expenses had to be added humanitarian, rehabilitation, and other economic recovery costs that member states ended up paying through their contributions to international organizations with budgets separate from the United Nations, such as the United Nations High Commissioner for Refugees (UNHCR), the World Health Organisation (WHO), the World Food Program (WFP), the United Nations Children's Fund (UNICEF), and the World Bank.[11]

Member states also paid for the increased costs associated with peace operations by directly financing two other types of initiatives: international humanitarian interventions and other peace operations–related costs. International interventions in the 1990s represented a major break with the past. They came to embody the willingness of the international community to address humanitarian crises with the possible use of force. Authorized by the Security Council (the intervention in Kosovo in the spring of 1999 is a debated exception), they were usually led by a nation or group of nations in command of the operation (most often permanent members of the Security Council). In Somalia, Haiti, Bosnia, Kosovo, and East Timor, these interventions amounted to major expenses for the countries that played a leading role in their implementation.[12] In Somalia, the military operations aspects of the international interventions Operation Restore Hope and the Unified Task Force (UNITAF), created to coordinate the various aspects of the international intervention, cost the United States more than $1 billion from December 1992 to May 1993.[13] The U.S.-led intervention in Haiti between September 1994 and March 1995 cost American taxpayers $2 billion.[14] In Bosnia, the NATO-led multinational Implementation Force (IFOR) cost participating countries $5 billion from December 1995 through the end of 1996.[15] The cost of air operations conducted in Kosovo in the spring of 1999—close to $4 billion—was covered by the NATO countries, primarily the United States.[16] For East Timor, Australia had to pay a significant amount of the costs generated by the International Force for East Timor (INTERFET), which opened the way to the deployment of the United Nations Transitional Administration in East Timor (UNTAET).[17]

The other expenses associated with peace operations directly covered by member states were also very significant. For example, in Haiti, the United States' costs for humanitarian aid, rebuilding, refugees, and other matters were more than $1 billion.[18] In the Balkans, substantial costs were borne by nearby countries to which hundreds of thousands of Bosnians fled; Germany played host to almost half of the 700,000 Bosnian refugees in Europe. The total cost between 1992 and 2000 came close to $10 billion.[19] Although theoretically it is Bosnia's problem, in practice the international community (the European Union in particular) is ultimately paying the estimated $60 billion to rebuild Bosnia's economy.[20] The same applies to Kosovo, where the European Union is destined to pay most of the reconstruction bill.

Human resources allocated for peace operations are another indication of the unparalleled investment made by the international community in peace operations in the 1990s. Around 400,000 military and civilian personnel were deployed between 1991 and 2000 in the context of peace operations. Because the United Nations has no army or standby forces, each time the Security Council calls for the creation of a new operation, its components must be assembled from scratch. This is a challenging task, considering that contributions of personnel to peacekeeping forces are not obligatory for UN member states. In addition, a troop-contributing country retains the right to withdraw its personnel from an operation. With so many personnel present in the field, fatalities were unavoidable. Approximately 900 fatalities occurred among the UN personnel during the 1990s, with peaks in 1992 (59 fatalities), 1993 (252), 1994 (168), and 1995 (127), with a number of countries paying a particularly high price.[21] By way of comparison, between 1948 and 1990 there were 851 fatalities among the personnel deployed on the ground.[22]

In addition to the troops deployed in peacekeeping missions, member states, especially the United States, France, and the United Kingdom, contributed massively in personnel within the framework of the international forces used to lead the humanitarian interventions. At its peak, the Unified Task Force in Somalia counted 37,000 troops, of which 28,000 were provided by the United States.[23] The Multinational Force (MNF) in Haiti was initially a 21,000-member force, composed primarily of U.S. troops. In Bosnia, close to 60,000 troops were deployed in December 1995 in the context of the Implementation Force; one year later, at the end of 1996, the establishment of the Stabilization Force (SFOR) led to the deployment of 36,000 troops, including 30,000 NATO and 6,000 non-NATO troops.[24] The United States, France, and the United Kingdom were major participants in these operations. Kosovo benefited from a similar situation: the Kosovo Force (KFOR), established in June 1999, reached full strength at 50,000 troops, with a large participation from the United States, France, and the United Kingdom, and less substantial participation from other NATO and non-NATO countries.[25]

QUALITATIVE CHANGES IN PEACE OPERATIONS

The peace operations of the post–Cold War era continued to perform the tasks that had been initially envisioned for peacekeeping. Interposition of forces, monitoring of cease-fires, and maintenance of buffer zones went on either in the context of operations that had been initiated during the Cold War and were still in action or within the framework of newly established peace operations. However, peace operations also went through major qualitative changes in the 1990s that brought critical alterations in their conception and implementation, entailing measures taken at three stages of the crises: before the eruption of conflicts, during the unfolding of internal conflicts and humanitarian crises, and during the postconflict period of those crises. The measures mainly concerned prevention (before the eruption of conflicts); humanitarian assistance and peace enforcement, including use of force and sanctions (during the conflicts); and peacebuilding (in the aftermath of conflicts).

The United Nations did not wait until the 1990s to discover the importance of conflict prevention. The theme of preventive diplomacy is touched on in the UN Charter, and Secretary-General Dag Hammarskjöld argued in the early 1960s that preventive action should be viewed as one of the main tools to maintain international peace.[26] But it is mainly with Secretary-General Boutros Boutros-Ghali and his *Agenda for Peace,* published in 1992, that prevention began to be taken more seriously.[27] For the first time, the deployment of UN troops, either in interstate or intrastate disputes, was viewed as a major component of international diplomacy and peace operations. Not long after, preventive military deployment in the context of peace operations became a reality. In the Former Yugoslav Republic of Macedonia (FYROM) in 1993, the first—and, so far, only—preventive peacekeeping operation was undertaken.

While local conflicts and humanitarian crises unfolded, the following initiatives came to occupy the forefront of peace operations, introducing major changes compared to past peacekeeping: humanitarian assistance; a mixture of humanitarian assistance and peace enforcement; sanctions; and, to a certain extent, ad hoc international criminal tribunals.

Peace operations were launched explicitly for humanitarian assistance delivery purposes (and no longer primarily with interpositioning in mind). Humanitarian assistance included providing food and shelter to victims and restoring essential supplies, such as water and electrical power. Most of the time, this humanitarian assistance was taking place while wars were still unfolding. With one or more parties at war often blocking UN attempts to deliver food, the world organization was first forced to negotiate for the delivery of humanitarian aid. Over time, when the negotiations failed to produce the desired conditions, the temptation grew to call upon the UN Charter's Chapter VII to ensure that humanitarian assistance would reach its intended recipients. Allowing the use of force to protect relief convoys and services to civilian populations became the option of last resort. The United Nations' involvement in Somalia and Bosnia serves as a case in point.

The enforcement dimension of peace operations was often closely associated with interventions envisioning the use of force. These interventions, principally launched to help ease humanitarian crises, happened before peace operations were deployed. This was the case of Operation Uphold Democracy[28] in Haiti in September 1994, Operation Allied Force in Kosovo in March 1999, and the International Force for East Timor in September 1999. They also happened in the midst of a UN involvement. This was the case of Operation Restore Hope, which took place in Somalia when the United Nations Operation in Somalia I (UNOSOM I) was already on the ground. Finally, the interventions happened after a long and substantial UN engagement, as in Bosnia with IFOR and SFOR as successors to the United Nations Protection Force (UNPROFOR). Unlike UNPROFOR, IFOR and SFOR envisioned use of force beyond self-defense.

The use of sanctions in the midst of conflicts was another way in which peace operations evolved qualitatively in the 1990s. Whereas the Security Council had imposed sanctions only twice in the first forty-five years of the United Nations (against Rhodesia in 1966 and South Africa in 1977), during the 1990s it adopted more than fifty resolutions dealing with sanctions issues.[29] The sanctions that the Security Council imposed against Iraq (1990), Libya (1992), Sudan (1996), and Afghanistan (1999) did not concern peace operation matters.[30] But all the other sanctions that it adopted in the period were related to peace operations. The sanctions against the former Yugoslavia (1991, 1992, and 1998), Somalia (1992), Cambodia (1992), Haiti (1993), Angola (1993, 1997, and 1998), Rwanda (1994), and Sierra Leone (1997) have to be seen in this light.

The qualitative changes that peace operations went through in the 1990s were partly the deepening of a tendency that had already started in the late 1980s.[31] This tendency entailed increasing attention given by peace operations to peacebuilding measures after the end of conflict. Departing from the concept of postconflict peacebuilding first outlined in Boutros Boutros-Ghali's *Agenda for Peace*, peacekeeping developed a more holistic and structural outlook, with the mission not only to hinder violence before or during conflict, but also to "prevent the recurrence of violence among nations and peoples" after conflict.[32] In more practical terms, peacebuilding measures tackled in a rather straightforward manner two main sets of issues: military and political—that is, *institutional* (although the pursuit of justice through the ad hoc international tribunals can be included in these peacebuilding measures).

For the peace operations of the 1990s, moving away from the military culture that dominated the period of conflict implied primarily getting rid of military equipment that had been used during the wars, implementing demining programs, and ensuring the voluntary demobilization of combatants and their reintegration into civilian society. On the political side, peacebuilding measures entailed multiple tasks for the reconstruction of political institutions, amounting in the long run to accountability, transparency, and legitimacy, if not democracy. These measures included, to various degrees, strengthening the rule of law (for example, through the training and restructuring of local police, as well as judicial and penal reform), improving respect for human rights through the monitoring and investigation of past and existing abuses, providing technical assistance for democratic development (including electoral assistance and support for free media), and promoting conflict resolution and reconciliation techniques.

Most of the peace operations after 1991 had one or several of these military and political (institutional) aspects of peacebuilding. This was the case of the United Nations Mission in El Salvador (ONUSAL), the United Nations Transitional Authority in Cambodia (UNTAC), the United Nations Angolan Verification Missions (UNAVEM II and III), the United Nations Mission for the Referendum in Western Sahara (MINURSO), the United Nations Operations in Mozambique (ONU-MOZ), the United Nations Mission in Somalia II (UNOSOM II), the United Nations Mission in Bosnia-Herzegovina (UNMIBH), the United Nations Mission in Kosovo (UNMIK), and the United Nations Transitional Administration in East Timor.

If in the early 1990s the establishment of the ad hoc international tribunals was limited to the former Yugoslavia and Rwanda, later on international criminal jurisdiction became a tool also used in postconflict reconstruction efforts in Sierra Leone and East Timor.

ASSESSING PEACE OPERATIONS: A LESS IMPRESSIVE PICTURE

On reflection, the quantitative and qualitative growth of peace operations in the 1990s is less impressive than first appears. The mobilization of resources and the results were, indeed, fairly modest.

COLLECTIVE SECURITY AND ITS MEAGER RESOURCES

Comparing the United Nations' peace restoration efforts with the commitments of member states, especially major member states, to their own interests and agendas helps to show that these efforts remained marginal. In most cases, the troops committed to peace operations by key member states in the 1990s were minimal—a fraction of their overall national capacities. For example, in 1994 the United Kingdom supplied 3,800 personnel to UN peace operations, France provided 5,200, and the United States provided 1,000. By comparison, the United Kingdom had 406,000 active duty military and civilian defense personnel; France, 614,000; and the United States, 2,760,000.[33] Thus, the United Kingdom provided the United Nations with 0.9 percent of its available force; France, 0.8 percent; and the United States, less than 0.04 percent. As a result, peace operations suffered chronically from two ills: delays in the deployment of personnel and shortages in the troops deployed.[34]

The differences between national defense budgets and the amount of funds allocated to UN peace operations are another telling indication of the limited commitment of member states to peace operations. While total UN expenditures for peace operations for the 1990s amounted to $19.9 billion, total world military expenditures for 1991 to 1999 amounted to approximately $6.9 trillion.[35] The contributions of member states to the United Nations to confront the crises that arose in the 1990s were equal to only 0.3 percent of the total amount that world governments spent on their militaries. On average, for every $1 spent on peace operations during the 1990s, $349 were spent on the militaries of the member states. Even among Western powers that contributed significantly to peace operations, this ratio remained massively in favor of national military spending. This is true first and foremost of the United States, the biggest military spender ever. The total U.S. federal budget outlays for national defense functions between 1991 and 1999 were approximately $2.5 trillion, or 125 times greater than the total UN peacekeeping budget.[36] In 1994, the most expensive year of the 1990s for peace operations, the United States was assessed $1.08 billion for UN peacekeeping missions and spent $281.6 billion for its national defense. During the same year, France was assessed $0.15 billion for peacekeeping and spent $42.6 billion on its national defense. The United Kingdom was assessed $0.23 billion for peacekeeping and spent $42.7 billion on defense. Thus, for every $1 spent on United Nations peace operations, the United States spent $290, France spent $282, and the United Kingdom spent $182 on their respective national defense needs.[37]

The percentage of a country's gross domestic product (GDP) spent on peace operations is also a telling indicator.[38] Figures for France, the United Kingdom, and the United States (shown in table 1) indicate that although defense spending made up an important portion of overall spending in the 1990s, peace operations expenditures were so minor in the overall economic picture as to be almost negligible.

As a result, while significant and unparalleled vis-à-vis the past, peace operations efforts remained relatively modest in the 1990s. They were not

**Table 1. Defense and Peacekeeping as a Percentage of
Gross Domestic Product (GDP), 1990–1999**

Country	Defense Spending as % of GDP					UN Peacekeeping Operations Spending as % of GDP		
	1990	1992	1994	1996	1998	1994	1996	1997–98
France	3.6	3.4	3.3	3.0	2.8	0.0146	0.0179	0.0049
United Kingdom	4.0	3.8	3.4	2.9	2.7	0.0219	0.0254	0.0048
United States	5.3	4.8	4.1	3.6	3.2	0.0171	0.0256	0.0035

Source: *Report on Allied Contributions to the Common Defense: A Report to the United States Congress by the Secretary of Defense* (Washington, D.C.: Office of the Secretary of Defense, various years), tables: "Selected Country Responsibility Sharing Indicators and Contributions" for France, the United Kingdom, and the United States (1995); "Selected Country Responsibility Sharing Indicators and Contributions" for France, the United Kingdom, and the United States (1997); and table E-5 (1999).

really commensurate with the crises that they tried to solve and the public attention that they received. What this state of affairs also indicates is that major powers continued to view the local conflicts and humanitarian crises in which they led the United Nations to get involved as marginal compared to their immediate national priorities. In the process, they were exposing the United Nations to the risk of being unable to fulfill the responsibilities to which they were committing it.

THE MIXED RECORD OF PEACE OPERATIONS

Regarding the evaluation of the peace operations of the 1990s, two questions come to mind: What exactly is being evaluated in peace operations? And what are the criteria of evaluation?[39]

What is evaluated is only what could be reasonably achieved by peace operations considering the crises in which they got involved. In this regard, three elements have to be underlined. To start with, the peace operations launched to address humanitarian crises and complex humanitarian emergencies could not solve all the problems encompassed by them.[40] This is especially the case since peace operations usually took place in "failed" states crippled by political, social, and economic disintegration, often carrying the stigmas of a long legacy of traumas and grievances. Consider how long it took for the Western industrialized nations, how many crises and conflicts they had to go through, to reach their current state of stability and prosperity. It cannot be fundamentally different for the less developed countries of today. In addition, the United Nations was not the sole actor involved in the handling of the crises. As part of a group of actors (including states) operating at various levels to solve the crises, peace operations must therefore not be considered the sole agent accounting for the outcomes, positive and negative, of the situations in which they engaged. Moreover, the diversity of tasks at hand in peace operations implies various timelines of evaluation, with the demarcation of what is and what is not assessable at a given moment. While a number of missions or aspects of a mission were designed to produce short-term results and can consequently be evaluated on this basis, others were supposed to produce results over a longer period.

These elements are the broad context in which the criteria for evaluating peace operations have to be understood. It is important to keep them in mind when referring to the ambitious mandates of the peace operations of the 1990s—mandates that constitute the baseline used to measure peace operations.[41]

In setting up the mandates of peace operations, Security Council resolutions outline their goals.[42] They indicate what is to be realized by peace operations for them to be viewed as successes. In the process, they provide benchmarks of evaluation.[43] From the resolutions of the Security Council dealing with peacekeeping in the 1990s, we can identify three sets of objectives, or criteria, around which most of the peace operations were built.

First, the Security Council resolutions assign to peace operations the main goal of stopping the conflicts in a relatively short time. This is an overarching and primary objective mentioned by all the resolutions that address conflict situations. In this connection, the resolutions call for a variety of measures, depending on the stage, specific nature, and depth of the crises.

The second set of goals on which the Security Council resolutions focus concerns the delivery of humanitarian assistance and respect for human rights. These are two recurrent themes in most of the resolutions of the 1990s, as important as putting an end to conflicts. Depending on the stage of the crisis and its nature, the attitude of the parties in conflict, and the commitment of the international community, the measures envisioned by the Security Council vary.

The third set of goals entails peacebuilding. Peacebuilding measures include initiatives concerning not only military and police institutions, but also elections, judicial institutions, and the political system in general.[44]

Using these goals as the main criteria of evaluation, and keeping in mind the qualifications alluded to at the beginning of this section, the picture that emerges from the overview of the major peace operations of the 1990s is one of mixed results. The major peace operations of the period fall into three categories: peace operations that can be considered as having succeeded, operations that are neither a success nor a clear failure, and operations in which the sense of failure predominates.[45]

In the 1990s, four peace operations can be considered overall success stories. These operations have three main characteristics: They were conducted with the consent of the parties on the ground; they did not entail peace enforcement aspects; and success was met preventively—that is, when the operations tackled issues before the conflict had erupted (prevention)—or after combatants had made a real commitment to ending the conflict and asked the United Nations to contribute to the reconstruction of the country (peacebuilding). These success stories are the UN missions in Macedonia, El Salvador, Mozambique, and Guatemala.

One area in which the United Nations can be credited with a success in prevention is the United Nations Preventive Deployment Force (UNPREDEP) in Macedonia.[46] It is the general view that the mission played a significant role in preventing the war from spreading and contributed to the internal stabilization of Macedonia.[47] Regrettably, when a permanent member of the Security Council (China) vetoed a further extension of the mission's mandate in February 1999, UNPREDEP came to an end.[48] Had the operation continued, many negative developments along the Macedonian border with Kosovo in early 2001 probably would have been avoided.

In El Salvador, Mozambique, and Guatemala, the United Nations intervened at the end point of the conflicts, when the parties had exhausted their will and capacity to fight. Peacebuilding aspects, launched on the basis of peace agreements, represented the bulk of the United Nations' responsibilities. With the help of the United Nations Observer Mission in El Salvador,[49] in less than a decade the country was transformed from one whose name was synonymous with death, torture, and destruction into what many consider to be a model of rather successful reconciliation. To be sure, certain reforms continue to encounter obstacles to this very day, reforms in land tenure being a case in point.[50] Also, El Salvador's society continues to be among the most crime-ridden in the Americas, especially because of violent street gangs. When it completed its mandate in April 1995, however, ONUSAL had had a very positive impact on the evolution of the country.[51]

The United Nations Operation in Mozambique can also be viewed as quite successful when it comes to peacebuilding.[52] Of course, the UN involvement was not flawless: A number of opportunities were missed, and, at the end of the two-year UN operation in December 1994, much still needed to be done, including clearing land mines from the fields so that agriculture could resume, providing health and educational facilities, and removing weapons.[53] Moreover, Mozambique had increased rather than shaken off its dependence on international financial and humanitarian assistance, and the voices of ordinary Mozambicans were in danger of being drowned out by the agendas of international development agencies. Nevertheless, the principal purpose of the mission was achieved: ONU-MOZ had played a critical role in helping to steer a large, war-torn country firmly in the direction of peace. By December 1994, the United Nations could claim that not only had it succeeded in keeping Mozambique's warring factions, Frelimo and Renamo, from returning to war, but that it had also organized elections that had helped to put the country on the path to political recovery.[54]

The United Nations Verification Mission in Guatemala (MINUGUA) also had a positive influence on the evolution of the country. Having the responsibility of observing the cessation of hostilities between the government of Guatemala and the Unidad Revolucionaria Nacional Guatemalteca (URNG), principally in separating forces and helping in the demobilization of URNG,[55] the UN mission acted as a confidence-building mechanism. In addition, MINUGUA observers provided a channel for international assistance by contributing to the pacification of a highly militarized and economically and socially stratified society.[56] These were no small achievements in a country that had been ravaged by war for close to forty years.

Several peace operations were neither clear successes nor clear failures. Among them, two main categories stand out: either the United Nations' involvement in the crises was successful in one of the generic goals that the Security Council resolutions outlined but failed regarding the other sets of objectives, or it encountered mixed results in the overall goals of the peace operation. The UN missions in Haiti, Sierra Leone, and East Timor fall under the first category. The peacebuilding initiatives in Cambodia, Bosnia (following the Dayton Accords), and Kosovo (in the aftermath of the air campaign of spring 1999) belong to the second category.

In Haiti, the involvement of the U.S.-led Multinational Force and the United Nations brought a number of positive results between the fall of 1994 and the spring of 1995, first and foremost being the ouster of the military government in September 1994.[57] But in subsequent years, the peacebuilding efforts of the United Nations did not produce significant improvements. The situation in Haiti remained bleak. The institutions that the

United Nations committed to help reform (the police and judiciary) are to this day in poor shape and certainly not functioning as initially expected.[58] In 2004, the situation worsened as major protests and political violence precipitated an abrupt change of government and two tropical storms produced humanitarian crises. After having authorized rapid deployment of a Multinational Interim Force (MIF) to stabilize the country, on June 1, 2004, the United Nations established MINUSTAH, the sixth peacekeeping mission in Haiti since 1993.[59] Against this background, the situation continues to be serious in Haiti, particularly regarding the failure of disarmament efforts and the failure to achieve a certain degree of political stability.[60] The presidential elections that took place (after having been delayed several times in 2005) on February 7, 2006, in the presence of MINUSTAH, and returned former President René Préval to office are unlikely to be enough to improve the political situation drastically. Furthermore, the country has not progressed economically. In other words, achieving the broad UN mandate (to put democracy on firmer ground in Haiti) is perhaps more than ever an elusive goal.

The prospects for the restoration of peace in Sierra Leone are reasonably good in spite of the persistence of local endemic problems—political corruption in particular.[61] The outcomes of the United Nations Mission in Sierra Leone (UNAMSIL), established in October 1999, are therefore rather positive, the situation having especially changed on the ground after the British-led intervention in May 2000.[62] The "Security First" approach of the international community, which brought about the disarmament of all armed groups, the full deployment of some 17,000 UNAMSIL peacekeepers across Sierra Leone, the restoration of government authority in the countryside, and a clearer understanding of the threats posed by regional insecurity, are results for which the UN peace operation can be credited. UNAMSIL logistical support also went a long way toward minimizing the administrative challenges confronting the National Electoral Commission and the organization of the presidential elections of January 2002. Later that year the United Nations, together with the government of Sierra Leone, reached an agreement on the establishment of a Special Court for Sierra Leone to try war criminals.[63]

The international and national commitment to peacebuilding has been clearly expressed in Sierra Leone, and the final publication of the Sierra Leone Truth and Reconciliation Commission in 2004 marked the turning point from the painful past to a new beginning.[64] Still, it is not possible to give a fully positive assessment of the UN experience with Sierra Leone: The disastrously ineffective approach to Sierra Leone during the second half of 1990s, including the poor showing of the United Nations Observer Mission in Sierra Leone (UNOMSIL) between July 1998 and October 1999, is not easy to overcome.[65] Moreover, UN efforts have not yet produced a stable state capable of exercising the full range of sovereign responsibilities on behalf of the population. Although the international presence is diminishing, it remains necessary.[66]

Regarding East Timor, the conditions in which the United Nations oversaw the end of the Indonesian domination and the referendum for independence cannot be perceived as a success.[67] The destruction of its infrastructure, the massive dislocation of its people conducted in late summer 1999 by pro-integration militias and Indonesian forces (after the East Timorese people voted for independence in the UN-supervised referendum of August 30), and the bystander attitude of the United Nations Mission in East Timor (UNAMET) can easily be considered a failure for the world organization.[68] On the other hand, the peacebuilding track record of the United Nations Transitional Administration in East Timor, established in October 1999, was quite positive.[69] It certainly had a long-term positive impact on the evolution of East Timor, as the peaceful and successful access of East Timor to independence (as the state Timor-Leste) in May 2002 has shown.[70] The follow-on peacekeeping mission of the United Nations Mission of Support in East Timor (UNIMSET),[71] from May 2002 to May 2005, and the United Nations Office in Timor-Leste (UNOTIL, mandated for one year) that succeeded it, presided over the replacement of peacekeeping activities by the consolidation of peace measures.[72] However, in May 2006, after new breakouts of violence, international forces (mainly Australian troops) re-entered the country to help contain the rebels.

Cambodia, Bosnia in the aftermath of the Dayton Accords, and Kosovo are cases where the overall goals of peace operations encountered mixed results. In Cambodia, the task awaiting the United Nations appeared a daunting one. UN involvement in the country came after more than twenty years of turmoil. Between 1970, when a military coup ended Prince Norodom Sihanouk's rule, and 1991, when a peace accord was signed in Paris, Cambodia went through a great deal: a civil war that raged between 1970 and 1975; the brutality of the Khmer Rouge, which between 1975 and 1978 presided over mass executions and deaths in slave labor camps; a Vietnamese invasion in 1978 that toppled the Khmer Rouge regime; and Hun Sen's Vietnamese-installed communist government fighting a war against the remaining Khmer Rouge guerrillas. Following these dramatic events, UN involvement certainly helped to stabilize the country.

The United Nations Transitional Authority in Cambodia facilitated the return of refugees, encouraged the formation of Cambodian nongovernmental organizations (NGOs), and engaged in human rights education. More important, the multiparty election that the United Nations organized in 1993 proved a success. But because the Khmer Rouge and the government balked, and because the United Nations did not put massive pressure on them, the peacekeepers could not carry out two key peacebuilding provisions of the peace accord: disarming the factions and overseeing the security apparatus.[73] As a result, fractious politics continued to be a feature of the Cambodian political landscape. Hun Sen muscled his way into power through a coup in July 1997, leading to the execution of dozens of his opponents. International efforts have left Cambodia without an independent or neutral legislature, judiciary, army, police force, civil bureaucracy, or other major institutions to check and balance government and guard civil rights.[74] The country suffers from poverty; it is weak and largely controlled by Hun Sen's party. Such a state of affairs is certainly not the one that UN peacebuilding efforts were initially meant to bring about, and hence, the United Nations is devoting more and more attention to the problem of impunity and accountability in Cambodia.[75]

Peacebuilding in Bosnia also shows a mixed record. The bulk of the UN peacebuilding mandate was outlined in the Dayton Accords, which gave the United Nations a rather modest role.[76] It assigned the United Nations Mission in Bosnia and Herzegovina the function of forming a local police force, and, although some progress has been made, it was not as much and as quickly as initially envisioned.[77] This left Bosnia with three separate police forces—Bosniak, Croat, and Serb—each with its own jurisdiction. The first two have merged, at least nominally, but the Republika Srpska has refused all efforts to reform structures or integrate them with those of other ethnic groups. Moreover, the Serb force was filled with war criminals and actively supported persons indicted by the International Criminal Tribunal for the Former Yugoslavia in The Hague. In this context, the police forces throughout the country have remained highly politicized, acting at the behest of politicians to obstruct implementation of the Dayton Accords—in particular, refugee return—and are heavily involved in organized crime.[78] Thus, police malfeasance and security continue to be a problem in the region and hamper the peacebuilding process.[79]

There is also a mixture of success and failure in the UN peacebuilding involvement in Kosovo.[80] On the one hand, the United Nations has recorded a number of accomplishments, notably improvement of law and order and the development of democratic self-governing institutions.[81] In the first instance, both the Kosovo Force and the United Nations Mission in Kosovo deserve credit for the demilitarization of the Kosovo Liberation Army (KLA). They also deserve credit for preventing a civil war that threatened to break out in the chaotic and violent conditions of immediate postwar Kosovo between supporters of the KLA and Ibrahim Rugova's League of Democrats of Kosovo (LDK). These preventive measures played a critical role in laying the minimum foundations for respect for law and order in the province. An equally important accomplishment has been to put in place an effective framework of institutions. Local government elections in October 2000, which gave significant institutional responsibilities to the municipal level; the election for the legislative assembly in November 2001; and the agreement reached in February 2002 concerning the designation of the president of Kosovo, the president of the assembly, and the prime minister are major results springing largely from the work of the UN mission.[82] Despite the low participation of Kosovo Serbs, the Kosovo Assembly elections in October 2004 furthered these institutional achievements, as a large majority of the Kosovars participated in peaceful democratic elections, expressing an overall wish for accountable leaders.[83]

However, the failures of the UN peacebuilding efforts in Kosovo cannot be overlooked. First, after achieving the KLA's agreement to disarm, there was little follow-up and very few serious attempts to move against elements within the KLA who are widely believed to operate underground quasi-criminal networks. Second, the inability to come up with any credible strategy for dealing with the Serbs in Kosovo is a major problem. After the war, approximately 150,000 Serbs fled Kosovo; perhaps 100,000 remain in enclaves or in a solid Serb sector north of the divided city of Mitrovica. Here the stakes are high: Failure to reintegrate the Serbs would likely lead to the formalization of Kosovo's de facto partition along the Ibar River, which divides the northern and southern portions of Mitrovica. In that event, the Serb enclaves in the rest of Kosovo would probably be swept away in a renewed round of violence.[84] Third is the issue of Kosovo's status, which remains a sensitive issue.[85] The situation worsened somewhat when President Ibrahim Rugova died on January 21, 2006. With him, an important symbol of Kosovo's pacifist struggle for independence, and perhaps the only clear and unifying leader of the country, disappeared. Although Kosovo's independence is moving closer to becoming reality, in order for the talks on the future of Kosovo's final status to be successful, extensive groundwork is essential to address the complex of issues.[86]

The role of the United Nations in Bosnia before the Dayton Accords, in Somalia, Angola, and Rwanda, can be listed as peace operation failures. In these cases, the sense of disappointment spans, in one way or another, the three areas on which Security Council resolutions focused in the peace operations of the 1990s: bringing the conflict to an end in a relatively short time, providing humanitarian assistance, and peacebuilding. These failures are not entirely attributable to the United Nations. Rather, they are associated with an unwillingness of the parties in the conflicts to arrive at a genuinely peaceful settlement; but this fact does not eliminate UN responsibility in what happened.

In Bosnia, before the Dayton Accords of fall 1995, the United Nations' involvement that corresponds to the period of UNPROFOR (between 1992 and 1995), combining peace enforcement and humanitarian assistance, constitutes a dramatic failure. UNPROFOR did very little, or at least did not take decisive action, to stop the killing of more than 100,000 people.[87] It came more or less to accept the fact that the delivery of humanitarian assistance would be constantly hampered by Bosnian Serb combatants. The inability of UNPROFOR to protect the populations trapped in the so-called safe areas—in Srebrenica especially—and, more generally, the tendency of its forces to adopt a bystander attitude as civilian populations were killed and displaced are hard facts that epitomize the shortcomings of the United Nations in Bosnia.[88]

The failures of UN peace operations appear even greater in the context of Africa. The importance of the humanitarian assistance delivered to the people of Somalia from 1992 to 1993 should never be underestimated. It certainly saved many lives, but in the end, the United Nations' involvement in Somalia can be considered a failure.[89] Neither the peace enforcement nor the peacebuilding components of the UN involvement managed to produce peace and put the country back on track. More than ten years after the events, Somalia remained crippled by political and economic disintegration. It still had no central government, and the country was plagued by numerous localized conflicts among rival militia groups backed by regional powers.[90] Moreover, terrorists were taking advantage of the state's collapse to attack neighboring countries.[91]

Angola is another failure for the United Nations, which succeeded neither in stopping war nor delivering humanitarian assistance and ensuring peacebuilding. The UN mission was never able to bring peace between the government, built around the forces of the Popular Movement for the

Liberation of Angola (MPLA) and its leader José Eduardo dos Santos, and the National Union for the Total Independence of Angola (UNITA), the rebel movement headed by Jonas Savimbi. The two had been fighting for control of the country since it gained its independence in 1975. Throughout the years of war, the MPLA government drew on support from the Soviet Union and Cuba; the United States and South Africa backed UNITA. The United Nations began its involvement in Angola in January 1989 with the United Nations Angola Verification Mission (UNAVEM I), whose mandate to help oversee the withdrawal of Cuban forces was successfully fulfilled with the cooperation of the parties. UNAVEM I lasted until June 1991. After that, things went downhill. UNAVEM II, in place between June 1991 and February 1995, had neither adequate resources nor the authority to help the parties to stop fighting.[92] In particular, the United Nations was unable to convince Savimbi to accept the results of the September 1992 elections that it had helped to organize. As a result, soon after, the country was plunged into another war. UNAVEM III, deployed between February 1995 and June 1997, achieved only a very shaky peace.[93] In the process, the initial phases of peacebuilding were hampered. The two single conditions that would have been strong signs of progress—the demobilization of UNITA's military forces and the extension of the government's administrative authority throughout the country—were not implemented. Ultimately, it took Savimbi's death in February 2002 to show the need for a real cease-fire.

The lack of real effort by the United Nations to prevent the genocide in Rwanda in 1994 is another failure, and probably the biggest one for the United Nations in the 1990s. Here the failure is about preventing internal war, humanitarian disaster, and genocide. A quotation of the opening lines of the *Comprehensive Report on Lessons Learned from United Nations Assistance Mission for Rwanda (UNAMIR) October 1993–April 1996*, published by the Lessons Learned Unit of the UN Department of Peacekeeping Operations in December 1996, helps to illustrate the extent to which the United Nations failed the people of Rwanda during this period:

> 1. From April to July 1994, between 500,000 and 800,000 Rwandese, mainly of the Tutsi ethnic group, were massacred in Rwanda. Without a resolute and immediate response from the community of nations, the slaughter continued in the presence of the United Nations Assistance Mission for Rwanda (UNAMIR), a lightly armed and equipped peacekeeping force sent to the country in October 1993 to assist in the implementation of the Arusha Peace Agreement, which had obviously collapsed. Genocide was committed while UNAMIR was left with only

400 peacekeepers without a clear mandate, the means or necessary support to stop it.

2. From its inception until its eventual withdrawal, UNAMIR seemed always to be one step behind the realities of the situation in Rwanda. It was deployed in October 1993 to assist in the implementation of a peace process that seemed to have stalemated even before it began. At the height of the crisis, the unilateral decision of some Governments to withdraw their national contingents left the remnants of UNAMIR even more vulnerable and unable to provide protection to civilians at risk. Even when the strength of UNAMIR was increased in May 1994 in response to the continued killings, by the time the authorized strength of 5,500 was reached it was November 1994, the civil war was over and the needs of the country were no longer assistance in the maintenance of security, but assistance in national reconstruction.[94]

Subsequently, the United Nations was unable to stop the spread of war beyond Rwanda and the development of a regional conflict that embroiled the DRC and others, at the expense of several million civilians' lives.

By launching multiple and complex peace operations at more or less the same time, the United Nations was taking a considerable risk. Although peace operations benefited from more resources and attention than in the past, they remained relatively low on the priority list of the major powers—hence the mixed record of UN peace operations in the 1990s. In this regard, the successes and failures of peace operations tended to echo the time lines of the conflicts. Successes were likely when the United Nations got involved before the eruption of the crises (prevention) or toward the end of the conflicts (peacebuilding activities). Failures were encountered most when the peace operations were deployed in the midst of the crises, when parties were still at war. This shows that peace enforcement was not well suited for peace operations. Using force as a way to coerce local actors into negotiating peace proved to be difficult.

The overall impression in the review of UN peacekeeping during the 1990s is that the international community did both so much and so little to address the humanitarian crises of the period. Why such an ambivalent attitude, such a mixture of extended and limited commitment on the part of the international community vis-à-vis humanitarian crises? This is the central question addressed from different perspectives in the next three chapters, beginning with a look at the relative ineffectiveness of the international community's response from the perspective of the principal international organization—the United Nations as an international bureaucracy.

CHAPTER 2

THE UNITED NATIONS AND ITS SHORTCOMINGS AS AN INTERNATIONAL BUREAUCRACY

T HE UNITED NATIONS IS THE FIRST SOURCE for a comprehensive explanation of the ambiguous results of peace operations. This initial focus entails analyzing the impact of the political and operational limitations of the United Nations as an international organization. To examine the political shortcomings of the UN, it is necessary to concentrate on the problems created by the different viewpoints on the conception and implementation of peacekeeping operations—first, between the UN secretary-general and the Security Council, and, second, among the permanent members of the Security Council. As for the impact of the operational aspects of the United Nations, they have to do with three issues: the tensions between the diplomatic culture shaping UN headquarters and the demands of the field, the gap between the administrative capacities of the United Nations in New York and the needs on the ground, and the endemic communication difficulties within the United Nations itself.

POLITICAL SHORTCOMINGS: THE SECRETARY-GENERAL AND THE SECURITY COUNCIL

The relations among key decision makers inside the United Nations are meant to be cooperative. Short of this, decision makers quickly reach a stalemate. The fact that cooperation among the major actors by and large prevailed in the 1990s allowed the United Nations to tackle major humanitarian crises around the world. However, this cooperation proved to be far from smooth. The disagreements between the secretary-general and the Security Council were a political factor that undermined the ability of the United Nations to project decisiveness, coherence, and consistency—that is, effective leadership.

THE SECRETARY-GENERAL AND THE SECURITY COUNCIL'S POWER: THEORY AND PRACTICE

Before looking into the impact of the disagreements between the UN secretary-general and the members of the Security Council on the United Nations' approach to Somalia, Bosnia, and Rwanda (three of the defining crises of the 1990s), a few words are necessary to outline, in theory and practice, the interplay between the secretary-general's and the Security Council's power, which will help to clarify the framework of deliberation and decision making of the United Nations.

In the United Nations Charter, the respective status and roles of the secretary-general and the Security Council are clearly defined. What is also clearly established is the disparity of power between them. The Charter gives an advantage to the Security Council over the secretary-general.

It is essentially in the five articles of Chapter XV of the UN Charter, focusing on the Secretariat, that the status and powers of the secretary-general are defined.[1] Article 97 indicates the status of the secretary-general, who is described as the chief administrative officer of the organization, and it is from this title that the extent and limits of the secretary-general's responsibilities derive. Article 98 stipulates that in terms of administrative capacity, the secretary-general represents the United Nations in the meetings of its various organs. Article 99 addresses the question of the political power of the secretary-general. It merely stipulates that the "secretary-general may bring to the attention of the Security Council any matter which in his opinion may threaten the maintenance of international peace and security."[2] It would be difficult to make it shorter. The power of the secretary-general entails a power of qualification regarding crises that affect international order. Nonetheless, the expression "may bring to the attention of the Security Council" does not serve as an endorsement for strong powers to be attributed to the secretary-general vis-à-vis the Security Council. There is no indication that the secretary-general can mandate the Security Council, for example, to take an initiative that it would not want to take. Article 100 outlines guidelines for the ethics of the secretary-general's role, as well as that of the UN staff—essentially, impartiality and objectivity.[3] It puts the secretary-general above the particular interests that may animate the member states and makes this official the representative of the United Nations as a whole. Finally, Article 101 indicates the institutional responsibilities of the secretary-general regarding the composition of the United Nations and its professional qualities and moral standing.

In comparison to the secretary-general, the amount of attention dedicated to the Security Council and the powers given to it by the Charter are considerable. The Security Council is described as the executive organ of the United Nations—the one that holds the key to the main policy and operational decisions relating to international peace and security issues. Three elements stand out. First, the Council decides who qualifies for United Nations membership, who is admitted or not into the United Nations.[4] It also decides who continues to be a member of the United Nations or is expelled.[5] Second, the decisions and actions of the Security Council have a representative character; they speak for the entire United Nations organization on behalf of its members.[6] This is especially the case in the prime task of the United Nations and the Security Council: the maintenance of international peace and security.[7] Third, there are the powers of the Security Council concerning the maintenance of international peace and security. The bulk of these powers is addressed in Chapters VI, VII, and VIII of the UN Charter.

In Chapter VI, the Security Council is given the power to determine whether or not a dispute threatens international peace and security.[8] The Council is also given the power to help through pacific means to solve the dispute among the parties. In this context, the Council enjoys a wide range of possible initiatives—including negotiation, enquiry, conciliation, arbitration, judicial settlement, and resort to regional agencies or arrangements—to help in finding a solution.[9] Furthermore, should the parties to the dispute be unable to find a solution, the Security Council can recommend appropriate procedures or terms for pacific settlement.[10]

Chapter VII epitomizes the key role of the Security Council in handling threats to the peace, breaches of the peace, and acts of aggression; it begins in Article 39 of Chapter VII with the power given to the Security Council to qualify and determine the existence of a threat. This power of interpretation and qualification is crucial: It provides the foundation for international action. The measures at hand to deal with the threats to international peace and security are part of a gradation that goes from sanctions to ultimately (if there is no other way) the use of force.[11] Articles 43 to 51 of Chapter VII best indicate the extent of the Security Council's powers regarding the use of the force. According to these articles, the Security Council has the power to decide on the use of force; but further, it may call upon member states to contribute militarily and logistically to the use of force and decide with key member states how the contributions will be used.[12]

Chapter VIII of the Charter outlines the role of regional organizations in the maintenance of international peace and security. Once again, it makes the Security Council an essential organ in this area. From a general point of view, the Council is granted a *droit de regard* in regional affairs. For instance, Article 54 of Chapter VIII requires the Security Council to be informed of any initiative taken at the regional level to address disputes. The Security Council can also take initiatives on its own to address regional disputes.[13] When it comes to enforcement and the use of force as a way to maintain international peace and security, Article 53 could not be clearer: It gives the Security Council leadership and monopoly of initiative concerning authorizing the use of force through regional arrangements. Regional organizations cannot act on their own; they are dependent upon the green light of the Security Council. As a result, the Council has in principle an uncontested grip on collective security, be it at the global or regional level.[14] With these powers, the Security Council is certainly an overwhelming force compared to the secretary-general. The fact that the secretary-general is elected by the General Assembly, upon the recommendation of the Security Council, drives home this reality.[15]

Although the Charter engineers a huge disparity of power between the secretary-general and the Security Council, this does not imply that the role of the secretary-general is of little significance. In practice, the secretary-general can play a more substantial role than is apparent in principle. A number of elements suggest the importance of the secretary-general's power in the quotidian functions of the position.

The fact that the UN Charter so briefly defines the realm of action of the secretary-general is not necessarily an indication of truncated powers of the office. Less can also mean more. By not precisely describing and regulating the power of the secretary-general, the Charter leaves open possibilities that perhaps would not exist otherwise. To a certain extent, it leaves the drawing of the boundaries of the office's power to the discretion of the situations and the people in place. Accordingly, secretaries-general have had the tendency to fill in the blanks associated with the definition of their powers by interpreting them as much as possible to their advantage; even those who have traditionally been labeled as weak have not been reluctant to do so.[16] Moreover, the institutional tools of the secretary-general, as part of the decision-making process of the UN Secretariat, give the position notable powers. The reports of the secretary-general, in particular, are an important vehicle to make suggestions and to make known personal preferences to the Security Council. (Boutros Boutros-Ghali especially used his reports to the Security Council in this way.) In addition, the secretary-general is not, in reality, just an administrative figure; the secretary-general is also a political actor. The posting at the top of the United Nations puts the secretary-general in a position to engage in dialogue and negotiate with the national representatives to the United Nations and, more generally, with heads of state. The multilateral dimension of UN politics encourages the secretary-general on this path; it profiles the secretary-general as a natural go-between among the member states, especially when they are at odds with each other, particularly during a crisis.

In this regard, the secretary-general carries a symbolic and moral power that adds to the position's political stature. As more than the sum of the United Nations' parts (the member states), the secretary-general is meant to embody the spirit of the United Nations. Compared to the always tempting self-serving initiatives of the member states, including the permanent members of the Security Council, the symbolic power of the secretary-general is a key asset that he or she can call upon to help bring about solutions to crises.[17] It puts the secretary-general in the position of being a "last resort" actor. Furthermore, the personality of the individual holding the position of secretary-general can enhance the visibility, if not the influence, of the office. Take the case of Boutros Boutros-Ghali. To be sure, the 1990s, especially in the early years of the decade, were not a typical period for the world organization (if ever there was one). The unstable character of the Cold War's aftermath made it a favorable terrain for a secretary-general eager to make his mark. Yet it was Boutros-Ghali's choice to embrace the newfound centrality of the United Nations in international life and try to capitalize on it by engaging and challenging member states on their international responsibilities.

The Impact of the Disagreements between Boutros-Ghali and the Security Council on Peace Operations: Somalia, Bosnia, and Rwanda

One of the keys to the success of UN involvement is an agreement between the secretary-general and the Security Council on how to handle crises. In the case of Somalia, Bosnia, and Rwanda, the secretary-general and the Security Council (more specifically, the leading members of the Security Council: the United States, the United Kingdom, and France) were never able to fully bridge the gap between their understanding of the crises and the appropriate response. This situation undermined the coherence, credibility, and effectiveness of UN involvement in these countries, resulting in significant negative outcomes.

The decision to intervene in Somalia in December 1992 did not generate much disagreement between the secretary-general and the Security Council. For some months, pressure had been mounting from relief organizations and the international media, leading most international actors to think that something drastic had to be done to put an end to the starvation and death of hundreds of thousands of Somalis. Hence, the decision was made in November 1992 to dispatch up to 30,000 troops under U.S. leadership to Somalia in an attempt to stop the humanitarian crisis.

However, the division of labor regarding who would do what in Somalia generated major disagreements between the secretary-general and the United States, the key member of the Security Council for the international involvement in Somalia. The disagreements concerned both the U.S.-led Operation Restore Hope and the UN mission to follow, UNOSOM II (following UNOSOM I, which operated between 1991 and 1992). Specifically, the disagreements concerned the duration of the presence of U.S. troops in Somalia; the meaning of the mandates of the two missions, especially when it came to restoring security; and the direction and coordination of the various stages of the international operations.

The question of the duration of the U.S. presence was posed in the context of Operation Restore Hope and in the context of U.S. support to UNOSOM II. Regarding Operation Restore Hope, Washington was preparing the withdrawal of U.S. troops even before they arrived in Mogadishu. From the start, President George H. W. Bush and his foreign policy team had planned Operation Restore Hope to be a short undertaking to be deployed for a few weeks, after which the UN mission would take over. Bill Clinton's victory in the November 1992 presidential elections made this initial plan all the more pressing. Bush did not want to impose upon the new administration a major operation that it had not initiated. Consequently, with the transition under way in January 1993, the Pentagon prepared plans for what it called a seamless takeover by the United Nations in Somalia.

These plans did not fit Boutros-Ghali's views. He acknowledged that the operation should be "limited in time, in order to prepare the way for a return to peacekeeping and postconflict peacebuilding."[18] Nevertheless, he considered that this limitation presupposed that by the time of withdrawal, Operation Restore Hope would have achieved one of its principal mandates: calling upon the U.S.-led force, UNITAF, "to use all necessary means to establish as soon as possible a secure environment for humanitarian relief operations in Somalia."[19] The establishment of a satisfactory level of security on the ground was a condition for the withdrawal of UNITAF and the deployment of UNOSOM II.

Evaluating whether or not this had been achieved became a point of contention between the United States and Boutros-Ghali. By the end of January, the United States argued that the situation was secure enough.[20]

The view at UN headquarters was quite different.[21] In March, the secretary-general's assessment of the security situation was still rather negative.[22] Nevertheless, the U.S. position prevailed. Although security had not been achieved in Mogadishu and other parts of the country, on March 26, 1993, UN Security Council Resolution 814 authorized a UN takeover with a force of 28,000, plus the U.S. Quick Reaction Force.[23] The handover officially took place on May 3, 1993, after the Americans had already started to withdraw, tired of what they regarded as UN foot-dragging.[24]

The fact that the UN secretary-general and the United States could not come to an agreement on the duration of UNITAF jeopardized UNOSOM II from the start. Lacking the deterrence and credibility of the U.S.-led force, it was difficult to see how UNOSOM II would be able to ensure a secure environment for humanitarian relief operations. Six months later, the inability of the secretary-general to convince the United States to remain involved in Somalia, following the deaths of U.S. Army troops in Mogadishu on October 3, 1993, would have even greater consequences for the fate of the UN mission. The other participating nations decided to follow the lead of the United States and withdraw, essentially ending UNOSOM II.

The issue of the duration of the U.S. presence in Somalia became linked with the question of establishing a secure environment because the secretary-general and the United States clashed on what the mandate of securing the environment meant for the American-led UNITAF forces. The interpretations of the secretary-general and the United States diverged deeply. In his report of December 19, 1992, Boutros-Ghali noted that the success of Operation Restore Hope rested on two main conditions—the deployment of UNITAF forces throughout the entire Somali territory and the disarmament of factions:

> Since Resolution 794 (1992) was adopted, I and senior members of my staff had a number of meetings with representatives of the United States Government to discuss, inter alia, how and when the transition to continued peacekeeping operations could be made. In these discussions I have laid emphasis on two conditions in particular, whose importance I also stressed in a letter of 8 December 1992 to President Bush. The first condition is that the Unified Task Force should take effective action to ensure that the heavy weapons of the organized factions are neutralized and brought under international control and that the irregular forces and gangs are disarmed before the Unified Task Force withdraws. . . . The fulfillment of this condition demands action on two fronts. First, it is necessary to establish or consolidate agreements with the leaders of all

the organized factions for effective cease-fires in the various conflicts between them. . . . Secondly, it is necessary to disarm the lawless gangs who have been the principal threat to humanitarian operations. . . . The second, and equally essential, condition is that the authority entrusted to the Unified Task Force should be exercised throughout Somalia. Paragraph 10 of Security Council Resolution 794 (1992) imposes no geographical limitation, other than "in Somalia," on the mandate it confers. . . . In addition to the humanitarian argument for countrywide deployment of the Unified Task Force, there is also a compelling security argument. The objectives of the Unified Task Force would not have been achieved, nor the conditions created for the transition to peace-keeping operations, if heavy weapons and lawless gangs simply withdrew from parts of Somalia controlled by the Unified Task Force to continue their action in other parts while waiting to return and resume their harassment and exploitation of the international relief effort after the Unified Task force had handed over control to a less numerous and powerful United Nations force.[25]

On these two issues, Washington had a different view. Its position was stated in the report that the United States addressed to the president of the Security Council on January 16, 1993.[26] In the report, there is no mention whatsoever of planning to extend the authority of UNITAF throughout Somalia. As for disarming the factions, it is described as an occasional effort more than as a genuine and systematic policy.[27]

Whose interpretation of the mandate was right? In his letter to the Security Council of November 29, 1992, outlining the mandate of UNI-TAF, the secretary-general mentioned a countrywide deployment of UNITAF as a possibility, not as a strict condition. As a result, and logically, in Resolution 794, there is no specific indication of the necessity to deploy all over Somalia; the UN resolution discusses Somalia in general. Thus the U.S. interpretation of the geographical scope of UNITAF's mandate, although a minimalist one, is correct. To be sure, the secretary-general's reasoning on the need to deploy countrywide, which he later expressed forcefully in his December 8, 1992, letter to President Bush and in his December 19 report to the Security Council, made sense (in fact, probably more sense) in terms of securing the country. But he was then, as the United States argued at the time, trying to change the goalposts in the middle of the game.

What about the issue of the factions' disarmament? Here it seems that the secretary-general's interpretation is the correct one. In his November 29, 1992, letter, he explicitly mentioned getting rid of heavy weapons as a critical condition for restoring security.[28] Resolution 794, which interpreted and endorsed the recommendations made by the secretary-general in that letter, thus gave a clear mandate on the issue of disarmament. Nevertheless, the United States, unwilling to risk the casualties expected in going after heavy weapons, stayed away from the task; it let the opportunity for disarmament pass.[29] This was all the more unfortunate considering that the Somali militias had initially expected to be disarmed and were surprised at the inaction of the U.S.-led force. The more the militias realized that UNITAF was unwilling to take away heavy weapons, the more they took their chances and moved away from the subdued attitude that they had adopted at the outset of Operation Restore Hope. As the tensions steadily increased between UNITAF and the militias in the early months of 1993, the United States grew more and more eager to hand over the operations to the United Nations. In the end, with the failure of the United States to take on the task of removing the heavy weapons, the burden fell upon UNOSOM II—what Boutros-Ghali had feared all along. This would prove to be a daunting task for UNOSOM II.

Security Council Resolution 814 (adopted on March 26, 1993) was unprecedented in the history of the United Nations. It authorized UNOSOM II to use force under Chapter VII to implement the following mandate: to create a secure environment throughout Somalia; to promote political reconciliation; to establish the rule of law; to ensure compliance by all Somali parties, including movements and factions, with the commitments they had undertaken in signing the Addis Ababa Accords of January 1993, especially in relation to the implementation of the cease-fire disarmament provisions; and to assist in the repatriation of refugees and the resettlement of displaced persons.[30] Yet this impressive mandate could not hide the fact that, despite continuing U.S. military participation, UNOSOM II was much weaker than UNITAF, a widespread view among Somalis. Thus it seemed only a matter of time before the factions' leaders, Mohamed Farah Aidid in particular (whose power UNOSOM II was designed to eradicate), opposed the United Nations. The denouement came on June 5, 1993, when twenty-four Pakistani peacekeepers were killed while conducting an inspection of the Aidid faction's arms depot. This put the United Nations and Aidid on a collision course. Security Council Resolution 837 (June 6, 1993), after identifying Aidid's faction as responsible for the attack, authorized "all necessary means against all those responsible for the armed attacks."[31] Ultimately, the security situation continued to deteriorate in the summer of 1993 in the midst of the hunt for Aidid. This led to the October killing of U.S. soldiers and, a few months later, to the end of the international community's effort in Somalia.

The October debacle should not have come as a surprise, considering the complex and thus fragile chain of command in UNOSOM II. This issue brings up the question of the direction and coordination of operations in Somalia, the third main point of contention between the UN secretary-general and the United States.

The direction and coordination of operations were already sources of tension between Boutros-Ghali and the United States in the context of Operation Restore Hope. Although Boutros-Ghali was very much in favor of the U.S.-led intervention, he did not want the United Nations to give carte blanche to the United States. Consequently, he proposed a number of mechanisms to coordinate the U.S.-led mission with the United Nations as a way to monitor it. This was accepted in principle by both the Security Council and the United States and outlined mainly in paragraphs 13, 15, and 18 of Security Council Resolution 794.[32] In practice, however, the secretary-general was largely unable to convince the U.S. administration to comply with them.

In the context of UNOSOM II, the issues of direction and coordination proved even more problematic. To achieve the Resolution 814 mandate, the Security Council agreed to dispatch 20,000 UN peacekeepers and 2,000 civilians to replace UNITAF. The U.S. contribution to the twenty-nine-nation UNOSOM II force was 8,000 logistical troops and a Quick Reaction Force of 1,200 troops; the United States also provided a third of the initial estimated cost of $800 million. The person placed in charge of UNOSOM II was retired Admiral Jonathan Howe (a former deputy national security adviser to President Bush), who served as the secretary-general's special representative. The U.S. logistical forces came under UN command and control. As the first U.S. troops to serve under UN command, their integration did not pose any major problems. Far different was the case of the Quick Reaction Force. Neither the report of the secretary-general of March 3, 1993, which analyzed in particular the military concept of UNOSOM II, nor Resolution 814, which established UNOSOM II, mentioned precisely what the relations would be between UNOSOM II and the Quick Reaction Force. Article 14 of Resolution 814 stipulated only the following on the issue:

> [The Security Council] requests the Secretary-General, through his Special Representative, to direct the Force Commander of UNOSOM II to assume responsibility for the consolidation, expansion, and maintenance of a secure environment throughout Somalia, taking account of the particular circumstances in each locality, on an expedited basis in accordance with the recommendations contained in his report of

March 3, 1993, and in this regard to organize a prompt, smooth, and phased transition from UNITAF to UNOSOM II.

This provided little guidance because the report of the secretary-general limited itself to indicating the following: "A tactical quick reaction force of at least a battalion strength to be provided by the United States will be available in support of UNOSOM II."[33] The mention of "support" fell short of indicating under exactly whose command and authority the Quick Reaction Force would be. Furthermore, when mentioning the rules of engagement, the report did not allude at all to the Quick Reaction Force: "The rules of engagement would be defined by the UNOSOM II force commander. They would authorize and direct commanders to take certain specific actions if they were judged necessary to fulfill the mandate."[34]

How can this lack of clarity on such an important issue—involving the use of force—be explained? The answer is simple. Because the matter was critical, the lack of clarity was of the essence. Rather than clarifying the issue, which, in showing the extent of the disagreement, would have run the risk of jeopardizing U.S. involvement, the rules of engagement were left vague. Eager to have the U.S. military contribution to UNOSOM II, Boutros-Ghali accepted this setting because of the unwillingness of U.S. troops facing the possibility of using force to be put under UN command.[35] In the midst of this vagueness, the Quick Reaction Force was at least supposed to act in coordination with UNOSOM II. This hardly happened. Even worse, although its increase would have been critical and necessary with the intensification of the tension between UNOSOM II and Aidid's faction, coordination diminished parallel to it.[36]

The situation unraveled entirely with the arrival of the elite U.S. forces, the Delta Force and Army Rangers. Deployed in Somalia in August 1993, after the United States began incurring casualties, their mission was to protect the U.S. troops of the Quick Reaction Force and to participate in the hunt for Aidid.[37] To accomplish this mission, they benefited from more autonomy vis-à-vis UNOSOM II than did the Quick Reaction Force; in fact, they were outside the formal UNOSOM II command structure. The Rangers took their orders from U.S. Central Command at MacDill Air Force Base in Tampa, Florida, and all their subsequent operations against Aidid were approved by senior military officials in Washington.[38] The secretary-general and the United Nations as a whole were left more or less in the dark, yet the U.S. troops' actions had far-reaching consequences on the ground.[39] Moreover, they would lead to the events of October that precipitated the end of UN involvement in Somalia and, ultimately, its failure.

Regarding Bosnia, the fact that Boutros-Ghali and the three Western permanent members of the Security Council were at odds—first, on whether or not to have the United Nations involved and, second, on the modalities of its involvement—undermined the credibility of UN policies and their capacity to help end the war.

From the start, and throughout the conflict, Boutros-Ghali was not disposed to having the United Nations involved in the Balkans. He recognized that something had to be done, but he was wary of a UN engagement; he never really thought that the conditions on the ground met the criteria for a viable peace operation. Because the parties to the conflict felt that the battlefield was a better way for them to secure their respective goals than a political settlement at an early stage of the war, their authentic consent to the deployment of the peace operation was lacking—thus, Boutros-Ghali felt that there was no peace to keep.[40] Also, in his view the conflict in Bosnia diverted the attention of the international community away from other humanitarian crises in other parts of the world. For him, the African crises were as important, if not more, as those in the Balkans, yet they were receiving far less consideration and resources. Boutros-Ghali probably would have resented the selective attention of the Security Council less had he thought that the United Kingdom, France, and the United States were really committed to solving the war in Bosnia as quickly as possible. But this was not the case. With these three countries in the Security Council insisting on having the United Nations involved in the Balkans and yet sharing, each in its own way, an unwillingness to make the kind of commitment that seemingly would have been necessary to bring a rapid end to the conflict, the secretary-general regarded UN involvement as unlikely to succeed.[41] He saw it as a slippery slope, knowing that in case of failure the United Nations would be turned into a scapegoat.[42] As a result, unlike in the case of Somalia, he tended to take a back seat regarding Bosnia: He adopted a reactive attitude by and large; most of the time, he limited himself to responding to the pressures coming from the ground as well as to those exercised by member states.

To be sure, Boutros-Ghali was wrong to think that the United Nations could stay away from Bosnia. There was too much pressure on Western governments for them to allow the United Nations to ignore the Balkans. But he was right to fear UN involvement under the wrong conditions. In this regard, the lack of accord between the secretary-general and the Security Council came down to four main issues: means put at the disposal of the United Nations to achieve the goals assigned, chain of command, use of force, and confusion of mandates.

In the Security Council, the United Kingdom, France, and the United States were giving numerous and complex mandates to the United Nations, but the means to implement them never met the expectations. Troops to be dispatched on the ground often arrived late, and they were deployed in smaller numbers than initially proposed. The case of the "safe areas" is a telling example of this situation: The Security Council had established a safe area for Srebrenica in its Resolution 819 (April 16, 1993). In Resolution 824 (May 6, 1993), it had decided that Sarajevo, Tuzla, Zepa, Gorazde, Bihac, and their surrounding areas should also be treated as safe areas. The secretary-general, in his report to the Security Council of June 14, 1993, had informed the Council that approximately 34,000 additional troops would be required if deterrence through strength was to be obtained to protect the safe areas. The Security Council rejected this recommendation and opted for a light approach, envisioning the deployment of only 7,600 troops, but even this minimum requirement was not met by the troop contributors, thus severely limiting UNPROFOR's presence in the safe areas.[43]

Another point of contention between the UN secretary-general and the Security Council was the issue of the chain of command. Boutros-Ghali recognized that the involvement of countries in the operations on the ground justified their having a certain amount of control in the field. The very low capacity of the UN Secretariat to plan, support, and command even the simplest aspects of peace operations, let alone peace enforcement, begged for such control. Furthermore, it was understandable that countries whose nationals were deployed in the field would want to be as responsible as possible for their safety. This was especially the case for countries like France and the United Kingdom, whose troops constituted the backbone of the UN operations in Bosnia. France and the United Kingdom were eventually given senior positions of command in UNPROFOR. On the other hand, Boutros-Ghali considered that the countries' wish to have a say in command operations should not affect the organization of UNPRO-FOR, already dangerously undermined by the dispersion of its military structure.[44] Consequently, the extent to which the permanent members of the Security Council involved in the management of the Balkan crisis insisted on having the upper hand on the piece of operation in which they were most engaged was destined to create problems. The inability to reach an understanding on this matter led UNPROFOR to be decentralized to the point that it lacked coherence and efficiency.

This situation was never more visible than with the use of force in the context of air strikes. The mandate and setting of UNPROFOR did not allow it to venture explicitly into the use of force on the ground. Air strikes were therefore the only conduit for the use of force. Assessing who—the United Nations or NATO—would be responsible for the decision to launch air strikes grew to be a major element of friction. Boutros-Ghali was keen to preserve for himself or, at a minimum, his special representative the final decision on air strikes. The United States wanted the commander-in-chief of Allied Forces South in Naples to command the use of air strikes with full freedom. The major troop-contributing countries, France and Canada in particular, wanted the UNPROFOR commander to have a veto on any use of airpower.[45]

A compromise was eventually found with the establishment of a complicated "dual-key" procedure: NATO would conduct air strikes only in agreement with UNPROFOR—an arrangement meant to minimize the risks to UN troops. Crucially, approval for the first such strike had to be given by the special representative of the secretary-general, to whom the latter had delegated his authority. The complexity of the procedure, along with the debates associated with the decision-making process over air strikes, did little to enhance the deterrent power of the international community. In fact, this procedure (highly impractical from an operational standpoint, and far from facilitating airpower, as the United States had hoped) made the secretary-general's special representative, Yasushi Akashi, reluctant to authorize its use.[46]

The confusion of mandates was a final point of tension between the UN secretary-general and the Security Council. Initially, UNPROFOR's mission was to achieve three goals: alleviating the consequences of war, notably through helping in the provision of humanitarian aid; containing the conflict and mitigating its consequences by imposing constraints on the belligerents through the establishment of such arrangements as a no-fly zone, safe areas, and exclusion zones; and promoting the prospects for peace by negotiating local cease-fires and other arrangements, maintaining them where possible, and providing support measures aimed at an overall political settlement. However, the lack of consent of the parties on the ground made it impossible to accomplish these goals. Gradually, UNPRO-FOR became a mixture of peacekeeping and peace enforcement. The by-product of this situation was the increasing difficulty in getting a clear picture of what UNPROFOR was about, what its priorities were, and what it was attempting to achieve. While Boutros-Ghali viewed this as a recipe for disaster, the United Kingdom and France argued, at least until the late spring of 1995, that short of the full use of force (which the United Kingdom, France, and the United States refused to contemplate), it was better than nothing.

In the end, the disagreements between the UN secretary-general and the leading members of the Security Council contributed to seal the fate of UNPROFOR; they led to the perception of the UN operation in Bosnia as a tentative and shaky endeavor. The disagreements also undermined its ability to function well, leading the United Nations to come up with procedures and schemes that, already looking very dubious on paper, could only engender catastrophes when put to the test on the ground. The role of the cumbersome dual-key arrangement in the tragedy of Srebrenica is a case in point.[47]

When it comes to how the relationship between the secretary-general and the Security Council played a role in the tragedy of Rwanda, three points must be emphasized: the initial refusal of the Security Council to endorse the secretary-general's proposition, in the fall of 1993, to have a modest mission in Rwanda; the gradual alignment of the secretary-general and his senior staff on the Security Council's hands-off approach; and the role of the United States.

At the outset of UN involvement in Rwanda, the Security Council was unwilling to establish a mission as strong as that suggested by the secretary-general. The Arusha Accords, signed on August 4, 1993, were comprehensive and wide-ranging, providing for political, military, and constitutional reform in Rwanda.[48] They were meant to bring a peaceful resolution to the conflict that had pitted the Hutu government of President Juvénal Habyarimana against the Tutsi-led Rwandan Patriotic Front (RPF), and they envisioned Rwanda as having a broad-based transitional government until a democratically elected government could be installed. They also called for a neutral international force to help implement the agreement. The parties to the agreement asked the United Nations to assume responsibility and command the force, which the parties requested to assist in the maintenance of the country's overall security, searches for weapons caches, neutralization of armed bands, demining, and demobilization of armed forces and all aspects of the new national army and national gendarmerie. In addition, the parties to the agreement wanted assistance in the delivery of humanitarian aid and the repatriation of refugees and resettlement of displaced persons, essentially Tutsi.[49]

In his report to the Security Council dated September 24, 1993, Boutros-Ghali argued that Rwanda needed a traditional peacekeeping mission and not a peace-enforcement mission. He took the wishes of the parties to the Arusha Accords into account with two major exceptions: Based on his experience with Somalia, he knew that the Security Council was unlikely to endorse the Arusha Accords' requests to guarantee the overall security of the country and to seize arms. He therefore limited his own recommendations in this area to ensuring security in and around Kigali and simply monitoring the securing of weapons.[50]

In light of these two exceptions, the UN mission in Rwanda was going to be weak, hardly able to perform its peacekeeping tasks, if the lessons of Somalia were a precedent. Yet the Security Council was unwilling to go along even with such a limited mission. The United States in particular made it clear that it opposed a number of the secretary-general's recommendations; it insisted that the priority was to minimize spending.[51] The United States stated that it wanted only a symbolic presence of one hundred soldiers. To cut costs further, the United States argued for a reduction in the role of the peacekeepers.

On October 5, 1993, the Security Council passed Resolution 872, mandating a small and cheap peacekeeping mission in Rwanda, the United Nations Assistance Mission in Rwanda. As a compromise, it was a half-hearted commitment. The Security Council had finally agreed on 2,548 troops, but the scope of their mission was narrow; it would only "contribute to the security of the city of Kigali inter alia."[52] Moreover, while the Arusha Accords and the report of the UN secretary-general of September 24 asked that the peacekeepers assist in providing security for the refugees returning home, the mandate of Resolution 872 was for peacekeepers only "to monitor the process of Rwandese refugees."[53] Not a word was mentioned of their security. Furthermore, as it soon became clear on the ground, the equipment and the readiness level of the 2,000 troops who were eventually deployed bore no relationship at all to what even the reduced mandate of UNAMIR required.[54]

Overall, this meant that the Arusha Accords were gutted. It is difficult to say whether or not the accords would have helped to achieve their proclaimed goals of democratizing and bringing peace to Rwanda. Critics argue, for instance, that President Habyarimana, not being sincere when he negotiated and signed the accords, had no intention of contributing to their implementation.[55] But what is clear is that the UN mission as mandated by the Security Council was ill designed to succeed, as it lacked even the barest of essentials; this was especially the case as the situation deteriorated in Rwanda in the winter of 1994.[56]

At this point, the prospects for a stronger UN commitment to Rwanda were bleaker than ever. By then, the reluctance of the Security Council to get involved further in peacekeeping operations had grown stronger with the Somalia debacle and the worsening situation in Bosnia and Angola. The secretary-general and his senior staff could not fail to recognize that

Rwanda was not a priority for the three big Western powers, regardless of what was brewing there. Boutros-Ghali was left warning the various Rwandan delegations he met with in the course of the winter that the international community (i.e., the influential permanent members of the Security Council) had no intention of getting seriously involved in Rwanda, that Rwanda was on its own, and that the way Rwanda would go—peace or war—was essentially up to the Rwandan political leaders. Although this atmosphere of disillusionment helps to explain the hands-off approach that Boutros-Ghali and his senior staff ended up adopting in the winter and early spring of 1994, it cannot serve as an excuse—for they have their share of responsibility.[57] There is no doubt about that.

To begin with, between January and April 1994, the UN Department of Peacekeeping Operations (DPKO) overlooked the increasingly alarming information on weapons caches and mounting violence that the force commander of UNAMIR, General Roméo A. Dallaire, was sending to UN headquarters.[58] Perhaps even worse, as the DPKO leadership, headed at the time by Kofi Annan, feared that too much bad news would lead the UN Security Council to decide to pull UNAMIR out of Rwanda altogether, such information was not communicated to the Security Council.

Boutros-Ghali's attitude does not come across any better. When the news of the beginning of the mass killings broke out, he was on a mission in Europe. In spite of the dramatic character of the situation in Rwanda, he did not judge it necessary to go back to New York immediately. As a result, he reported directly to the Security Council only upon his return on April 20, almost two weeks after the massacres had begun. Thus, he missed a window of opportunity that existed between April 7 and 21 for containing the genocide.[59] Moreover, in the report that he presented to the Security Council on April 20, Boutros-Ghali portrayed what was happening in Rwanda in terms of a two-party confrontation and civil war, assigning the burden of responsibility for the mass killing to both sides, and not as a systematic and well-organized killing campaign launched by Hutu extremists against the Tutsis.[60] As such, he probably helped to undermine the moral case for military intervention and certainly prepared the ground for Resolution 912, adopted on April 21, 1994. The resolution, which reduced the UN force to a token level of 270 personnel, was tailored exactly to fit a situation in which a civil war was prevailing.

On the other hand, it is not as if the members of the Security Council had themselves been eager to take action.[61] In addition to their already noted reluctance to commit significant resources to Rwanda in September–

October 1993, a number of elements point toward the Security Council's continued negligence as the tragedy approached. To start with, some of the permanent members of the Security Council were probably better informed on the situation in Rwanda than Dallaire himself.[62] France, most notably, and the United States, most likely, had extensive information at their disposal gathered by their intelligence services.[63] Had they wanted to act in the months and weeks preceding the killings, they could have done so.[64] But the discussions that took place in the Security Council in April, when the massacres were in full swing, showed the extent to which the leading members of the Security Council had been unwilling to act all along: the possibility of a military intervention in Rwanda was never envisaged.[65] When a reinforcement of UNAMIR was discussed, it was not in the context of taking action against mass violence, but in the context of rescuing expatriates.[66]

Had the secretary-general and his senior team been pushing for action, they still would have had to face the opposition of the United States. The enactment of the Clinton administration's Presidential Decision Directive 25 (PDD 25) by early May made it even more difficult for the secretary-general than in the previous months to convince the Security Council (waiting for U.S. leadership as ever during this period) to approve an international intervention in Rwanda. The review was months in preparation and came in the wake of the Somalia fiasco. It was the first comprehensive review of U.S. policy toward multilateral peace operations in the aftermath of the Cold War, setting strict conditions on future support for UN peacekeeping. From now on, specific criteria would have to be met for the United States to get involved, including U.S. interests at stake; a threat to world peace; a situation of urgent humanitarian disaster; a clear mission goal; a working cease-fire; acceptable costs; congressional, public, and allied support; specific and streamlined command and control; and a clear exit point.[67] Rwanda failed every condition but one: urgent humanitarian disaster coupled with violence. Adoption of Security Council Resolution 918 (May 17) shows that this criterion was not enough for the United States to get involved.

In early May, Boutros-Ghali's attempts to find alternative solutions for troop contributions for Rwanda had failed.[68] As the killing in Rwanda continued, he turned again to the Council. He suggested in his report to the Security Council of May 13 an operation that would airlift a standing brigade into Kigali of some 5,500 well-armed and well-trained soldiers to protect civilians at risk and to provide security for humanitarian operations.[69] The mission's rules of engagement would not contemplate enforcement action. These suggestions contained certain aspects of Dallaire's original plan outlined in a cable sent to New York on April 8. It was a minimally viable force, Boutros-Ghali told the Security Council, but there were immediate complaints about the plan from the American diplomats. Madeleine Albright, the U.S. ambassador to the United Nations, was now championing the new presidential directive on peacekeeping. In accordance with the directive, her staff said that the plan for Rwanda was inadequate and lacking in field assessment. As a result, although Resolution 918 ultimately authorized 5,500 troops for UNAMIR, it was a sham.[70] By then, the world had shut the door on Rwanda for good.

Reflecting on the Impact of the Relationship between the Secretary-General and Security Council on Peace Operations

As the examples of Somalia, Bosnia, and Rwanda show, the disagreements between Secretary-General Boutros-Ghali and the Security Council had negative effects on the conception, implementation, and results of the peace operations. This was all the more the case considering that the topics of discord concerned key issues. Moreover, the discrepancies between the secretary-general and the Security Council did not go unnoticed by the parties in conflict, to whom the display of unity of view and purpose was essential to project credibility. In addition, the fact that the Somalia, Bosnia, and Rwanda crises did not represent international security threats in the traditional sense of the term, and therefore called for doing the right thing mainly from an ethical point of view, gave more weight to the disagreements: The lack of decisiveness that the divergences illustrated encouraged further complacent, if not cynical, policies vis-à-vis the humanitarian crises. Short of an absolute imperative to intervene, discord became a convenient excuse for action initiated more for the sake of doing *something* than with the clear goal of stopping the conflict at hand.

Could things have turned out differently? Could more convergence between the secretary-general and the Security Council have avoided the toll that their tense relationship ended up taking on the UN involvement in Somalia, Bosnia, and Rwanda? It is tempting to think so. Antagonizing the actors he needed most was not the wisest thing Boutros-Ghali could have done.

In this regard, Boutros-Ghali had good relations with France, Russia, and China. The relationship between the secretary-general and the United Kingdom was one of ambiguity. Although there was no open hostility between him and the United Kingdom, a sense of mutual defiance tended to be the undercurrent of the relationship. Boutros-Ghali's relationship with the United States was the most problematic. The negotiation and interpretation of the UN mandate in Somalia generated much acrimony on both sides. The acrimony turned into mutual resentment from fall 1993 onward, which was, of course, unsettling for Boutros-Ghali's standing as secretary-general. The more the United States withdrew its support from him, the more he needed it. As his prestige took a nosedive with the United States, he was less able to mobilize other key member states or to make their support meaningful enough; as they looked to the United States for leadership, they could not balance or make up for the secretary-general's loss of American backing. This created a dynamic that spiraled downward, the last episode of which was Boutros-Ghali's defeated re-election bid. Notwithstanding the fact that he managed to line up most member states in support of his re-election, any analyst could guess even before he was vetoed on December 13, 1996, that his re-election campaign was somewhat of a lost cause. American hostility made member states' support a fickle one.

Thus we can see that by putting the Security Council on the defensive, Boutros-Ghali was not encouraging it to strengthen its political, financial, and logistical support. Ultimately, although the dramatic character of the unfolding crises called for taking a moral high road and avoiding personal acrimony, the tensions generated bruised egos and got in the way of conducting business. Perhaps a less abrasive secretary-general could have helped to improve the conception and implementation of peace operations and their results.

That being said, the tale of Boutros-Ghali's successor, Kofi Annan, introduces a sobering note. Annan had certain human qualities that, considering the nature of the secretary-general's job, amounted to political benefits.[71] He was a listener, whereas Boutros-Ghali tended to be more focused on transmitting. Annan brought people in, whereas Boutros-Ghali was prone to be less inclusive. Annan had a nonthreatening and nonabrasive attitude, and he had a sense of collegiality and team spirit that his predecessor was not so strong on. Yet for all these personal qualities, and for all the good relationships that he had with the Security Council, by and large Kofi Annan was unable to achieve more than Boutros-Ghali when it came to getting the Council to display a strong commitment to solving humanitarian crises. The reluctance of the Security Council to address, for instance, the Sierra Leone and Great Lakes Region crises in the second half of the 1990s shows that excellent relations and an endearing character are not necessarily enough.

POLITICAL SHORTCOMINGS:
THE SECURITY COUNCIL

Although nonpermanent members of the Security Council at times play an important role, the influence of the permanent members, because of their veto power, counts the most in international politics. The 1990s were no exception.

Instrumental to addressing the humanitarian crises of the period, the permanent members displayed similarities as well as differences of opinion. All permanent members were open to the idea that humanitarian crises could not be ignored by the Security Council. They recognized that, with the end of the Cold War, times had changed and that the Council had to take some sort of responsibility in these new political developments. On that basis, they were able to work well together in many instances. Yet there were also major differences among the permanent members, especially when peace operations entailed peace enforcement; these differences ended up playing, in one way or another, a negative role.[72]

There were (and still are) two distinct groups among the permanent members: China and Russia on one side, and the United States, France, and the United Kingdom on the other. China and Russia tended to favor the maintenance of the status quo and were not keen on international intervention and the use of force. The United States, France, and the United Kingdom were willing to adopt a more active, flexible, and forceful approach. In both groups, there were additional disparities stemming from the national peculiarities of the countries. Ultimately, the split between China and Russia, on the one hand, and the United States, the United Kingdom, and France, on the other, as well as the differences of points of view among the three Western powers, significantly shaped peace operation modalities, the manner in which they were perceived on the ground and in the world at large, and their outcomes.

China's and Russia's Positions and
Their Influence on Peace Operations

China and Russia were more or less on the same side of the political chessboard vis-à-vis the humanitarian crises addressed by the Security Council. Favoring the systematic pursuit of diplomatic and political channels and mediation, they were wary of the combination of peacekeeping and peace enforcement. It was not so much the confusion that this mixture introduced and the operational difficulties it generated that made these two countries uneasy; it was, rather, the breach of national sovereignty and the possibility of the use of force in the name of human rights and humanitarian imperatives. The fact that enforcement was becoming over time an almost routine option in face of humanitarian crises contradicted China's and Russia's views of international relations and went against some of their vested interests.

The enforcement dimension of peace operations was certainly at odds with China's view on international relations as a whole. From a general standpoint, China considers that enforcement contradicts the principles of mutual respect for sovereignty and territorial integrity, as well as noninterference in one another's internal affairs, which it sees as key for the stability and justice of the international system. As a result, China historically has favored the peaceful settlement of disputes and has been consistently unwilling to endorse the use of coercive means to impose the United Nations' will on a sovereign country. Hence, the People's Republic has been uncomfortable with the use of force under Chapter VII, even in situations of clear-cut foreign aggression and invasion.[73] It has also been reluctant to support sanctions (economic, diplomatic, and other), especially if the conflict is internal in nature.

The Chinese refusal to override territorial integrity and intervene in the internal affairs of sovereign countries grows stronger when external intervention is based on humanitarian and human rights concerns. China does not see humanitarian catastrophes and human rights violations as a strong enough justification to violate the principle of noninterference in the internal affairs of sovereign countries. More specifically, China is concerned that peace operations encompassing humanitarian interventions may further enhance the international influence of the West, and primarily that of the United States. The Chinese commitment to the balance of power as a way to construct and preserve global stability makes it wary of initiatives that could contribute to the spread of a hegemonic model of international order.[74] The fact that the areas of humanitarian interventions were all located outside the developed world reinforced this defiance. Also, its own vested interests at home and along its borders made China uneasy about the characteristics of the peace operations of the 1990s. Considering the criticism under which it finds itself when it comes to its human rights track record and that of the immediate periphery under its control (Tibet in particular), the Chinese government feared that peace operations on humanitarian and human rights issues would be viewed as a precedent that could be used against it in the future. All this amounted to the fact that China considered traditional peacekeeping, with a deployment based on the consent of the parties on the ground, as the main—if not only—means of action.

Despite its opposition to peace enforcement, China adopted a moderate attitude in the Security Council. It did not want to be perceived as playing an obstructive role and being insensitive to human suffering. Moreover, the "failed" nature of the countries where interventions were mandated weakened the sovereignty and territorial argument as well, as the collapse of the state was producing anarchy and making internal order impossible. China tended to be satisfied as long as its lobbying efforts to dilute the key resolutions on humanitarian interventions and human rights—in particular, by having them mention the exceptional character of the initiatives— were successful. As a result, China used its veto power extremely rarely, usually in situations associated with Taiwan.[75]

Most of the time, either in the use of force or sanctions dealing with protection of humanitarian aid delivery and stopping human rights violations, the Chinese government limited itself to abstaining to show its disagreement. China abstained on several resolutions concerning Bosnia.[76] In the case of Rwanda, it abstained on Resolution 929 of June 22, 1994, which created the French-led Operation Turquoise under Chapter VII in the wake of the April–May mass killings.[77] Other peace operations triggered similar reactions. China abstained from voting on Resolution 940 of July 31, 1994, which authorized a multinational coalition to assist in restoring Haiti's exiled President Jean-Bertrand Aristide to power. Later on, China abstained on Resolution 1244, adopted in June 1999, to establish the UN mission in Kosovo within the context of Chapter VII.[78]

In the end, it was only in the case of Somalia that the Chinese government endorsed the use of force by voting in favor of Resolution 794 (December 3, 1992), which established UNITAF. During the vote on the resolution, Ambassador Li Zhaoxing stated that China considered UNITAF an "exceptional action" taken "in view of the unique situation in Somalia," that military operations should cease as soon as a "secure environment" had been established, and that control of the operation be put under the authority of the Security Council and the UN secretary-general.[79]

In the early 1990s, Russia's ability to project internationally was reaching a nadir. For forty years, the Soviet Union had been the main counterweight to Western power, and suddenly it was reduced to being practically a nonplayer. Its international influence was minimal because it was too busy looking after itself. With the disintegration of the power structure that had made the Soviet Bloc band together, Russia had to try to salvage what remained of the former Soviet Union through the Commonwealth of Independent States (CIS).[80] It was also facing huge economic and political domestic difficulties associated with its transition.[81] In this context, how could Moscow have been other than inwardly focused, giving little attention to multilateral issues? Why and how could Russia have invested more than the bare minimum of capital in multilateralism and the humanitarian crises of the period (nontraditional security conflicts void of national interest considerations) when its own fate was at stake? Besides, the successive Russian military campaigns against Chechnya in the course of the 1990s did not place Moscow on strong bargaining ground to express forcefully its discontent with the policies advanced in the Security Council by the United States, France, and the United Kingdom. It may even have been one of Russia's strategies to think that the less it voiced its concerns vis-à-vis the humanitarian-assistance positions of the three Western powers, the more they would be inclined to silence theirs regarding Russian foreign policy in the Caucasus. In short, Russian involvement in UN affairs was limited and selective in the 1990s, geared primarily toward the UN engagement in the Balkans.

A political presence in the Balkans was not openly articulated as Russia's official goal. Nevertheless, the Balkans were implicitly one of Russia's most significant regional interests. More than the mere sharing of Slavic culture, the necessity to prevent developments in the area from being completely controlled by the West accounted for Russia's stand on the Balkans. In both Bosnia and Kosovo, Moscow favored a political solution. Concerning Bosnia, after having acknowledged in the early phase of the conflict that Belgrade bore the heaviest responsibility for the Bosnian war, Russia ended up advocating an evenhanded approach, placing responsibility on all sides.[82] Russia pushed forward its position within the framework of the Vance-Owen Plan, which it supported, and then by participating actively in the work of the Contact Group.[83] Russia tended to disapprove of relying upon Chapter VII to solve the conflict; it liked neither sanctions nor the use of force, particularly because it felt that they were biased against the Serbs.[84] Despite frequent threats, Russia only exceptionally used its veto power to express its opposition. It used its veto on the arms embargo issue on December 2, 1994, and surely it would have done so again concerning the use of air strikes in Kosovo if the occasion had arisen.[85]

Apart from these rare examples of the use of its Security Council veto, Russia opted for other ways to state its position on the Balkans vis-à-vis the policies of the three Western permanent members. It repeatedly attempted to counter the measures of coercion by introducing as many amendments as possible in the adopted resolutions, either to slow down the decision-making process and the actions on the ground or to water them down. Although Russia's efforts failed because of a lack of support—and in some cases outright opposition from other Security Council members—it also tried to counter coercive measures by attempting to draft a Security Council resolution, supported by China, to condemn NATO's bombing of the Bosnian Serbs in early September 1995.[86] More generally, Russia expressed its disagreement and discontent through abstentions: Between 1993 and 1995, Russia abstained fives times on Bosnian issues.[87] Concerning Kosovo, it abstained twice: on Resolution 1203 (October 24, 1998) regarding agreements for the verification of compliance with the provisions of Resolution 1199 (1998) on the situation in Kosovo; and on Resolution 1239 (May 14, 1999) concerning relief assistance to Kosovo refugees and internally displaced persons in Kosovo, the Republic of Montenegro, and other parts of the Federal Republic of Yugoslavia.[88]

China's and Russia's attitudes did not have major consequences on the conception, implementation, and immediate results of the peace operations of the 1990s. As long as Security Council resolutions took some of their concerns into account, they were satisfied to stay away from the day-to-day handling of the missions. Hence, Chinese and Russian reluctance did not significantly affect how peace operations unfolded. Even in the Balkans, Moscow did not get in the way much. Of course, it tried to influence the course of the UN-Western engagement. But, ultimately, in neither Bosnia nor in Kosovo were the UN policies designed and implemented with much attention paid to the Russians. Their point of view was not forgotten, but it was not a primary factor for the decision makers.

Nevertheless, in the long run, the fact that China and Russia distanced themselves from the other permanent members through abstentions exacted a price on the credibility of peace operations. Despite the fact that Russian and Chinese abstention has been viewed in the West largely in a positive light, as a form of goodwill and cooperation, over time it tended to weaken the case of peace operations as a way to address humanitarian crises. It deprived their launching and implementation of the political gains and the normative justification that consensus within the Council would have helped to achieve. In short, the humanitarian stance of the Security Council became more and more identified with the West.

As such, in the end, the international solidarity that was supposed to support the spirit of peace operations ran the risk of being supplanted by visions of conspiracy, implying the hidden intent to instrumentalize solidarity to advance Western influence. The decision of the Western permanent members of the Security Council to act forcefully in Kosovo without formal UN authorization only encouraged the perception of an increasing divide between the West and the rest of the world. Paradoxically, the ambiguous commitment of Western powers to the resolution of humanitarian crises—their sense of solidarity echoing and varying to a large extent with the degree to which their interests were at stake in the regions in conflict, the disagreements that this occasioned among them, and the negative effects that it had on the results of peace operations—only sharpened this perception in the non-Western world.

THE UNITED STATES, FRANCE, AND THE UNITED KINGDOM: CONSEQUENCES OF AN UNEASY LEADERSHIP ON PEACE OPERATIONS

With China and Russia in a largely subordinate decision-making role, it fell to the United States, France, and the United Kingdom to take the lead in the Security Council regarding the humanitarian crises of the 1990s. The relative reluctance and, at times, the significant disagreements that marked their leadership were not without negative effects on the mandates, implementation, and results of peace operations.

A bedrock agreement characterized the positions of the United States, France, and the United Kingdom in the Security Council on the humanitarian crises of the 1990s. The three countries shared the general notion that the crises were too important to be ignored and that something had to be done. This basic sentiment led them to place humanitarian crises on the Security Council agenda and play a key role in their handling; these countries were a critical factor in efforts to end humanitarian conflicts in the aftermath of the Cold War. However, although the three Western powers shared the view that it was their responsibility to try to solve humanitarian crises, they also believed that these crises were not vital to their national interests. Thus the bedrock agreement was a qualified one; as such, it amounted to a limited commitment. At best, action was taken within limits (this is the scenario that most peace operations followed); at worst, hardly anything was done, as the Rwandan example shows.

Far from silencing the differing viewpoints of the United States, France, and the United Kingdom on how the humanitarian crises should be handled, this limited commitment allowed discrepancies to endure over time; lack of decisiveness, of a firm course of thought and action, prevented the crises from being addressed seriously, let alone eliminated. This state of affairs tended to create problems for peace operations when divergences concerned sensitive issues—particularly in cases involving the use of force and the dangers in executing it. Bosnia is a case in point.

Disagreements separated France and the United Kingdom, on the one hand, and the United States, on the other, on three key aspects of the Bosnian crisis: the use of force, the arms embargo, and the Vance-Owen Plan.

France and the United Kingdom opposed the use of force (namely, air strikes) and the lifting of the arms embargo, while the United States was inclined to support them. France and the United Kingdom feared that air strikes would endanger the troops that they had deployed on the ground. The arms embargo also de facto targeted Bosnia, even after its secession had been formally recognized by the international community. Nonetheless, France and the United Kingdom considered that lifting the arms embargo was likely to fuel the war and put their troops at greater risk of harm, whereas the United States felt that the Bosnians were entitled to defend themselves. In addition, the United States did not endorse the Vance-Owen Plan that France and the United Kingdom favored.[89] These differences of opinion proved to be highly problematic for UNPROFOR, underscoring three main shortcomings in the peace operation.

At the political level, because the United States had wanted to avoid leadership from the outset of the war, it would have been essential for America to support the Security Council's attempts to find a solution as quickly as possible; a united front was all the more necessary considering that the European ability to broker a solution depended largely upon clear U.S. backing. Instead, the U.S. refusal to support the policies put forward by the French and British undermined the Security Council's credibility, and that of UNPROFOR.

From a strategic point of view, the divisions separating France and the United Kingdom from the United States in the Security Council were sending the wrong signals to the warring parties; they were an invitation for them to harden their respective positions and shun compromise. U.S. support for air strikes and the lifting of the arms embargo, as well as its reluctance to endorse the Vance-Owen Plan, signaled to the Bosnians that help was on its way and that they should hold on. The opposition of France and the United Kingdom to air strikes and the arms embargo indicated to the Bosnian Serbs that they could continue on their violent path without much fear of retaliation.

From an operational standpoint, differences of opinion introduced contradictions into the mandates of UNPROFOR and made them impossible to implement properly. A number of Security Council resolutions, although envisioning and calling for the use of force, continued to ask for the respect of previous resolutions aimed at peacekeeping activities presupposing the consent of the parties. This led to a combination of peacekeeping and peace enforcement that required the simultaneous performance of two opposite tasks. The confusion of peacekeeping and peace enforcement put the humanitarian activities in jeopardy as well; it polarized the attitudes of the parties at war, making the delivery of humanitarian aid a stake—and thus increasingly difficult. Also, the fact that the Western powers sponsored resolutions that entailed the possible use of force without being really committed to it exposed the UN operation to the danger of losing on two fronts: on political negotiations and on deterrence. This was making the balance of the carrot and the stick hard to achieve.

The more peace operations entailed complex aspects, including the use of force, the less the three Western powers could afford to present a disunited front. Differences of perspectives on rather secondary matters were acceptable. The change of their positions over time on how to approach a crisis was also acceptable; after all, the evolution of situations occasionally calls for adjustments in positions in order to open new venues. Flexibility and changes in positions can play a positive role as long as they are part of a calculus of adaptable plans and strategies to solve the crises, and as long as they are engineered and projected in a convincing manner, so that the changes introduced do not disorient and distract the parties involved. But for the Western powers to conduct several policies at the same time on key issues was a recipe for failure.

OPERATIONAL SHORTCOMINGS OF THE UNITED NATIONS AND THEIR TOLL ON PEACE OPERATIONS

The concrete conditions in which the United Nations implemented the peace operations of the 1990s are another factor that explains their mixed results. The conditions amounted to three gaps between headquarters and the missions deployed on the ground: a culture gap between the Security Council and peace operations in the field; a resource gap between the UN Secretariat departments monitoring peace operations (the Department of Peacekeeping Operations and, secondarily, the Department of Political Affairs) and the needs of the missions on the ground; and a communication gap between UN headquarters in New York and the field—and, eventually, the outside world.

THE GAP BETWEEN THE DIPLOMATIC CULTURE OF THE SECURITY COUNCIL AND THE DEMANDS OF THE FIELD

Security Council resolutions reflect, directly or indirectly, key aspects of international life at a given time—in particular, the distribution of power and the corresponding constraints and possibilities to address the conflicts of a specific period. As such, the Security Council resolutions of the 1990s mirrored the changes that were altering international relations in the aftermath of the Cold War through the great number adopted and the variety and novelty of the issues that they addressed. But the fact that Security Council resolutions are a good entry point to the dynamics of international politics does not imply that they offer a total transparency of intent and goal and are part of a straight causal line running between decision and action; the connection between the resolutions and their implementation is not always clear. Resolutions are often ambiguous in their formulations and the goals they pursue; this was especially the case in the 1990s, and this accounts to a significant degree for the poor performance of peace operations at that time.

In the 1990s, as in previous years, Security Council resolutions served by and large six main purposes: to bring unfolding crises to the Security Council's attention and agenda; to formulate expectations or demands for the parties in conflict; to qualify the nature of the crisis; to justify and authorize appropriate action on behalf of the international community, with the legitimacy it bestows; to outline the initiatives to be taken; and to empower the actors identified to conduct these initiatives. These generic characteristics and the conditions under which they were realized gave a strong operational and political determinacy to the Security Council resolutions. They indicated what the Council wanted to do and how it wanted to do it, sometimes in extremely precise terms. Still, a noteworthy number of the resolutions that addressed the humanitarian crises and the peace operations devoted to them also entailed substantial indeterminacy; they were ambiguous and open-ended in their objectives and their methods of achieving them.

Reasons abound for the lack of clarity characterizing peace operations resolutions. The very nature of a Security Council resolution itself is one factor. Even a resolution that is geared toward action is not a directive that constitutes a detailed work plan. Although resolutions can be used to delineate the mandate of the peace operations (and may do so in specific ways), they do not generally concern themselves with the micromanagement of their implementation. Traditionally, it falls to the UN Secretariat (in particular the Department of Peacekeeping Operations and the reports of the secretary-general to the Security Council), and the member states engaged in the peace operation to work out the details of the implementation. Diplomatic rules of the game and the manner in which they help to shape Security Council resolutions are other elements contributing to the ambiguity of peace operations resolutions. Diplomacy differs from a zero-sum game; it entails bringing actors in a negotiation process closer to each other and having them believe they are getting something out of the exercise.

This implies compromise as well as, frequently, some uncertainty about what is agreed upon. Ambiguous formulation and the relatively indeterminate meaning associated with it help to bring on board actors who could be reluctant to do so were things stated explicitly. Obviously, the appropriateness of ambiguity is a matter of degree. Short of the proper degree, the agreement becomes deceiving and, ultimately, counterproductive. As an expression, product, and tool of international diplomacy, Security Council resolutions are no exception to this modus operandi; in fact, ambiguity is particularly important at the multilateral level of the Security Council, where permanent members can often have different points of view and divergent agendas. Allowing ambiguity in the text of the resolutions may be necessary to mitigate the differences so that no veto is cast.[90]

The transitional character of the international context in the aftermath of the Cold War emphasized this dimension of mandate formation. Considering the disagreements among the five powers on how to address humanitarian crises, accommodation was required at times in the Security Council so that the resolutions would be adopted and action taken. It was required to prevent China and Russia from voicing their concerns by using their respective vetoes. It was also required to prevent the divisions among the United States, France, and the United Kingdom from dominating the Security Council's deliberations. Moreover, the three Western powers, while taking the lead in tackling the unfolding crises, were unsure of the route to take and uneasy about risking too much in getting involved. From this perspective, opting for a rather open-ended course of action could be viewed as presenting significant political benefits. By having the resolutions point alternately or at the same time in different directions (e.g., combining peacekeeping and peace enforcement), the Western permanent members in the Security Council were aiming for a win-win political strategy. In an international environment in which they viewed humanitarian crises as not vital enough for them to project absolute determination but sufficiently important to necessitate doing something to stop them, the ambiguity of the resolutions could embody a double advantage: serving various goals and their respective supporters while picking none of them as the defining one with which they could be identified and held accountable. In the process, while echoing the uncertainty of the time and expressing the limits of their commitment, the Western powers were embedding in the resolutions policies that they could embrace or distance themselves from, depending on how things turned out on the ground. Either way, they could hope to escape some criticism for having done too little or too much.

Needless to say, the gains ambiguity permitted from the diplomatic and political standpoints were lost from the perspective of implementation. The indeterminacy of the Security Council resolutions exacted a toll on the realization of peace operations and their results. The more complex and sensitive the issues, the more straightforwardness and focus were required in the mandates and the conditions to achieve them. Yet the opposite happened in critical instances.

The nadir was reached with peace enforcement. When it comes to the use of force, more than any other issue, clarity of directives and rules of engagement are fundamental; this is one of the key aspects of military culture and of the chain of command that goes with it. Yet most of the Security Council resolutions of the 1990s did not offer the purposefulness and single-mindedness that would have been critical for successful military engagement. As the case of Bosnia shows, for the force commanders of the peace operations, trying to implement the use of force in an environment conditioned by diplomatic and political aims proved to be close to impossible.

The Gap between the UN Secretariat and the Field

The divide between the key departments for peace operations at UN headquarters and in the field was also quite damaging to the implementation and outcomes of peace operations. Three elements are of particular importance in this regard: the shortage of human resources in the UN Secretariat compared to the needs on the ground; the limited expertise in the UN departments concerning the areas and issues at the center of the peace operations; and a tendency in New York to combine "formal universalism" and a "headquarters approach" in the handling of humanitarian crises.

The quantitative and qualitative changes that peace operations underwent in the aftermath of the Cold War dramatically increased the need for UN headquarters to provide guidance and support to the field operations. Thus in the early 1990s, a number of initiatives were taken to enhance the capacity of the UN Secretariat. In the spring of 1992, peace operations, which up to then had been the responsibility of the Department of Political Affairs, were taken up by a new department entirely dedicated to them: the Department of Peacekeeping Operations. At the same time, the Department of Humanitarian Affairs was created. Additional efforts were made in 1993 to strengthen the human resources capacity of these departments and a number of other programs dealing with issues related to humanitarian crises.[91] The establishment of a Situation Room in April 1993, meant to function twenty-four hours a day, was also viewed as a way to reinforce the capability of the Secretariat.[92] Nevertheless, the efforts to improve UN headquarters' capacity to support peace operations could not hide the fact that an enormous gap persisted between the needs in the field and the human resources at their disposal in New York. To have an idea of how this state of affairs affected the implementation of peace operations, it helps to know a bit about the responsibility of the Department of Peacekeeping Operations vis-à-vis the missions.

By and large, as the interface between UN headquarters and the field, the Department of Peacekeeping Operations has the task of monitoring the various aspects of peace operations. Its responsibility entails three major functions: to collect information coming from the ground to ensure that decision makers in the Secretariat (the secretary-general and his immediate advisers, the heads of the departments, and the members of the Security Council) are properly informed on unfolding events and can make sound decisions; to draw up policy suggestions on the basis of the information collected (here desk officers play a significant role in drafting the secretary-general's reports on the conflicts that are on the UN agenda); and to relay to the field the directives coming from the Security Council, the secretary-general and his office, or DPKO itself. DPKO's interface is critical, because while peace operations on the ground have minimal autonomy to interpret mandates, the authorization for action usually comes from New York.

In order to perform these three critical functions satisfactorily, appropriate staffing was the minimum requirement. Yet, even after the efforts made in the early 1990s, a huge disconnect between the tasks at hand and the existing personnel persisted. For example, between 1992 and 1994 Bosnia was tracked in the Department of Peacekeeping Operations by only five staff members—including desk officers, a division director, and intelligence officers. During this period, DPKO had one desk officer for the entire region (UNPROFOR, Croatia, and Former Yugoslav Republic of Macedonia), who received assistance from the director for the Europe and Latin America Division of DPKO in handling day-to-day operations. Until 1996, only one desk officer was working full time on UNPROFOR with the director. Three military officers (of whom two were gratis personnel) assisted in all missions. The Field Administration and Logistics Division (FALD) of DPKO had one desk officer who handled administrative matters for several UN peacekeeping missions. The Department of Political Affairs had one desk officer for the Balkans.[93] The situation was no better when it came to the African crises. Between April 1992 and March 1995, Somalia was monitored by one desk officer in the Department of Peacekeeping Operations and one desk officer in the Department of Political

Affairs. The same applied to Rwanda between October 1993 and March 1996. The situation was clearly absurd. In view of such inadequate levels of personnel, the criticisms addressed at the time to the United Nations (particularly by the United States) that it was an overstaffed bureaucracy appear ludicrous, to say the least. More to the point, in light of such a shortage of human resources, the best that the UN Secretariat could do was little more than damage control. Obviously, this was far from enough.

The negative influence of the UN Secretariat's human resources shortage was aggravated by another problem: the weakness in expertise on the areas and issues of concern. The problem was more visible in the Department of Political Affairs than in the Department of Peacekeeping Operations.[94] The conflicts and operations that DPKO was monitoring created a level of pressure that helped to keep its officers prepared and up-to-date. On the other hand, the Department of Political Affairs often fell short of providing cogent and substantial background analyses on the countries where crises were about to erupt or were starting to simmer. These analyses would have been more than useful to help tailor solutions adapted to the characteristics of the regions in conflict and the nature of the crises that they were facing. Indeed, the countries where the United Nations is likely to intervene tend to be located in the developing world. Removed from the main channels of international power, they are often understudied, if not ignored, by scholars and policy experts. As such, coming up with solutions to the conflicts that affect them requires all the more an intellectual effort to understand what has led to the conflicts. But for each officer eager to extend expertise as much as possible in the areas under his or her supervision, too many did not go beyond reading the UN reports, cables, and media dispatches.

Moreover, weakness of analysis was deepened by the lack of institutionalized professional bridges *(passerelles)* between UN headquarters and the field. The staff of the Political Affairs and Peacekeeping Operations departments should have been the most aware and sensitive to the working conditions and needs of the people in the field. Yet most of them had very little or no field experience and often no desire for it. The widespread lack of field experience in the Secretariat prevented the kind of knowledge that would have been critical for New York headquarters to better understand what was happening on the ground and the kinds of problems the field officers were confronting. Without shared knowledge between desk officers at headquarters and in the field, it was also difficult for the personnel in the Secretariat to aid in the development of an integrated approach to the missions. The lack of shared knowledge between headquarters and the field, which were on separate career paths with little overlap (which remains the case to a large extent even after the reform efforts in the 2000s), had to do with a weak sense of belonging to the same institution; this created an institutional barrier to strong cooperation. Although desk officers would have benefited from taking field assignments, the fear of not being able to return to headquarters prevented them from doing so. The greater stability and prospects for advancement at headquarters compared to those in the field only reinforced bureaucratic biases and shortcomings, and at times discouraged an atmosphere of mutual appreciation. In the end, an atmosphere developed in which the center looked down on the field, and the field resented the center.[95] In this context, it was difficult to monitor and liaise properly with the field personnel.

To manage humanitarian crises, the UN Secretariat assumed that methods and skills could be transferred across contexts; it considered that the tools used in one situation could be applied more or less in other situations—for instance, what had worked in Cambodia could work in Bosnia. This uniform approach echoed the UN tendency, as in other international organizations and large bureaucracies, to engender formal and universal categories—more or less by design, inattentive to particular concerns—to address pressing problems.[96] This assumption was useful: It provided a road map to peace operations. But when pushed too far, it could become counterproductive. In overlooking a commonsense factor (i.e., to resolve a conflict, it is essential to understand the local conditions; how the warring parties and civilians think; what their motivations and values are; the historical, economic, political contexts, etc.), the ability to work out the problems was diminished; this was the case in several instances. Somalia was certainly one of these instances. Rather than approaching Somalia as if the characteristics of the local environment did not really matter, had the international community made an effort to comprehend the specifics of Somali society and its interplay with clan culture, a number of deadly mistakes could have been avoided.[97]

The fact that the universalism of the UN approach to conflict management cohabited with an organizational culture at times designed more to respond to the demands associated with the politics of UN headquarters (including internal politics in the Secretariat, the Security Council, and among member states in general) than to trigger real action addressing issues on the ground did not help. The combination of a decontextualized understanding of the conflicts and the inward considerations of UN headquarters further hampered New York's ability to service the field with the right assessment of the situation. The political dependency of the United Nations fed this dynamic: It encouraged UN senior staff to anticipate the reactions of the member states (especially powerful member states) before making any decision and to settle for an overly cautious course of action, one that would be the least controversial.[98]

The UN philosophy of impartiality pushed in the same direction, contributing to the deepening sense of the Secretariat's institutional disconnectedness. The UN commitment to impartiality resides at the core of its approach to tensions and conflicts in general, except in clear situations of international aggression. Impartiality is at times criticized as a refusal to take a stand when necessary. But it is also a tool that has strong moral and political justification. It reflects the UN philosophy that assumes that each member state is a good international citizen from whom cooperation is expected. In the context of embedded respect and reciprocity among member states, of which impartiality is a part, each international actor is to be treated in good faith and with the benefit of the doubt until proven guilty of aggressive or rogue behavior. Thus the use of force is a last resort. Using force is acknowledging that the community bond and structure on which the United Nations is based has been broken by one of its members and needs to be protected and reinstated by force, by socializing the delinquent member perforce. Yet UN impartiality is not without institutional timidity, if not bureaucratic indifference.[99] In the context of the 1990s, UN decision makers, remote and estranged from the field, glossed over the dramas on the ground. As the gap between Dallaire's assessment of the situation in Rwanda and the reaction of UN headquarters shows, the conflicts appeared far less real from New York and, thus, easier to discount, than from the field. As a whole, the inability to maximize the minimal resources at hand could not facilitate a win-win outcome for the humanitarian crises.

The Costs of the Communication Breakdown

Critical for the success of peacekeeping, communication proved to be another major weakness in the peace operations of the 1990s.[100] This was especially true for missions having complex mandates and calling on the use of force. Problems existed at two main levels. There were difficulties of internal communication not only between the UN headquarters and the field but also *within* the missions deployed on the ground. And there were communication problems outside the United Nations realm, vis-à-vis the local populations in the areas where the United Nations was intervening and with the world at large.

The divide between UN headquarters and the field operation was the mark of an institutional communication stalemate. Still, there were also more prosaic but equally important communication difficulties. All too often, communication between the field and New York, even in dramatic circumstances, was slow and erratic. When life-or-death decisions had to be made on the ground, the delays damaged the functioning of the missions and their credibility—and the credibility of the United Nations as a whole.[101]

Communication problems also affected the field itself. Lack of proper communication and integration among the various components of the peace operations was a recurrent problem on the ground. The number of nationalities deployed in the field, although partly the strength of peacekeeping as it reflects its seeming universality, did not ease communication. But it is the complexity and evolution of the mandates (often with the subsequent change in the names of the missions) that proved to be major obstacles.[102] Bosnia constitutes a case in point. The mandates of the United Nations in Bosnia were complicated at the outset, and they became even more complex. As a result, they were difficult to understand even for the people meant to implement them on the ground. In addition, as the two maps of UNPROFOR in Bosnia in 1994 and 1995 show (figures 1 and 2, respectively) the layout of UN troop deployment and what it meant in terms of chain of command of UNPROFOR was confusing at best.[103]

Under these conditions it was close to impossible for peace operations to perform well, so it could not be expected that communications with the outside world would be any better. How could an organization that did not offer clarity of function and purpose to its own personnel be portrayed in the best light, if portrayed at all, to outsiders? This was one of the challenging questions that UN peace operations had to face in the 1990s. Lack of clarity in the peace operations affected their relations with local populations where they were deployed. This was particularly the case with peace operations that encompassed multiple tasks and had an enforcement component; such a situation often translated into reluctant cooperation, if not disapproval, from the local populations. The failures of the peace operations in this regard often boosted the confidence of the groups that were fueling war on the ground and on whom the UN presence was meant to have a constraining effect.

The United Nations also demonstrated an inability to convey its message to the world at large.[104] The need to make its case and that of peace operations was not fulfilled. From a general standpoint, the dimension of public information and communication is a key element for the United Nations; it is indeed crucial for the world organization to build for itself a constituency and receive support. One of the best ways to do so is to explain to the public what it does, why it does it, how it does it, and why it is not easy to accomplish it. In recent years, the United Nations has made progress on this front, namely through the Internet. Opened in 1996, the UN Web site has become a major tool of public information and communication. It offers information in six languages on all aspects of United Nations' activities. In 2004, www.un.org received 32,010,640 visits. In 2006, the number increased to 34,423,923.[105]

Figure 1. UNPROFOR Deployment, 1994

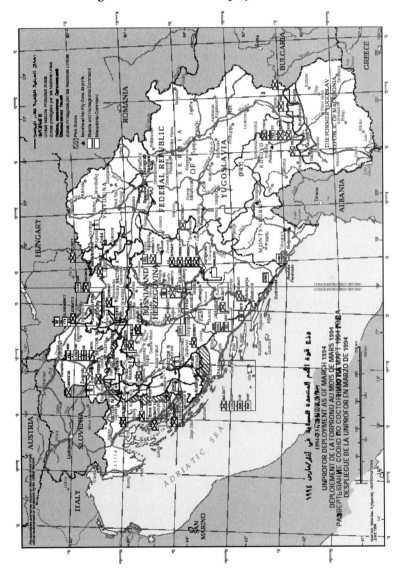

But in the 1990s, as the United Nations became heavily involved in complex peace operations, a successful communication policy was absent. While Western major powers played a key role in involving the United Nations in humanitarian crises, the extent and limits of their willingness to commit themselves was conditioned to a certain degree by public opinion.[106] The need for the United Nations to reach out was therefore critical.

Figure 2. UNPROFOR Deployment, 1995

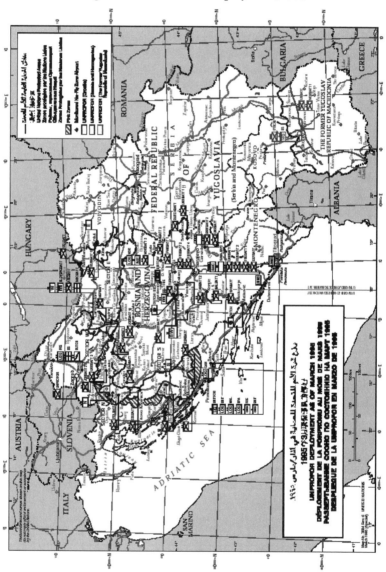

Furthermore, Western governments were not eager to take the blame when peace operations went badly. Too often the member states most involved in the management of the conflicts acted as if they had nothing to do with it. Although it would have been essential for the United Nations to tell its side of the story to retain public and political support, it failed on this score. The media, especially in the United States, echoed more than anything else the viewpoints of governments, showing in the process how ambiguous their role is when it comes to humanitarian crises. More than in the past, the media play a positive role in pushing the international community to get involved in humanitarian crises; by covering them, they generate public awareness and a sense of outrage that pressures Western powers to act. Yet the way the media operate introduces major problems for multilateral action in humanitarian crises. Their commitment to the crises is fickle, and they can also be easily manipulated by governments.

In general, the political shortcomings of the United Nations during the 1990s amounted to weak leadership. It was divided and indecisive. Operational shortcomings amplified its limitations: its tendency to take an ad hoc approach (lacking systematic and institutionalized procedures) and its inability to capitalize on the lessons of the past. This is not to say that the United Nations alone should bear full responsibility for the ambiguous results, including failures, of peace operations in the 1990s. The effectiveness or ineffectiveness of any organization cannot be ascribed to considering it as an autonomous entity. Although institutions (be they national or international, public or private) are effective or ineffective based on their ability to rationalize and maximize their resources, their level of effectiveness must also be assessed in connection with their environment, as well as in relation to their partners.[107] This is especially true when the partners are stakeholders, when they are not only contributing to define the environment in which institutions operate but are largely deciding their policies as well. The relationship between the United Nations and key member states falls into this category.

In this regard, the political vision and collective strategies stemming from the structure of international politics are crucial in assessing how far the projection of international solidarity, as expressed in the peace operations addressing humanitarian crises, can extend. Considering the way international politics is structured, it is not surprising that the United Nations was limited in its dealing with the humanitarian crises of the 1990s. This is the subject of the next chapter.

CHAPTER 3

THE STRUCTURE OF INTERNATIONAL POLITICS AND THE DILEMMAS OF SOLIDARITY

N O MATTER HOW IMPORTANT the political and operational short-comings of the peace operations and their ambiguous results in the aftermath of the Cold War, they alone cannot explain the deficiencies. They are only the tip of the iceberg. To comprehend their full meaning, they have to be understood within the broader picture of the structure of international life and the role of the key member states in the 1990s (the United States, the United Kingdom, and France, especially as permanent members of the Security Council) regarding humanitarian crises. Analyzing the problem from this perspective sheds light on the mixture of conservatism and progressivism, and on the extent and limits of international political will in the area of human rights and humanitarian affairs.

This chapter addresses four main issues: First, what led to a greater awareness vis-à-vis human rights and humanitarian matters in the aftermath of the Cold War? Of critical importance were the relaxation of the logic of global confrontation and its impact on multilateralism, the democratic values at the core of the three Western permanent members of the Security Council, and the socialization of international politics. Second, why, in spite of a better responsiveness to human rights and humanitarian crises, did the extension of international solidarity remain restricted in the 1990s? The limitations of modern democratic solidarity and the continuing national bent of international life, which have stymied a legally binding sense of international solidarity, provide an answer. Third, the chapter illuminates the fact that the hybrid character of international politics (constituting the internationalist obligations associated with human rights and humanitarian concerns, on the one hand, and more traditional state demands, on the other) framed the Security Council's deliberations and decisions regarding what to do about humanitarian crises in terms of dilemmas. Fourth, the chapter reflects on the ambiguous contribution of major Western democratic powers to the structure of international life and the diffusion of international responsibility and solidarity.

THE ENHANCEMENT OF INTERNATIONAL SOLIDARITY IN THE AFTERMATH OF THE COLD WAR

Two factors contributed to international solidarity in the 1990s: the easing of the logic of global confrontation that followed the end of the East-West showdown and what it meant for multilateralism and its peacekeeping activities, including the humanitarian area, as well as for the key state actors of the period; and the values of solidarity underwritten and promoted at home and abroad by the three Western permanent members of the Security Council.

THE RELAXATION OF THE LOGIC OF GLOBAL CONFRONTATION

The end of the Cold War introduced changes that significantly modified the distribution of international power and multilateralism. This modification benefited major Western democratic powers and, among other things, allowed them to pay more attention to the humanitarian crises than they had previously. For the purposes of this study, four fundamental changes in the post–Cold War era are notable: the alteration of the standing of the United States, United Kingdom, and France (the key countries in the peace operations of the 1990s) and their new international projection of power; the increased importance of multilateralism as a modality of global governance—along with its institutions and operations; the adjustment, in various degrees, of the three Western powers to the characteristics of the post–Cold War multilateral moment (and its constraints and possibilities); and the triggering of a sense of international responsibility and solidarity vis-à-vis people caught in the midst of conflicts, thereby connecting the local and global levels of international life.

The possibility of global conflict that had structured much of international relations since the beginning of the Cold War lost a great deal of its ability to shape international politics with the end of the East-West showdown. The emphasis on this transformation does not imply that the prospect of confrontation vanished altogether from the international landscape during the 1990s. Preparing for the worst continued to dominate the defense and foreign policies of most nation-states. This was all the more the case since "replacement" candidates somehow quickly filled at least part of the void created at the global level by the disappearance of the East-West divide. "Rogue" states and international terrorism, in particular, were presented as the new enemies, their threats more diffuse and unpredictable than traditional threats and therefore especially dangerous. But it is clear that the end of the Cold War modified the international distribution of power: the disappearance of the Communist Bloc and the collapse of the Soviet Union ended the bipolar (or, more precisely, bipolycentric) balance of power that had prevailed for decades. The West found itself at the top of the hierarchy of international power and hardly challenged. Clearly, it is for the United States, the United Kingdom, and France that these changes mattered principally. The three Western powers, especially the United States, were among the chief beneficiaries of the shift of international power. The responsibility to steer a course and set a tone in international affairs also fell primarily upon them. In this regard, the increased margins of security (material and psychological) generated by this "victory" made the imperatives of survival and national security less of an obsession. They now had the luxury to give more consideration than before to matters of nontraditional national interest. This led them as well to revisit their conception and use of multilateralism.[1]

In its most fundamental sense, multilateralism is a way for three or more states to coordinate relations according to certain principles. It usually manifests itself in glimpsed statements about collective visions and, sometimes, declarations about concerted joint action on a specific international problem, such as the degrading of collective security regimes.[2] One of the bases of the multilateral collective security design is that balances of power are inherently unstable. In contrast, multilateralism as a community of powers working together and identifying with a number of key principles of international behavior augurs well for international stability. The commitment of multilateralism to the upholding of the fundamental values of democracy, human rights, civil society, and the rule of law is supposed to be a great help. Against this background, if the Cold War had largely paralyzed the multilateral vision and practice of international politics, its demise made multilateralism possible again. The leading Western democratic powers took a renewed interest in multilateralism, its institutions, and the resources for action that they offered.

In this context, peacekeeping became a more valuable option than in the past. As a result, it went through a certain reorientation of its fundamental purpose, placing a more normative weight behind its tasks.[3] This applies not only to the United Nations but also to NATO specifically; the collective defense pact meant that security was indivisible: an assault on one (presumably a European member)[4] meant an assault on all, requiring in particular an immediate U.S. response to a Soviet invasion. In the post–Cold War era, non–Article 5 missions not only required a comparable commitment to collective security but also called for a much broader and deeper commitment among all the leading powers.[5] In the absence of the Soviet threat, NATO's peacekeeping repertoire gradually transformed the organization from a collective defense to a collective security pact.[6] Gone were the days of NATO's planning for a Soviet assault. Now was the time to engage in crisis planning for failed and rogue states. The leading powers in the Atlantic Alliance, and in the UN Security Council, adhered to a "Western" reconceptualization of international security—from threat to risk assessment. The international democratic solidarity that had characterized multilateralism since the Cold War transformed from a strategic concern buoyed by a shared threat to a concern with crisis management and the promotion of international stability. The assumption of collective security increasingly came to project international democratic solidarity into countries and regions that had few encounters with democratic principles.[7] This entailed propagating a new normative rationale for intervening in the humanitarian crises of the post–Cold War era.

The fact that the 1990s put the United States, France, and the United Kingdom in a leading position regarding the multilateral handling of humanitarian crises called for some adjustment on their part, and such adjustment was certainly smaller and easier to make for the United Kingdom and France than for the United States. The reworking of foreign policy required of France and the United Kingdom to adapt to the new international situation did not imply drastic transformations; their international power standing fit the new context. Indeed, by the end of the Cold War, France and the United Kingdom had long lost their great power status and the worldwide reach associated with it.

In this context, the image of the enemy had largely ceased to play a pivotal function in the foreign policy of the United Kingdom and France. Even during the Cold War, they were inclined to view the Soviet Union more as an adversary not to be trusted than as an enemy to be defeated. This state of affairs played a role in their reluctance to challenge the status quo built around the East-West divide. Incidentally, there were also differences in the French and British perceptions of the Soviet Union. The United Kingdom, as one of the closest allies of the United States and a key actor in NATO, was more adamant than France in keeping Moscow in check. This was all the more the case considering that a constant feature of France's foreign policy, from De Gaulle to Chirac, has been to try to balance American influence. This has led France to appear at times more resentful of the

United States' sway than fearful of any other threat. Furthermore, the shaping of the British political landscape by a tradition of political liberalism not keen on social revolutionary ideals pushed the United Kingdom away from the Soviet Union, while the long history and influence of leftist ideas on French social and political life created somewhat of a bridge between Paris and Moscow.

If the reduced international stature of the United Kingdom and France had relieved them of the pressures of international competition at and for the top, it had also deprived them of the global influence that they had enjoyed as great powers. As a result, they came to value the United Nations over time, as they were able to see beyond its role in the decolonization movement that brought about the dismemberment of their empires. They retained to some extent their old attachment to the balance of power, as well as to realpolitik and the relatively cynical view of the conduct of foreign policy that goes with it. Nevertheless, they also came to see the United Nations as a useful venue for the management of international problems, as well as a way for them to continue to be influential internationally. Logically, therefore, they welcomed the resurgence of the United Nations' relevance in the 1990s. The fact that the United Nations was now a channel that could not be easily ignored for the handling of crises—actually, more than ever, one of the key *legitimate* means to address conflicts—gave them a weight in international affairs that had eluded them for a long time. Moreover, while major wars encompassing global strategic stakes would have been likely to make the United States' leadership indisputable (at best, asking for their endorsement via the Security Council and then largely pushing them to the sidelines of day-to-day decision making and implementation), the local scope and the humanitarian nature of most of the crises of the period suited the limited international power projection of France and the United Kingdom and, consequently, gave them a significant place in the management of such crises.

The situation was quite different for the United States. Although it had done the most to bring about the demise of the Soviet Bloc and the resulting international changes, in a way it had a greater and more difficult gap to fill to adapt to the context of the 1990s; the extent and difficulty of the adjustment were commensurate to the importance of America's international role in the previous decades. Since the end of World War II, the atmosphere of global competition had helped the United States to acquire a largely unchallenged leadership over its allies. It also tended to provide justification for unilateral international interventions whenever necessary and possible in its spheres of influence or in the ideological fault lines. In addition, the severity of global competition fed into the belief that America's peculiarly democratic values should be spread around the world, with the mixture of idealism and righteousness that went with them. The aftermath of the Cold War put these features under scrutiny, amounting to the need to partly redefine and redirect the American sense of international responsibility and solidarity. Three significant adjustments appeared to be required from American foreign policy.

First, the United States had to address the growing separation of its national interest from those of its friends. Since the fading dangers of global confrontation were breaking the close bonds between America and its allies (in the West and elsewhere), the argument that U.S. national interests were its allies' national interests would no longer suffice to make the case for U.S. foreign policy. Second, the significant demotion of what had been traditional strategic interests and reasons for involvement overseas, and the media and public attention given to humanitarian crises, called for revisiting the why and how for engaging internationally. Third, there was the need to tackle the fact that unilateralism was now less of an option and multilateralism more an imperative for the United States. Making these adjustments proved to be challenging for American foreign policy. Along with the idiosyncrasies in British and French foreign policy, U.S. foreign policy changes certainly affected the ways in which the UN peace operations handled the humanitarian crises of the 1990s.

The strategic competition associated with the Cold War had contributed to connect, if not intermesh, local conflicts and global concerns. The East-West showdown gave a strategic meaning to local crises, and local conflicts had global implications. It generated some sort of "solidarity of fear," with each side of the ideological divide marshalling its allies against the other and often putting local conflicts at the service of the global agenda. Does this mean that the bridge between local crises and global stakes disappeared with the meltdown of the Soviet Union? Certainly not. The bridge was largely reconfigured. The "New World Order" championed by President George H. W. Bush was already an attempt to push forward a new type of connection between local conflicts and global concerns. The Bush administration sold the idea of the New World Order as a vision and a commitment to reinforcing civilized standards of international conduct and setting new precedents in international cooperation. It was presented as a post–Cold War world order paradigm, in which nations from East and West, North and South, including great powers, would come together to ensure strong respect for the rights of the weak, to pursue peace and justice, and to enhance the rule of international law.[8] However, essentially referred to in the context of Operation Desert Storm, the idea was short-lived. Rather than being the harbinger of a new international paradigm, the New World Order constituted an isolated slogan.

More successful as part of the reconfiguration between the local and the global was an enhanced sense of international solidarity and responsibility. This emerged from the French, British, and American willingness to recognize the need to address the humanitarian crises of the period and to adjust, to a certain extent, their foreign policies in order to do so.

Building on the Normative Commitment to Solidarity

The lifting of the "struggle for survival" associated with the Cold War moved the existing normative commitment to an ethics of solidarity to a more significant place internationally. The changes unfolding in the international order pushed the United Nations Security Council to adopt, in its deliberations and resolutions asking for action, a reading of international legal principles and their interrelationships (which provide the normative and political framework of the Security Council) that was more favorable than before to human rights and humanitarian concerns. In addition, the historical contribution of the United States, France, and the United Kingdom to the solidarity-based aspects of international law and the United Nations (based on the projection at the international level of some of the key democratic values of solidarity with which they identified at home) made them receptive to the idea of actively pursuing the sense of international solidarity toward individuals that the new international landscape rendered possible.

There was no need for the Security Council to start from scratch to motivate and justify international involvement in the humanitarian crises of the 1990s. The Council was simply required to be sensitive to the human rights and humanitarian considerations already laid down in the UN Charter and international law. Four elements help to clarify this: the nature of international principles at the core of international law; the role international legal principles play in the socialization of international relations; the influence that the distribution of international power and its evolution has on the interpretation and way key international actors (here, the three Western permanent members of the Security Council) apply international principles and their relations; and the consequences of this process on the sense of international legitimacy and the normative, ethical, and political guidelines that it provides.

The post–World War II mechanism of formulating international principles to regulate international relations that took place through the work of the UN Special Committee on Principles of International Law Concerning Friendly Relations and Cooperation among States lasted for several years. On October 24, 1970, a Declaration on Principles of International Law Concerning Friendly Relations and Cooperation among States, in accordance with the Charter of the United Nations, was adopted by consensus in the UN General Assembly.[9] The declaration listed the critical principles at the core of the international rule of law, allowing a modicum of relatively smooth international relations. The following major principles were endorsed: sovereign equality of states, nonintervention in the internal or external affairs of other states, negotiating in good faith, self-determination of peoples, prohibition of the threat or use of force, peaceful settlement of disputes, respect for human rights, and international cooperation.[10] The principles of sovereign equality of states, nonintervention (at least in its role as a precept designed to protect states from traditional interferences in their domestic affairs), and negotiating in good faith are strongly embedded in the classical pattern of international relations. Self-determination of peoples, ban on force, peaceful settlement of disputes, respect for human rights, and cooperation among states are indicative of the post-Westphalian model of sovereignty—a model that reflects the changes in the international order brought about by universal values that have emerged in the twentieth century.[11]

The socializing role that these principles play in international relations can be broken down into three complementary functions: inclusion, outlining of the international rule of law, and enhancement of the sense of community at the international level. Inclusion is served by the fact that international principles bring a variety of value-ideals into the international system. Their recognition and incorporation is a key element of the intersubjective dialogue among actors, as well as of their interactive relations throughout history.[12] Because the value-ideals at the basis of international legal principles are identified with and viewed as valid by strategic actors, their endorsement as international principles is a condition of the interaction of these actors and, as such, an indispensable feature of the establishment of a workable international system. International principles achieve their second socializing role (the outlining of the international rule of law) in two ways. To begin with, the architecture of international order is envisioned and set up largely in connection with these principles; and international norms, rules, regulations, and standards are associated with these principles, directly or indirectly. In addition, playing conjointly the roles of axiological foundations, guidelines, and ends, international principles are meant to encourage a predictability of interactions within a dynamic of reciprocity of rights and duties that is geared toward regulating the present and future of relations among actors. The third function of the socialization of international principles is to express a sense of community at the international level. In delineating the overall setting of the "logic of appropriateness" in international interactions, the principles point to what is required from actors to participate as members of an international community, to be part of it. They design the ins and outs of the experience of international community. In doing so, they define the ethics of international affairs within the realm of a perceived international community. Ultimately, these three functions make international principles an essential element (an expression and a tool) of the construction of international order and its claims to justice and legitimacy.[13] They are at the core of the deliberations, decisions, and actions of those eager to take the rules of the game seriously.

The socializing role of international principles takes place through the relations of compatibility and competition that are at the core of the international system. As the most basic aspect of international socialization, compatibility among principles is critical for the existence and functioning of the international system as a whole; compatibility ensures that international principles pull the international system in the same direction and also makes international principles mutually reinforcing. For instance, the prohibition of the use of force, peaceful settlement of disputes, and international cooperation express, defend, and promote a similar philosophy of international relations and work together in the service of the regulation of the international system. But international principles are also in competition. Take, for example, the principle of nonintervention in the internal affairs of other states and that of respect for human rights. They are apt to be at odds with one another and, thus, in competition.

Moreover, competition can exist not only among principles but between *interpretations* of a principle as well. The conflicting interpretations of the sovereign equality of states in the 1990s, echoing to a certain extent debates that were not new, serve as a case in point. Some advocated a territorial understanding of sovereignty, basically associated with the view that nations are independent realms within which national political institutions are entitled to exercise almost unlimited and unchallenged power. (Here, the autonomy of the state vis-à-vis the international realm was conceived largely as nonnegotiable, reinforced by the principle of nonintervention in the internal affairs of other states.) Others put forward an interpretation of sovereignty that emphasized its democratic dimension, insisting on the significance of the individual and human rights. The principle of respect for human rights was called upon to support this reading. The former view tended to be favored by the non-Western world, particularly by developing countries already deeply penetrated by dominant powers or fearing such penetration. The latter was the preference of the Western democratic nations; however, these nations, especially the most powerful among them, tended to rein in their advocacy for democratic sovereignty whenever it infringed upon their own autonomy of decision making, as was for instance shown by the U.S. reservations regarding the International Criminal Court.[14]

Although competition among principles or their interpretation can be a source of incoherence, it also constitutes a key instrument of international socialization, as critical as compatibility: Competition allows bringing in principles or interpretations of principles that may be cause for disagreement but on which there is enough accord to acknowledge that they are an essential part of the mechanism of international socialization.

The mixture of compatibility and competition among international principles results in a creative tension of "indeterminate determinacy" that encourages international socialization.[15] As long as competitive principles are neither denied nor judged as wholly contradictory (scenarios that are likely to undermine the stability and legitimacy of the international system), socialization occurs in such a dynamic of compatibility and competition. International socialization happens through the normative hierarchy and prioritization (and reprioritization) that the international distribution of power fosters among international principles. In this regard, international principles are not equal. The distribution of international power brings about a hierarchy that favors certain principles or interpretations of principles over others. This normative hierarchy indicates the value-ideals to which the international system attaches a prevailing significance. For instance, before the 1990s the territorial reading of the principle of sovereignty was the predominant paradigm, making it difficult to launch and justify international interventions in the name of human rights and humanitarian considerations.[16]

The normative hierarchy is not fixed in stone. As a product of history, it evolves with the transformations affecting the international system. This does not imply that international transformation is a one-way process, triggered only by alterations in the material distribution of power that are then incorporated at the normative level. Value-ideals can themselves contribute to international changes.[17] For example, if the appeal for the respect of human rights was not the sole element that brought about the collapse of the Soviet Bloc, it certainly had an impact.[18]

Transformation is what happened to a certain extent with the end of the Cold War. The changes in the international reality and its perception modified the interpretation of international principles and their relations put forward by the three Western permanent members of the Security Council. In the "arc of interpretation" (connecting principles, unfolding events, and the international distribution of power) that they leaned on to deliberate and decide, these countries factored in the new international landscape, putting on display the historicity, and relative plasticity, of international legitimacy. In this regard, when a transformation in the international distribution of power is radical, it can account not only for the emergence of a new approach to the hierarchical relationships of principles, but also for the changes of international principles themselves.[19] The ability of international law and the institutions underwriting it to be relevant and handle change depends upon balancing international principles, their relations, and interpretations.

In the 1990s, the somewhat altered sense of international legitimacy made it important to embark on a reading of international principles keen on addressing human rights and humanitarian issues. As a result, not only did most peace operations of the period have a strong human rights component, but attention to human rights and humanitarian matters also led the Security Council to challenge the traditional understanding of the principle of sovereignty for the sake of humanitarian interventions. Perhaps propelling human rights and humanitarian concerns even further was the establishment by the Council of the international criminal tribunals for the former Yugoslavia and Rwanda, which certainly helped lead to the creation of the International Criminal Court in 1998. At the same time, the post–Cold War transformation in the normative rationale for multilateral interventions signaled a more profound change in peacekeeping itself, best exemplified by NATO and its parallel transformation.[20]

International democratic solidarity had been the hallmark of NATO since its founding in 1949—the linkage of the world's leading democracies in a pact designed to ward off conquest by the world's leading communist power. Yet in the Cold War's aftermath, that solidarity transformed from a strategic concern buoyed by a shared threat to a concern with crisis management and the promotion of international stability. In short, NATO transformed from a multilateral regional grouping of democracies focused solely on collective defense to a regional collective security organization focused primarily on the stability of a newly enlarged democratic region. NATO's principal vehicle for such a transformation was an expansion of its membership and, beyond that, "out of area" peacekeeping tasks. The fundamental premise with both modalities was the same that served as the Atlantic Alliance's raison d'être in the early years of the Cold War and throughout: to maintain the bulwark of democratic values that originally served a collective defense organization. Nevertheless, NATO also faced a fundamental change of mission with the collapse of the Soviet Union, and it had to redefine its basic goals for the sake of organizational survival. In short, NATO had to reorient its peacekeeping rationale toward a more "robust" agenda that included peacebuilding—the move toward state building that includes establishing more representative institutions.

Beyond the threat to cohesion of collective defense alliances, international democratic solidarity is actually the basis of the philosophy and international political theory of early collective security designs, as propounded by Immanuel Kant and Woodrow Wilson. To be sure, President Wilson's vision for the League of Nations admitted some of the realities of international—particularly European—politics, but both men adumbrated a *community of power* comprising nations whose political composition was consonant with the shared values, norms, and rule-of-law principles that could indeed sustain a community. These polities, in Kant's and Wilson's view, could be nothing other than democracies. Both held the conviction, in David Yost's words, "that the legitimacy of governments should be based on constitutional and democratic self-determination, rather than on the power of despots or the prescriptive right of hereditary autocrats."[21]

Balances of power were inherently unstable, Kant and Wilson believed, simply because the nations that balanced them—particularly at the time of their respective observations—were inherently unstable as well. A community of power augured well for international stability because of the very stability that characterized its democratic members: "[B]oth believed in the political *solidarity* of democratically governed states [and] the ethical authority of enlightened public opinion. . . ."[22]

In short, collective security regimes focused on upholding fundamental values of democracy, human rights, civil society, and the rule of law. These shared democratic norms among NATO's members have been a constant ever since the organization's inception, but their mutual sharing as the basis for international democratic solidarity was obscured by the Cold War's emphasis on defense planning and threat assessment. With the ultimate dissolution of that threat in 1991, when the leaders of the Union of Soviet Socialist Republics declared their empire no more, international democratic solidarity had a new emphasis in the response to the new humanitarian crises that seemed to be sprouting across the globe, and that new emphasis manifested itself—at least in theory—quantitatively and qualitatively.

Quantitatively, international democratic solidarity no longer meant a phalanx of allied powers whose "solidarity" (or, to be precise, "solidity") relied on numerical strength, such as that constituting balance-of-power arrangements and defense alliances. With the dissolution of the Soviet Union and the concomitant demise of the Warsaw Pact, NATO no longer had to enlist like-minded democratic neighbors to oppose a roughly equal number of communist states to the east. NATO's subsequent enlargement sought to draw former adversaries into an inclusive community of democratic values whose shared expectations strengthened the new, normative solidarity.

The related qualitative change was that the new emphasis in international democratic solidarity seemed to get well beneath the level of the nation-state as the locus of concern in multilateral endeavors. In NATO's transformation from a collective defense to a collective security organization, with the latter's embrace of democratic values (human rights foremost among them), international democratic solidarity now seemed to touch *individuals* directly. In both its quantitative and qualitative changes, international democratic solidarity seemed to make a tremendous intellectual and operational leap within Émile Durkheim's sociological schema—from the *mechanical* solidarity of traditional collectivities based on simple division of labor to the *organic* solidarity of modern societies, whose members' specialized individual actions are crucial to the functioning of the society as a whole and, further, are maintained daily by the same normative and role expectations of a *community*—that is, expectations that are not based on arbitrary or contingent decisions but, rather, on the independent and purposeful rule-of-law governance that respects individual rights.[23]

The historical commitment and contribution of the United States, France, and the United Kingdom to the solidarity-based aspects of international law and the United Nations is another factor that made them receptive to the idea of actively pursuing the sense of international solidarity toward individuals. In this regard, the massive human rights violations associated with the humanitarian crises of the 1990s contradicted a principle (respect of human rights) that these countries, each in its own way, had worked to put on the international agenda and that is key to the expression and extension of a sense of solidarity to individuals beyond borders. Indeed, based on their respective support of human rights, the United States, France, and the United Kingdom played a critical role after World War II in the transformation of the idea of constitutional rights into the internationalization of human rights by contributing in various ways to the creation of international legal instruments.[24] It goes without saying that they alone should not be credited with the recognition of the importance of human rights at the international level. They could not have done it on their own; they needed the commitment of other countries, Western and non-Western. Moreover, although major Western powers led the way in the development of key international rights, they were at times circumspect about the inclusion of some of them. For instance, although they favored the International Covenant on Civil and Political Rights, they were less eager to promote economic and social rights. It was the Soviet Bloc and the developing countries that were instrumental in the worldwide adoption of the International Covenant on Economic, Social, and Cultural Rights. (Although the Soviet Bloc's critique of civil and political rights was self-serving—it echoed the reluctance of socialist states to recognize their validity at home—it was also a revival, this time at the international level, of the Marxist negative appraisal of the formalism of liberal rights.)

Now that the East-West confrontation no longer provided a justification for getting internationally involved mainly out of national interest considerations and calculations, the three Western permanent members of the Security Council could not let the humanitarian tragedies of the period go totally unchallenged without undermining the credibility of their claimed commitment to human rights.

Doing nothing would have been all the more problematic for the three countries, given that their ability to contribute to the establishment of a sense of solidarity at the international level was rooted in values and rights at the heart of their domestic democratic culture. The internationalization of solidarity that they helped to bring about was largely the result of the externalization of the values of universality and equality of human rights. The formal universalism—the equality of rights and freedoms—and the betterment of people's conditions at the core of American, British, and French constitutionalism were decisive factors in the internationalization of human rights. Consequently, not responding to feelings of international empathy and solidarity would also have meant betraying their own principles. For this reason, each of them in accordance with their brand of democratic culture felt compelled to tackle the humanitarian crises of the period.

It should be added that the differences in the democratic cultures of the United States, France, and the United Kingdom partly account for the variety of ways in which they envision the international realm and how to engage it. These differences affected the American, French, and British approaches to the humanitarian crises of the 1990s and the solutions they recommended to stop them. For example, the specific characteristics of the French and American democratic cultures impacted their views on the Bosnian conflict, although with quite opposite effects. France's historical vision of integration via cultural assimilation (stemming from an uneasiness with minority rights and multiculturalism) was behind its endorsement, particularly in September 1993 in the context of the European Union's so-called Invincible Acquis proposal, of the idea of dividing Bosnia along ethnic lines. The feeling that integration via cultural assimilation was at this point an unachievable goal militated for breaking up Bosnia.[25] With respect to the United States, a multicultural mode of social integration that has increasingly recognized, along with the rights of individuals, the cultural groups to which they might belong (be they ethnic, racial, religious, or gender-based) played a role in shaping the U.S. position of favoring the policy of a multiethnic Bosnia at all costs, to the point of imposing it on the parties at Dayton rather than having them agree to it.[26]

THE LIMITS OF INTERNATIONAL SOLIDARITY

While the context of the post–Cold War allowed international solidarity to be extended further than before, it remained essentially constrained in the 1990s. Three major factors explain this state of affairs: the structure of modern solidarity; the national bent of international life; and, as a consequence of these two factors, the moral—more than legal—character of the obligations entailed in international solidarity.

MODERN SOLIDARITY AND THE INTERNATIONAL REALM: FROM POSSIBILITIES TO LIMITATIONS

In traditional forms of social organization, solidarity connotes a tight bonding among people (kinship), which renders it imperative for the group to look after its members. The sense of solidarity runs deep and permeates the group's internal relations. The other side of this "thick" solidarity is its sharply exclusive character. The "us-versus-them," "in-versus-out" divides that traditional societies tend to exhibit have a heavy bearing on who benefits from solidarity and who does not.[27]

Compared to traditional solidarity, modern solidarity that springs from democratic values and rights is wider and more diffuse.[28] Rather than being locked in forms of membership that tend to be narrow and exclusive, modern solidarity seeks the broadest inclusion possible. The values and rights of universality and equality at the core of democratic culture introduce and call for a connectedness among people that initiates an experience of community going far beyond the boundaries of the immediate society. This type of solidarity-driven process entails three facets.

First, democratic values of universality and equality and the rights associated with them celebrate the identicalness of people based on equality and universality being shared by as many as possible. From this derives, second, a sense of obligation. Because "the other" (whoever and wherever he is) is not foreign, his fate triggers responsibility for his co-members. They are the repository of his rights. Responsibility makes them accountable to help ensure that others' rights are respected. Third, the spreading and embracing quality of values and rights of universality and equality, by recognizing individuals in their variety as members of one world, provide them the tools to build a case for their rights and consequently fight for their better inclusion. Historically, these three facets have worked in favor of widening and deepening solidarity at the national level and, at least ideationally, at the international level.[29] To some extent, international law is a product of this state of affairs.

To be sure, the beginnings of modern international law have been an exceedingly self-serving exercise for the major European powers.[30] And throughout their history up to the present, the economic and political interests of the most powerful (Western) nations have remained integral parts of the making of international law—a consideration that the weak countries at the receiving end of international power must continuously address.[31] At the same time, international solidarity concerns geared toward individuals have not been absent. Early on, the discovery of new worlds and their ruthless subjugation by European powers led some to favor a better treatment for non-European people. What was humanly, ethically, and legally owed to them came to occupy the work of a number of scholars reflecting on international law, such as Bartolomé de Las Casas and Samuel von Pufendorf. But the real break came much later, in the twentieth century, with the internationalization of democratic values and rights of equality and universality. The spectacular development, after World War II, of the universalization of human rights is what really highlighted international solidarity exercised in favor of individuals.

However, the values and rights of universality and equality that trigger international solidarity are also part and parcel of what accounts for its limitations. From a general standpoint, what constrains solidarity in key democratic values and rights occurs at three levels. Modern democratic solidarity, although wider than traditional solidarity, tends to be thinner. This is the first problem. Arguably, universality and equality introduce a distance among people that lessens the level of social solidarity among them; it places a boundary between bonding and belonging. In other words, as solidarity widens, it becomes attenuated. What brings people together is also what keeps them apart.[32] A second problem is that values and rights of universality and equality get rid of neither the ideas of priority and of hierarchy that go with it, nor of the need for them. How could they, considering that making priorities and establishing hierarchies are essential to human life, partly because without them no direction can be given to it, and partly because the limited resources at hand ask for choices in their allocation? The result is that the values and rights of universality and equality cannot impede the hierarchy of priorities from playing a selective, and therefore restricting, role in the projection of solidarity. Third, in this perspective, as the circle of the human community expands under the influence of the values and rights of universality and equality, the ability to relate solidarity with people becomes more and more abstract and fragile. As such, the extension of democratic solidarity itself has the tendency to give a renewed importance to traditional bonds of proximity, including kinship ties.[33]

We can imagine how the cumulative effects of these constraints maximally play on solidarity at the international level. As the largest circle of humanity, the international realm does not benefit from strong identification and participation (that is, it does not support relations that exist at the national level, at least in unified nations). The "pull" power of international solidarity is weakened further when self-interested considerations enter—and they often do—into its calculus. The inconsistency that comes with self-interest prevents such solidarity from being fully credible and, consequently, from being taken seriously as an imperative. In these conditions, despite the rhetoric of universality and equality, it is hard not to view international solidarity as a secondary characteristic of international life.

INTERNATIONAL SOLIDARITY IN THE NET OF INTERNATIONAL POLITICS' NATIONAL BENT

International solidarity's secondary status will continue to deprive it of its power to contribute to collective security as long as international politics remain structured by a national bent—that is, as long as our understanding of international politics is centered on the nation-state. The fact that the state-centric paradigm of international life has endured certainly has hampered a greater projection of solidarity at the international level.

In the aftermath of the Cold War, increased economic interdependence (especially under the pressure of globalization) and innovation in international governance, along with the lessening of global security competition, have boosted the internationalization of social reality.[34] But these forces have not fundamentally altered international life, which is still based on the interactions of nation-states. As a result, in the 1990s, three trends associated with the state-centric paradigm continued to have limiting effects on international solidarity.

The political community of the nation-state remained the principal context of individuals' socialization. People went on experiencing identification, participation, expectation, and obligation—four key elements of socialization—chiefly at the national level, despite the parallel local and international affiliations they may have had. The national realm remained the main reference point of identity, and the various forms of social participation in which individuals engage (political and economic) mostly took place at the national level. People directed their expectations as members of the community toward the national spheres of activities and services. As for obligations, they remained essentially geared toward fellow citizens. National politicians thus continued to focus on domestic needs; even in countries that espoused a commitment to international solidarity, politicians continued to assess and apportion it in relation to the primacy of national wants.

Also, the end of the East-West showdown did not change the fact that national power commands international influence. Relations between international organizations and great powers illuminate this reality in a variety of ways. Powerful nations, for example, are those that have the strongest impact on and in international organizations, formally and informally. Equally illustrative is the fact that the level of support of powerful countries decisively shapes the authority of international organizations: Historically, the World Bank and the International Monetary Fund have owed much of their influence to their support from the advanced industrial democracies. Conversely, the United Nations has suffered from the reluctance of the United States to back it up. Absent the support of countries other than advanced industrial democracies, international organizations face a major challenge—the erosion of their influence. The different manifestations of the "pull" and "push" powers of international organizations oscillate as well with the level of countries' power: International organizations' powers tend to be strong vis-à-vis weak states, and weak vis-à-vis strong states.

The 1990s stressed this critical correlation between national power and international influence in their own dramatic way. The West, led by the three Western permanent members of the Security Council, dominated the agenda of the international community. At the same time, Russia turned into a debilitated power: Barely able to attend to the welfare of its own people, Russia was largely incapable of making its views heard on one of its historical areas of interest—the Balkans. In this respect, the Russian story confirmed that in order to do good internationally, to extend international solidarity, a country must be doing well itself at the national level as a whole.

Moreover, despite all the talk in the aftermath of the Cold War on the emergence of an era of enhanced cooperation among nations, Russia's loss of standing delivered another clear message to the world: International competition remains a key factor of international politics, and any country caught in a position of weakness is destined to pay dearly for it. In other words, international solidarity cannot be the sole aspect of a foreign policy. The United States, France, and the United Kingdom did not miss the point: Although leading the charge of international solidarity throughout the 1990s, they extended it with parsimony.

Solidarity and the Limits of International Legal and Moral Obligations

The parsimony displayed by the three Western powers matched another factor constraining the extension of international solidarity: the lack of real international legal obligations to act decisively to stop massive human rights violations in other countries—hence, the need to resort to a sense of moral responsiveness, particularly to justify humanitarian intervention. Whatever their merits, ethical considerations constitute a rather weak foundation on which to base international action to uphold human rights. This proved to be a significant impediment.

Democratic values and rights historically have been enough of a collective cultural pressure for the importance of human rights to be acknowledged in international law. Nonetheless, it does not follow from this recognition that international law and its institutions are the principal guardians of human rights. International legal instruments stipulate that states look after their own human rights first and foremost (i.e., guarantee that they are properly expressed, protected, and enhanced nationally). Human rights is one of the defining values enshrined in the UN Charter, and as members of the United Nations and parties to international human rights conventions, states must ensure the respect for human rights within their borders as part of their responsibility.[35] Thus, legal obligations regarding human rights are by and large meant to be internally exercised. Although this situation has positive aspects (it helps, for example, to empower national institutions), a problem arises: What happens when states do not respect their obligations to human rights? What are the legal remedies offered by international law to protect against massive violations of human rights in the national realm? Is there any legal recourse that can be called upon to justify and trigger action by the international community?

The fact is that there is hardly any provision in international law to address this issue.[36] When human rights violations hamper the development of friendly relations among states, it is possible to take action. The coupling of human rights problems with questions of international peace and security generates an incentive and a justification. But international law alone does not really offer an antidote to human rights abuses. It does not entail mechanisms to force states to live up to their human rights commitments.[37] It neither envisions nor organizes an international right to intervene to stop massive human rights violations. The fact that the consent of a state is necessary to deploy international troops on its territory where a humanitarian crisis is happening illustrates that external intervention in the name of human rights, as superseding the state's sovereignty right, is no right in itself. The obligation or duty of humanitarian intervention is even less of a possibility. Even in a case as extreme as that of genocide, there is no legal imperative to get involved. The Genocide Convention does not clearly concede an obligation for states to intervene.[38]

The lack of a legal responsibility to intervene in order to put an end to massive violations of human rights shows how the "public good" dimension of the international system remains restricted. Far from being communal, the international realm is, to this day, interstatal.[39] As such, it leads to the preservation of the idea of self-contained national sovereignty taking at times a toll on the respect for human rights. It also induces the international community to fall back on moral suasion to address humanitarian crises.

In the absence of a legal hierarchy that would put the protection of human rights explicitly ahead of and above sovereignty, international law cannot oblige nation-states to save strangers; hence, intervening or not becomes principally an ethical or moral question. For the international community, humanitarian intervention, possibly encompassing the use of force, tends to be a collective matter of feeling compelled, or not, to do the right thing. In this context, ethics is not foreign to international relations, contrary to conventional thinking. The relatively low level of international legal protection for human rights, in light of their importance, contributes to making morality a significant aspect of the thinking and practice of international affairs. This is better than nothing, but notwithstanding the merits of acting internationally on a moral basis, it is still a more perilous path than action grounded in and backed by law and its various institutions.

Generally speaking, this refers to the paradoxical status of morality vis-à-vis law. Although morality is one of the foundations of law, morality alone is weaker than law. In the humanitarian context, the weakness of a moral or ethical source for intervention that lacks legal backing comes down to the shortage of normative resources in the international realm, where morality suffers compared to law. Intervention based simply on moral considerations does not offer the benefits of the institutionalization and socialization that a right and obligation enjoy when they are a matter of law. Law is based upon the recognition and implementation of moral or ethical values that are considered so fundamentally important in terms of each individual's life and relations among people that they are established in legal rights and their corresponding duties. Values receive the legal endorsement that makes them the foundations, guidelines, and horizon of reality geared toward socialization, and they become part of the rule of law that guarantees their respect.[40] In the rule of law, guarantees entail access to claims and challenges, as well as enforcement mechanisms—social pathologies are apt to be both prevented and prohibited. Consequently, doing the right thing morally and abiding by the law are meant to work together; they have convergent and cumulative effects. Law offers a set of mechanisms aimed at securing the realization of the vision of morality with which society identifies.

On the other hand, when doing the right thing is more or less a matter of moral judgment, and one somewhat at odds with standard law, it is destined to be problematic. It may not be subject to what can be the limitations of law—namely, proceduralism. But it does not profit from the social and political qualities associated with law. In particular, it does not proceed along a predictable course. The "right thing" cannot be counted on; its occurrence is largely voluntary, a question of choice and good will. It is up to the principal international actors—states—to act morally or not.[41] Furthermore, initiatives based on moral considerations that lack legal endorsement are likely to encounter difficulty mobilizing the type of support from actors and institutions that is the foundation of international law and that is often necessary for proper implementation. Calling upon moral justification in the absence of legal backing—as happened for the humanitarian interventions in the 1990s—generates even more controversies and questions: Because there is no agreement on the envisioned action that the moral stand seeks to justify, it does not become enshrined as an international legal principle. The fact that the action is caught in conflicts of legitimacies (between the various value-ideals and constituencies that enter into the substance of international legitimacy) explains why it is not part of the obligations explicitly codified by international law. Making a decision becomes a difficult choice. This is certainly not an invitation to boldness; rather, it encourages caution, if not operational timidity, and the adoption of a conservative political course.

It is in this constraining context that the three Western powers came to deliberate in the Security Council on what to do about the burgeoning humanitarian crises in the 1990s. As the crises created a moral and political pressure that they could not ignore, *something* had to be done. Short of finding in international law and the UN Charter a legal obligation for international involvement, the Council stretched Article 39 of Chapter VII of the Charter and the definition of a "threat to the peace" to justify UN intervention in internal conflicts and humanitarian crises that previously had been considered matters of domestic jurisdiction under Article 2 (7) of the Charter.[42] Nevertheless, the incentive to address these crises always remained relatively low: The de facto lack of international legal obligation to stop massive human rights violations echoed the reluctance of major powers to engage fully in the international realm for reasons other than conventional international peace and security matters.

HUMANITARIAN CRISES AND DILEMMAS OF INTERNATIONAL SOLIDARITY

The tensions created by the elements favoring international solidarity and those hampering it shaped the ways the international community handled the humanitarian crises of the 1990s. The Western permanent members of the Security Council paid more attention to issues of international solidarity but did not focus exclusively on them. They maintained their primary responsibilities toward the national realm. The deliberations, decisions, and actions initiated by the Security Council, echoing the hybrid structure of international life, tended to address conjointly the demands coming from the national and international levels—and the competing character of some of them made such deliberations a difficult exercise. It led the decision-making process to a series of dilemmas. When difficult choices had to be made between obligations to national constituencies and responsibilities to international solidarity, primacy (although not always an easy decision) was given to the former.

The deliberations and decisions of the Security Council and their implementation in terms of dilemmas that reflected (inside the Council) and projected (in the areas of conflict as well as in the world at large) the extent (and ultimately the limits) of international solidarity are examined here along three dimensions: first, the notion of a dilemma; second, the principal dilemmas of ends and means that shaped the deliberations and decisions of the Security Council regarding the humanitarian crises of the 1990s; and third, the changing nature of international democratic culture and the strain generated by the moral communities that are part of it.

DECISION MAKING IN A WORLD OF DILEMMAS

A dilemma arises when the benefit that is envisaged in adopting a decision and following the course of action that goes with it, and the justification and motivation to act that it provides, are balanced by a trade-off. The dilemma involves being unable to pursue a gain without being exposed to the drawback that it implies. The more the two conflicting sides of the problem appear in close proximity, the more difficult it is to assess the pros and cons, and the greater the stalemate. This state of affairs forces the decision maker to address a tricky predicament—what is to be done and how is it to be done, considering that the incentive to decide and act in one direction goes hand in hand with an outcome that tends to deprecate the benefit initially foreseen. Usually the deliberation process—begun as a benefit-maximization endeavor only to turn into a deadlock—attempts to overcome the impasse by adopting the option that constitutes the smallest loss possible.[43]

The social context largely accounts for the emergence of dilemmas. Three factors explain this situation. First, the appearance of a stalemate requires that the environment allow the possibility of a plurality of choices. Facing a dilemma is unlikely when there are no options at hand. The larger the number of options (and the drive to maximize benefits associated with them), the more likely a quandary will arise. Second, the unpleasant perspective, embedded in the terms of the dilemma, of losing the gain envisioned at the outset has to be understood in connection with the identity of the context. What is valued as an end or goal is linked with the overall scale of social worth in which the decision maker operates. Third, for a valued end or goal to contribute to the creation of a dilemma, not just any assignment of value will do. The end goal has to be valued, but not valued above everything else. If it is not valued at all, there is no reason to pursue it. If it is absolutely valued, an end goal will nip in the bud any possibility of dilemma: It is destined to prevail over other considerations, be they other end goals or restrictions on means to achieve them.

Dilemmas are likely to have a significant bearing on the individual and institutional decision-making process, especially in a social environment in which democratic values prevail. The scope of possibilities (and consequent choices) that are offered to people and institutions to deliberate is larger in this context than in any other. The commitment of democratic values to a relatively open and maximization-driven way of organizing reality guarantees such a social context. In addition, the pledge to pluralism has an impact on the creation of dilemmas. While this pledge is at the core of the inclusive character of democracy, it adds complexity, especially because it puts the need to balance the trade-offs that inclusiveness through pluralism introduces at the center of democratic governance. Although key democratic values are difficult to reconcile, their more or less equally valued quality forbids any of them from being overlooked. Think, for instance, of the challenge of pursuing equality and freedom simultaneously. These values (neither of which can be ignored) are meant to be mutually reinforcing, but they can also be at odds. Thus, the quest for democratic legitimacy amounts to an open-ended progression of trying to implement critical democratic value-finalities as much as possible while mitigating the tensions existing among them.

In the 1990s, the Security Council had to address the necessity of attending to a plurality of value-finalities and the dilemmas that this entails. The transitional nature of the international system at the time played a decisive role in bringing about this state of affairs. The alterations associated with the end of the Cold War enhanced the need for the international agenda to accommodate the importance of internationalist concerns regarding human rights and humanitarian issues; this undermined the quasi-monopoly that traditional considerations (essentially revolving around national interest) had previously enjoyed, but it did not end their crucial relevance. This mixed picture militated for attempting to find equilibrium between the traditional and internationalist value-finalities. It led the decision-making process of the Security Council to be caught in a series of dilemmas in its handling of humanitarian crises.

The three Western powers of the Council endorsed their leadership function of tone- and trend-setters by adopting a middle-ground course. They tried to service national as well as international solidarity demands. In their treatment of humanitarian crises, both internationalist and traditional national interest considerations influenced their deliberations and decisions. The conjoint pursuit of ends that their respective priorities tended to put at odds with one another framed the discussions in the Security Council, the drafting of the resolutions, and their implementation in a dilemma mode.

DILEMMAS OF INTERNATIONAL ACTION AND THE
SECURITY COUNCIL IN THE 1990s

It is easy and tempting to overlook the activity of the Security Council and disregard it as the expression of international political expediency—if not cynicism—reflecting mainly the double-talk, double standards, and self-interested positions and policies of major powers on international issues. The diplomatic posturing and rhetoric, the disconnect with the tragic reality on the ground, and the delaying tactics that often crowd the statements and resolutions of the Council encourage this point of view and can lead observers of the United Nations to believe that its dealings are the epitome of hypocrisy. Yet there is more to the deliberations and decisions of the Security Council than keeping the world at arm's length and catering to the interests of the powerful countries. In spite of all its shortcomings and the frustrations that its output may generate in those eager to see the globe's problems addressed and solved fully and at once, the Council has an important and constructive role. While it is true that during the Cold War its ability to influence international matters was severely constrained, in the 1990s the Security Council found itself one of the principal conduits of international action, and it emerged as a principal source of international legitimacy.[44] Its deliberations and resolutions, and the actions and results that they triggered, led the Council to be at times conservative, at times progressive, in its contribution to the socialization of international life.[45]

The deliberations and decisions of the Security Council came to be shaped by two related sets of dilemmas: dilemmas of ends and, mostly derived from these, dilemmas of means.

Dilemmas of ends, humanitarian crises, and international involvement. Historically, dilemmas of international action are understood mainly in the relation between ends and means, especially in the need to try to have means accorded (normatively, politically, and operationally) to ends. In the case of use of force, in particular, it has come down to finding a point of equilibrium between *jus ad bellum,* which seeks to identify the reasons that force can be used legitimately (answering the question *why?*) and *jus in bello,* which defines *how* force can be employed in ways that make it legitimate.[46] The 1990s were no exception to this state of affairs. Nonetheless, the dilemmas of international action (including use of force) in the aftermath of the Cold War within the framework of the United Nations present two characteristics: From a general standpoint, when the United Nations takes up the use of force, it does so more with the purpose of bringing peace than winning a war. In the 1990s, the primary motive for the United Nations to get involved with the possible use of force was to address humanitarian crises. These two factors, rather than making the ends of international engagement unquestionable, installed them at the center of the deliberations.

In deliberating on what should be the political ethics guiding the engagement of the international community in attempting to solve humanitarian crises, the leading members of the Security Council believed that the pursuit of an internationalist agenda through international solidarity should not take place at the expense of their commitment to national priorities. Hence, in the Council debates, dilemmas revolved around weighing the value of humanitarian and human rights protection. Dilemmas entailed assessing the pros and cons of (1) the justification and motivational power of the imperative to defend human rights versus the demands of national interest associated with threats to international peace and security, (2) selective interventionism, and (3) the minimization of the risks incurred in the intervention.

Humanitarian crises and massive human rights violations do not neatly fit the scenario of a threat to or breach of international peace that the Charter stipulates for justifying international intervention. But as the crises of the 1990s could not be totally ignored, the Western permanent members of the Security Council advanced a combination of two arguments to validate and motivate international involvement: the need to protect human rights, which responded to the humanitarian crises, and the need to reframe traditional threats to international peace and security in order to admit these post–Cold War crises. In such a way, the crises would more directly touch on the national interests of member states—by far the strongest rationale for triggering international action. This strategy made sense in the transitional context of the Cold War's aftermath. Yet there were advantages and disadvantages to such a course, which introduced a quandary.

Using the defense of human rights as a justification for international engagement had its shortcomings, domestically and internationally. At the national level, the protection of human rights tended not to be a compelling rationale for international intervention. Indeed, although the three Western Security Council members have been key contributors to the modern discourse on human rights and are dedicated in principle to these rights internationally, neither their foreign policies nor their public opinion consider the respect of human rights abroad as enough of a *strategic* matter to justify a strong international commitment. This is particularly the case with the United States. Calling upon human rights as a justification for international involvement in humanitarian crises also generated problems at the international level. Not only were Russia and China destined to be uncomfortable with this type of rationale and the actions it motivated, but most of the developing countries felt uneasy about going down such a path as well, not simply because of self-serving motives (their own human rights track records, for instance) but also for more tangible concerns (such as respect for national sovereignty).

The other justification for international involvement in these new crises—responding to a threat to international peace and security and the demands of national interest—was equally problematic. Invoking the national interest was a double-edged sword. Its use in the West to generate domestic political support for international intervention (especially from conservative constituencies) created problems nationally and internationally. Nationally, the perception of the lack of real strategic interest in humanitarian crises diluted the national interest justification. In the United States in particular, such an argument made the commitment to international solidarity tentative. Internationally, calling upon the national interest rationale tended to aggravate the opposition of non-Western and developing countries to humanitarian interventions. It invited them to conclude that the West was using interventions for self-serving reasons. The fact that the national-interest justification was a significant aspect of the American rhetoric only increased the suspicion. What was needed in the domestic American environment to help justify acting in a multilateral setting (making the case that it was a matter of national interest) cast the international engagement of the United States in the shadow of self-centeredness. The national-interest argument showed the oddity of the most powerful nation basing its international role first and foremost on domestic calculations. In times of relative peace, it may have made sense for the foreign policy of the predominant power to be guided essentially by inward considerations. But it certainly did not show international leadership. This state of affairs brings home the difficulty of balancing and reconciling national and global constituencies. To gain national support, multilateralism has to be sold to a certain extent to domestic public opinion on the basis of self-interested motives; yet if limited to these motives, it fails to appeal internationally.

The issue of selective interventionism created another quandary. The impossibility of addressing all the humanitarian crises (because of resource constraints and the inability to be on all fronts at the same time) implied that choices had to be made. With those choices came the dilemma of selective interventionism. At stake was justifying and weighing what was gained and what lost in adopting a discriminatory approach to humanitarian intervention, in stepping in to protect human rights here but not there. When disinclined to involve the United Nations, the Western permanent members of the Security Council tended to argue that intervening would not make a real difference. The conflicts were depicted as based on old hatreds, tribal in nature, and therefore too pervasive and deeply rooted for outside intervention to solve in the short or long term. This rationale was used not only in Africa but also in the Balkans. The Council's unwillingness to invest much in Africa, where the wars were most numerous and had the gravest humanitarian consequences, tended to make a mockery of the idea of international solidarity's universality.[47]

Assessing the risk of casualties involved in humanitarian interventions confronted the Security Council with the following choice: accept the eventuality of a significant number of casualties as a risk worth taking, or make their avoidance a central concern. The trade-offs inherent in both options amounted to yet another difficult dilemma. On the one hand, viewing casualties as unavoidable was likely to generate discontent at home for the Western permanent members of the Security Council, particularly in the United States. On the other hand, elevating the avoidance of casualties to a key goal undercut the moral and political value of the humanitarian intervention and the sincerity of its promotion.[48] Being worried about casualties first and foremost sent a dubious message: To intervening forces (primarily Western soldiers and more specifically U.S. soldiers) it sent the message that they were good enough to use force and eventually kill others, but too good to be killed themselves. To people and areas in crisis, it sent the message that they were worth helping but not worth sacrificing for, with the caveat that upholding this limited commitment to them tended to depend upon their cultural, geographical, or strategic proximity to the West.

From the dilemmas of ends to the dilemmas of means. The dilemmas of means the Security Council faced had to do with problems of implementation: balancing political and military measures, choosing local partners for the conduct of negotiations, applying sanctions, and deciding the most efficient ways to use force.

Balancing political and military measures was particularly challenging. Although the search for politically negotiated solutions to the conflicts was the international community's preferred course of action, as the crises dragged on, it became only one aspect of a wider portfolio of measures, including the use of force. Trying to end the conflicts through political means backed by the threat or use of force made sense. But in the context of the humanitarian crises of the 1990s, the inherent tension between the logics of negotiation and force made the Security Council undertake a complex calculation: The right balance between the pursuit of negotiations and the use of force, with either too much and not enough negotiation, as well as either too much and not enough coercion, proved to be a hard calculus.

Part of this difficulty overlapped with a second quandary—that of deciding whom to engage as negotiation partners in the areas of conflict. It was almost unavoidable that talks would involve those in power or fighting for power; their military and political clout made them impossible to ignore. Nonetheless, choosing the most effective party as interlocutor had drawbacks. In many cases, local military and political leaders were directly or indirectly responsible for the abuse of human rights. To bring people who were the primary causes of the problem into the negotiation process without empowering them further was not easy. An alternative was to move away from the centers of power and attempt to work with midlevel leaders who were likely to be more democratically minded, such as grass-roots leaders, academics, elders, or religious leaders, to build trust with the communities outside the power centers.[49] But this strategy entailed dealing with actors with little political power: In the environment of failed societies lacking democratic foundations, midlevel leaders with democratic leanings tended to be politically isolated.

Sanctions were another dilemma for international decision makers. The fact that, at times, they ended up hurting the people they were meant to help more than those they were targeting could not be overlooked. In the Balkans, their implementation took a particularly bitter tone. The arms embargo imposed on Yugoslavia between 1991 and 1995 inadvertently conferred a military advantage on the Serbian forces.

The dilemmas raised by the use of force were the most challenging, clearly shown by the difficulty of choosing between calling upon ground forces or limiting the use of force to airpower. Ground troops were likely to be the most effective use of force. Their use demonstrated a genuine commitment to end the crises as quickly as possible. On the other hand, their deployment posed logistical difficulties and, more to the point, exposed peacekeeping forces to the possibility of significant casualties. Airpower appeared to have the advantage of limiting the risk of casualties, at least for those countries that did not have troops deployed on the ground. But its deterrent effect was less than that of ground troops; it demonstrated a rather low level of commitment.[50]

Another context in which the use of force created dilemmas was in the delivery of humanitarian assistance. In particular, using force in a tentative manner contributed to two more dilemmas at the implementation level. The first was how to provide humanitarian assistance in a hostile environment when the international community was not really prepared to ensure its delivery by force. For a long time, no satisfactory answer was given to this problem, so humanitarian assistance was likely to be used (particularly in Somalia and in the Balkans) as a bargaining chip by the parties at war to manipulate the situation to their advantage. Indeed, once the use of force was being considered—albeit reluctantly—humanitarian assistance tended to be "instrumentalized" by belligerents, threatening in one way or another to hamper its distribution.

The second dilemma was how to use force effectively and credibly (from the military and political perspectives) when the declared purpose for using it (human rights protection) was supported by no more than a hesitant endorsement that largely conditioned and limited its modalities of employment upon the avoidance of casualties. This quandary was not easy to resolve, especially considering that in this context the use of force was perceived as a lose-lose situation in traditional military terms.[51] Consequently, not only did the low commitment to addressing humanitarian crises decisively determine in a restrictive manner how and where force would be used (including narrow interpretations of the peace operations mandates) but also the goal of ending the humanitarian crises was destined to be achieved as a secondary priority, as the side effect of an implicit primary objective (minimizing the risks taken by the military troops in the midst of intervention)—with the mixed results that this implied.

The use of airpower in Kosovo in 1999 and the dilemmas associated with it constitute a telling illustration of this state of affairs. In this regard, although the intervention in Kosovo had a unique character, it also conveyed a sense of déjà vu.

To be sure, there are differences between the international community's involvement in Kosovo and previous interventions. First, while the peace operations in Bosnia, Somalia, and elsewhere unfolded within the UN framework, the intervention in Kosovo was a NATO-led operation. Second, unlike the UN peace operations of the 1990s that displayed a mixture of peacekeeping and peacemaking, the NATO-led operation in Kosovo was clearly a military venture. Third, failure was not an option for the NATO intervention. Once under way, there was a real U.S. commitment to bring it to a successful military conclusion—the credibility of NATO and of the United States was at stake. It was out of the question to let Slobodan Milosevic emerge as the winner of the confrontation.[52]

Yet the debates among the Western permanent members of the Security Council concerning the modalities of intervention in Kosovo and the way it took place were reminiscent of critical aspects of the UN approach to other crises earlier in the 1990s. In particular, the refusal to envision and plan a ground war and the decision (at least in the first six weeks or so of the campaign) to restrict the military intervention to what for most of the conflict took the form of a high-altitude bombing campaign using laser-guided weapons, cannot be explained solely by the massive airpower and high-technology devices placed at the disposal of NATO, principally by the United States.[53] In light of the general dilemma that shaped international engagement in humanitarian crises in the aftermath of the Cold War, Kosovo was the shining example: to respond to humanitarian crises, yes, but at minimal cost.

Although the air campaign ultimately played a crucial role in the resolution of the Kosovo conflict (especially by precipitating the end of Serbian rule), it had three dramatic negative effects: Air bombardments created an open field that the 40,000-strong Yugoslav National Army and special police forces exploited to empty (temporarily) Kosovo of most of its 1.8 million ethnic Albanians in a few weeks. Although Belgrade had planned the implementation of a systematic ethnic cleansing campaign in Kosovo weeks, if not months, before the first of NATO's bombs fell in March 1999, the exclusive use of airpower in the intervention fueled rather than ended the ethnic cleansing. Also, the tactical choice to fly planes at high altitudes as part of a "zero casualty" imperative incorporated a calculated risk of misinterpreting the identity of the targets on the ground and hitting civilian and refugee populations. It took several cases of gruesome civilian casualties, widely publicized by the Serb authorities, before NATO planes began flying lower in order to identify their targets. The intensification of human rights violations that the modalities of military intervention adopted by NATO allowed to happen during the two months of the air campaign, from the end of March until mid-May 1999, further diminished the possibility of reconciliation among Kosovo's various ethnic groups after the war. Thus in Kosovo, as in Bosnia and Somalia, dilemmas of decision making, with the uncertainty on ends mainly commanding deliberations on means, showed that the hope was to achieve success on the basis of limited commitment.

INTERNATIONAL SOLIDARITY AND MORAL COMMUNITIES

The dilemmas examined above are part of the survey of international democratic culture's status in the 1990s; as such, the survey sends a highly mixed message: On the one hand, when confronted with extending a sense of solidarity and responsibility at the global level for nontraditional strategic reasons, the key international decision makers of the period, while advocating international engagement, favored the national realm and its ends over the international realm, offering a sobering view of the reality of moral obligations to people beyond borders. The moral community of the national realm continued to prevail over the moral community of the international realm. On the other hand, the mere fact that the Security Council addressed the conflicts of the period through dilemmas admitting humanitarian and human rights considerations demonstrates progress. It marked the recognition that nation-states' rights are not the only thing that matters at the international level.

Because of the conflicting legitimacies and constituencies at work in the international system, the Security Council tried to address massive human rights violations and humanitarian crises by searching for an acceptable balance between competing demands. This implied weighing the political and normative appropriateness of being either conservative or progressive in the evaluation of the situations and in responding to them. The weighing process concerned the fate of the populations in the areas of conflict. It also concerned the standing and reputation of the major democratic powers and of the international system that they contributed to underwrite. Moreover, it addressed how the period would set the tone of international response in the future.

In this regard, it should be acknowledged that the "cosmopolitan" ideas put forward by the international community and called upon by local actors to motivate external powers to come to their rescue were hijacked at times by the nationalist agendas of some of these same actors (such as the Kosovo Liberation Army), a situation that only furthered the international community's reluctance to pay a high price in the name of internationalist engagements.[54] As a result, the international community at times became increasingly embittered by the realization that, in the process of helping to stop conflicts, it was inadvertently empowering ethnic nationalist ideas, as well as authoritarian and corrupt practices. The early years of independence in the aftermath of the recent Balkan wars illustrate this situation. One can well understand how countries and people that have been structured by social, economic, and political pathologies for decades could not turn the corner of transition in a short time. Nevertheless, the reluctance on all sides of the Balkan conflicts (on the criminal perpetrators' side as well as on the victims' side) to assess the share of responsibility of everyone in the tragedy was problematic. The tendency for both perpetrators and victims to retain an entitlement mentality made it difficult to move beyond the authoritarian and selective rights culture that got the region in trouble to begin with. This also applies to the Hutus and Tutsis (each in their own way) in Rwanda after the genocide.[55]

To be sure, what was at stake in charting a course between conservatism and progressivism was the evolution of the international order, of its defining aspects and qualities, considering the role of its various actors and key interests and values. Specifically, what was at stake was that the policies the international community adopted in responding to the humanitarian crises of the 1990s would stretch the historicity of international norms of legitimacy.

In the balancing act among the moral, political, and legal obligations with which it struggled in the 1990s, the UN Security Council recognized the growing obligations of the international community to individuals beyond borders, whoever and wherever they are. Such recognition of the moral community of the international realm was far from perfect because it took place within the realm of selective internationalism, reactive and restorative justice, and the portrayal of concerns for human rights in terms of traditional national interest to create the minimum incentive for action. However, addressing the conflicts in terms of dilemmas acknowledged more than ever the increasing legitimacy of a moral community beyond borders. It admitted the fact that the community of obligations toward others does not stop at the border. The centrality of dilemmas in the Security Council deliberations showed that the global moral community beyond the national moral community was now strong enough to force decision makers to think of international engagement for purposes of solidarity and responsibility in terms of trade-offs.

THE HYBRID NATURE OF INTERNATIONAL POLITICS AND THE RESPONSIBILITY OF MAJOR DEMOCRATIC POWERS

The fact that the governments of the most powerful nations could not walk away entirely from humanitarian and human rights imperatives and thus had to subsume somewhat their national interests to international moral obligations was a change for the better. Whether this reorientation could become a constitutive rule of the international system is still an open question. Reflecting briefly on the hybrid nature of international politics helps shed some light on the issue.

At the heart of the contemporary political role of the three Western permanent members of the Security Council is a paradox of a somewhat schizophrenic nature. On the one hand, these democratic countries have done and continue to do much for the development of democratic ideals and the constitutionalization of modern politics, both nationally and internationally.

On the other hand, they have made and continue to make the pursuit of national interests the defining element of their foreign policies.

The commitment to the politics of national interest and realism that the major democratic powers have shown throughout their history, combined with their close association with democratic values and their diffusion, leaves an ambiguous legacy. This legacy makes them the primary source of the contemporary hybrid nature of international politics, inhabited and structured by both national and international interests.

The diffusion of these powers' liberal democratic values in the international realm advanced a sense of sameness, equality, and shared destiny worldwide that more than anything else has helped to shape formal transnational communities of like-minded countries. When this is added to their contribution to the establishment of the United Nations and their endorsement of key international treaties in the field of human rights and humanitarian law, the leading Western powers appear to serve as a central force in a contemporary international democratic culture. On the other hand, they also contributed the most to keeping countries and people apart by relating to other countries as competitors, if not enemies, perpetuating the strategic culture of national interest that continues to dominate international affairs. Moreover, the very Western values whose diffusion contributed to the development of an internationalist vision of international relations are also those that historically fueled the rise of nationalism and competition among nations. The modern values of powerful democratic nations gave the countries that they tried to dominate both the normative foundations and the political reasons to oppose them. In the process, the competition of national interests became one of the key defining elements of modern international politics.

The historical contributions of the three Western permanent members of the Security Council to the hybrid nature of the modern international system, made up of internationalism and national interest, also partially explains their ambiguous attitude toward the United Nations: They are committed to it because it is largely their creation and the projection of their normative culture into the international realm. Yet they are suspicious of it because they remain committed to the politics of national interest.

To be sure, the redistribution of international power in the aftermath of the Cold War allowed the three countries to revisit and reassess the two dimensions of international life—its internationalist and national-interest dimensions—and their relations to them. The peace operations of the 1990s gave them the possibility to reflect on where their priorities lay. As democratic nations, they had the values affiliation and identification that put them in a good position to accept the challenge of pushing forward the sense of international solidarity and responsibility. As major powers, they had to deal with the temptation to continue to ally themselves with their traditional politics of national interest. As *powerful* democratic nations, they ended up staying on a middle course, acknowledging to a certain extent internationalist demands while favoring the national realm. They alluded to a sense of international solidarity and responsibility while respecting their national interests. In such a way, although instrumental for the extension of solidarity and responsibility at the international level, they also greatly limited it.

If there is one country that wrestled with this particular dilemma of democratic power and of the obligations the national and international realms entail, it is the United States. The next two chapters examine whether and how two leaders of the sole superpower chose to reconcile the U.S. national interest and the "nagging" moral imperatives of international intervention in humanitarian tragedies.

Bill Clinton came to office as a genuine internationalist, but his vision of international peace relied on free trade and increased economic interdependence. His approaches to international intervention were largely hemmed in by a reluctant military and an overbearing Congress. The result was a selective multilateralism that echoed somewhat ineffective UN mandates, and when the mandate promised to exclude the prospect of forceful action in Kosovo, such multilateralism avoided a UN mandate altogether.

George W. Bush's foreign policy seemed to preclude multilateral peace operations, in keeping with the traditional conservative suspicion of international organizations, the United Nations chief among them. Moreover, as the Bush administration's foreign policy was framed early on by the terrorist attacks on American soil on September 11, 2001, the Bush Doctrine was explicit on the extent to which it would enlist America's European allies in multilateral endeavors in the war against terrorism—now, the mission would determine the coalition, not vice versa as in the past. In time, this would mean that the administration's determination to depose Iraq's Saddam Hussein would plunge the Atlantic Alliance into perhaps its most severe rupture since the Suez Crisis.

CHAPTER 4

CLINTON'S FOREIGN POLICY AND THE QUANDARY OF NATIONAL AND INTERNATIONAL INTERESTS

THE ROLE OF THE UNITED STATES IN THE 1990s vis-à-vis humanitarian crises was a mixture of decisiveness and reluctance. It was decisive in the sense that it was instrumental in triggering and implementing some of the defining international interventions of the period. American support was, for instance, essential to Operation Restore Hope and the United Nations' subsequent involvement in Somalia. It was also critical in the summer of 1995 to end the war in Bosnia and, in the fall of the same year, to negotiate the Dayton Accords. The Kosovo campaign in the spring of 1999 would not have happened without the leadership of the United States. Later, in September 1999, America helped to find a solution to the East Timor predicament—namely, by giving diplomatic and logistical support to the Australian deployment.[1]

However, the United States also showed reluctance to address humanitarian crises. The tentative interest taken by the Clinton administration in the Bosnian war until the spring of 1995 and its unwillingness to stop the genocide in Rwanda in 1994 are cases in point. At a time when America was more or less free of global threats and thus in a good position to act upon the internationalist values that partly shape its identity and foreign policy, how can we account for its ambivalence concerning humanitarian crises? And to what extent did the U.S. approach affect the international community's actions?

U.S. FOREIGN POLICY AND INTERNATIONALISM: BRIDGING THE PAST AND THE PRESENT

The Clinton administration could not ignore the local conflicts and humanitarian crises that had been overlooked in previous years. Nevertheless, it was not in a position to address them in an entirely new manner.

Like any other administration, it had to take into account and adapt to the principal parameters of American foreign policy. It had to work around two related strictures: the built-in conflicts in the United States' foreign policy between isolationism and internationalism, as well as between realism and idealism; and the paradoxical relationship between America and the United Nations, with the former being the single most important country in the establishment and functioning of the latter, and yet not fully committed to it.

From U.S. National Interest to Internationalism

Defending American interests has always been a key concern of U.S. foreign policy. Isolationism and internationalism, as well as their realist and idealist justifications, have all along been called upon in defense of the national interest. Each in its own way, as well as in their intertwined relationship, serves as a guideline to make America safer and stronger in the international realm.

The choice of isolationism entails a restriction of relations with other countries. Initially, in the early days of the republic, it had roots and motivations in U.S. idealism (that is, in the presupposed superiority of the American system and the need to guard it from the shortcomings of the rest of the world). The conviction that Europe's constant wars were the result of its cynical method of statecraft militated for America's staying away from world politics, at the time essentially conducted in and from Europe. The geopolitical situation of the country supported this idealist message. The security conferred on it by the ocean that separated it from the European powers protected America from being implicated in European balance-of-power struggles. In addition, the policy of isolationism was flexible enough to leave room for pragmatism and realism. For instance, throughout the nineteenth century, the United States did not carry its rejection of the Old World to the point of forgoing territorial expansion. Later on, between World War I and World War II, U.S. isolationism again proved to be selective: The U.S. refusal to be bound by the League of Nations did not amount to an absolute retreat from the world stage. From the relative comfort of its isolation as political and military tensions increased around the world and war loomed larger on the horizon of the 1930s, the United States defended its interests wherever it saw fit, and on its own terms.

Internationalism is the other major trend of U.S. foreign policy, and it tends to be seen in idealist terms. President Woodrow Wilson's philosophy of power and international relations did much to create this view. His vision encompassed four key beliefs that had been at the core of American conventional wisdom since Jefferson: (1) America's special mission transcends day-to-day diplomacy and obliges it to serve as a beacon of liberty for the rest of the world; (2) the foreign policies of democracies are morally superior because they are inherently peaceful; (3) foreign policy should reflect the same moral standards as personal ethics; and (4) the state has no right to claim a separate morality for itself. Wilson's contribution to American internationalism was to restate these four core beliefs in internationalist terms.[2] From his standpoint, universal law (not power equilibriums) and national trustworthiness (not national self-assertion) were the foundations on which international order should be established. His formula was basically an international system built upon democratic nation-states in the political sphere, coupled with a worldwide liberal economy and an interdependent structure of collective security in the League of Nations. The League was viewed as a way to institutionalize the moral international consensus on peace that Wilson's Fourteen Points advocated.[3] In essence, Wilson was proposing a world order in which resistance to aggression would be based on moral considerations rather than geopolitical calculations. In addition to asking themselves whether an act was threatening, nations would ask themselves whether it was unjust.

U.S. internationalism also encompasses a realist dimension; it does not lose sight of U.S. national interests. After all, the moral considerations put forward by Wilson were not meant to serve only others' interest. They were also envisioned as a tool to be put at the service of U.S. interests. What separated Wilson and the opponents to the League (in particular to Article X of the League Covenant, which envisioned the use of collective force to oppose and punish a nation for violating the sovereignty and territorial integrity of another) was not a matter of ends, but one of means: Although Wilson and opponents of the League agreed on the primacy of U.S. national interests, they disagreed on the way to achieve them. Mainstream conservatives in particular saw the obligation that the League imposed upon the United States as compromising American sovereignty by subjugating it to a supranational institution. As a result, the United States Senate, which at the time had a Republican majority, rejected the treaty and refused participation in a global institution designed to manage international order.

Subsequently, the limits imposed upon U.S. sovereignty by global institutions continued to be a major point of contention between internationalists, who see the commitment of the United States to global institutions as a potential source of benefits for the world and for the United States, and those who see such a commitment as a source of problems for the world and for the United States. But both those who support global institutions and those who are skeptical about them agreed at least that, no matter what, the U.S. national interest had to come first. This agreement was destined to make the relationship of the United States with the United Nations a contentious one.

THE UNITED STATES' RELUCTANT EMBRACE OF THE UNITED NATIONS

Although America is the country to which the United Nations owes the most, particularly in its internationalist and idealist aspects, it is as well a country whose realist and self-interested understanding of the United Nations leads it to have misgivings about the world body.

The central place that America came to occupy after World War II meant that its international engagement was required for the preservation of both its interests and the solidity of the international system.[4] The position of power predominance that the United States had achieved by the end of World War II convinced President Franklin D. Roosevelt that the country had enough power to structure the international system according to American principles. American values of internationalism and idealism also made this contribution possible. Roosevelt was determined to have the international environment embody the quintessential internationalist and Wilsonian principles of collective security and national self-determination, to which was added that of decolonization, which Wilson had been unable to push forward at the end of World War I because of the resistance of the old colonial European powers.[5] Roosevelt, a realistic Wilsonian, favored a consortium of the great powers to manage international peace and prevent future acts of aggression. As a result, the United Nations was given the power of the Security Council.

There is, nonetheless, another side to the story of the U.S. relationship with the United Nations. It concerns the reservations that America has toward the United Nations and the negative effects associated with them. They are rooted in the fact that, from the establishment of the world body, America has also related to the United Nations as a venue for the pursuit of its national interests. The U.S. approach to the United Nations in national interest terms is not surprising; as for any other country, national interest is a key motivation for getting involved in it. Moreover, to a point, America identifies its moral values with its political interests. It conceives their diffusion and realization in the world at large as an intrinsic part of the fulfillment of its national interest. Moral nationalism coincides with political universalism, and moral universalism with political nationalism. This view is destined to create problems. By virtue of the progressive American values themselves, the United Nations, although allowing much room for national interests, is not meant to serve them exclusively and narrowly, let alone serve the U.S. national interest above all. It is therefore difficult for other member states to accept the notion that America's national interest is an absolute, that any other national interest is secondary in importance (if not lacking fundamental validity), and that its national interest is the *international* interest.

The tension at the heart of the U.S. relationship with the United Nations came to a head during the Cold War. As the United Nations became a bastion of power for non-Western countries (with the Soviet Bloc and a number of developing countries challenging America), the United States realized that the United Nations and the exercise of multilateralism that it had done so much to create was not a one-way affair. Rather than endorsing an agenda that it disapproved, the United States chose to see the United Nations as deprived of its moral quality and stopped viewing itself as a primary stakeholder in the institution. Retreating and holding on to its Security Council seat, the United States ended up perceiving the General Assembly, its organs, decisions, and actions as part of a global scheme in which it wanted no part. True, the United Nations required much institutional improvement in the 1980s; however, President Reagan's demands for UN reform were probably more of an attempt to exert power over the world organization than a genuine appeal to bring the place up to satisfactory working standards. America's commitment to containing the expansion of Soviet power was then very much designed in opposition to the type of internationalism that the United States helped to endorse and promote with the establishment of the United Nations. America's guiding principle was to do what it thought best largely outside the United Nations, through a system of strategic alliances, economic aid programs, and the promotion of American-style democracy and capitalism as well as covert operations, controlled insurgencies, and the manipulation and overthrow of governments.[6]

In the 1990s, the disappearance of a sense of external and global threat after the collapse of the Soviet Union changed the international landscape, which no longer offered strong justification for the pursuit of unilateral policies, even when carried out within the framework of alliances. Ironically, the triumph of the United States introduced limitations on the use of its power. In fact, the end of the Cold War corresponded with a decades-long international movement pushing for greater respect of human rights and, more generally, the democratization of international life. America was due to meet the international world of multilateral expectations and obligations that it had created for itself and other countries more than forty years earlier.

President George H. W. Bush recognized that the United States had a new chance to express its commitment to the internationalism embodied in multilateralism and the United Nations. On September 21, 1992, in a speech to the United Nations, President Bush recommended a strengthening of UN peace operations capabilities and American support for them. He set out five areas that required improvement: better peace-keeping equipment and training at the national level; enhanced interoperability, planning, and training of multinational forces; an improved system for providing logistical support; enhanced capability for planning, crisis management, and intelligence; and adequate and equitable financing of UN operations.[7] Bush saw Mikhail Gorbachev as a genuine partner in the remodeling of the international system after the end of the Cold War. But, again, although Bush acknowledged that multilateralism and the United Nations were now viable options, he did not imply that he was overlooking the U.S. national interest.[8] For Bush, following the UN route was in fact serving the U.S. interest. In addition, had Bush remained in power, it is not certain that he would have invested much in and made a priority of the handling of the humanitarian crises of the 1990s. After all, the ways in which he approached the early stages of the conflicts that made the headlines during most of the period show some concern for the moral dimensions of the crises bridled by careful strategic considerations.[9] In other words, the sea change brought about by the end of the Cold War did not radically alter the structure of American foreign policy and, ultimately, the primacy it gives to national interest. William Jefferson Clinton's tentative support of humanitarian and human rights further illustrated the continuing significance of this state of affairs.

CLINTON'S INTERNATIONALISM: AT ODDS WITH CONGRESS AND THE MILITARY ESTABLISHMENT

Addressing wholeheartedly the conflicts of the 1990s and the humanitarian crises associated with them called for a type of American internationalism less concerned with traditional national interest and security issues. In spite of its initially declared internationalism, the Clinton administration did not break away from the inherent constraints on U.S. foreign policy and the strategic choices that they engender. Although more open than previous administrations to the idea of tackling nontraditional security emergencies and of doing so in a multilateral framework, the Clinton administration's attitude vis-à-vis the United Nations and humanitarian and human rights crises did not essentially disentangle itself from American foreign policy traditions. Ironically, far from helping to make its case with Congress and the military establishment, Clinton's tentative internationalism undermined it.

THE RHETORIC AND REALITY OF CLINTON'S INTERNATIONALISM

As a Democrat, Clinton was assumed to be an internationalist. The criticisms that he addressed to the Bush administration during the 1992 presidential campaign for not doing enough to stop humanitarian crises encouraged this impression. Bush tilted toward a realist vision of international relations, with the tendency to define the national interest in geopolitical terms rather than in terms of universal principles. Clinton insisted that U.S. foreign policy should not be divorced from the moral principles at the core of American democracy. Nonetheless, his support for a U.S. foreign policy committed to internationalist values proved to be somewhat tenuous. All along, the priorities of the Clinton administration focused on domestic issues—the economy foremost—so it should not come as a surprise that the administration's internationalism was in fact rather limited—or, at most, selective.

The foreign policy team that President Clinton put together echoed his declared belief in internationalism as a significant aspect of American foreign policy. People like Secretary of State Warren Christopher, National Security Adviser Anthony Lake, Ambassador to the United Nations Madeleine Albright, and special adviser Strobe Talbott (a close friend of Clinton) had four internationalist threads in common.[10] First, they expressed an aversion to the "cynical calculus" of pure power politics. They believed that balance of power and traditional geopolitics were ill suited to a new era and were no longer sufficient reasons to spend national wealth or send American troops abroad. Second, they believed that U.S. foreign policy had to pursue more humanitarian goals than in the past. In this regard, enlarging the realm of democracies had to be a priority, as did the protection and advancement of human rights.[11] Third, they held the view that the use of force should not be limited to the defense of vital interests defined in traditional terms; it should also be extended to interventions conducted in the name of moral or humanitarian principles and, if required, should be discreet and carefully applied. Fourth, they believed it was wrong for America to "go it alone." In the areas and on the issues mentioned above, the United States should conduct as much as possible a multilateral foreign policy that should, at least partly, insert itself into the mechanisms of collective security, centered on the United Nations. This conception and application of internationalism, built around spreading democracy to other nations, adhering to the importance of principles, and stressing the need for involvement, had a practical and political base: Multilateral cooperation would facilitate the initial predisposition of the Clinton administration to support a more interventionist U.S. foreign policy.

It is against this background that the Clinton administration conducted its review of UN peace operations. Presidential Review Directive 13, signed in early February 1993, provided an all-encompassing mandate to assess the entire spectrum of peace operations, from traditional peacekeeping to large-scale peace enforcement falling just short of war. The review asked four basic questions: When is it appropriate to engage in UN peace operations? Who should conduct peace operations: the United Nations, regional organizations, or ad hoc coalitions? How can peace operations be improved? And how can the U.S. governmental machinery be enhanced to support peace operations? To examine these issues, the Presidential Review Directive sought to devise a plan for the long-term strengthening of UN peace operations and America's capacity to participate. By July 1993, the essential framework of the document was in place. Notwithstanding the failure to resolve differences over financing and lead responsibility, the draft represented a major change in U.S. foreign policy toward peace operations. Most critical was the general tone of the document, which favored a greater use of peace operations and fully committed the United States to support them in all their political, military, and financial dimensions.[12]

Yet in only a few months, the nature of the presidential review was transformed radically. Its final version, published on May 5, 1994, under the title of Presidential Decision Directive 25 (PDD 25), was a marked departure from the statements put forward by the Clinton administration in the first half of 1993. PDD 25 effectively increased constraints on American engagement in the framework of peace operations.[13] The document addressed six major areas of reform and improvement: making disciplined and coherent choices about which peace operations to support; reducing the United States' costs for UN operations; clearly defining U.S. policy concerning the command and control of American military forces in peace operations; reforming and improving the United Nations' capability to manage peace operations; improving the way the U.S. government manages and funds peace operations; and creating better forms of cooperation among the executive branch, Congress, and the American public regarding peace operations.[14]

Three aspects of PDD 25 stood out. First, it insisted on the limited role played by peace operations in the United States' national security and defense policy. It indicated that the goal of U.S. policy was neither to expand the number of peace operations nor to enhance U.S. involvement in them. Rather, its aim was to ensure that the use of peace operations was selective and more effective. Second, PDD 25 provided a set of strict conditions for U.S. engagement in peace operations, including a specified time frame tied to immediate or final objectives, and an integrated political/military strategy to be coordinated with humanitarian assistance efforts. Additional, and even more rigorous, conditions applied when a significant U.S. participation in UN Chapter VII operations that were likely to involve combat was envisioned. Third, usefulness of peace operations was assessed largely in connection with national security and national interest. PDD 25 offered this final assessment:

> Properly constituted, peace operations can be one useful tool to advance American national interests and pursue our national security objectives. The U.S. cannot be the world's policeman. Nor can we ignore the increase in armed ethnic conflicts, civil wars, and the collapse of governmental authority in some states—crises that individually and cumulatively may affect U.S. interests. This policy is designed to impose discipline on both the UN and the U.S. to make peace operations a more effective instrument of collective security.[15]

This was hardly an endorsement of the ideals that had initially been the core of Clinton's internationalism. With the justification of involvement based on national-interest concerns, this looked like a new form of realism applied to any multilateral engagement. The full American support for peace operations mentioned in the early months of the Clinton administration had now receded.[16]

The effects of the Somalia debacle help explain this change. After October 1993 until the end of his presidency, Clinton turned defensive regarding peace operations and made it close to impossible to put American soldiers at risk in that context. Somalia was less a source of Clinton's policy change than a trigger for modifying a course that was in all probability destined to be taken eventually. The events in Somalia had a decided impact because the nature of the Clinton administration's overall foreign policy allowed them to have a great deal of significance; the administration's focus on economic issues could only push humanitarian questions backstage.

Clinton made American economic success and free trade the defining aspect of his presidency; in fact, this emphasis was closely related to his conception of international affairs. Believing that the dominant factors of international relations were shifting from traditional security to economic issues, he saw international affairs mainly in economic terms. This was not surprising: Since the late 1970s and increasingly during the 1980s, international economic issues had become more and more crucial in the structuring of the international system. Furthermore, in the 1990s, Clinton's tenure coincided with a historic convergence of technological and political trends, including open markets, porous borders, democratization, and the rise of the Internet. Globalization offered a wealth of opportunities, and Clinton viewed the global economy as a vehicle for increasing American prosperity, as well as a medium for enhancing international stability.

The focus on the economic dimension of international relations nevertheless had its disadvantages. The reconciliation of the aggressive economic nationalism that animated Clinton's foreign policy (involving a concern with achieving exclusive access to markets) with liberal free trade policies proved to be rather unconvincing to international competitors.[17] More to the point, the emphasis on trade and economic questions meant that all too often other international issues were not given sufficient consideration; this was especially true for humanitarian and human rights problems. Except on occasions of great urgency, Clinton spent minimal time on them, particularly during his first term.[18] And yet the demands associated with tackling them in their various aspects (diplomatic, political, military, etc.) in more than a reactive manner could be met only, if at all, by the president's sustained attention. For all Clinton's declared good intentions vis-à-vis internationalist values, such was not the case; although significant, his commitment to humanitarian and human rights issues was secondary to other concerns.

Clinton's capacity for empathy (epitomized in the "I feel your pain" line during his first presidential campaign) applied to the international realm. He felt the necessity of extending a sense of solidarity and responsibility at the international level to stop the wave of post–Cold War humanitarian and human rights crises. There is no reason to believe, for example, that his concern for the fate of Bosnian civilians was not genuine. However, his reluctance to make the case to the American people of the need to adopt a proactive course to address these crises showed that they were quite insignificant to his and his administration's agenda. President Clinton often explained his reluctance by indicating that the American people were unwilling to have the United States involved internationally for humanitarian and human rights motives. Yet in a study conducted in the middle of the 1990s, Steven Kull and I. M. Destler argued that the Clinton administration's response to the humanitarian emergencies was less a result of the disinclination of the American public than of his own uneasiness about pursuing a risky course.[19]

TENSIONS OVER PEACE OPERATIONS: THE UNITED NATIONS BETWEEN CONGRESS AND THE WHITE HOUSE

The Clinton administration's public display of a halfhearted commitment to internationalist values created problems. Trying to have it both ways presented the political advantage of allowing Clinton to keep his options open; and when the handling of the crises turned sour, it offered the possibility of an exit. The rather ad hoc approach of the Clinton administration to humanitarian crises also had the advantage of combining pragmatic idealism and opportunism. But the strategy had its faults. Among other things, it jeopardized the cooperation of the two pillars of American power the administration required to implement what little commitment it made to the internationalist components of its foreign policy: Congress and the military.

One of the central stories of the 1990s concerning the relations between the Clinton administration's foreign policy team and Congress was their mutual effort to shape the U.S. position regarding peace operations. Eventually, Congress acquired a critical role, often driving the policies of the White House; this was especially the case during Clinton's first term and to a large extent during his second. It is in this context that the peace operations budget allocation and modalities of U.S. military involvement in a multilateral setting developed into major points of contention between Congress and the Clinton administration.

The tensions that unfolded throughout the 1990s between Congress and the Democratic administration concerning peace operations stemmed from three sets of conflicting visions: the general difficulty of convincing Congress of the need for the United States to get involved internationally for motives other than national interest; the reluctance of Republican leaders in Congress to go along with nontraditional security policies conducted in a multilateral UN framework; and the misgivings of the administration itself about engaging America in attempts to resolve humanitarian and human rights emergencies.

The notion of separation of powers was a key component to good government in the eyes of the framers of the American Constitution. In the area of foreign policy, this was clearly the wish of the drafters, as they bestowed upon Congress the power to declare war, ratify treaties, and raise an army through taxation and spending, while reserving for the president the role of commander in chief of the armed forces. One of the main reasons for the founders' determination to vest the decision to go to war in the legislative branch was a determination not to let such a decision be made easily. The founders assumed that peace would (and should) be the customary state of the new republic and sought to fashion the constitution so as to assure that expectation. Their assumption was not that Congress was any more expert on the subject of war than the executive branch (if anything, they assumed the contrary) but, rather, that requiring its assent would reduce the number of occasions on which the United States would become thus involved.[20]

Notwithstanding its positive effects, this constitutional arrangement was also an invitation to tension. It had the potential, should the legislative and executive branches disagree, to lead them into a confrontation over a policy, particularly regarding the decision to deploy the nation's armed forces. Risks of divergence proved to be limited in times of great danger. In the absence of doubt about the reality of an external threat, the power of the White House has had the tendency to overshadow that of Congress.[21] On the other hand, with the lessening of danger, the power of the executive branch has tended to diminish and that of the Congress to increase. It is in this configuration that possibilities of disagreement have been most likely to occur between the legislative and executive branches.

As it happened, the end of the Cold War and the disappearance of the Soviet threat introduced a debate between Congress and the White House, and within Congress itself, over what threats existed to U.S. interests in the new environment. With the Soviet danger now a fading memory, Bill Clinton learned firsthand that members of Congress were more likely to disagree among themselves and with the president over what constituted the national interest. He learned as well that in this changed international context, Congress was open to challenging presidential decisions on U.S. military involvement abroad and the use of force. The domain of peace operations, more than any other, saw the shift in the relationship between Congress and the executive branch. As the controversies that raged in 1993 and 1994 concerning Somalia, Bosnia, and Haiti attested, taking risks in areas that did not entail an explicit stake for U.S. national interests generated much opposition in Congress. For its members (and not always only Republicans), humanitarian and human rights motivations were not sufficient to justify engaging American power overseas.

Projecting U.S. power in the context of the United Nations to end humanitarian crises was also at odds with the Republicans' conception of the goals and means of American foreign policy. It went against their idea that the national interest is the primary, if not the sole, touchstone of U.S. foreign policy. In addition, Republicans were uncomfortable with the support (even if tentative) of multilateralism and the United Nations put forward by Clinton and his foreign policy team. They viewed with suspicion the mixture of national and international interests at the heart of the multilateral and UN worldview. This was especially the case considering the conservative leanings of the Republicans dominating Congress at the time.[22]

Republicans were all the more eager to critique the U.S. involvement in nontraditional security crises in a UN setting because they were also trying to gain political benefits from their opposition to such engagements. Engaged in a fierce partisan battle, they saw the use and instrumentalization of UN issues as fair game, particularly when peace operations ran into trouble.[23] Criticizing President Clinton's stewardship of American foreign policy regarding the United Nations and peace operations became a way to undermine his administration. The fact that in November 1994 Republicans won control of both houses of Congress for the first time in forty years facilitated such a strategy. Although their resistance to Clinton's internationalism had been achieved mainly through skillful mastery of congressional rules before 1995, the new majority in Congress made their opposition much easier.

It was only when U.S. troops were deployed in Bosnia (after the Dayton Accords) and Kosovo (starting in 1999) under NATO's umbrella that Republican attacks over the engagement of U.S. soldiers in the Balkans diminished. The United States' identification with NATO, much stronger than its identification with the United Nations, made it de facto a matter of national interest to support NATO and its actions.

The Republican opposition to Clinton's policy vis-à-vis the United Nations and peace operations was assisted by the misgivings of the Democratic administration itself. Although recognizing that attempts to solve humanitarian and human rights crises had to be part of its foreign policy agenda, risking as little as possible was its principal concern, which explains why Clinton never really put all of his weight on Congress to back up his multilateral and peace operations policies. This also explains why, in the second half of the 1990s, in the congressional debates on the deployment of NATO troops in Bosnia and Kosovo, the Clinton administration insisted on the importance of American national interest as the key motivation for involvement and intervention rather than the moral and humanitarian considerations and the need to cooperate with multilateral bodies such as the United Nations. The focus of the discussions of the 106th Congress was not on humanitarian matters but on the question of whether NATO air strikes in Kosovo were in the United States' national interest.[24]

For these reasons, Congress acquired a critical role in curtailing the White House's policies on the handling of humanitarian and human rights emergencies. It happened in two main ways. First, Congress utilized the power of the purse. Congressional Republicans made sure that restrictions on the funds allocated to peace operations would limit U.S. involvement as much as possible. For example, in its first budget submission, the Clinton administration requested a total of $913 million for peace operations, almost twice the $460 million budget during the last year of the Bush administration. The figure included two add-ons—a supplemental request for $293 million in fiscal year 1993, and, as part of the $620 million in fiscal year 1994, a contingency fund of $175 million to be spent on unspecified, unanticipated peacekeeping bills. Despite the fact that these funds were badly needed, as the administration claimed, Congress rejected the two add-ons.[25] This set the tone for the difficulties that the administration encountered in trying to finance peace operations, especially in the first term of Clinton's presidency.

Most payments to the United Nations, including those for peace operations assessments, fall under the jurisdiction of the House Commerce-Justice-State Subcommittee. In that subcommittee, the United Nations must compete with domestic programs aimed at crime, immigration, trade promotion, and community economic development, so the peace operations account is often viewed as a source of cuts that can be used to support domestic needs. Moreover, the jurisdiction of the subcommittee over peace operations places the UN account in direct competition with operating funds for the State Department, a fact that can temper the department's advocacy on Capitol Hill for peace operations. Requesting additional resources for peace operations was not a welcome move in the 1990s, considering that the budget of the State Department was itself reduced.[26] What also did not help was the fact that Congress generally does not favor contingency funds because such funds violate a central premise of congressional oversight that specific dollars are tied to specific activities. The problem was especially acute for a budget item that was going through a substantial increase over a short period of time. Furthermore, Congress tends to be even more concerned about oversight for activities that could lead to U.S. involvement in military conflicts, particularly when the mixed results of the involvement give the impression of dragging the United States into foreign quagmires.[27]

Of course, this institutional funding mechanism in Congress would not have represented a major obstacle if the peace operations had been a matter of national interest. However, their secondary nature in the Clinton administration, combined with their political instrumentalization by the Republicans, gave them much resonance. Eventually, the funding difficulty not only sabotaged the administration's relations with Congress on peace operations policy but also affected the peace operations themselves. The inability of the United States to meet peace operations requirements generated arrears that posed serious problems: The bigger the debts, the longer the United Nations took to pay salaries for troops, and the harder it was to get nations to contribute troops.[28] The debts also made it more difficult for the United Nations to fund the kind of improvements in management of peace operations sought by the United States. After 1996, funding problems became less of an issue; with the number of peace operations decreasing in the second half of the 1990s (before rising again at the end of the decade), the call for congressional approval and the tensions associated with financing peace operations lessened. Nevertheless, Congress continued to take any occasion to curtail UN peace operations through budget-related questions.[29]

Congress also used reservations over the conditions of deployment of U.S. troops in peace operations as another way to challenge the Clinton administration. It expressed five principal concerns. First, it wanted to be consulted regarding the commitment of U.S. forces to peace operations. Many members insisted on the necessity of congressional approval if U.S. troops were to be placed at risk. A second issue was the question of whether U.S. troops in peace operations should serve under the command or control of foreign officers. The issue of command was at times posed in symbolic terms, reflecting larger concerns about U.S. leadership in the world and the use of collective security mechanisms, but it also involved a pragmatic side: whether the United States should entrust its citizens' lives to the judgment of foreign officers.[30] A third concern was whether U.S. military forces were by character, doctrine, and training suited to carry out peace operations. Soldiers cultivate the instincts and skills of fighters, while the skills and instincts needed for peacekeeping more resemble those of law enforcement. Fourth, the issue of casualties often stood at the center of congressional discussions on deploying U.S. contingents in multilateral operations.[31] Fifth, readiness—the degree to which the armed forces are prepared in terms of training and equipment to defend the country—was a constant theme in congressional debates over the extent to which U.S. troops should engage in peace operations. The fact that the U.S. military was increasingly called upon to perform peace operations while it had been significantly downsized since the end of the Cold War worried members of Congress, leading them to question whether U.S. military forces could perform their core mission (i.e., national defense where U.S. vital interests are threatened) if they engaged extensively in other activities.

Clinton's Tentative Internationalism:
At Odds with the Military Establishment

It was not solely in its relations with Congress that the Clinton administration had to deal with the oversight of American foreign policy. It faced a similar situation with the military establishment, whose influence on the foreign policy decision-making process could not be ignored. The influence of the military establishment on U.S. foreign policy reflects America's status as a global power and the extent to which it is implicated in international security affairs. There is no equivalent level of military sway in other Western democracies. In the United Kingdom and France, for example, armed forces are relatively marginal in the foreign policy decision-making process. Against the background of a problematic relationship with the Democrats, the military establishment favored a doctrine of engagement that left little room for tackling humanitarian and human rights crises and peace operations.

By the time Bill Clinton took office, the relationship between the Democrats and the military establishment tended to be one of relative acrimony, suspicion, and growing political distance on the part of the armed forces, making it harder for the Clinton administration to get the military establishment on board with its internationalist foreign policy.

The tension between the Democrats and the military went back to the Vietnam War. Two Democratic presidents, Kennedy and Johnson, had been the principal architects of the ill-advised escalation in Vietnam. At the same time, most of the antiwar protests had come from the liberal-left faction of the Democratic party, along with some moderate centrist Republicans. This made the military establishment doubly unhappy with the Democratic party, resenting it for having allowed an escalation that lacked public support at home and that it was not willing to sell forcefully to the American public. It also resented the Democrats for having permitted just a gradual and incremental escalation, consequently making the war effort indecisive from the military establishment's standpoint and forcing the military to conduct a war in an unwinnable way. Furthermore, the foreign policy track record of the Democrats and the use of the military since the Vietnam War did not speak in their favor. For the military, the fact that by 1992 the Democrats had held power for only four of the last twenty-four years (between 1976 and 1980, under President Jimmy Carter), and that during those four years U.S. foreign policy and use of the armed forces had not really been successful, was not encouraging. The disastrous April 1980 Iranian hostage rescue attempt, in the last year of Carter's presidency, stood as a telling illustration of the Democrats' difficulty in handling international crises and projecting American power effectively.

The political evolution that the armed forces went through between the 1970s and the 1990s, amounting to a distinctive partisan affinity, played an additional role in its uneasiness vis-à-vis the Clinton administration. Neutral servants of the state continued to be the role of the armed forces, but the officer corps in particular developed a rather idiosyncratic political coloration: The percentage of officers who identified themselves as independent (or specified no party affiliation) dropped from 46 percent to 27 percent, and the percentage who identified themselves as Republican nearly doubled (from 33 percent to 64 percent). In the early 1990s, while the country's governmental and business elite and the mass public were split more or less evenly, for every Democratic military officer there were eight Republicans.[32]

Various factors contributed to the "Republicanization" of the officer corps.[33] These factors include the ways in which the American military was involved in the crises of the past thirty years and the outcomes that followed, both in the handling of the crises and the evolution of the culture of the military institution. Here, of course, the fallout from Vietnam obviously has a special importance. Factors include as well Democrats abandoning the military and Republicans embracing it, an increase during the 1980s in the proportion of young people identifying themselves as Republicans and expressing an interest in joining the military, and the Reagan-era military buildup.

On top of this, perceived missteps at the time of his ascendancy to power did not help Bill Clinton win the trust and good graces of the military. Two elements stood out. The first was the draft issue. In January 1992, when Clinton was campaigning for the New Hampshire primary, a story appeared in the *Wall Street Journal* indicating that he had manipulated the draft in 1969 so that he would not have to serve in Vietnam. Eventually, he was able to overcome the problem. After all, he had not been the only young American to avoid the draft, among them some of the other men who were emerging as national political figures.[34] Nonetheless, the sense of entitlement that the incident displayed would not be forgotten by U.S. military leaders, especially by the person who was, in 1992, the chairman of the Joint Chiefs of Staff, General Colin L. Powell. When Clinton's issue was being debated, one of the nation's not-so-hidden secrets was being unveiled: America's educated and privileged had by and large not served in Vietnam, and Powell despised the discrimination that had presided over decisions on who would go to Vietnam and who would not.[35] Second, the fact that

Clinton made the question of gays in the military one of the more visible issues of the first months of his presidency alienated the military establishment. Integrating openly gay people into the armed forces was a campaign promise, and the decision to go ahead with it was made entirely by Clinton and his political advisers, against the advice of the conservative military institution. Once elected, Clinton dove straight into the matter, got his nose bloodied, and ultimately backed off.[36] This placed him again in a defensive position vis-à-vis an already suspicious military establishment.

It is against this background that the declared internationalism of the Clinton administration, even if tentative, ran contrary to the armed forces' worldview. Getting involved in humanitarian crises and peace operations, including peace enforcement, did not mesh well with three core elements of the American military doctrine: the primary mission of the armed forces to fight wars, the modalities of engagement with which the military identified, and the determination to minimize casualties in any deployment.

Throughout the 1990s, the various defense-related studies issued by the U.S. Department of Defense at the request of Congress were meant to reshape U.S. military strategy in light of the downfall of the Soviet Union and the end of the Cold War.[37] These studies consisted of the Base Force Structure, the Bottom-Up Review, the Quadrennial Defense Review (QDR) of 1997, and the 1997 National Defense Panel.[38] None of these studies, or the follow-up reports, transformed U.S. military strategy in ways that recognized the importance of humanitarian crises and peace operations.

In the early 1990s, General Powell coined the term "base force" to designate a proposed structure representing the minimum armed forces necessary for the United States to meet the national security objectives defined by policymakers, notably the ability to conduct two major theater wars simultaneously. This concept was the main force shaping the 1993 Bottom-Up Review, which acknowledged the considerable changes in the global security environment and articulated a strategy whereby the Department of Defense sought to prevent conflict by promoting democracy and peaceful resolution of conflict; yet it also continued to focus on the two-major-wars scenario (at the time, Iraq and North Korea as the most likely adversaries), and peace operations remained extremely marginal.

The strategy outlined in the Quadrennial Defense Review of 1997 did not fundamentally alter this state of affairs. The report mentioned that the military must contend with new threats, including the proliferation of weapons of mass destruction, advanced technologies, drug trafficking, organized crime, and uncontrolled immigration. It also envisaged the possibility of "smaller-scale contingency operations,"[39] but the QDR retained the two-major-wars scenario as its force-shaping criterion and did not recognize that more importance had to be attached to the multilateral handling of humanitarian crises. The perception of failure that had accompanied the deployment of UN peace operations in the previous years encouraged the armed forces in this line of thinking.

The 1997 National Defense Panel, although criticizing the two-wars scenario as a means to justify a Cold War force structure, once again presented peace operations as a minor item in U.S. military doctrine. Follow-up reports from the Pentagon did not drastically transform the assessment of peace operations either. Presidential Decision Directive 56 (PDD 56), entitled "Managing Complex Contingency Operations," is a case in point.[40] Although it envisioned the improvement of capacities for humanitarian assistance and peace operations, it stopped short of enhanced coordination for coercive and other early-action preventive strategies.[41]

The perceived lack of importance of multilateral operations within the U.S. military establishment may have fluctuated with the personalities in charge, the new chairman of the Joint Chiefs of Staff in particular. General John M. Shalikashvili, chairman of the Joint Chiefs of Staff between 1993 and 1997, was more open to American military involvement in multilateral operations at the service of humanitarian causes than was General Powell.[42] However, no matter who was heading the armed forces, UN operations and human rights emergencies were by and large considered minimally significant; they simply did not fit the types of conflict and motivations for engagement that the military establishment valued the most. It is therefore not surprising that during the 1990s, the peace operations and conflict prevention units at the Pentagon remained small.[43]

The modality of involvement in humanitarian crises in a multilateral context was another issue that made the armed forces uncomfortable. Four main areas of concern stood against the ways most of the peace operations were launched and conducted: clarity of mandates and objectives, including entry and exit conditions; use of force and rules of engagement; command; and nature of the missions.

The imperative of clarity of mandates and goals went back to the military establishment's visceral need to avoid another Vietnam (and another Beirut).[44] It went back as well to the so-called Weinberger Doctrine (after the Reagan administration's secretary of defense), which made the clarity of mandate and objective one of the key requirements for military force to be considered as a policy option.[45] The continuity of some critical aspects of this position was assumed in the Bush administration, as well as in the early years of the Clinton presidency, with the appointment of General Powell as Joint Chiefs of Staff chairman.[46] Once given a chance to plan and implement interventions himself, Powell stayed true to the credo of his former boss, so much so in fact that the ideas put forward by Secretary Caspar Weinberger became reincarnated over time as the Powell Doctrine. This approach was to be applied to military operations led by the United States, unilaterally or in a multilateral setting, in crises where its vital interests were at stake. Although the Powell Doctrine had not been initially envisioned in this context, it also became a factor in peace operations. In fact, it turned out to be a major tool that the U.S. military used to limit as much as possible U.S. involvement in peace operations and even military interventions of a broader order.[47] The peace operations of the 1990s, besides dealing with conflicts not really endangering the American national interest directly, unfolded in ways that lacked clarity of purpose and objective. The manner in which they took place on the ground and through which they were handled in diplomatic circles, deeply marked by ambiguity and messiness, was a warning to the military. Moreover, "nation building," a key component of the peace operations, only further obscured the debates on the need for military engagement from the armed forces' standpoint.

The conditions on the use of force in peace operations were equally at odds with the military establishment's views. Overwhelming force was not an option; in peace operations, the use of force tends to be limited because it does not seek to achieve military victory as such. Far from being a tool meant to defeat an enemy, the use of force is called upon to exercise pressure on the parties at war. The fact that the Clinton administration was often inclined at best to merely "do something" undermined all the more, in the armed forces' opinion, the meaning of using force in these situations. The quandary was that although Powell's all-or-nothing doctrine of decisive force was inadequate for most of the smoldering conflicts of the 1990s, the United States could not ignore them altogether because of its global power status.

Command was another issue. Throughout the 1990s, the military resisted putting U.S. troops under foreign command in a multilateral setting, although it was more accommodating with NATO. The reservations applied especially to the United Nations: Unless the commander was American, there was refusal to put forces under the UN flag. The concerns grew from what the military viewed as the shortcomings of the United Nations as an institution and the way the peace operations were conceived and implemented. U.S. commanders' worries included lack of protection, poor planning, weak communications, and underfunding. The irony was that a number of these limitations had partly to do with the reluctance of important member states, and primarily the United States, to pay their contributions to the United Nations.[48] Furthermore, in Somalia—the UN operation that had one of the greatest impacts on the American foreign policy regarding multilateral involvement—the shortcomings of command and communication that led to the deaths of U.S. Army Rangers were not principally the making of the United Nations; they were largely rooted in the U.S. chain of command. Had the U.S. troops not been operating largely on their own in Mogadishu, chances are that events would have turned out much less tragically.[49]

Another important concern was the nature of the peace operation missions. In this case, the military was reluctant to get involved in certain assignments because it felt that the mission statement of the armed forces did not fit the tasks required of peacekeepers. The sense of disconnect concerned the use of force, which, in a peace operation context, is by definition restricted. It had also to do with the fact that the military was often asked in the 1990s to perform police functions in the areas of deployment, functions for which it did not see itself to be designed and trained.[50] There are indeed fundamental differences between the roles of soldiers (in particular, U.S. soldiers) and those of police. Soldiers protect the nation from external threats; police protect against internal ones. Soldiers traditionally fight wars; police protect the peace. Soldiers, when acting as soldiers, fight enemies; police, when acting as police, protect citizens. Soldiers are trained to consider the maximum allowable force to accomplish the mission; police are trained to consider the minimum allowable force to protect the community and use deadly force only if someone poses a threat to others. Moreover, people who "break the peace" in peace operations are more likely to be criminals than combatants.

The U.S. military also felt it was ill equipped, compared to other national armed forces, for the policing tasks required of peacekeepers. The more a military force has been led over time to perform civilian police or quasi-police functions, the more the gap between the military and the police has narrowed and can be bridged. Usually, armed forces in countries not exposed to major security responsibilities or threats have a narrower gap with police. This is the case, for instance, in the Nordic countries and increasingly in former European global powers such as France and the United Kingdom. (Incidentally, the involvement of British armed forces in Northern Ireland has allowed them to acquire a policing expertise that few other national militaries possess.[51]) On the other hand, the global power status of the United States and its security responsibility and exposure do not induce it to have a "police culture" become part of a military culture. Furthermore, the police culture in the United States is somewhat "militarized": American police are more likely to use force than any other police force among Western democratic nations.[52]

Casualty aversion was another key issue for the U.S. military establishment. Although to a certain extent the positions of the different services varied (and continue to vary to this day), it was a shared concern among the branches of the armed forces.[53] While casualty aversion is a general trend in Western democracies, with military commanders ever mindful of their soldiers' safety, a number of factors made casualty aversion particularly acute in the U.S. military context. Once again, the unhappy legacy of Vietnam played a role. The feeling that thousands of young American draftees had died for reasons that hardly appeared justified at the time and that were viewed as less and less so as years passed was the source of a deep trauma. This concern became an increasingly important aspect within the process of reorientation of the U.S. military in the aftermath of the Vietnam War. The shift from a draft to a volunteer army introduced a change of attitude vis-à-vis enlistees. Soldiers came to be seen as an asset of great value rather than simply the rank and file.[54]

The technological superiority of the U.S. military (with a growing reliance on high technology, including airpower and precision weaponry such as cruise missiles), allowing troops to engage the enemy with minimal risk, gave a concrete expression to casualty aversion on the battlefield.[55] For the United States, none of the conflicts associated with humanitarian crises in the 1990s was a war of survival or put its national interest at stake (two circumstances in which historically it had accepted the likelihood of high casualties); hence, casualty aversion was elevated to an almost obsessive level. In Operation Desert Storm (the one conflict of the 1990s that closely fit the national interest requirement), casualty aversion had been a significant concern; in the humanitarian crises context, it was destined to be a decisive one.[56] Ultimately, the tentative support the armed forces could hope to receive from the Clinton administration played into the institutionally embedded tendency of the military establishment to be at odds by tradition and mission with internationalist and multilateralist foreign policy.[57]

Would the attitude of the military establishment have been different had it felt that it could count fully on the political support of the Clinton administration? It is possible that it would have been more flexible about the lack of importance of the humanitarian crises in terms of mainstream military doctrine, the conditions of military engagement, and casualty aversion. However, the tentativeness with which Clinton and his administration approached the humanitarian crises, amounting to indecision about what to do and how to do it, deepened the uneasiness of the armed forces. The fact that the White House was calling upon the military to address humanitarian crises, yet was itself halfheartedly committed to its declared internationalism, made the military establishment ever more cautious: If things went wrong, the administration, perhaps like any administration, would not assume full responsibility but, rather, shift the blame to the military if necessary.[58]

THE IMPACT OF AMERICAN PRIMACY ON PEACE OPERATIONS

To be sure, the centrality of American power in the post–Cold War era gave much resonance to the debates on the extent to which internationalism should shape U.S. foreign policy. Greatly influencing the multilateral handling of the humanitarian crises of the 1990s, the debates affected the conception and implementation of the peace operations.

THE UNITED STATES AND PEACE OPERATIONS: MAXIMUM INFLUENCE FOR MINIMUM INTEREST

As the U.S. role played in the peace operations in the 1990s shows, occupying a key international position is critical for being able to have an impact on the international agenda, its modus operandi, and the policies that are launched and implemented, even in those areas that are of little concern for the sole superpower.

For a medium power, to have a noted international influence takes a lot of concerted commitment and effort over time. Short of having the capacity to affect the whole international agenda, a medium power can be influential only by focusing on the areas, issues, and institutions that are the most likely to be responsive to its level of power. This is mainly why the Nordic countries and Canada, for example, view multilateralism as a significant way for them to have a voice internationally. The weaker the position of an international actor, the more strategic its thinking and course of action should be to have a chance of success with its foreign policy goals. In this regard, the political and institutional weakness of the United Nations vis-à-vis major powers makes it critical for it to have a strategic approach in order to be of relevance. At a minimum, a strategic approach entails having a good knowledge of the inner workings, motivations, and interests of the most important member states, the United States in particular.

On the other hand, a country placed at the center of the international distribution of power does not necessarily have to evince much commitment and effort to exercise overall influence. To be sure, the fact that it occupies a pivotal international position presupposes that it has done much in the past to achieve it and that it continues to work hard to maintain it. Nevertheless, predominance guarantees significant power even in domains that the country does not see as a priority. This is typically the case of the United States.

In areas that are strategic to the continuation and enhancement of American dominance, successive U.S. administrations have always done what was required to remain ahead of other countries in the economic and defense realms.[59] This being said, one of the side benefits of predominance is that it reverberates in domains to which America does not give much attention and importance. This allows the United States to define the terms of the debates and hold the keys—even for issues about which it cares marginally. In this context, whatever position America holds, the centrality of its power tends to give it a critical influence. Not only can it play by the rules of the game or change them somewhat to its advantage, it can also bypass them by and large, officially or unofficially.

The peace operations of the 1990s serve as a telling illustration of the fact that, because of its international superiority, the United States can have a major impact even on issues that it perceives as secondary.

As noted before, the portion of the U.S. budget allocated to peace operations in the aftermath of the Cold War, although significant in and of itself, was minuscule compared to its annual national defense budget. As also noted previously, the number of people working exclusively on peace operations at the Pentagon was extremely small, echoing the fact that peace operations were marginal in U.S. military doctrine. Moreover, for the Clinton administration, humanitarian crises never represented a genuine concern to be addressed forcefully and consistently. Yet America influenced in decisive ways the peace operations of the 1990s, although they were a secondary concern for U.S. policymakers. Other countries could not compete with U.S. leverage in the international arena.[60]

THE U.S. IMPACT ON PEACE OPERATIONS

The "swing power" that the United States enjoyed in the aftermath of the Cold War and the critical weight that it had on peace operations do not suggest that the United States alone should be praised for the success of peace operations (when there was success) and blamed for their shortcomings (when there was failure). Other factors played positive and negative roles. As previously shown, the United Nations, the nation-centric structure of the international system, and the role of other actors must also be taken into account. However, the unparalleled international influence and leverage of America cannot be overlooked in the assessment of the multilateral handling of humanitarian crises. As it happens, the U.S. impact was mixed.

Without a doubt, America played a positive role in the search for solutions to the humanitarian crises of the 1990s. In most of the instances in which there was international involvement, the U.S. role proved to be essential. Although the United States was never as decisive as in more traditional types of conflict (Operation Desert Storm, for example), it was decisive enough to get the international community engaged in, if not to end, the crises. This was particularly true for Somalia, Bosnia, Kosovo, and East Timor.

It is quite probable that without the U.S. decision to lead Operation Restore Hope, other nations would not have gotten involved in Somalia. Once America decided to withdraw, the other countries involved in the UN operation followed suit, demonstrating how the U.S. engagement was decisive for moving the international community into Somalia. Bosnia is another example of the key role the United States played. It took America's commitment to a solution to the conflict, in the spring of 1995, for the war in Bosnia to end. In Kosovo, the U.S. decision to launch a NATO air campaign was central to international involvement there, and it paved the way for the subsequent UN operation. In East Timor, the political pressure exercised by the American government on Djakarta and the logistical support given to Australian forces were key to the deployment of international forces on the island.

Although the United States had a positive impact on some of the most defining humanitarian crises of the 1990s, there is a less inspiring side to the story; it concerns American shortcomings and their negative effects on humanitarian crises. In this regard, one element has to be singled out: The oscillation between reluctant leadership and outright refusal to get involved that characterized the U.S. attitude on a number of occasions had dramatic consequences on the multilateral handling of humanitarian crises.

Rwanda is one instance of how the U.S. refusal to get involved in humanitarian crises had negative consequences. In the spring of 1994, a few months after the Somalia fiasco and at a time when the Clinton administration was issuing restrictive guidelines on U.S. involvement in peace operations with PDD 25, the Rwandan crisis had little chance of attracting the attention of the White House. This was all the more true considering that the United States had no geopolitical interests strong enough in the country to be worth making the case for intervention.

Although it was becoming clear that mass killings of an unprecedented nature were taking place in May 1994, the Clinton administration refused to acknowledge that a genocide was under way.[61] It invoked in the Security Council financial constraints and operational difficulties to justify its refusal to get involved. Not only did the United States shun involvement, but it also opposed the involvement of the international community. Throughout May it blocked effective action for Rwanda by arguing against the plan devised by General Roméo Dallaire in the first days of the genocide to airlift a brigade to Kigali. Instead, the United States argued for the creation of safe havens on the border of Tanzania and Zaire.[62] This position was destined to have tragic consequences, as other countries used American reluctance as an excuse to turn their eyes away from the crisis.

Were there alternatives to the Clinton administration's policy? Despite the fact that throughout the genocide the administration presented its position as the only option, there were certainly alternatives. Samantha Power, in particular, suggests a number of them within or outside the context of the United Nations. Before the violence escalated, the United States could have agreed to Belgian pleas for UN reinforcement. Once the daily killing of thousands of Rwandans had begun, Clinton could have asked for the deployment of troops to Rwanda. The United States could have joined Dallaire's UNAMIR forces or it could have intervened unilaterally with the Security Council's backing, as France did in June.[63] The White House also could have threatened to prosecute those complicit in the genocide. It could have at least required the deployment of Pentagon assets to jam the inflammatory radio broadcasts from the Hutu-controlled Radio Milles Collines.[64] But in depicting the killings as anchored in ethnically embedded hatred, and arguing that America could not get involved everywhere, the Clinton administration conveyed the message that war and killing in Rwanda certainly created no strategic imperative but was, rather, an ambiguous moral dilemma. For the White House, Rwanda was simply not a priority. No matter the extent of the tragedy, it was too remote from more immediate concerns for the administration to pay it much attention.[65] As such, Rwanda fell into the type of neglect by the United States and other major actors from which African crises suffered throughout the 1990s. After all, the United States had decided to put Somalia on the agenda of the international community because initially it had been viewed as a more or less risk-free operation. At the outset, the intervention had also been designed to remain within narrow parameters. Once the mission statement unraveled (or widened, depending on the point of view) and casualties were incurred, the U.S. withdrawal was only a matter of time.

The other crisis in which America played an indirectly negative role in the 1990s was Bosnia. To be sure, the United States paid much more attention to the Balkans than it did to Africa. In addition, the American initiatives in the spring and summer of 1995 were crucial to ending the war and arranging for the postwar transition to peace and reconstruction. Yet the centrality of the United States' power as a whole led the ambiguities of the Clinton administration regarding humanitarian crises to have a rather negative influence on the handling of the war in Bosnia. By the time Clinton came to power in early 1993, the Vance-Owen Peace Plan was well under way. The new Democratic administration offered mild support for the plan in the beginning, before in effect withdrawing it with the claim that it favored the Serbs. The message sent by the Clinton administration in spring 1993 was that the Europeans would not be able to define a settlement on their own and on the best terms achievable; hence, the international community and, more important, the sides in the Bosnian conflict looked to the Clinton administration as the key to finding a solution to the crisis. As a result, neither the Bosnian Serbs nor the Bosnian Muslims endorsed the plan. However, for two years, between the spring of 1993 and the spring of 1995, the White House remained on the sidelines. Having torpedoed Europe's efforts, it did not have much of an alternative to offer for two long and bloody years.[66] While it had opposed an early settlement, it was not willing to fully engage in the management of the crisis. In the end, the settlement achieved at Dayton was not drastically better than the one offered by the Vance-Owen Plan.[67]

Throughout the 1990s, the Clinton administration was willing enough to factor in the emerging complexities of the post–Cold War era and extend the realm of concerns and involvement beyond a narrowly defined national interest. But it was unable to do so more than marginally. As a result, the gap between the rhetoric and the reality of international solidarity remained wide. To reduce the gap would have required U.S. foreign policy to fulfill a number of conditions. In short, it would have needed a road map, which was apparently missing in the offices of the Clinton foreign policy team. When it came to "soft" security issues, the Clinton administration was operating largely on an ad hoc basis. To reduce the gap would have required a disciplined and sustained effort, all the more difficult to achieve with a contingent approach to humanitarian crises.[68] And it would have required making the new crises of the post–Cold War era a significant and acknowledged part of the administration's political agenda, with the acceptance of the political risks involved. Short of meeting these conditions, Clinton's foreign policy could be only a simulacrum of strong international leadership put at the service of solidarity-based values: In foreign policy, as in any other aspect of political life, real gains and the legacy they support entail taking calculated risks, an ability that is much admired and respected in leaders (generating as well a sense of gratitude)—but it is indeed rare among not only select politicians but also the human collectivities called nation-states that they lead.

CHAPTER 5

THE BUSH "REVOLUTION" IN U.S. FOREIGN POLICY AND THE SIDELINING OF INTERNATIONALISM

COMPARED TO THE FOREIGN POLICY in the succeeding presidency of George W. Bush, President Clinton's commitment to multilateralism, the United Nations, and the agenda of international solidarity appears robust and determined. Radicalizing approaches that already existed in American foreign policy toward the United Nations and its procedures and values, Bush made a unilateral and security-driven conception of international affairs the hallmark of his foreign policy at the outset of his presidency. Such a conception was manifested after the terrorist attacks on American soil on September 11, 2001. What are the main points in which Bush's foreign policy has departed from Clinton's internationalism and how did it unfold in practice? How did Bush's dismissal of multilateralism affect the Atlantic Alliance (which played such an important role throughout the 1990s), and what price has the Bush administration paid for it? What to make of the issues that have been raised by Bush's foreign policy for world order? This chapter aims to answer these questions.

BUSH'S FOREIGN POLICY AND THE ECLIPSE OF INTERNATIONALISM

Embracing an all-security approach to U.S. foreign policy, George W. Bush came into office determined to ignore the international solidarity concerns expressed in the 1990s regarding UN peace operations and humanitarian interventions. The Bush administration has made unilateralism and the use of force its modalities of choice in statecraft. The depth of changes that have taken place in U.S. foreign policy since the early 2000s has even led some observers to talk about the Bush "revolution" in U.S. foreign policy.[1] Comparing Bush's conceptualization of foreign policy—what we could call his grand strategy[2]—with Clinton's, and examining how it shaped reality before and after 9/11, show how, in the matter of a few years, American foreign policy has probably become more self-centered than ever. President Bush indeed abandoned the internationalist patina of Clinton's foreign policy.

BUSH'S FOREIGN POLICY DOCTRINE VERSUS CLINTON'S

Each year or so, the White House submits to Congress a national security strategy outlining the president's vision for America's role in the world and discussing the administration's international priorities. Usually little publicity is given to the document, which tends to be viewed as an administrative formality without tremendous political significance. This changed in September 2002 with the publication of *The National Security Strategy of the United States of America*, which captured the attention of many in the United States and abroad.[3] Compared to past such documents, the Bush administration's *National Security Strategy* struck a notably different tone on a number of critical points.

The security strategy documents of the 1990s published under President Clinton listed three overarching goals for U.S. grand strategy: to sustain U.S. security, to enhance U.S. economic prosperity, and to promote democracy abroad—traditional objectives of U.S. foreign policy.[4] These goals have shaped U.S. foreign policy in general and can be found more or less in any administration, including the one of President George H. W. Bush.[5] These goals are also found in the 2002 *National Security Strategy of the United States of America*, but the ways they are pursued in Bush's foreign policy doctrine are quite distinct from those of the Clinton administration.

The national security strategy documents issued by the Clinton White House devoted a great deal of attention to the classical external threats against which the United States has sought to protect itself. As the 1990s unfolded, the national security strategy documents also acknowledged the growing menace of transnational threats—primarily terrorism—and the need to tackle them accordingly. Nevertheless, a cautious optimism about the state of the world and the U.S. role in it pervaded these documents: The challenges at hand were balanced by unprecedented opportunities, and international cooperation and trust could prevail over confrontation and suspicion.[6] President Clinton's strategy assumed that, on the whole, the world was at peace.[7]

The tone is radically different in the *National Security Strategy* of September 2002: Bush's basic assumption is that the world is at war. Four characteristics of the document follow. First is the largely confrontational conception of international relations. Cooperation and shared values among actors, especially allies, are mentioned as playing an important role, but the defining aspect of the international realm is the centrality of tensions and conflicts of interests, and the sense of mistrust associated with them. Second is the exceptional situation in which the world and America find themselves because of transnational terrorism—its unconventional nature as a global threat conveys a sense of exceptionalism, internationally and at home. A third characteristic is the ally-enemy divide, calling upon all states in the international arena to identify terrorists as the ultimate enemy and distinguishing those countries collaborating fully in the War on Terror from those reticent to give their unrestricted backing—who is not with the United States is against it. Fourth, building on the idea that there is a new form of global war under way and that the enemy is "evil" in nature, the Bush Doctrine credited the administration's worldview with a moral clarity presented as normatively superior. "In pursuit of our goals, our first imperative is to clarify what we stand for: the United States must defend liberty and justice because these principles are right and true for all people everywhere. No nation owns these aspirations, and no nation is exempt from them."[8] Bush's assessment of international reality and the crusading drive to reform it contrasts with the political pragmatism that accompanied, each in its own way, the realism of Bush père and Clinton's cautious foreign policy optimism. Here the largely pessimistic assessment of the reality of the world leads to a quasi-missionary zeal to eradicate terrorism and forcefully reshape the international landscape.[9]

Although giving priority to American national interest and security, the strategic security documents issued in the 1990s by the Clinton administration conveyed a sense of balance between these main goals and the two other overarching ends of U.S. grand strategy—economic prosperity and the promotion of democracy abroad. The documents also put forward a somewhat inclusive vision of the U.S. national interest and security, recognizing the need to articulate them with other nations' interests and security.

In contrast, the September 2002 document demonstrates a single-mindedness of purpose: It is foremost about the American national interest and homeland security. To counter its sense of vulnerability and insecurity, America must get as close as possible, through the neutralization of opponents—potential or real, present or future—to absolute security.[10] Self-centeredness (excluding genuine concerns for other nations' interests) and hierarchy (securing America at the apex of world order) are the underlying assumptions of the Bush Doctrine.

Not surprisingly, therefore, the measures evoked in the White House's 2002 *National Security Strategy* amount to a turning away from international norms, treaties, and security partnerships to which the United States had been traditionally committed—all the more in the immediate aftermath of the Cold War.[11] Five of the means that stand out in Bush's repertoire of tools are a striking departure from Clinton's foreign policy rationale: an ad hoc approach to international coalitions and alliances, unilateralism as the principal modality of U.S. statecraft, pre-emptive (or, more precisely, preventive) use of force, regime change, and the War on Terror.

Clinton's support for global institutions and belief in the value of international cooperation may have appeared at times more rhetorical than real, but when the U.S. national interest was at stake, his administration did not ignore the imperative of multilateral cooperation in tackling international problems. Although limited and tentative, the Clinton administration's commitment to global institutions and cooperation was nevertheless relatively genuine. In contrast, Bush's *National Security Strategy* document does not value institutionalized international cooperation. Rather, it shows a readiness, if not eagerness, to adopt an ad hoc approach: "America will implement its strategies by organizing coalitions—as broad as practicable—of states able and willing to promote a balance of power that favors freedom."[12] Although partly designed to overcome the institutional and policy rigidities of established regional security organizations and multilateralism in general, the approach is rooted in a deep and general suspicion of international agreements and international organizations in general, including the United Nations.[13] The rejection of the International Criminal Court, which the 2002 report emphasizes in its closing paragraphs, provides further indication of the circumstantial value attributed to the United Nations and multilateralism.[14]

Clinton was disposed to unilateral action when vital national interests were at risk, but he saw it as part of a larger portfolio of means: "We must . . . use the right tools—being willing to act unilaterally when our direct national interests are most at stake; in alliance and partnership when our interests are shared by others; and multilaterally when our interests are more general and the problems are best addressed by the international community."[15]

By contrast, the 2002 document envisages unilateralism as the principal means of acting in the international realm. The Bush administration's exclusive centeredness on U.S. national interests and its characterization of an imperiled America at war widen the idea of vital interest to *all* aspects of the U.S. national interest. As there is hardly any room left for shared or general interests, multilateral collaboration with other nations on issues beyond the War on Terror becomes secondary: "[W]e will be prepared to act apart when our interests and unique responsibilities require. When we disagree on particulars, we . . . will not allow such disagreements to obscure our determination. . . ."[16] To be as unconstrained as possible in tackling terrorism works hand in hand with the reluctance to recognize more than a circumstantial value in collective norms and institutions.

Like other U.S. presidents before him, Clinton recognized that America has the right to strike in the face of danger, but he acknowledged that the danger must be imminent. Short of such immediacy of threat, Clinton's foreign policy basically endorsed one of the fundamental tenets of American foreign policy since the Cold War: containment. The Clinton administration's handling of the threats posed by Iraq, Iran, and North Korea throughout the 1990s has to be seen in this light.[17] Containment is applied even to terrorism: Even though Clinton's counterterrorism policies called for both offensive and defensive actions, their goal was less to eliminate entirely the terrorist threat than to reduce it.[18]

The Bush administration has seen things differently. The concepts of containment and deterrence have been deemed outdated by and large, replaced by a more offensive posture, including, in particular, the preemptive (or preventive) use of force: "[A]s a matter of common sense and self-defense, America will act against . . . emerging threats before they are fully formed."[19] In this regard, the Bush Doctrine—the right to pre-emptive, unilateral self-defense against those *attempting* to acquire a particular warfighting capability—removes the traditionally accepted justification for pre-emption: that the threat be imminent. Terrorism, by its elusive nature, brings about an uncertainty regarding the immediacy of the threat. Pre-emption (or prevention) provided the Bush administration with a powerful incentive to take the initiative:

> For centuries, international law recognized that nations need not suffer an attack before they can lawfully take action to defend themselves against forces that present an imminent danger of attack. Legal scholars and international jurists often conditioned the legitimacy of pre-emption on the existence of an imminent threat—most often a visible mobilization of armies, navies, and air forces preparing to attack. We must adapt the concept of imminent threat to the capabilities and objectives of today's adversaries. Rogue states and terrorists do not seek to attack us using conventional means. They know such attacks would fail. Instead, they rely on acts of terror and, potentially, the use of weapons

of mass destruction—weapons that can be easily concealed, delivered covertly, and used without warning. . . . The greater the threat, the greater is the risk of inaction—and the more compelling the case for taking anticipatory action to defend ourselves, even if uncertainty remains as to the time and place of the enemy's attack. To forestall or prevent such hostile acts by our adversaries, the United States will, if necessary, act pre-emptively.[20]

The issue of regime change is another tenet in which Clinton's and Bush's foreign policy differ significantly. To be sure, on October 31, 1998, Clinton signed the Iraq Liberation Act of 1998, making it clear that the United States would support those elements of the Iraqi opposition that advocated the removal of Saddam Hussein from power and promoted the emergence of a democratic government to replace that regime. Yet the act certainly did not stipulate that the United States should act militarily against Iraq.[21]

Although the expression "regime change" is not used per se in the 2002 *National Security Strategy* document, the description of the danger that rogue states represent internationally, combined with the reasoning in the same document on the pre-emptive use of force and the not-so-tacit demonization of the enemy, call for the de facto elimination of these regimes:

> In the 1990s we witnessed the emergence of a small number of rogue states that, while different in important ways, share a number of attributes. These states: brutalize their own people and squander their national resources for the personal gain of the rulers; display no regard for international law, threaten their neighbors, and callously violate international treaties to which they are party; are determined to acquire weapons of mass destruction, along with other advanced military technology, to be used as threats or offensively to achieve the aggressive designs of these regimes; sponsor terrorism around the globe; and reject basic human values and hate the United States and everything for which it stands. . . . We must be prepared to stop rogue states and their terrorist clients before they are able to threaten or use weapons of mass destruction against the United States and our allies and friends.[22]

Finally, there is the War on Terror. The Clinton administration approached terrorism as one of the deadly security threats inherent in the tensions and conflicts of international life. Based on this assessment, it called for targeted measures, including limited use of force when needed. In contrast, President Bush elevated terrorism to a phenomenon of historical (almost cosmic) significance, as part of a global Manichean struggle of good versus evil. Therefore, his counterterrorism policies are not restricted to targeted military operations. Rather, it is a *global* war against terrorism and its sources.

Considering these differences of view between Clinton's and Bush's foreign policy doctrines, it is not surprising that what the *National Security Strategy* document of 2002 coins as "a distinctly American internationalism"[23] leaves no room for the international solidarity agenda that the Clinton administration selectively adhered to in the 1990s.

In the Clinton administration's national security strategy documents, peace operations were a noteworthy item. Their value was acknowledged, both in strategic terms for U.S. foreign policy and somewhat on moral grounds, as a useful tool to address the post–Cold War humanitarian crises.[24] In comparison, the 2002 *National Security Strategy* document mentions the term peace operation only once—in the context of Africa and then *en passant*.[25] By and large, peace operations were simply not part of the security mind-set of the Bush administration.

The gap between Clinton and Bush is even greater when it comes to humanitarian interventions. Clinton's peacekeeping doctrine envisioned the possibility of using force in certain circumstances to end humanitarian crises:

> There are three basic categories of national interests which can merit the use of our armed forces. The first involves America's vital interests, i.e., interests which are of broad, overriding importance to the survival, security, and vitality of our national entity—the defense of U.S. territory, citizens, allies, and economic well-being. . . . The second category includes cases in which important, but not vital, U.S. interests are threatened. That is, the interests at stake do not affect our national survival, but they do affect importantly our national well-being and the character of the world in which we live. . . . The third category involves primarily humanitarian interests. Here, our decisions focus on the resources we can bring to bear by using unique capabilities of our military rather than on the combat power of military force. Generally, the military is not the best tool to address humanitarian concerns. But under certain conditions, the use of our armed forces may be appropriate: when a humanitarian catastrophe dwarfs the ability of civilian relief agencies to respond; when the need for relief is urgent and only the military has the ability to jump-start the longer-term response to the disaster; when the response requires resources unique to the military . . . and when the risk to American troops is minimal.[26]

These are not options for the Bush administration. Surely, the 2002 document refers to the importance of providing humanitarian assistance in the specific case of Afghanistan, but typically in conjunction with eliminating the direct sources of terrorism: "As we pursue the terrorists in Afghanistan, we will continue to work with international organizations such as the United Nations, as well as nongovernmental organizations, and other countries to provide the humanitarian, political, economic, and security assistance necessary to rebuild Afghanistan so that it will never again abuse its people, threaten its neighbors, and provide a haven for terrorists."[27] The document also evokes a number of ways of helping regions and populations that have suffered from humanitarian crises, including economic, legal, and political aid.[28] But as U.S. national security is the sole metric of Bush's foreign policy, humanitarian crises in and of themselves are not enough reason to justify the use of force to stop them.

To be sure, the Bush foreign policy document stresses that the United States "champion aspirations for human dignity,"[29] that "America must stand firmly for the nonnegotiable demands of human dignity: the rule of law, limits on the absolute power of the state, free speech, freedom of worship, equal justice, respect for women, religious and ethnic tolerance, and respect for private property."[30] But human rights violations in the context of humanitarian crises are not enough to trigger a decisive U.S. reaction. Typically, if humanitarian crises in Africa—the continent where they have been the most endemic and lethal since the 1990s—are mentioned in the 2002 document, they are referred to primarily in the context of how they constitute national security and terrorism threats.[31] It is the danger represented by rogue and failed states, and not their track record of human rights violations, that causes them to forfeit their national sovereign rights and thus be exposed to military intervention from "coalitions of the willing," presumably led by the United States.[32]

BUSH'S FOCUS ON THE U.S. NATIONAL INTEREST IN THE INTERNATIONAL REALM

In practice, Bush's foreign policy has proved to be faithful to its main doctrinal aspects. Before and after September 11, 2001, particularly in the context of the war in Iraq (in the lead-up to the war as well as in its aftermath), the Bush administration has been consistent in disconnecting the ends and means of its foreign policy from those of most of the rest of the world.

During the 2000 U.S. presidential election campaign, Texas governor George W. Bush had not disputed the fact that, if elected, his administration would decrease U.S. involvement in peace operations, stay away from humanitarian interventions, and distance itself from the United Nations and multilateralism. Bush's senior foreign policy adviser, Condoleezza Rice (a scholar on the Soviet Union and a former National Security Council official in the administration of President George H. W. Bush during the late 1980s and early 1990s), foreshadowed the presidential candidate's position on humanitarian interventions in an issue of *Foreign Affairs* during the early stages of the campaign season:

> "Humanitarian intervention" cannot be ruled out a priori. But a decision to intervene in the absence of strategic concerns should be understood for what it is. Humanitarian problems are rarely only humanitarian problems; the taking of life or withholding of food is almost always a political act. If the United States is not prepared to address the underlying political conflict and to know whose side it is on, the military may end up separating warring parties for an indefinite period. . . . The president must remember that the military is a special instrument. It is lethal, and it is meant to be. It is not a civilian police force. It is not a political referee. And it is most certainly not designed to build a civilian society. . . . It is one thing to have a limited political goal and to fight decisively for it; it is quite another to apply military force incrementally, hoping to find a political solution somewhere along the way. A President entering these situations must ask whether decisive force is possible and is likely to be effective and must know how and when to get out. These are difficult criteria to meet, so U.S. intervention in these "humanitarian" crises should be, at best, exceedingly rare. This does not mean that the United States must ignore humanitarian and civil conflicts around the world. But the military cannot be involved everywhere. . . . Using the American armed forces as the world's "911" will degrade capabilities, bog soldiers down in peacekeeping roles, and fuel concern among other great powers that the United States has decided to enforce notions of "limited sovereignty" worldwide in the name of humanitarianism.[33]

Echoing a statement made in one of Governor Bush's campaign speeches, Rice emphasized Bush's position during an appearance on *The Charlie Rose Show,* saying that "he made very clear that he thought that militaries are essentially for the purposes of deterring, fighting, and winning wars, not for the purposes of civil administration and nation building and long-term peacekeeping":

> Condoleezza Rice: "[Vice President Gore] is sending a signal that any civil conflict is always going to be on the table for the American Armed Forces, and it's a bad signal because it will cause others to abdicate their responsibility in their regions for doing that work."

> Charlie Rose: "But you've said you would never say never to any possibilities where there were certain kinds of gross violations."

Condoleezza Rice: "I said you'd never say never, but I think it's pretty clear that we're saying hardly ever."[34]

The task of maintaining peace in the Balkans was held up as an example of precisely what the United States military should not be doing. Keeping the peace in the region was presented foremost as the responsibility of the Europeans. Withdrawing from the theater was therefore the best thing for U.S. troops to do. Once in the White House, after a few months of equivocation on the topic and protests from European allies, President Bush finally announced that U.S. troops would remain in the Balkans after all. But when fighting broke out in Macedonia in March 2001, despite the potential for a widespread confrontation between Macedonian Slavs and the country's sizable ethnic Albanian minority, the Bush administration essentially vetoed direct U.S. involvement. Later on, in August 2001, when NATO sent troops into Macedonia to disarm the Albanian rebels in the wake of a peace accord, the United States took a minimal role. Only U.S. troops already stationed in the region to support peace operations in Kosovo joined in, and their mission was restricted to providing European troops logistical support and intelligence.

George W. Bush showed no more inclination to have the United States involved in humanitarian intervention than he did for peace operations in general, and he remained true to Rice's observation in early 2000. Bush's foreign policy eschewed the humanitarian emergencies generated by war in the Democratic Republic of the Congo. And it did not manifest serious concerns for human rights violations in Afghanistan prior to 9/11.

While paying lip service to the United Nations and multilateralism, the Bush administration also took a number of initiatives making clear that it refused to be bound and constrained by them. Thus, the Bush administration radicalized a tendency already at work in Clinton's foreign policy: committed in principle to a multilateral brand of international governance but frequently compelled to act alone.[35] It rejected several compacts that the international community, and especially U.S. allies, had pushed forward in recent years: the Kyoto Protocol to the United Nations Framework Convention on Climate Change, regarding global warming; protocols enforcing a ban on germ warfare; an accord on illegal sales of small arms; and the ABM Treaty, limiting ballistic missile defenses.[36]

The Bush administration denied that such actions represented a blanket condemnation for collective action as a way of conducting world leadership; it denied quite simply that it was unilateralist. Rather, it argued that it viewed treaties as an antiquated means of global leadership whose usefulness would be judged one issue at a time, one negotiation at a time, one summit meeting at a time. "What you are going to get from this administration is 'à la carte multilateralism,'" said Richard Haass, at the time the State Department's director of policy planning, coining a term for the administration's approach in its pre-9/11 months.[37] Ultimately, the United Nations and multilateralism were to be assessed in a purely instrumental way, not seen as ends in themselves, based on their utility to the U.S. national interest. The War on Terror as envisioned by the White House, including Afghanistan and Iraq, served as a case in point.

In the aftermath of September 11, the main neoconservative voices behind Bush's "distinctly American internationalism" were somewhat at odds on what the extent of U.S. international engagement should be. Vice President Richard B. Cheney and Secretary of Defense Donald H. Rumsfeld, in particular, tended to favor a rather strictly national-security approach, including, for instance, a narrow interpretation of "regime change" with military interventions when needed, followed by a military presence designed around straightforward U.S. national security goals. Deputy Secretary of Defense Paul Wolfowitz favored a more comprehensive form of U.S. international engagement. His vision of regime change encompassed not only the removal of a government hostile to U.S. interests, but a whole rearrangement of the political culture of the country based on values that followed from "a belief in the uniqueness and the virtue of the American political system." Translated into foreign policy terms, that clearly meant the United States as a model for the world.[38]

Fundamentally, however, these officials agreed that "distinctly American internationalism" was first and foremost about the U.S. national interest and security projected in the international realm. The spread of American values, by force if needed, was not an end in itself (for the sake of human rights) but a means to enhance U.S. national interest and security. The leaders also shared the view that U.S. international engagement was best fostered not through international organizations and international cooperation but by American power and U.S.-led alliances and coalitions of the willing. After the adoption on September 28, 2001, of UN Security Council Resolution 1373, calling upon all states to take a variety of measures to curb terrorism, it did not take long for the Bush administration's handling of Afghanistan and Iraq to illustrate how serious it was about translating these views into reality.[39]

Afghanistan offers an example of cooperation between the United States and the United Nations. After the quick victory of the U.S.-led Operation Enduring Freedom against al Qaeda and Taliban forces in October–November 2001, the United States supported the establishment of the International Security Assistance Force (ISAF) in December to help the Afghan Interim Authority create a secure environment in Kabul and its surrounding areas.[40] In March 2002, it buttressed the creation of the United Nations Assistance Mission in Afghanistan (UNAMA).[41] Yet Afghanistan also serves as a telling case of the reservations of the Bush administration vis-à-vis the United Nations and its operations. In particular, although the Bush administration welcomed the help of the United Nations, it refused to contribute troops to ISAF.[42] This was in line with the administration's unwillingness to commit U.S. troops to peace operations, but it also showed that it was not going to go the extra mile to increase the chances of the UN mission's success.[43]

More than anything else in Bush's foreign policy, the war in Iraq has become the exemplar of its disregard for multilateralism and the United Nations. The dust of war had hardly settled in Afghanistan when the Bush administration turned its attention to Iraq and began preparing the international community for the fact that Iraq, as part of the "axis of evil," was next on the list. The argument put forward to justify going after Iraq was its assumed possession of weapons of mass destruction (WMD) and its links with al Qaeda.[44] In March 2002, Vice President Cheney traveled to Europe and the Middle East to build support for a confrontation with Saddam Hussein's regime.[45] In the following months, officials at the White House and the Department of Defense evinced a steely determination to do whatever it took, with whomever would join a coalition, to bring down Saddam Hussein.[46] To them, going through the United Nations was ill advised.[47] Moreover, as Cheney argued at the outset in an address to the Veterans of Foreign Wars national convention in Nashville on August 26, simply resuming UN inspections could give "false comfort" that Saddam Hussein was contained.[48]

However, not everyone in the Republican administration wished to ignore the options offered by the United Nations. Secretary of State Colin Powell favored building support for the U.S. policy toward Iraq via the United Nations, and he managed to convince the president.[49] In a speech to the UN General Assembly on September 12, 2002, President Bush stressed that his administration would work with the Security Council to adopt new resolutions as the instrument for forcing Saddam Hussein to disarm or, if he refused, as the basis for military action.[50] But he also warned the United Nations that it risked becoming irrelevant if it allowed Iraq's noncompliance with relevant Security Council resolutions to go unchallenged.

After a few weeks of intense negotiations, the Security Council unanimously passed a resolution with teeth. Approved on November 8, 2002,

Resolution 1441 set up an enhanced inspection regime with the aim of ensuring full and verified completion of the disarmament process established by Resolution 687 (1991) and subsequent resolutions of the Council. It stressed as well the imperative that Iraq disarm totally or face "serious consequences."[51] Yet the divisions within the Bush administration on the need for a UN endorsement hampered the effectiveness of the American efforts to bring other countries on board. While Colin Powell was soliciting member states for their support, at times it seemed as if the main goal of the more hawkish elements of the Bush administration was to undermine rather than support his diplomatic efforts.

In addition, the difficulty of convincing other member states of the existence of WMD in Iraq, compounded by the mixed reports of the UN weapons inspectors and the even greater challenge of demonstrating a link between Iraq and al Qaeda, proved to be a significant obstacle for the United States in the Security Council.[52] The more the United States and the United Kingdom insisted that they had a case (without supporting it with incontestable evidence) and the more they expressed the need to use force, the less the other permanent members (especially France) and the nonpermanent members (in particular, Germany) of the Security Council were willing to go along.

By January and February 2003, the primary rationale for going to war was put in serious doubt. In their various briefings to the Security Council, Hans Blix, executive chairman of the UN Monitoring, Verification, and Inspection Commission (UNMOVIC, the successor to the UN Special Commission), and Mohamed ElBaradei, director-general of the International Atomic Energy Agency (IAEA), indicated that, based on the information collected, the existence of weapons of mass destruction in Iraq could not be proved.[53]

For a U.S. administration quick to endorse a black-and-white approach to the issues at hand and eager to act, Blix's inconclusive assessment of the situation on February 14, and again on March 7, must have been a source of great annoyance, to say the least. Statements such as "One must not jump to the conclusion that they [prohibited weapons] exist. However, that possibility is also not excluded. If they exist, they should be presented for destruction. If they do not exist, credible evidence to that effect should be presented"[54] must have been seen at the White House as typical UN vintage, averse to taking a position and encouraging decisive action.

Nevertheless, the fact is that, although the White House would have welcomed a green light from the UN inspectors and, later on, in the first half of March, an endorsement from a Security Council resolution, it did not want its doctrine to be dependent on any decision by the United Nations. In this regard, while Powell was courting member states to obtain their support, the more doctrinaire officials in the Bush administration were undermining his efforts, not only attempting to keep the United States free of UN and multilateral entanglements but also making the point that the United Nations and multilateralism were not equipped to provide legitimacy to current U.S. foreign policy.[55] In the process, they were questioning the legitimacy of the United Nations itself. Combined with the lack of concrete evidence of the existence of weapons of mass destruction and of the link between Baghdad and al Qaeda, the Bush administration's disregard for multilateralism and the United Nations made the war in Iraq a battleground within the Atlantic Alliance itself.

FROM THE CHOICE TO THE BURDEN OF UNILATERALISM: BUSH AND THE TRANSATLANTIC PARTNERSHIP

Absent the key role the Atlantic Alliance played in the 1990s in the management of international security issues, chances are that humanitarian crises would have stayed off the UN Security Council's agenda. As noted earlier, there were at times significant differences in perspectives and policy among the United States, the United Kingdom, and France in the Security Council, as well as among other Western allies, on how to address the humanitarian crises. However, by and large, Western countries took the lead and worked together. George W. Bush's foreign policy relegated such multilateral cooperation to a last-resort option. Its unilateralism and total-security approach to international life had already generated much tension with European allies before September 11. The war in Iraq may not have destroyed the Atlantic Alliance, but it certainly created a tremendous fissure that will require much work to repair. It also proved to exact a heavy toll for U.S. foreign policy in Iraq—and beyond.

The Clash over Multilateralism and Iraq in the Transatlantic Partnership

Very early on, Bush's foreign policy initiatives claimed for America a margin of maneuver that it forbade to other nations. The "à la carte" conception of multilateralism amounted to reserving relative international duties and absolute rights for the United States, including absolute sovereignty for itself and the right to infringe on the sovereignty of others, and calling for other countries to have absolute duties and relative rights.[56] Not surprisingly, such a complex of assumptions did not go over well with other nations: Although they were willing to recognize that its predominant power gave America a special place and role internationally, they were not at all prepared to codify a double standard. This was especially the case in Europe.[57]

The rift between America and Europe brought a softening of the German position on the issue of European defense. It also encouraged a foreign policy rapprochement between France and Germany at the global level. This rapprochement had a significant impact when Iraq came to occupy the center of attention at the United Nations. Germany, which became a nonpermanent member of the Security Council on January 1, 2003, and held its presidency in February 2003, forged a partnership with France that turned out to be instrumental in opposing Bush's foreign policy. Arguably, German support helped France break out of its isolation in the Council and to hold its ground against Washington, ultimately denying the Bush administration a UN authorization for the war.

In the early years of the post–Cold War era, the overwhelming power of the United States fueled France's inclination to view multipolarity as a better way to guarantee world security. France's fear that excessive concentration of power by one state can be a destabilizing factor worldwide also led it to favor more than ever an international system in which rules and institutions play a significant role. In that regard, the French embrace of multipolarity worked hand in hand with a plea for multilateralism as well as for security management via the United Nations.[58] Needless to say, this preference for multipolarity and multilateralism over unipolarity and unilateralism was also as much a matter of principle as a question of realpolitik. The centrality of the Security Council, the principles and values of collective security that it embodies, gave France an international power that it could no longer claim on its own.[59] Against this background, the excessively "America-centric" nature of Bush's international worldview was from the start a matter of concern in Paris. Later on, Washington's insistence on going to war against Saddam Hussein, with or without UN support, was destined to clash with Jacques Chirac's government.

French opposition to the war should not have come as a surprise to the United States and the United Kingdom. It echoed what had been the attitude of France vis-à-vis Iraq since the end of Operation Desert Storm. Throughout the 1990s, France was indeed quite supportive of Baghdad. In particular, France over time moved to a position in favor of easing, if not lifting, the UN sanctions against Iraq.[60] This was in sharp contrast to the U.S. and British positions, which were eager to condemn the regime of Saddam Hussein as much as possible.

The relatively lenient French position toward Iraq in the aftermath of Operation Desert Storm was bolstered by three considerations. First, France was willing to give Saddam Hussein the benefit of the doubt. This was in line with its long-standing support of his secular regime, which was a continuation of the strong links that France had cultivated with Baghdad since the 1970s, in part based on its somewhat republican nationalist ideology.[61] Second, there was the genuine belief that the UN sanctions were hurting Iraqi civilians far more than was Saddam Hussein's regime.[62] In this regard, Paris felt that, although the sanctions were crippling Saddam Hussein's efforts to rearm, there was no doubt that they were also worsening the already very low standards of living of ordinary Iraqis.[63] A third consideration was French economic interests in Iraq: France's oil dependency on Iraq, the Oil-for-Food Program, oil concessions, and accumulated debt.[64] On the other hand, the French recognized that Saddam Hussein's lack of cooperation with the UN inspections, particularly since 1998 and the withdrawal of the UN Special Commission (UNSCOM), created a situation that could not go on forever. Bush's eagerness to take the lead and act against Iraq offered an opportunity for change.

Paris was not in agreement, however, with the course of action favored by the White House. France saw the Middle East as a powder keg that should be treated with caution to preserve the stability of the region; a "grand strategy" approach to the numerous problems and challenges facing the Middle East would be counterproductive. From this perspective, the French leadership continued to think that the central issue in the region was not Iraq but the Israeli–Palestinian conflict.[65] More to the point, the French assessment of Iraq was that it did not constitute a major security threat: Saddam Hussein's alleged links with terrorism were not much of a threat, regionally or globally. By the winter of 2002–03, France had indeed come to the conclusion that the disarmament policies conducted under the UN inspection regime during the 1990s had worked: The Iraqi army had been reduced to about half its previous size; its conventional weapons were out of date; its missiles had been used and not replaced; and most of its WMD arsenal had been destroyed by UN inspectors and various bombing campaigns. In addition, it was clear to France that Saddam Hussein's regime was not popular: In the north of the country, the Kurds were in almost open revolt; in the south, the Shiite majority had long resented its exclusion from government. This made the Iraqi regime all the weaker internally and not in a position to be a major danger externally. Furthermore, the French government thought that the links the Bush administration claimed existed between al Qaeda and Saddam's regime had no credibility. The lack of evidence of terrorist activities in Iraq or of links with transnational terrorist organizations contributed to France's rather skeptical outlook regarding the terrorist threat.[66] In France, as in other European countries, there was no sense of paranoia about terrorism and its Middle Eastern (particularly Iraqi) origins. Paris went along with the War on Terror after 9/11; it was concerned about possible terrorist attacks, but it did not trace their source directly to Iraq.[67]

French decision makers were also highly skeptical that regime change imposed from the outside would lead to a stable regime or that international security in the Middle East could be secured by war. Although no French official really mourned the prospect of the fall of Saddam Hussein's dictatorial regime, the French government sensed that the Bush administration did not have a clear vision of what a post-Saddam Iraq would look like. As a former colonial power that had experienced failed attempts to govern countries from afar, France was doubtful that the United States, or any other country for that matter, could successfully govern Iraq with a large occupation force. France also feared that in the absence of such a military force, once war had taken place, a quick handover of authority to a new Iraqi regime could fail, leading to internal conflicts over resources, ethnic and clan reprisals, and a possible intervention by a number of Iraq's neighbors. The ensuing chaos could then provide a fertile ground for terrorists.[68]

Ultimately, the use of force without a UN Security Council authorization was for France the worst of all options. Paris was keenly aware that if it refused to support a U.S.-led operation to deal with Iraq, the Bush administration might act anyway, alone or with support from other European allies. French officials worried about the precedent that would be set by an unauthorized UN intervention; they also argued that it could legitimize other attempts at pre-emptive war. A final concern was that the unauthorized use of force would undercut the credibility of the Security Council—and that of the United Nations in general.

In the late summer of 2002, President Chirac outlined a two-stage UN process to address the Iraqi crisis. It envisioned a first stage that would demand Iraqi compliance with a more rigorous weapons inspection regime. If Iraq failed to comply, the second stage would request that the Security Council take action to address the problem. Chirac declared that use of force was a possibility, provided that it was decided on by the international community and on the basis of indisputable proof, short of which the use of force should not be authorized by the United Nations.

A key aspect of France's cooperation with the United States and the United Kingdom in the UN Security Council in the fall of 2002 for the drafting and adoption of UN Security Council Resolution 1441 and the implementation of the inspection regime that followed was France's insistence that any new resolution on Iraqi disarmament and weapons inspections not contain an automatic recourse to force. From the French perspective, this conditionality had three main merits: It emphasized the ultimate authority of the Security Council, it denied the United States the right to unilaterally declare Iraq in noncompliance and thus the ability to go to war over Iraqi missteps, and it showed the world at large that the international community was going the extra mile to avoid war.[69]

All of this meant that the potential divergence between France and the United States (and the United Kingdom) was likely to come over the threshold for compliance, how it would be interpreted, and how the international community should act in the event of disagreement. This is exactly what happened. Deep differences soon emerged in the interpretation of the text of Resolution 1441 regarding whether it authorized UN member states to use force against Iraq.[70] The French position was that Resolution 1441 did not contain the signal words "use all necessary means," which traditionally have been considered vital to a Security Council authorization for the use of force.[71] This interpretation was supported by the fact that representatives of all the members of the Security Council, including the United States and the United Kingdom, had publicly confirmed at the time of its adoption that Resolution 1441 contained no "hidden triggers" or "automaticity" with respect to the use of force.[72] But this did not prevent the United States from envisioning acting unilaterally if it saw fit.[73]

Between December 2002 and March 2003, the accumulated evidence could not demonstrate in absolute terms the existence of weapons of mass destruction in Iraq. Yet it seemed that George W. Bush and Tony Blair were adamant about going to war, no matter what.[74] And the more eager the United States and the United Kingdom were to act, the less France was willing to compromise. What Chirac had envisaged as a possibility—the use of force—in the autumn of 2002 became an impossibility for him in March 2003. Ultimately, France gave more credit to Hans Blix and his inspectors' point of view than to that of the White House and 10 Downing Street. The French government was not disputing the horrific nature of Saddam Hussein's regime. It simply felt that war in Iraq was not justified on the grounds of weapons of mass destruction.

In the end, France could not be convinced to give its support to a second Security Council resolution that would have justified the military intervention in Iraq. After it became clear that the second resolution would not get a majority—and would get a French (and possibly Russian) veto—the United States, the United Kingdom, and Spain decided to withdraw the March 17, 2003, draft. The war began two days later, on March 19, 2003, without UN authorization. In the aftermath of the war campaign, the French position remained the same: The war in Iraq was not legal, because it did not conform to international law. Nor was it legitimate, because it was based on shaky justifications.

As the showdown in the Middle East was heating up in January and early February 2003, the United States asked NATO for help in the war in Iraq—specifically measures to protect Turkey, the only NATO member to share a border with Iraq. Although France, Germany, and Belgium opposed the move on the grounds that giving the go-ahead to NATO's planning would mean entering the "logic of war" and prejudging the findings of the UN weapons inspectors in Iraq, the other sixteen NATO members (including the United Kingdom, Italy, Spain, Poland, and Portugal) endorsed it. In early February, the so-called Vilnius Ten, a group of Central and East European nations (Albania, Bulgaria, Croatia, Estonia, Latvia, Lithuania, Macedonia, Romania, Slovakia, and Slovenia) established in 2000 to seek NATO membership, issued a declaration supporting the U.S. position in the Iraqi crisis. The Bush administration wanted to see in the backing of these European countries the emergence of a new transatlantic partnership, perhaps able to serve as a substitute for the creaky Atlantic Alliance that, at the United Nations, had presided over the post–Cold War international changes of the 1990s.

The fact that British prime minister Tony Blair rallied the Bush administration in its crusade against Iraq was not much of a surprise. In the 1990s, the United Kingdom had sided with the United States on the sanctions issue. On several occasions, London, along with Washington, had opposed lifting the pressure against Saddam Hussein. By May 1997, when Blair came to power, it had become clear that the Iraqi dictator was not going to back down. It appeared all the more the case in the early 2000s, as the inspections had reached a total stalemate. Bush's decision to go after Saddam Hussein thus might have looked to Blair like the least unpalatable option. There is evidence that the British prime minister allowed himself to believe that Iraqi WMD did indeed pose a long-term threat to both national and international security.[75] There is also evidence that he doubted that there could be effective Iraqi disarmament while Saddam Hussein remained in power. In addition, humanitarian considerations made him open to the idea of regime change, although he stated publicly that they could not be the reason behind going to war in Iraq.[76]

Blair's willingness to use force in Iraq did not mean, however, that he had aligned himself entirely with the Bush administration. In backing the United States, he wanted to show that Britain was a loyal ally. He was also eager to act as a bridge between Europe and America and to ensure that there was no serious division in transatlantic relations. But he fundamentally disagreed with the Bush administration's neoconservatives that the United Nations was irrelevant in managing the Iraq crisis. In fact, Blair was determined that Iraq's disarmament should be accomplished through the multilateral route, and that the United Nations should emerge from the crisis in a stronger position to confront the future threat posed by WMD proliferation.[77] Moreover, Blair was very uncomfortable with pre-emptive action without an imminent threat.

Given how much capital he had invested in trying to secure it, the failure to have a UN endorsement for the war in Iraq was a massive blow for Prime Minister Blair. At the same time, "there was no question of Blair breaking his word to Bush that Britain would support America over Iraq. It was a cardinal assumption of the prime minister that the world would be a more dangerous place if America acted alone. Blair feared that this would strengthen the unilateralists in the administration and set back the cause of multilateralism."[78]

Without British backing, the Bush administration's case against Iraq would have appeared even more dubious. Although it failed to enroll a majority of states at the United Nations, the White House could at least claim that it was working hand in hand with a permanent member of the UN Security Council. Moreover, chances are that without the United Kingdom at the side of the United States, it would have been harder for the Bush administration to garner the support of other European nations.

The fact that in the winter of 2002–03 both Spain and Italy—two countries committed to Atlanticism—had conservative governments facilitated their siding with Bush's foreign policy (Spain more forcefully than Italy). The two countries may have also seen their support for the United States as an occasion to enhance their global foreign policy visibility, if not to settle scores with France and Germany, which tended to treat other middle-power European nations as junior partners. Bush's determination and black-and-white approach in the War on Terror must have also fit well with Spanish prime minister José María Aznar's aggressive stance against the Basque terrorist organization Euskadi ta Askatasuna. With the United Kingdom taking the European lead on the War on Terror, Aznar and Italy's Silvio Berlusconi were encouraged to go against their nations' public opinion, which, as was the case with the rest of Europe (and, across the Channel, the United Kingdom), was overwhelmingly against the war.[79]

East European nations such as Poland, the Czech Republic, and Hungary had their own reasons to support the United States. Although they were on the verge of joining the European Union, which they knew would determine much of their future economic prosperity, they had a very fresh memory of the fact that it was to America first and foremost that they owed the demise of the Soviet empire in the late 1980s and, even more recently, their membership in NATO; the security guarantee offered by the United States took precedence over other considerations. Yet once again it is debatable whether these countries would have taken the risk of going against France and Germany in the European context had the United Kingdom not stood firmly by Bush's side.[80]

Could this truncated European support for Bush's foreign policy in Iraq be enough? Could it constitute a solid and credible substitute for the whole of the Atlantic Alliance? Despite the White House's minimization of the split between France and Germany on one side and the United Kingdom and newer continental allies on the other (and despite the bombastic geopolitical recasting of Europe by Secretary of Defense Donald Rumsfeld into "Old" and "New"), this type of European balking proved to be short of what was needed to ensure the "postconflict" success of the United States in Iraq. Ultimately, the United States went to war in Iraq with a coalition of the willing of thirty countries.[81] In the aftermath of the military campaign, although the troops of thirty-six countries came to join in the occupation of the country, the armed forces of the United States and the United Kingdom represented the bulk of the coalition deployment. [82]

THE PRICE OF GOING ALONE

As the war was unfolding in the spring of 2003, France and Germany indicated that they favored a UN presence in postwar Iraq, which presupposed the United Nations taking the lead in rebuilding the country and having a say in the modalities of the transition toward the restoration of full Iraqi sovereignty. The White House rejected at the outset the idea of giving the United Nations a central role: From the Bush administration's point of view, the United States had not taken the risk of going to war just to hand over Iraq to those (the United Nations and France in particular) who, in its judgment, had adopted a bystander and, worse yet, obstructionist position. The most the White House was willing to accept for the United Nations was the May 2003 appointment by the UN secretary-general of a Special Representative for Iraq—one without much power.[83]

The rejection of a key UN role in postwar Iraq was a missed opportunity to put the Atlantic Alliance back on track, setting the stage for the subsequent mishandling of the occupied country. And the price turned out to be pretty high: Between May 2003 and 2006, the difficulties associated with the insurgency, the mounting costs of reconstruction, and the problems surrounding the establishment of a legitimate government only increased. Despite the contribution of coalition members, addressing those massive postwar tasks became a huge challenge for the United States without the help and resources that it could have received, and indeed needed, from more European states and the United Nations.

On the occasion of his "Mission Accomplished" moment on the aircraft carrier USS *Abraham Lincoln*, off the coast of San Diego, California, on May 1, 2003, President Bush announced the end of major combat operations in Iraq. In a matter of a few weeks, the United States had managed to defeat Saddam Hussein and his regime, in effect terminating close to a quarter-century of dictatorial rule. A few months later, the picture had changed dramatically. The occupation and the reconstruction were running into major problems.

The lack of sustained military resistance that had surprised U.S. strategists during the "Shock and Awe" phase of the campaign, between March and the end of April, gave way to an insurgency that seemed to fragment and grow exponentially over time. From 735 insurgent attacks on coalition forces in November 2003, by August 2004 there were 2,700.[84] As of January 2006, the number of attacks remained just as high or even higher.[85] In November 2003, it was estimated that the strength of the Iraqi resistance nationwide amounted to 5,000 active insurgent fighters. By September 2004, the estimate had gone up to 20,000.[86] That same month, a *New York Times* article claimed that, one by one, Iraqi cities were becoming "no-go zones."[87] Falluja, Samarra, Ramadi, Karbala, and the Sadr City slums of Baghdad were now controlled by various insurgencies.[88] In January 2006, it was estimated that the strength of the Iraqi insurgency continued to be around 20,000,[89] including 700 to 2,000 foreign fighters (against 300 to 500 foreign fighters in January 2004).[90] Later in 2006, the number was estimated to have grown.[91] The deterioration of the security situation only underlined the difficulty for the United States of carrying the financial and personnel burden of the occupation alone. In the early summer of 2003, roughly 7 percent of the coalition forces deployed were non-American;[92] one year later, the situation was no better. The U.S. deployment represented close to 90 percent of the troops on the ground. In early 2006, this remained more or less the case.[93]

This meant that the United States was by and large carrying the entire financial cost of the Iraqi occupation. In July 2003, it estimated that the cost of the conflict and occupation of Iraq could reach $100 billion through 2004.[94] As of December 2005, with no end in sight for the occupation, its total costs had amounted to $251 billion; including estimates from the Congressional Budget Office, the total almost was destined to double, to $500 billion. Two months later, in February 2006, new estimates put the total costs at more than $2 trillion; the Bush administration originally estimated the cost at $50 to $60 billion, most of which would have been paid by U.S. taxpayers.[95] The deterioration of the security situation was likely to increase the spending. The overwhelmingly American character of the coalition meant also that U.S. troops accounted for most of the casualties. Perhaps even worse, during the military campaign of spring 2003, U.S. troops had suffered 109 casualties as a result of hostile action; 1,335 U.S. soldiers were killed between May 2003 and the beginning of January 2004.[96] By March 1, 2006, the number of U.S. fatalities due to hostile incidents had gone up to 1,805.[97] By June 2006, that figure had increased to more than 2,500.[98] Although the figures are tragic, it should be noted that they remain low compared to the loss of lives on the Iraqi side, estimated at several tens of thousands, depending on the source.[99]

Handling reconstruction proved to be equally challenging. According to the World Bank and the United Nations, Iraq will need $17.5 billion to restore infrastructure and public services to their March 2003 levels, which, it should be kept in mind, were not very high, considering the degradation that had taken place in the years before.[100] In addition, combined World Bank and Coalition Provisional Authority estimates in January 2004 put total needs in "reconstruction and development" for fourteen "priority sectors" and oil and security over the next four years at $55.2 billion.[101] Yet by the summer of 2004, the United States had allocated just $18 billion for Iraq's reconstruction, of which roughly $10 billion had been spent.[102] By the end of December 2005, $12.5 billion had been spent; by July 2006, the United States had appropriated $21 billion for the rebuilding of Iraq.[103]

It is difficult to say whether or not a European contribution beyond that of the United Kingdom and other European nations in the coalition would have helped in Iraq. Yet in terms of financial and troop contributions, the backing of the "old" European countries that refused to get involved, France and Germany in particular, could have made a significant difference. On the financial front, a stronger willingness of the European Union—led by France and Germany—to share the costs of the country's reconstruction would have been a welcome relief. At the international donors' conference held in Madrid on October 23–24, 2003, the European Union (EU) and other acceding countries pledged $1.25 billion, mainly in grants, for Iraq's reconstruction—significant but not much, compared, for instance, to the $4.9 billion pledged by Japan.[104] Moreover, France and Germany have certainly not shown strong leadership in the area of Iraqi financial reconstruction. In September 2004, they still had not transferred any aid, aside from that provided by the Europe Union; by June 2005, the overall aid situation had not improved much. Of the $13.6 billion non-American aid (including EU aid) pledged in 2004 toward Iraqi reconstruction, only $2 billion had been disbursed.[105] And as of November 2005, the European Commission had provided assistance to Iraq at the modest total sum of €518 million (including €100 million of humanitarian assistance and €418.5 million of support for reconstruction).[106] The European Commission allocated €200 million for Iraq in the 2006 budget year.[107] The lack of security and lack of coordination among donors, hampering effective aid management, have contributed to this reticent attitude. The problems have certainly been magnified by the political residue of the Iraq crisis and Europe's misgivings about the Bush administration's handling of Iraq.[108]

Troop contribution is the other area in which broader European support would have helped. The possibility of a French presence in Iraq (at times evoked but never realized) served as a case in point of how thin the coalition was stretched.[109] France's experience acquired in the course of the peace operations of the 1990s would have been useful on the ground, and it would have complemented the British approach well. A French contribution also probably would have been a signal for other countries to contribute. Equally important, a French military presence would have been synonymous with an agreement on the role of the United Nations in Iraq.

For the Bush administration, losing the support of the Atlantic Alliance over the war in Iraq and losing the support of the United Nations were one and the same. As mentioned earlier, a substantive and meaningful role for the United Nations was a key condition for the involvement of France, Germany, and others in the aftermath of the military campaign. But the Bush administration never seriously considered the possibility of a strong UN presence; the misgivings that had existed among Bush's hard-liners before the war persisted during the occupation. On the other hand, as progress in Iraq proved elusive, it became clearer and clearer that UN legitimacy could have been an asset at two levels—internally, in helping to fashion new political institutions and public security architecture; and externally, in smoothing diplomatic relations with Iraq's neighbors. Regarding the former level, as was noted in a July 2003 Iraq Reconstruction Assessment Mission report, the United Nations has valuable expertise in the area of policekeeping, a key element for the restoration of law and order in postconflict situations.[110] Throughout the 1990s, it had a considerable degree of accumulated experience, and over time, even its mistakes have been a source of learning and have led to a gradual improvement in UN police functions.

The United States could have benefited from this know-how.[111] The difficulties it encountered in establishing a secure environment in postwar Iraq strongly suggest that relying on military forces was not enough, and that there was a need for organized civilian policing expertise.[112] This would have required the United Nations to be politically distant from the Bush administration, or at least not be perceived as an instrument of its agenda. It was the only way for the United Nations to overcome the resentment built up against it in Iraq by years of UN sanctions in order to be credible as an honest broker and to minimize the risk of being targeted by insurgent groups intent on sabotaging the transition process. As the August 19, 2003, bombing of its Baghdad office grimly showed, the United Nations was certainly not immune from terrorist attacks. The August attack killed twenty-two people, including the mission chief, Sergio Vieira de Mello, and seemed to put an end to any intention that the United Nations might have had to get deeply involved in Iraq.

To avoid as much as possible accusations of establishing a puppet regime, the Bush administration felt enough of a need for UN legitimacy by the spring of 2004 to accept the help of Special Representative of the Secretary-General Lakhdar Brahimi with the negotiations on the transitional arrangements leading to the formation of the government and the transfer of sovereignty. Washington viewed UN Security Council Resolution 1546 (adopted on June 8, 2004), which endorsed the formation of an interim government for Iraq, as a useful way to secure the legitimacy of the nascent government and the process leading to elections in early 2005.[113] This resolution gave the United Nations Assistance Mission for Iraq the task of supporting the Independent Electoral Commission of Iraq for the election process, which it did for the January 30, 2005, elections for the Transitional National Assembly (whose primary mandate was to write a draft constitution for Iraq); the October 15, 2005, referendum on the constitution; and the December 15, 2005, Council of Representatives elections.[114]

For Washington, all this amounted to a painful recognition that the lack of full-fledged support from the United Nations was very costly in terms of how the international community viewed the occupation and regime change. The lack of such support affected America's diplomatic standing and, in doing so, threatened its ability to lead internationally. In addition to fueling opposition on the ground, the occupation of Iraq on U.S. terms isolated the United States and generated even more anti-Americanism worldwide.[115]

BUSH'S FOREIGN POLICY ASSUMPTIONS AND THE FUTURE OF INTERNATIONAL ORDER

Before and after September 11, as well as in the context of the war in Iraq, the Bush administration worked strenuously to convince the world that its foreign policy track was the only necessary one and that it was successful. It also labored to advance the thesis that a post-9/11 world required new ways to manage world order. In the process, the Bush administration sidelined the importance that the 1990s had given to multilateralism, the United Nations, and at least the prospects for a transformed and revitalized international democratic solidarity.

Bush's Foreign Policy: From Vindicated to Mistaken

At the heart of the most conservative foreign policy approaches in the Bush administration were four main assumptions: National security prevails absolutely over considerations of international democratic solidarity (including the importance given to humanitarian and human rights issues); the United States has the right to define on its own what is legitimate in American foreign policy; the United States has the power to influence international legitimacy and, subsequently, international law and norms; and U.S. foreign policy is largely accountable to no one but America itself.[116] Although the war in Iraq showed that these assumptions contained some element of truth, it proved them wrong by and large.

The predominant position of the United States in the post–Cold War international distribution of power gives to Washington ample room to define the international agenda and act unilaterally. Following the ways America conceived and conducted its own War on Terror in the aftermath of 9/11, the war in Iraq certainly makes this point. The skepticism and opposition of most nations toward the Bush administration's eagerness to act against Saddam Hussein were not enough to avoid war. The fact that the United States had the power to go to war on its own terms won the day—at least for a while. In that sense, the assumption that America has the power to act internationally as it sees fit was correct. But it does not mean that the United States enjoys a free hand and has the ability to redefine international legality and legitimacy. Neither does it mean that, because of the putative global primacy of its national interest, it is accountable only to itself. As previously noted, in Iraq the Bush administration learned firsthand how difficult it is to ensure security and reconstruct a rogue and failing state on its own—it found that it needed the political, military, financial, and logistical support of as many countries as possible. The Iraq intervention showed that U.S. national interest is not the sole metric to assess the legitimacy of foreign policy and international legitimacy as a whole, because in Iraq, America contributed less to the redesigning of international legality and legitimacy than to the weakening of its own credibility and legitimacy. The spurious reasons put forward by the Bush administration for going to war did not help. In June 2004, the 9/11 Commission found no proven link between al Qaeda and Saddam Hussein's regime.[117] Later on, in September 2004, as Iraq's putative weapons of mass destruction appeared to be more and more elusive, Charles A. Duelfer, the top U.S. inspector in Iraq, made public in a report that Iraq was a minimal weapons threat at the launch of Operation Iraqi Freedom in March 2003.[118] As if that were not enough, the ways U.S. troops on the ground used force turned out to be a problem as well. The ambiguous rules of engagement and the issue of torture (if not officially condoned, then at least encouraged and informally approved at the highest level[119]) did not boost America's reputation and ability to translate its power into influence and legitimacy.

From this perspective, the failures of Bush's foreign policy in Iraq illustrate the international social dimension of legitimacy—that is, legitimacy is not a self-declared phenomenon; it requires at a minimum the recognition and consent of others. As competition, tension, and confrontation tend to shape international life, any sense of international legitimacy must be a shared view.[120] This social dimension is a requirement of international legitimacy in general, but it is also a requirement for the legitimacy of any country's foreign policy. Considering America's global reach and democratic claims, such a requirement is of particular importance. The overwhelming international power of America affects other nations—particularly allies—tremendously, and if they are not consulted in the best spirit of multilateralism, a rift is destined to emerge. In short, the Bush administration's foreign policy, despite some positive effects, has had much negative impact on international order and on the norms and institutions underwriting it.[121]

Regarding the positive effects of Bush's foreign policy in Iraq, it is helpful to distinguish between intentional and unintentional. The main intentional positive effect was, of course, the elimination of Saddam Hussein and his regime.[122] The decisiveness with which the Bush administration acted against Iraq can be seen as another positive aspect. In the early 2000s, the willingness of the United Nations to leave the arms inspection issue in limbo suggested that no closure on the issue could come from the international organization. Yet the sanctions regime and the no-fly zones imposed on Iraq for more than a decade could not continue forever. Something had to be done, and the Bush administration's determination showed that there was an alternative to paralysis.

Among the unintentional positive effects of Bush's foreign policy in Iraq was the intellectual benefit it generated, which amounted to the fact that its radically innovative nature served as a wake-up call. Its departure from a routine approach of international relations served as an invitation to reassess not only the historicity of international life and its normative mechanisms, but also the very nature and role of the norms and institutions of international law, as well as their ability to change. Are international law and the United Nations—and the values, rights, and duties they promote—simply so much normative artifice to maintain the status quo, or should they be taken seriously and thus defended seriously? How do international law and multilateralism adapt to reality? Conversely, how does reality adapt to international law and multilateralism?

The radicalism of Bush's foreign policy vis-à-vis Iraq brought a political clarity that can be considered another unintentional benefit. For instance, European countries were forced to take a stand, to state the extent to which they value their alliance with the United States and transatlantic multilateralism. The ensuing political clarity helped define the extent and limits of the flexibility of international legality and legitimacy, of what is acceptable and what is not from the point of view of member states.

Another unintentional benefit of Bush's foreign policy regarding Iraq has been institutional—that is, vis-à-vis the United Nations. To be sure, the United Nations is today a rather politically weak organization. At the same time, the radical nature of Bush's foreign policy put it at the center of the debates on the normative environment of international political life and also contributed to UN stakeholders' becoming more aware of the challenges that the United Nations and multilateralism are likely to face if their limits are not acknowledged.

Yet these positive effects are only a small part of the Bush foreign policy's impact on the international order. To begin with, even the intentional positive effects of Bush's policy in Iraq are questionable. After the removal of Saddam Hussein from power, it is far from certain that the country will become a unified democratic nation; Iraq could remain unstable and a source of tension in the region and in the world at large. More to the point, Bush's Iraq policy had the cumulative impact of weakening international order at four levels.

The Bush administration's self-serving conception and discretionary use of multilateral mechanisms and obligations undermined the system of international legitimacy that multilateralism, within the confines of an international organization's mandate, seeks to provide. By promoting a double standard, Bush's foreign policy made it less attractive for other states to accept the constraints associated with international reciprocity, with the dynamics of rights and duties.[123] Its unilateral and self-centered approach to international affairs was an invitation for more unrequited reciprocity. The idea and possibility of a credible regime of international cooperation, of international legality and legitimacy, is endangered.

The credibility of the United States and of its historic credo concerning democratic values has been weakened. The spread of democracy at gunpoint, amounting to tens of thousands of civilian casualties, is a difficult sale. As a result, America's leadership role in the world, and especially its ability to rally other nations to the service of international law and multilateralism, is increasingly questioned. As such, it tends to deprive America of the important role that its foreign policy has had for the expression and tools of international legitimacy in the post–Cold War era. And considering the pivotal importance of the United States in the post–Cold War international distribution of power, it cannot help but be viewed as mismanaging the international order with a sense of international illegitimacy.[124]

The U.S.-led war in Iraq also sent a dubious message to rogue states. It conveyed the idea that unless they are in a position to deter an American attack—a very tall order—such an attack is a likely possibility. The incentive for them is to acquire nuclear weapons as quickly as possible and bargain for their survival through a subdued and drawn-out brinkmanship. The fact that the Bush administration more or less ignored North Korea only encouraged Iran "to go nuclear" in order to gain recognition and protect itself.

There was as well the negative effect of Bush's policy on the stability of the Middle East. Far from reducing terrorism, it contributed to its growth. Various prominent observers inside and outside Iraq have noted the descent of Iraq into a civil war. Moreover, the link between terrorism in Iraq, regional terrorism (namely in Saudi Arabia), and international terrorism has most likely been strengthened. To conclude the weighing of the positive against the negative consequences of the Bush administration's foreign policy by focusing on the case of Iraq, the relatively successful elections of January 2005 surely were a source of optimism. The elections did not turn into the Armageddon that the insurgency had promised; no major violence was unleashed on election day. Although most of the Sunni Arabs decided not to vote, Shiites and Kurds went to the polls by the millions. Yet in the aftermath of the elections, insurgencies and terrorist attacks did not cease. In the fall of 2005, after the constitutional referendum of October 15, it was still not clear how and to what extent it would be possible to bring Sunnis into the Iraqi political process. Finding ways through which the Shiite parliamentary majority would, in the long run, go along with the Kurds and, more important, with the once-privileged Sunni minority was not a settled issue.[125] By February 2006, sectarian fighting was dangerously on the rise, and on July 9, 2006, the serious escalation of violence between the Shiites and Sunnis expressed itself in actions of systematic violence that raised concern for a development that increasingly resembled ethnic cleansing.[126] What had in 2005 appeared to be the possibility for a positive development in Iraq and throughout the region had turned into a situation of heightened tensions a year later. By the middle of 2006, the future of Iraq, and of Bush's foreign policy, remained therefore very much an open question.

With the consequences of Bush's foreign policy not only on Iraq but also on international order at large still pending, there is a need to revisit the role of multilateralism, the United Nations, and the United States. There is also a need to re-examine what has to be changed and improved in each and in their relationship to one another. Eliminating the tensions between the United States and the United Nations and achieving a fully stable and just international order is a utopian goal. The national bent of international relations and the interstate structure that it gives to international order make tensions in and limits to international justice a fact of international life. Yet the necessity to reconcile international security and the collective security vision of international solidarity calls for trying to make some recommendations in this direction and to implement them as much as possible. This is the subject of the next, concluding chapter.

CHAPTER 6

TOWARD THE INTERNATIONAL
RULE OF LAW

T HIS FINAL CHAPTER will answer the following questions: First, what are the lessons of the analyses presented in the previous chapters? In particular, where do they leave us regarding the projection of a sense of international solidarity and responsibility? Second, where do we go from here? More specifically, is there room for enhancing the sense of international solidarity and responsibility and, in the process, the international rule of law? And if that is the case, what are the changes that could make it happen?

A FEW LESSONS FROM THE 1990s AND 2000s

The topical lessons drawn from the previous chapters center around four main issues: the United Nations and, more specifically, peace operations; international norms and principles and the issue of humanitarian intervention; the hybrid nature of contemporary international politics—a dynamic of national and international interests; and the United States and its relations with the rest of the world.

PEACE OPERATIONS AND THE LIMITS OF THE UNITED NATIONS

Had the funding, logistical support, and human resources available for peace operations in the 1990s been deployed in the context of a few traditional peace operations (that is, simple interposition operations stipulated by negotiations and a peace agreement), they would have been sufficient. However, at a time when the number of peace operations and the complexity of the issues required comprehensive and impeccable institutional support, what was put at the disposal of the United Nations, both in the Secretariat and in the field, crippled the organization's ability to perform well. Moreover, as the use of force often became a feature of peace operations, UN operations needed firm and clear political support from member states, in particular from the permanent members of the Security Council that were taking the lead in the multilateral engagements. Yet tentativeness, rather than decisive support, dominated decision making.

The fact that the United Nations was prone to view communication issues as a matter of nonstrategic importance proved also to be a serious mistake. The magnitude of the humanitarian crises, the complexity and risks encompassed in the various international interventions, and the involvement of major powers led the UN peace operations to receive concerted media and public attention. Any shortcomings of UN communication with the local population, between headquarters and the field, among the various agencies in the field, with the member states involved and, perhaps most important, with the world at large were destined to backfire. These shortcomings were especially evident when peace operations ran into major difficulties: No member state participating in the peace operation would rush to take responsibility, and in the communication war that ensued, the member states involved would usually manage to have their own responsibility overlooked. UN public information was no match for the powerful media outlets of member states enrolled, directly or indirectly, in describing the course of the operation.

Against this background, a variety of reports have been produced since the second half of the 1990s to address the shortcomings of peace operations.[1] Kofi Annan commissioned reports on the Rwanda genocide in the spring and fall of 1994, and on Srebrenica in July 1995.[2] In addition to identifying the technical and institutional shortcomings of UN peace operations, the reports were meant to acknowledge the responsibility of the United Nations in what had gone wrong. By acknowledging that the United Nations had failed the people that it had pledged to protect, the reports were meant to provide the United Nations some sort of apologia.

The *Report of the Panel on United Nations Peace Operations,* headed by Lakhdar Brahimi and published in August 2000,[3] represented the most comprehensive and genuine effort to come to grips with the technical and institutional problems that the peace operations had repeatedly encountered throughout the 1990s. Not only did the report offer a diagnostic of the institutional shortcomings in strategic areas of peace operations, it also made a number of targeted recommendations to redress them.[4] It focused on four main areas: doctrine, strategy, and decision-making operations; the United Nations' capacities to deploy operations rapidly and effectively; headquarters resources and structures for planning and supporting peacekeeping operations; and peace operations and the information age.[5]

The "Brahimi Report," as it came to be known, benefited from a better follow-up than any previous report of its kind. Within a few months of its publication, the UN Secretariat was able to put together a number of documents assessing in very precise terms what the institutional requirements would be for the Secretariat to have the report's recommendations fulfilled.[6] By summer 2003, major progress had been made in a number of areas, one of which was the second broad area of reform—namely, rapid deployment of personnel, which had become easier thanks to both standby arrangements with governments and the development of extensive on-call rosters for civilians in various specialist areas. Progress had also been made in the third broad area of reform, that of headquarters resources and structure for planning and supporting peacekeeping operations. The headquarters of the UN Department of Peacekeeping Operations was now at a strength of almost six hundred people. Thanks to this increase in personnel, the headquarters now had serious planning capacity. The progress in the last major area of reform, dealing with peace operations in the information age, had also been quite significant.

It is in the first area of the Brahimi Report—that of doctrine, strategy, and decision making for peace operations–that the least progress was made. In particular, the recommendation that Security Council resolutions remain in a draft form until the secretary-general had firm commitments of troops and other critical mission support elements was not approved.[7] Moreover, while the Brahimi Report was predicated on the idea of "robust" peacekeeping, in the 2000s, EU-NATO countries, which, more than any other UN member states, could provide such capacity for peacekeeping, grew increasingly reluctant to get involved in UN peace operations. In fact, these countries have hardly contributed troops in any great numbers to UN peacekeeping. This is particularly bad news for Africa, whose African Union cannot, as yet, play the role that NATO or the European Union has been able to play in the Balkans.

The suggestions for change in the Brahimi Report can help to reinstate the credibility of the United Nations. But there is more to do, especially in terms of the UN leadership's taking responsibility for the mistakes made. The Srebrenica and Rwanda reports marked progress regarding the United Nations' recognition of its own responsibilities. Still, this was very limited progress. Of course, one should not overlook the complexity of the multilateral decision-making process and the difficulty of finding out where the ultimate line of responsibility lies. But without mechanisms of political accountability—whatever the sanction may be—for those international leaders who have the authority and responsibility to do the right thing but fail to do so, the message sent to the victims is destined to be politically ambiguous and morally uncertain. In the end, the accountability of international leaders boils down to what the international community owes to victims. An apology can only be a start: While it points to a moral sense of international responsibility, it also calls for its translation into terms of political and legal responsibility.[8]

The Normative Dimension of International Politics and the Question of Humanitarian Intervention

We have seen throughout this study that the normative dimension of international politics that informs the principles at the core of international law and multilateralism is not detached from the goals and day-to-day tasks of collective security and, more specifically, peace operations. The normative dimension constitutes a framework in which the deliberations and actions of the major powers and the international community take place. For states, especially the most powerful of them, it is always tempting to break out of established multilateral frameworks and go off on their own. Nevertheless, ignoring altogether the guidelines and constraints posed by international principles is, in the long run, a risky proposition: Turning one's back on the negotiated and consensual way of conducting international politics means that, down the road, others could do the same.

Undeniably, there is a certain amount of normative convergence in international principles and the frameworks they establish. Yet as emphasized in chapter 3, there is also some element of competition among these principles, and this creates tensions in the international order. International principles factor in relatively different constituencies and values; hence, discrepancies arise between the principles, the degree of states' adherence to them, or even between the various interpretations of a given principle. Yet although these discrepancies may generate tensions, they are also indicative of normative change and the ongoing socialization of international life. Such creative tension also serves the purposes of international legitimacy. In this regard, the organization and distribution of international power and its evolution play a decisive role in the interpretation and application of normative guidelines formed by international principles. The guidelines influence the normative hierarchy that tries to balance the various demands (their compatible and competitive aspects) of international principles by favoring certain interpretations of principles. The 1990s saw a change of normative emphasis in the interpretation and application of international principles, but this does not mean that we have witnessed since the 1990s a paradigmatic sea change at the international level. The changes that have taken place have not radically transformed the norms that sustain the international order.

As the example of humanitarian intervention shows, there is now a greater willingness for countries to accept it, and a greater tolerance for countries to consider the option of international intervention for humanitarian reasons. Nonetheless, the limited commitment that it generates from the intervening powers is particularly noticeable in the selectivity of the humanitarian crises and in the ambiguous means employed—at times, designed more to ensure the security of the intervening personnel than the immediate safety and, ultimately, relief of the victimized populations. The notion of justifiable humanitarian intervention did not arise as a new international norm. At best, it was elevated in the international normative hierarchy as a morally nagging responsibility that is still too complex to evaluate and implement in consistent, balanced, and reliable terms. On April 7, 2004, as the world looked back on the failure of the international community to prevent or stop the genocide in Rwanda ten years earlier, the United Nations held a commemorative panel on "A Decade After Rwanda: The United Nations and the Responsibility to Protect." The motto of the day was "Never Again." It so happens that at exactly the same time, in Darfur, Sudan, for more than a year a thousand civilians per day had been dying from starvation, disease, and warfare, and a million had been forced from their homes, with the international community doing close to nothing. Since then, nothing much has changed in Darfur.

THE HYBRID NATURE OF INTERNATIONAL POLITICS AND INTERNATIONAL ETHICS

The 1990s emphasized the hybrid nature of contemporary international politics—that is to say, it was not solely about interstate politics and the pursuit of national interests, but also about individual rights, the international interest, and a nascent sense of supranational politics. To those (conventional realists and neorealists in particular[9]) who believe that the national realm and its interests are essentially what account for state motivations and behavior at the international level, the engagement of the international community in crises lacking traditional strategic stakes showed that projecting a sense of international responsibility and solidarity, with no immediate and clear major national gains, is also relevant. In the 2000s, although in a very different context, the Bush administration's foreign policy leads to a somewhat similar conclusion: It did not succeed in winning the hearts and minds in Iraq, nor in the world at large.

Now, if realism or traditional national interest considerations alone no longer win the day at the international level, this does not mean that ethics is a central benchmark for foreign policy. After all, the attitude of the international community in the 1990s did not fully indulge the tenets of internationalism.[10] While internationalist elements certainly motivated the international community's deliberations, decisions, and actions regarding the humanitarian crises and human rights violations, they did not lead states to neglect the demands of their national realms. Nation-centrism was mitigated, but the international system continued to be nationally based.[11] Moreover, states (especially powerful Western states) remained largely unaccountable for their international misconduct by omission or commission. The governments of the Western nations involved in the multilateral responses to the humanitarian crises have not had to face a sense of international accountability for their part in the failures that at times have undermined these responses. Surely, on April 16, 2002, almost seven years after the tragedy of Srebrenica, the Netherlands, following an official report that criticized the attitude of the two hundred Dutch peacekeepers at Srebrenica in July 1995, recognized its responsibility, and the government resigned. But the Dutch case is an exception. For instance, France, also involved in the Srebrenica tragedy (because Dutch peacekeepers were under the command of the French general Bernard Janvier) has thus far rejected any responsibility.[12] The United Nations also has not been held accountable for its shortcomings in this context.

The Quandary of Multilateralism and American Primacy

The redistribution of international power in the 1990s that left the United States as the sole superpower introduced the analytical rubric of unipolarity (or quasi-unipolarity[13]) into the study of world order. It also confirmed four U.S. foreign policy tropisms: the unequal relationship between the United States and the United Nations; the primacy of security issues in U.S. foreign policy; the priority given by the United States to national interest considerations; and the self-centered American conception of multilateralism, with the unilateralist temptation it entails. These four characteristics of U.S. foreign policy were manifest during the George W. Bush administration.

In the 1990s, as the United Nations stretched its capabilities by taking on numerous crises and embarking on actions beyond mere interpositional peacekeeping, the political, logistical, financial, and military support of its key member states became increasingly vital. The stronger the United Nations grew in its mandates and international interventions, the more dependent (and, in a way, the weaker) it became vis-à-vis the United States.

The United Nations led actors on the ground and in diplomatic circles to think that nothing of importance could be done without the United States. The U.S. eagerness to enjoy as much as possible its de facto veto power outside the UN Security Council, its insistence on having a final say (in one way or another) on the policies to be adopted, and the inability of its allies (key European powers in particular) to assume real leadership on their own only encouraged this situation. This was the case even when the United States was doing little or had little idea of what should be done to solve a crisis—for example, regarding Bosnia in the early part of the first term of Clinton's presidency.

The same unbalanced relationship between the United States and the United Nations and its impact on international life have been at work during the Bush administration, only this time in an even more dramatic fashion. After 9/11, Bush's foreign policy forced the United Nations and the international community to reopen the Iraq dossier, which the United Nations had left lingering. Later on, the inability of the United Nations to deter the United States from going to war in Iraq and, after the military campaign, to negotiate with the White House a significant and meaningful role for itself was another display of how deep the imbalance of power had become between America and the world organization.[14]

In the aftermath of the Cold War, internationalist considerations caught the attention of U.S. decision makers. Nevertheless, traditional military questions continued to be the prime concern around which the United States designed the core of its foreign policy and military strategies, and it apportioned its resources accordingly. The ways America handled the humanitarian crises of the 1990s showed that the prioritization of security is less contextual than deeply embedded in the national-security mindset and culture of U.S. decision makers. American reluctance to project power internationally in favor of internationalist issues contrasted with a relative openness to get involved (including military intervention if need be) in conventional security crises. The almost absolute priority of security issues over internationalist concerns left human rights and humanitarian crises unable to provide a strong enough justification to move U.S. decision makers unfalteringly.

The foreign policy adopted by the Bush administration offered a radical confirmation of this state of affairs. Its exclusive focus on national security issues left hardly any room for addressing human rights or humanitarian considerations in the international realm. The logic of national security has dominated and shaped Bush's foreign policy; in the case of Iraq, the inability of the United States to find weapons of mass destruction led the Bush administration initially to use the human rights violations by Saddam Hussein's regime as an additional justification for going to war. Over time, the establishment of a democratic regime also became an increasing source of legitimization for the American presence in Iraq. Yet these motivations cannot hide the fact that, compared to a strong national security rationale, all other foreign policy considerations occupied a very, very distant second.

The national bent of the international system calls for all countries to take into account in essential ways their own national interests in the formulation of their foreign policies, and such accounting may perhaps concern the United States more than any other country. As the international hegemon, it is exposed to more threats than less powerful nations. Its overwhelming power and preponderance become part of its weakness, as less powerful nations can make it a target of their envy. The changes of the 1990s, rather than shifting the prioritization of the national over the international interest, underscored its continuing relevance and significance in U.S. foreign policy. Eager to divert as few resources as possible and to expose itself minimally to political risks in support of internationalist causes, the Clinton administration satisfied itself with a "service minimum" compared to overall American power and capacity. The United States may have done more than, let us say, Canada to help address humanitarian crises in the 1990s; however, considering its unmatched power and capacity, America did comparatively less, allocating very few of its resources. Being the country that was doing the most did not exclude the United States from also being one of the countries that was doing very little.

Later on, 9/11 and the War on Terror provided the Bush administration the opportunity to go further on this path. Comparing the amount of resources allocated to national defense to the amount of resources allocated to UN peace operations—viewed by the Bush administration as largely lacking strategic value—serves as a case in point. Since 2001, the U.S. government's base defense budget per fiscal year has regularly increased: from $330.6 billion for 2003, to $358 billion for 2004, to $401.7 billion for 2005, to $419.3 billion for 2006, to $439.3 billion for 2007.[15] During the same period, peacekeeping operations figures remained extremely low and at times even decreased: requested budgets for peace operations were $150 million for fiscal year 2000, $134 million for 2001, $150 million for 2002, $108.25 million for 2003, $94.9 million for 2004, $104 million for 2005, $196 million for 2006, and $200.5 million for 2007.[16]

National interest is not in and of itself the enemy of multilateralism. Multilateralism is based upon and meant to serve the national interest of member states as long as its pursuit fits in with and abides by the rules of cooperation and reciprocity that joint international action seeks to express and promote. Multilateralism favors international socialization out of a national-interest approach to international relations, albeit an approach that is channeled into and constrained by a social or principled conception of relations among states—that is, geared toward reciprocity and consensual relations. Multilateralism is the art of balancing and managing the tensions between these two aspects. The difficulty for U.S. multilateral relations is that the superpower status of America generates a disequilibrium that encourages the United States to focus on national interest at the expense of the socially principled dimension of multilateralism. That was the case during the Clinton administration, and it has been even more the case under President George W. Bush.

Since the early 1990s, unipolarity has made it challenging for the United States to resist the temptations created by its overwhelming preponderance of power. It has been alluring for America to put itself above the rules of multilateralism while insisting that those rules apply to others. From this perspective, except with the U.S. attitude in the context of Operation Desert Storm (where America exhibited genuine multilateral leadership), the aftermath of the Cold War has shown that the United States has been rather consistently inconsistent. It has been consistent in its self-centered and self-absorbed (and therefore hardly multilateral) interpretation of multilateralism. This was already the case under Clinton (particularly in economic and trade negotiations) and has gone even further with the Bush administration and its almost exclusive focus on U.S. national security issues. In the process, not only have the socializing effects of multilateralism become endangered, but the very belief in the validity of the socializing values and aims of multilateralism is at stake. Indeed, why should such values and aims be taken seriously, considering that their most important underwriter, viewing them as conditional and malleable, tends to undermine them?

TOWARD A BETTER INTERNATIONAL RULE OF LAW

If the agenda of international solidarity was weak in the 1990s—a period during which international solidarity was given more attention—it has become even weaker in the 2000s. In the process, solidarity and security have grown apart. So have power and legitimacy. This is a perilous course of action. The goal of international solidarity is to bring countries together at the international level to solve common problems; its weakness plays into the gap that already exists between them and tends to deepen it. This situation makes the pursuit of order and justice in the international realm more elusive.

How then to rectify this state of affairs? First, some of the minimum requirements for promoting a better international rule of law should be identified: finding a better balance internationally between what is and what is not negotiable; between the need for decisive leadership and the need to factor in others' perspectives; between the need to build support for international action and the need to use force; between the need to defend and push for the enhancement of democratic values and the need to respect cultural diversity; and between the need to empower people and the need to recognize their desire to be the masters of their own destiny.

Four concomitant changes could contribute significantly to the pursuit of such minimum requirements. First, dovetail solidarity and security at the international level and consequently, embed power into legitimacy. Second, enhance the norms of international solidarity and take the democratic empowerment nature of multilateralism more seriously. Encourage the United Nations, member states, and regional and nongovernmental organizations to join in a comprehensive reassessment of their mutual tasks in a number of limited but critical areas in multilateral interventions, which would be a third source of welcome change. Fourth, make U.S. leadership more consensual and reciprocal, which would contribute vastly to a more stable and more just international system.

International Rule of Law and the Public Policy of Solidarity

If it is difficult for multilateralism to overcome its nation-centric bonds, an instant response to this study's title appears quite readily: Beyond the national interest is, simply, a reconceived national interest that is less narrow than its predecessor. Such a reconceived national interest is not self-centered or exclusive; it is decidedly inclusive in its factoring in the interests of other countries. Identifying issues on which there is overlapping, or common, interest among countries thus becomes the key to a more inclusive, socializing conception and pursuit of the national interest.

In the context of international crises that seem to elude the traditional strategic imperatives of international security, such a reconceived national interest, dictated by international democratic solidarity, provides some clues about how it already contributes to the international order; to what degree—and under whose auspices—it introduces change in that order; and whether such change, when it involves multilateral interventions, can be viewed as effective and an improvement in the conditions surrounding the crisis and in the international order as a whole.

At the national level, public policy has informed international democratic solidarity since the rise of the modern bureaucratic state. Accepting the needs and rights of individuals as the principal impetus of governmental decision making has led all branches at all levels of democratic government to establish effective policy mechanisms, including resource allocation and enforcement mechanisms, to ensure the promotion of not only civil and political rights but also social and economic rights—all in the service of social integration and stability.[17] The differences among the demands and responsibilities of public policy in the welfare state and the liberal state generate differences in their respective notions of the rule of law; yet in both cases, public policy as an expression and instrument of the rule of law seeks social inclusion based on fairness and accountability.[18] The West's advanced industrial democracies recognize a sense of responsibility toward their citizenries, and such recognition goes beyond mere "nagging moral or ethical questions"; it is essentially a function of social-contract obligations and is, to be sure, a very large part of the government's legitimacy.

Could such a public-policy approach to the consolidation of democratic solidarity work at the international level? The democratic creed of the leading Western powers and their "good governance" philosophies in the management of their own domestic polities (as illustrated through the tacit nurturing of civil society and the enduring assumptions in the distribution of public goods) serves as at least the *basis* for the projection of those values and underlying assumptions into the international realm. This "functionalist" foundation can be seen in the orientations of the relevant national agencies that are dedicated to international action: the U.S. Agency for International Development's Office of Foreign Disaster Assistance, the United Kingdom's Department for International Development, and the European Community's Humanitarian Aid Office of the European Union. These agencies had their origins in the Cold War competition for the "hearts and minds" of the Third World, where humanitarian gestures from the West went a long way in keeping such countries out of communism's orbit. Over time, these agencies' missions, much like that of NATO, have evolved toward the kind of new international democratic solidarity that NATO now exhibits in its role as a collective security organization.[19]

The functionalist orientation can also be seen in the relative support of leading democratic powers for multilateral responses to international crises. Indeed, these responses are separate—yet somewhat coordinated—

national endeavors based on broad common assumptions about and approaches to the crisis at hand, whether the commonality comes in the form of a coordinated peacekeeping force to separate warring factions in a country or, beyond that, broad peacebuilding functions that include good-governance practices, economic and political reform, and electoral assistance. After all, because an intervention in a failed or failing state occurs in the international realm does not mean that the interveners play by an entirely separate set of rules that are "out there," stipulated by international society—quite the contrary, as emphasized throughout this study: International society is conditioned and socialized by its leading actors, principally the leading democratic powers that have contributed to the development of international law.

In this regard, international democratic solidarity in a multilateral operation means that advanced industrial democracies, with decades of sophisticated public policy and public administration approaches to domestic problems, bring to the targeted country the organizational and administrative skills that they are familiar with in their own nations' domestic settings to prevent the recurrence of conflict in the multilateral operation's targeted state. At the center of this approach are the "core" values of international democratic solidarity—dispute resolution through deliberation, transparency, accountability, representativeness, inclusiveness, and respect for individual human rights.

Yet such orientations obviously fall short of an *international* public-policy framework that would institutionalize and routinize international solidarity in a substantial way through appropriate enforcement mechanisms and, as a result, strengthen the international rule of law. Such orientations fall short of projecting into the international realm public policy (designed to guarantee the rights of individuals within domestic society on a daily basis) at work in well-functioning national democracies, or even in the regional integration context of the European Union.

The international order is not, of course, structured this way. The projection of democratic solidarity is still marginal, underinstitutionalized, and weakly structured at the international level. As such, it is far from being conducted in public policy terms, far from manifesting itself as *organic* solidarity, far from serving as a constitutive referent for the structural organization of international life. For a number of nation-states, especially nondemocratic ones or those lacking a sophisticated governmental apparatus, this state of affairs is good enough. In the United States and in Asia, where the shield of sovereignty is strong or support for the idea of supragovernmentalism is weak, the attachment to national sovereignty is not conducive to projecting a public policy approach of solidarity beyond national borders.

In the end, it is in Europe that the idea of a global public policy of solidarity at the fringes of global governance is the most palatable. But even there, although it is felt that such global public policy is required as a way to engineer a more inclusive, democratic, and stable international order, it is also recognized that the institutional machinery (deliberation and decision making) and the distribution mechanisms (allocation of resources, evaluation of public goods provided, accountability, and so forth) of such public policy remain to be invented.[20] In this context, the development of a "human security" approach to international security issues and the increasing sophistication of studies devoted to global public goods may be good starting points for such an investigation.[21] But much more needs to be examined regarding the conceptualization and concrete conditions behind the implementation of a global public policy of solidarity—including its financing, the nature and the extent of the rights that it would defend and promote, the duties and responsibilities that it would confer on global actors (state or nonstate), and the decision-making and institutional mechanisms through which such a global public policy approach could come about.

However, the international community is not entirely bereft of institutional machinery for such a global public policy approach. Robert Keohane has identified familiar concepts of democratic public-policy formation regarding the United Nations, focusing on the legitimacy deficit the world body suffers in terms of its mandates for multilateral interventions.[22] Keohane suggests more inclusiveness and "epistemic reliability" in the operation of multilateral institutions. For instance, adherence to the principle of sovereignty in current multilateral interventions renders their decision-making procedures less legitimate if nondemocratic states "can express preferences that are not desired by, or in the interests of, most people residing within their territories."[23] Epistemic reliability seeks to rectify this defect in multilateral inclusiveness by incorporating the views of transnational activists and, presumably, the ultimate "clients" of the UN's mandates and programs—in much the same fashion that public policy in advanced industrial democracies in urban renewal, crime prevention, and welfare has evolved into client-based programs that canvass the recipients' needs. "The UN," Keohane observes, "is . . . too inclusive of states and not inclusive enough of the views of individuals and potential groups within authoritarian states."[24] Such "input legitimacy" has a strong empowerment component, providing the international organization with an enhanced legitimacy in conflict zones, and giving those whom the intervention seeks to assist or protect a sense of being stakeholders in the outcome of the intervention.

The legitimacy of a multilateral intervention also depends on its decisiveness and effectiveness. Highlighting the transparency and accountability of democratic states in their governance and policymaking, Keohane suggests a "league of democracies" to supplement UN Security Council deliberations on the urgent deployment of multilateral peace operations that may be subject to vetoes by nondemocratic member states.[25]

Short of solidarity's becoming an integral part of international policy formulation and implementation, security—national and international—remains a precarious and uncertain undertaking. Making international solidarity a secondary concern, not adhering to international law and emergent international norms, puts security itself at risk. For as much as it is the case at the national level, at the international level the rights of all are not secured when the rights of each are not fully recognized and protected. Over time, local conflicts can become a fertile ground for the nurturing and spreading of threats. Violence associated with weak, failed, or embattled states tends to spread beyond borders. Violation of people's rights is an invitation to contest regional norms that attempt to maintain stability in volatile areas of the world and, beyond that, in the international order as well.[26] It also fuels a geopolitics of ideological passions—of envy, hatred, nationalism.[27]

The intertwining of geopolitics and ideological passions is not new. Over the centuries, more often than not relations among countries have been dominated by competition, conflict, victory and defeat, rise and decline, feelings of superiority and inferiority. This has given passions—particularly negative passions such as distrust, resentment, envy, jealousy, and hatred—a significant place in the national and international dimensions of politics. Modernity has only furthered this condition. In particular, what has made it possible for the West to advance—with its relentless push in terms of technological progress and trade, the exponential increase of interactions across borders, and the neoliberal restructuring of economies and societies—is also what tears the world apart. Each technological, political, economic, and normative advance continues to generate conflicting tendencies among and within states. For lack of a better rubric, this globalization is exemplified by the fact that Western norms of universality and equality, while having done much for the recognition of the intrinsic value of the individual at the international level, have also ignited struggles between traditional and modern forms of socialization. Moreover, the intensification of global communication, by making developmental tensions sharper and more resonant, deepens the difficulty for non-Western societies to reconcile such tensions and for the West and the non-West, developed and developing countries, to come to terms with one another.

In the multilateral context, the push for solidarity in international interventions is an uphill battle. Because of the intergovernmental structure of international organizations, the tendency for each country's representatives to push for their own state's interests remains an important feature. When this tendency dominates the organization's mission, it affects the credibility of the multilateral system, weakening the security of all, nations and individuals. The shortcomings of the United Nations regarding solidarity are part and parcel of this landscape and play a role in the United Nations' serving as a weak security provider, with collective security more or less a paper tiger. The most powerful Western democratic nations are not immune to these circumstances, and this includes the main underwriter of the multilateral system—the United States. The responsibility that it bears as the unipolar actor in the world order in failing to secure the solidarist values of multilateralism contributes to the portrayal of America as culpable in the maintenance of the international system's pathologies. As such, it is a primary target for disenfranchised actors. The war in which the United States and transnational terrorism find themselves is an aspect of this story. Focusing on security at the expense of solidarity weakens all the more the very quest for security, considering that it comes with a gap between power and legitimacy. When power is unable to root security in solidarity—to root security in the recognition of others' right to the same and the (legally imposed) policy imperative to act upon it—the legitimacy of power, the way it is exercised, is at stake.

The tension between power and legitimacy is an enduring feature of the international system. The post–World War II period brought such tension into sharp contrast: The United Nations was paralyzed by the East-West showdown, the two blocs representing two competing forms of power and legitimacy. In the process, the international legitimacy meant to be embodied by the United Nations was drained of most of its significance. To be sure, global strategic competition in a bipolar world order did much to render acceptable the power and legitimacy disconnect during the Cold War; the alternatives that the two mutually exclusive world visions offered provided a de facto check-and-balance order that constrained the two superpowers.

But the structure of unipolarity that characterizes the international order now renders the disconnect between power and legitimacy more problematic—and perhaps even more dangerous. The United States argues that the pursuit of its national interest advances the international interest, but the argument appears increasingly unconvincing of late. This is all the more the case considering that, following the rise of China and India, the resurgence of Russian power, and the quagmire of the Iraq War, international life seems to be re-entering a world of multipolarity—a world of contending regional powers that will certainly be very different from the stable bipolarity of the Cold War and that is destined to have profound implications for the functioning of multilateralism.

Although the reality of international life admits huge discrepancies of power among countries, the idea that international norms could endorse a de jure hierarchy in the international system (in the form of an empire) presumes that the normative shape of the world has not progressed beyond the colonial era. Yet the historical progress of international norms puts a fundamental constraint on dominating powers, let alone on the hegemon: No legitimate foreign policy, and no legitimate international order, can be maintained by a conception and exercise of power that is exclusively self-centered.

As the world now lacks the type of check-and-balance mechanism that bipolarity offered, and as the awareness of democratic governance spreads, it becomes increasingly difficult to separate power and legitimacy, and to defend the unipolar condition. A unipolarity that is unable to, or overlooks the need to, embed power into legitimacy—that is, short of also seeking security through solidarity elevated to an international public policy level (and not simply limited to a moral stance)—is prone to generate instability as a systemic (not only a localized) feature of the international system. The results would be increasingly ominous for the United States, for the United Nations, and to world order in general. On its sheer power alone, America would still be able to project its influence internationally, but maintaining such influence would be difficult. From a material point of view, as the Iraqi case shows, the United States would have trouble handling on its own the troop deployments and the financial demands associated with global long-term commitments, especially in areas of conflict. From a diplomatic standpoint, the questioning of the legitimacy of America's foreign policy, if not the very nature of its political system, could increase with its overexposure. The United Nations would be in similar straits. Without the support of the United States, its already narrow role in the management of world order would shrink further—and with it, the venue for international legitimacy that it seeks to provide.

As for world order, a complete divorce between America and the United Nations would increase global instability. Because most countries favor a multilateral approach, bitterness toward the United States would grow. Moreover, as the rest of the world, including Europe, is neither willing nor able to take up the task of collective security on its own, the mission of preserving international security could end up facing two opposite but equally challenging predicaments: too much concentration or too much diffusion of power. In the first instance, the United States alone would be more or less in charge of global security, with the various dangers and limitations mentioned before. In the second instance, left to the care of regional hegemons, *international* order could remain largely neglected.

The gap between solidarity and security, and the discrepancy of incentives, means, and commitment that the gap generates are not as absolute and immutable as is usually assumed in academia and policy circles. International solidarity is about doing the right thing; but through the recognition and implementation of rights and duties in a public policy framework that is legally imposed (constitutionally or legislatively), solidarity can also bring the international realm closer to enjoying a key advantage of the rule of law—security. These two aspects are mutually reinforcing: The more actors identify with the moral dimension of solidarity, and the more solidarity is implemented through a public policy framework, the more it contributes to security. Conversely, to ignore solidarity is to invite violence. If the powerless have an opportunity to lash out, they will do so. Hence, solidarity is strategically important for the stability and well-being of a community and its members, disenfranchised and elite alike.

Provided that the implementation of solidarity's entitlements does not generate a complacent attitude, all people in all countries can share in and gain from the sense of security, the "tranquility of spirit," that solidarity as part of the rule of law provides.[28] The dovetailing of solidarity and security helps "secure security" materially and psychologically, because it both presupposes and brings about the embedding of power into legitimacy. As Rousseau famously said, "[t]he strongest is never strong enough to be always the master, unless he transforms strength into right, and obedience into duty."[29] The mutual dependency associated with the intertwining of rights and duties creates a structure of cooperative solidarity among actors. This process is also the one by which legitimacy of power is achieved.

The continuum among security, solidarity, and legitimacy—at the national and international levels—is especially relevant in the contemporary political context, in which democratic values have acquired much importance in defining the normative guidelines of good governance. These values infuse power with legitimacy (and, hence, security) through the imperative to deliver key services that make up a public good. These goods, in turn, are part and parcel of solidarity and centrally structure the community. Most advanced liberal-capitalist democracies have adhered to such a public policy rationale for decades. Yet the lesson of linking social stability, the legitimacy of power, and the distribution of collective goods seems quite lost on the international community. The European project is unlikely to happen on a global scale for any foreseeable future. A gap will therefore remain between solidarity and security at the international level. Still, it is imperative for nation-states to work on closing the gap as much as possible. But because no state alone has the political, normative, and financial resources to bridge the gap between solidarity and security–between power and legitimacy—at the international level, we are left to rely on inchoate UN mandates and insufficient rationales for multilateral interventions. Yet for all their limitations, they are still the best tools at our disposal to envision and implement the international rule of law. Building on the acknowledgment of the need to bring solidarity and security closer, another instrument of change and progress for the international rule of law is to enhance the democratic character of international life's normative framework.

Multilateral Norms of Democratic Empowerment and the Enhancement of International Solidarity

The more challenging it is for the United Nations and multilateralism to address international crises, the more the following questions come to the fore: How to balance the status quo and change in the international order? Where to place the cutoff point between what new tasks can be added to the UN and multilateral agendas, and what must be left out? To what extent should the international community be firm or flexible in the interpretation and implementation of the United Nations' multilateralist values and goals so that they are not betrayed and so that member states, regardless of their different approaches, stay on board and play an active role in multilateral endeavors? Examining what needs to be changed at the normative level of international life to strengthen the incentive for states to embrace international solidarity helps in the search for answers to these questions. Such an examination entails taking seriously and promoting the responsibilities and policy implications embedded in the legitimacy and empowerment qualities of the international principles at the core of multilateralism, particularly of those associated with democratic values. This in turn requires exploring the meaning and consequences of the following ideas.

Multilateralism's leitmotif is about constantly envisioning and implementing a system of international legitimacy. It is about defining and redefining the rules of the game in the socialization of international life. In its coordination of relations and cooperation among states on the basis of general principles, multilateralism implicitly strives for nothing less than the validation of the rule of law at the international level. The key tenets of collective security are sovereign equality of states, nonintervention in the internal or external affairs of other states, self-determination of peoples, prohibition of the threat or use of force, peaceful settlement of disputes, respect for human rights, and international cooperation.

These principles define what is possible and what is prohibited in multilateral interventions. They also express the value-ideals that significant actors—states and, increasingly, nonstate actors (including individuals)—consider indispensable in the quest for a workable and equitable international system, one that is conducive to their representation and participation. These principles are also meant to regulate states' interactions in a consensual fashion that favors consistency and thus predictability in their relations; in doing so, the principles pursue the overall coherence of multilateralism and the framework of international legitimacy that it attempts to fortify.[30]

Within the framework of international legitimacy, multilateralism is a system of empowerment. The principles that regulate the interactions of states engaged in multilateral action enable coordination and cooperation among them in order to empower them to act in the international realm. Only within such a multilateral system are states willing to enter into collective coordination and cooperation and to be constrained by it, including the relative surrender of part of their sovereignty in decision making and action.

In the *best* conditions, multilateralism as a goal-oriented structure of cooperation among states brings about some benefits of empowerment. The first is the move away from a primarily zero-sum (and short-term) approach in dealing with other states. Multilateral empowerment envisions reiterated interactions that require sustained recognition and accommodation of the interests of all. This in turn brings about a second empowering element: It makes the pursuit of self-interest inclusive, which has systemic and temporal dimensions. The systemic dimension can be summarized as follows: The minimization of losses that multilateral cooperation provides for most states creates a collective good in the international realm. The temporal dimension of multilateral empowerment resides in states' ability to anticipate the opportunities associated with some sense of community and a collective future—the dividends that multilateral empowerment generates. In a market context, multilateral cooperation is what brings states together to share in the exchange of a collective good.

The empowering benefits of multilateralism take place at two levels. The first deals with the crucial but rather elementary goals of securing the existence and coexistence of states: In the multilateral domain of collective security, sovereign equality of states, prohibition of the threat or use of force, and nonintervention in the affairs of other states are principles that outline the sine qua non of states' existence and coexistence. The second empowerment level has a more qualified character: the quality of empowerment *within* states. Principles that are concerned with the democratic aspects of multilateralism, such as respect for human rights, self-determination of peoples, and national sovereignty (as understood and interpreted in connection with popular sovereignty and human rights), fall into this category.

Multilateralism's interplay of legitimacy and empowerment takes place through an intertwining of international rights and obligations that express, defend, and promote the principles at the core of multilateralism and prescribe the code of conduct that states ought to follow. Some of these rights and obligations echo the basic goals of the existence and coexistence of states. In the area of collective security, prohibitions against the threat or use of force and adhering to the principle of nonintervention in the affairs of other states have been by and large either restrictive (the imperative not to infringe upon other states' prerogatives) or reactive (the imperative to redress a violation). To some extent, the Bush administration's pre-emption doctrine has changed this: By lowering the threshold of threat, it has introduced a proactive dimension.[31]

The rights and obligations deriving from the principles dealing with the democratic aspects of multilateralism—namely, self-determination and respect for human rights—have been challenging from the start. In a world marked by a diversity of cultures and political systems (let alone levels of development), agreeing on where human rights begin and where they end (including, for example, agreeing on where to draw the line between human rights and individual rights) and, consequently, assessing whether or not they are violated (and to what extent) has never been easy for the international community; deciding what to do about human rights violations is even more problematic. In this respect, the debates that have taken place around the world since the early 1990s concerning humanitarian crises and humanitarian interventions show how unsettling the issue has been. The challenge is only destined to grow as the increasing recognition of the individual as actor in the international system creates more and more pressure on the international community to formulate clear standards for making such assessments.

Wanting to have it both ways—that is to say, trying to maximize multilateral benefits and minimize multilateral constraints, to focus on the self-serving multilateral aspects and disregard those that are costly—is tempting for all states. Their dual identity as independent states (sovereign entities) and member states (entities embedded in multilateral networks) naturally encourages them to want it both ways. The temptation is especially strong for powerful countries and for those at the lower end of the international distribution of power, whose unprivileged situation can induce their leaders to feel entitled to rights and exempt from responsibilities and duties. However, when the temptation takes over multilateral relations, the sense of reciprocity that is supposed to be at the core of multilateralism may disappear—and with it, multilateralism itself. Consistency—that is to say, avoiding as much as possible an à la carte approach to the interpretation and implementation of general principles and the rights and obligations associated with them—is essential to the credibility and socializing role of multilateralism.

That said, a certain level of inconsistency is probably unavoidable. Furthermore, noncompliance with the rules and regulations of multilateral regimes does not erode support for and functioning of multilateral relations as long as it remains marginal and rather isolated and within the limits of acceptable and, at times, required flexibility. Nevertheless, there is a threshold of tolerance for such inconsistency: It must be justifiable—that is, motivated by factors that are disconnected as little as possible from the reasons and guidelines offered by multilateral rights and obligations. For instance, it is consistent, and therefore acceptable, to take action against country X to defend human rights and not to do so against country Y based on the gravity of the respective situations, with one satisfying the threshold justifying action and the other not. But the inconsistency is not justified if two similar situations generate different responses because of self-serving considerations.

Furthermore, the normative pluralism of multilateralism's supporting principles does not facilitate consistency; the fact that these principles are both compatible and competitive accounts for this situation. For example, upholding the principles of both nonintervention in the affairs of states and respect for human rights can be challenging; and yet the integrative aim of multilateralism makes it imperative that these principles cohabit. Otherwise, the normative framework of legitimacy and empowerment that such principles seek to convey and advance runs the risk of being even weaker than it is already.

When decision makers keep in mind that following the injunction of a given principle should not lead them to ignore entirely the injunctions of others, it helps them address the quandary. More important, though, the connection between the relationships of power shaping the international system and the international principles' priorities at a given time helps decision makers address the quandary. During the Cold War, the international community, influenced by the environment of superpower competition and "bipolycentrism," emphasized the basic concerns of multilateral legitimacy and empowerment in acknowledging the existence and coexistence of states. In the aftermath of the Cold War, the removal of strategic competition, while not getting rid of the primacy of the national level and of basic multilateral legitimacy and strategic empowerment considerations, made it possible to place more emphasis on human rights and humanitarian issues. It brought to the fore considerations of *democratic* legitimacy and empowerment: States are no longer the sole or primary actors and rights carriers at the international level. The rights that they enjoy and the duties and responsibilities that fall upon them derive more from the individual level, from their ability to respect and fulfill individual and human rights.

Although this new emphasis does not fundamentally affect the international complex of principles regarding the coexistence of states, it has a bearing on the issue of international intervention in the name of human rights. In this international environment, the rights of states, especially those connected closely with the principle of sovereignty and noninterference, become conditional, and they depend partly on the willingness and capacity of states (specifically, of the government or regime in power) to fulfill the duties and responsibilities that come with democratic rights, particularly human rights. The qualification (conditionality) of rights of states does not amount to advocating the liquidation and disappearance of these rights, or of nations themselves. Nation-states will remain one of the cornerstones of international life and of the attempts to socialize it. Their rights constitute an enduring value and a key element of the socialization of international life, international legitimacy, and empowerment. Nevertheless, by no longer making the basic requirements of existence and coexistence of nation-states the sole pillar of international socialization, the conditionality of rights of states deepens the impact of democratic legitimacy and empowerment within and among nations.

The transformation of quasi-absolute rights into qualified and, therefore, challengeable rights concerns primarily countries with human rights track records that do not satisfy any sort of international measures.[32] In such a context, sovereignty ceases to be a "refuge for scoundrels." For example, the military intervention in Kosovo in the spring of 1999 may have been illegal (lacking a proper endorsement from the UN Security Council), but the authoritarian character of Slobodan Milosevic's regime and the denial of basic individual rights to ethnic Albanian Kosovars did much to undermine the Federal Republic of Yugoslavia's legitimacy. The horrific nature of Saddam Hussein's rule went a long way beyond the putative WMD threat in justifying the Bush administration's belief that it was authorized to attack Baghdad. It also encouraged the international community to go along with the ouster of the Baathist regime even while it denounced the false pretense on which the war was launched. As such, Saddam Hussein's authoritarian regime not only undermined its own political legitimacy but also endangered Iraqi state sovereignty.

This shows that the conditionality of the rights of states, by bringing the failed or failing among them under scrutiny, is a form of accountability that seeks to correct their social and political pathologies. Equally important, this also shows how such conditionality is not meant to be unidirectional or give cartes blanches to developed and powerful countries. Although it may open the door to a range of options for international measures by Western democratic nations to address mass human rights violations in a given country (usually, if not always, in the Third World), the conditionality of rights introduces scrutiny over them as well.

The salient possibility emerging from the human rights dimension of multilateralism and its development is that international intervention becomes a *viable* option, albeit a constraining one. The constraints, partly originating in "just war" theory and partly residing in demands associated with multilateral legitimacy, can be described as follows: The violations must be proved (evidentiary grounds) to justify an encroachment on sovereignty. The goal of the intervention clearly has to be the ending of the crisis. The ways in which action is taken have to be as much as possible in line with multilateral requirements; in the present institutional arrangement of multilateralism, this calls upon the UN Security Council to provide legality and legitimacy to the intervention and to outline its modalities. The modalities of intervention (i.e., the means) must be proportional to the crisis situation, with force being the last resort and used only with precaution. Finally, there must be a reasonable chance that the consequences of (military) action will not be worse than inaction.[33]

Member states, regardless of their power and the nature of their regime, cannot ignore these guidelines. The guidelines are crucial because today, more than ever, the legitimacy and empowerment values with which most identify make overriding sovereignty justifiable only in very specific circumstances. It is justifiable not for the advantages that a state could gain from it, but when the well-being of people is truly at stake. Basic security and human rights represent the minimum desire of people the world over. When they are willing and eager to let the international community help protect this desideratum, particularly when local governments have a role in its systematic violation, it is on the condition that the intervention will not advantage any of the intervening powers. The debates of the 1990s concerning humanitarian interventions and those of 2003 regarding the war in Iraq put this condition in stark relief. Ultimately, whether or not powerful democratic Western nations are consistent with and abide by the constraints of multilateralism, their foreign policies have a global impact, shaping the extent and limits of the validity of their claims to be the models, repositories, and key instruments of democratic legitimacy and empowerment, nationally and internationally. Their collective attitude and actions serve as an indication of the extent to which the world should or should not believe and embrace such claims and the international system they underwrite.

INTERNATIONAL ACTORS AND THE ENHANCEMENT OF INTERNATIONAL SOLIDARITY

Before turning to what changes in the foreign policy of the most important international actor—the United States—would help consolidate the agenda of international solidarity and international security, let us touch upon some of the adjustments required of the following actors: the United Nations and its member states, regional organizations, and NGOs.

The United Nations is an organization that is politically important and at the same time, politically weak. This duality accounts for both its central role in world affairs and its inability to play it well and decisively. The significant UN involvement in peace operations activities and its rather disappointing results are a case in point. Although this reality is unlikely to change profoundly in the coming years, a number of targeted adjustments could help the United Nations to better fulfill its global mandates in bringing international security and international solidarity closer together. Improvement of the functioning of peacekeeping operations, the international civil service, and the Security Council are among the much-needed adjustments.

Peace operations will continue to be one of the most visible areas of activity of the United Nations, and one in which it can have an impact. The lessons learned in the 1990s, brought together in the *Report of the Panel on United Nations Peace Operations* and acted upon in its implementation, have made it possible to achieve tangible progress.[34] In this regard, as seen earlier in this chapter, the creation of a significant number of posts in the Department of Peacekeeping Operations in the late 1990s and early 2000s has helped considerably.[35] Yet more needs to be done, especially considering that the demands of peacekeeping operations are growing in scale. The surge in peacekeeping activity raised the total number of peacekeepers in October 2004 to 54,200; of civilian police, to 5,900; and of civilian staff, to 11,600.[36] By the fall of 2005, the eighteen peace operations deployed around the world constituted 83,000 troops, police, and civilian personnel, out of an authorized capacity of 87,250—a fivefold increase in field personnel since 2000; by the fall of 2006, the number increased to 93,000 men and women.[37] Moreover, peacekeeping demands are growing in complexity. With many of their tasks increasingly focusing on peacebuilding in postconflict transitions, peace operations are now linked to longer-term social and economic development approaches, which presuppose integrated programs from both within and outside the UN system.

Appearing before the Fourth Committee of the UN General Assembly in the fall of 2004, Under Secretary-General for Peacekeeping Operations Jean-Marie Guéhenno identified two areas that require urgent attention:[38] First, the need to get the right capabilities on the ground in time to implement the mandates of peace operations, including troops, specialized components, and civilian police and other personnel. Finding those capabilities can mean the difference between success and failure for a peace operation; the right capabilities must be available not only over the duration of the mission but also in the early, crucial phase of the deployment. The second area of priority relates to how these capabilities are best organized on the ground and how DPKO officials "integrate and rationalize the joint efforts of the UN system and the rest of the international community to assist the consolidation of a sustainable peace."[39] Addressing the issues of integration and rationalization entail in particular solving the discrepancy between the financing of different activities in today's complex peace operations. Certain security activities are indeed traditionally covered by assessed contributions, while reconstruction or development activity must rely on voluntary contributions; yet the success of a peace process depends on both. As Guéhenno noted, "peacekeeping budgets today will largely cover the disarmament and demobilization costs of former combatants but not activities designed to reintegrate them or the large numbers of women and girls associated with the fighting forces, back into society."[40] Making sure that the development programs' budgets do not come late, or are incomplete, is thus necessary to avoid unmet expectations and failure. "We run the leanest field operations organization in the world," concluded Guéhenno. "Our personnel in the field—your troops and police—operate in many instances on a more-or-less permanent state of shortfall."[41] Two years later, in his remarks before the Fourth Committee on the status of peacekeeping operations' personnel, doctrine, organization, and resources, Guéhenno, while recognizing tangible improvements in planning and deploying peacekeeping operations, indicated that the global increase in the demand for peacekeeping had created a new urgency.[42]

The United Nations has the reputation of being a huge bureaucracy, but in actuality it is understaffed, considering the array of tasks it handles. In 2005, the number of people employed worldwide by the United Nations in all capacities—nearly 16,000 people by the UN Secretariat (the UN Secretariat employs some 7,750 staff members under the regular budget, and some 8,230 under special funding) and some 63,450 by the entire UN system, including its related programs and specialized agencies—was remarkably small for an organization engaged on a global scale in promoting peace, furthering development, and organizing humanitarian relief.[43] Compare these figures with the U.S. federal government, which employs more than 89,000 civilians overseas alone.[44]

With so meager a staff (and budget), can the United Nations do its job as well as it should? Probably not. In addition to its limited size, the UN workforce has come to suffer from two other impediments: instability and low institutionalization of the international civil service (with short-term contracts and truncated career tracks becoming the rule rather than the exception) and poor human resources management.

Regarding the first problem, after decades of "cushy" job security, the UN civil service is growing rather unstable, which, combined with a shortage of personnel, tends to lead to a "UN work style" that often amounts to no more than damage control (if even that). To work better, the international civil service, like any federal bureaucracy, should strike a balance between too much security (which invites complacency) and too much insecurity (which generates paralysis). Improving human resources would certainly go a long way in helping to achieve this goal. All too often, indeed, the problems created by the United Nations' shortage of personnel and what is now an unstable international civil service are furthered by an inability to make the most of the human resources available.[45] Bad human resources management makes it also all the more difficult to make the case for the need to create more positions at the United Nations. To approach the UN reform process with the aim of producing real and concrete changes and results (with the sustained effort, stamina, imagination, and investments that this presupposes) would be a welcome move.[46]

The changes required from the Security Council concern the political side of the United Nations. As noted throughout this study, since the early

1990s the role played by the UN Security Council has been both conservative and progressive. Although national considerations and preferences have tended to prevail over internationalist concerns, the dilemmas in which the deliberations, decisions, and actions of the Security Council were framed showed progress in realizing the sense of international solidarity and responsibility.

Instead of moving back to a traditional understanding and handling of international politics and crises, the Security Council should continue to push further the internationalist dimension that it developed in the 1990s: The Council should give more recognition to the importance of the *democratic* character of multilateralism. Without renouncing the basic requirements of legitimacy and empowerment, it should allow more room for democratic imperatives at the international level.

Such a clearinghouse role in favor of international democratic legitimacy and empowerment presupposes in particular that the leading democratic powers in the Security Council are acutely aware of the responsibilities that their permanent status and their stated commitment to democratic values impose on the Council's formation of mandates. Because they have so much power, they also have a great deal of responsibility, especially with regard to democratic values and imperatives. This calls for them to view multilateral obligations as a set of obligations beyond the national realm. Such a perspective would allow the Security Council to help bridge the gap that continues to separate it from the United Nations' ultimate clientele and source of legitimacy: the world's people. In this context, it is rather disappointing to see that the latest debates on the reform of the Security Council at the September 2005 World Summit were unable to include the prospect of new permanent members and engineer a vision of a Security Council more responsive to more people's needs. Analysts and concerned observers of the world body hold out the hope that the envisioned collaboration between the Security Council and the newly established UN Peacebuilding Commission will get the Council more involved in the reconstruction of postconflict societies and development in general—and thus in the improvement of the conditions of those who need help the most.[47]

Considering the interstate structure of the current world architecture, UN member states have a critical role to play in enhancing international solidarity. Two types of change are required: first, the democratization of states and its implications for the enhancement of international solidarity; second, the improvement of member states' collective attitude toward their responsibility vis-à-vis the United Nations and the international community that it represents.

More "waves" of democratization would certainly have a positive effect on international solidarity. The dynamics of universal solidarity that democratic values introduce at the national level have a tremendous potential to spread beyond borders and reach out and shape the international realm and its framework of legitimacy. The primacy of the national realm and competition among countries (including economic competition, as the side-effects of globalization show) may impede this global democratic mechanism, but it cannot deny it altogether. Also, national democratic leaders are likely to take the demands of international solidarity more seriously than their non-democratic counterparts in other countries, if only for the reason that the latter project into the international realm the same type of paranoia that structures their human and political vision and their national policies. Provided that it is not simply a rhetorical discourse, democratization also encourages nation-states' social, economic, and political integration: Doing well nationally puts countries, at least in principle, in a position to do "good" internationally. Success and the sense of security that it provides allow countries and their leaders to be open to international solidarity. The Nordic countries are a case in point.

The further spread of democratization can ease states' dual-identity problem—with one side leading them to conform to multilateral requirements and imperatives, and the other encouraging them to try to evade them as much as possible. If multilateralism is a key tool in constructing a general will at the global level, it can happen only if each state sees the overall benefit of transcending particular interests. Democratization, with its focus on the creation and equitable distribution of public goods, can help to achieve this universalization of interests. Upon this condition rests the possibility of countries coming together and reaping the benefits of collective action and long-term cooperation—and, also, the possibility for the United Nations to be in a stronger position in its frequent competition with other international actors, such as regional and nongovernmental organizations.

Member states best serve the United Nations when they are engaged with and supportive of it, while respecting it as much as possible. Any alignment or perception of alignment of the United Nations with the specific interests of a member state, especially a powerful member state, can undermine its credibility globally and its ability to work on the behalf of the international community. This basic requirement serves as a starting point for the kind of attitude that member states outside the realm of the United States could adopt to help the United Nations better assert its status at the service of the international community.

European countries can help in three ways. First, although Europeans are always eager to present themselves as the most committed to internationalist multilateral policies (in the context of the United Nations and other international organizations), in reality this commitment is often hampered by a strong attachment to the status quo. Europe's insistence on negotiated solutions is at times a way of hiding its uneasiness with rapid and drastic change. This approach must be reconsidered. Second, there is a reluctance among Europeans to call upon decisive means to solve a crisis. If the United States is too eager to use force in certain situations, Europe's diffidence in doing so is a limitation that must be addressed. (One positive sign that it is beginning to be addressed is that the European Union is developing a military capacity—notably, the European Union Military Staff, which had already undertaken a number of tasks by the end of 2005, including early warning, situation awareness, and strategic planning within the framework of "out of area" crisis management and peacekeeping.[48]) Third, and perhaps most important, Europe can play a significant role in helping to build bridges between the United States and the rest of the world. It could bring to the United States the concerns of the developing countries and vice versa.[49]

Developing countries also have a role to play in the enhancement of international solidarity, which presupposes their going beyond the "victim's entitlement" positions they frequently adopt. For the purposes of enhancing solidarity, it is not enough for Third World countries simply to be either at the receiving end of international initiatives or in a reactive mode to them. Their international projection of the image of victimized countries may contain an emotive trigger for more foreign assistance, but it also perpetuates an unproductive dependency path. Dependency is not synonymous with solidarity—far from it. Fulfilling national responsibilities is essential to their contribution to a better United Nations and international system. A great deal of progress will have been made when rulers in the developing world understand that taking the interests of their people truly to heart (respecting their civil, political, economic, and social rights) is the best way to defend the national interest of their countries as well as to ensure their meaningful participation in the international community. Similar rationales—particularly in their implications for international democratic solidarity—can be found in the good governance criteria that inform the assessments of the International Monetary Fund, the World Bank, and the United States' Millennium Challenge Account program for the developing world.

Asian countries have a key role to play in terms of international solidarity. To be sure, the conceptual, normative, political, and operational management of the international realm is still very much a transatlantic affair. But if the United Nations' mandates are to become truly global (or globalized), Asia must be encouraged to bring its comparative advantage into multilateral affairs. The various ways in which it is a bridge between developing and developed countries, the West and the non-West, and the fact that it is (with Europe and the United States) one of the models of industrialization and global trade puts Asia in an ideal position.

In this regard, one has to concede that the issue of China in such a regional future of enhancing international solidarity is a paradox.[50] It is an economic powerhouse among the region's rapidly industrializing economies, and it has taken up the slack in flagging peacekeeping deployments around the world, particularly in Africa.[51] But its commitment to international *democratic* solidarity is problematic: Besides the speculation on the geo-economic motivations for China's involvement in African UN peacekeeping operations, its track record of private-sector initiatives on the continent run the risk of being tarnished by cozy relationships with repressive regimes.

The trend in recent years has been to give more responsibilities to regional organizations in the handling of collective security and humanitarian crises. The role played by NATO in the Balkans and, later on, in Afghanistan illustrates this trend. The operational limitations of the United Nations account for much of this tendency. Subcontracting matters of collective security to regional organizations is helpful and useful; however, it also creates problems. Because of the polemics surrounding how the NATO bombing campaign was conducted in Kosovo, many of these problems revolved around the question of whether or not a UN authorization is required for regional organizations (under the UN Charter's Chapter VIII) to take action. Yet besides this question, there are even more critical issues: What will happen to areas of conflict that fall outside of the purview and range of action of regional organizations? What will happen in Africa, in particular, whose regional and subregional organizations are too weak and certainly not operational enough to make a difference? Is the United Nations going to be led to explicitly endorse a laissez-faire policy for more "coalitions of the willing"? If so, what will become of international solidarity, let alone global security?

Consequently, the international community cannot view regional organizations as a way to free itself from its global responsibilities. It cannot afford to view NATO as a way to dovetail international solidarity and international security, for NATO is a regional organization. The capabilities that NATO encompasses, the ways it has been used, and the autonomy that it has demonstrated on some occasions have an exceptional character, and other regional organizations should not be expected to replicate it. If regional organizations can have a role in global security and international solidarity entailing the use of force, such force should take place through a division of labor considered within the framework of the United Nations.

What about NGOs and their relations with other international actors? The relationships between states and NGOs, as well as those between the United Nations and NGOs, should be conceived as an asset to establish a collaboration that builds on their respective strengths and a way to obtain better results in the area of international solidarity. NGOs have what states and international organizations are missing in terms of flexibility and ability to act quickly in zones of conflict. What is out of reach for nongovernmental organizations, particularly when it comes to scope of resources (let alone the use of force), is accessible to entities such as states and international organizations. Their complementary character indicates that any attempt to enhance an internationalist agenda cannot, in the end, be achieved by a logic of "either/or." The internationalist agenda must try to benefit from the various comparative advantages of international actors and create synergies among them.[52]

The Need for Change in the Worldview of America's Political Leaders

Since the end of the Cold War, the power and international influence of the United States have been unparalleled—to the point that, at the international level, most change begins and ends with the remaining superpower. Thus, it seems appropriate to conclude this chapter by reflecting on the changes required in U.S. foreign policy so that it can continue to make a positive, effective contribution to the socialization of international life. Bringing closer together power and legitimacy, and solidarity and security, at the international level requires at least several fundamental changes in U.S. foreign policy: finding a better balance between national and international interests; coming to terms with the foreign policy implications of American democratic values; exercising leadership within multilateral constraints; overcoming the parochial characteristics of U.S. foreign policy; and facilitating the learning ability of the U.S. foreign policy community regarding the changes required.

Calling for a better balance between national and international interests does not imply that U.S. foreign policy has so far ignored the importance of this balance and has not tried to attain it. The U.S. contribution to the development of multilateralism and the United Nations has been the result of trying to achieve such a balance. Yet somehow, America's belief in its exceptionalism, which has reached new heights since the beginning of the twenty-first century, leads it to view other countries' national interests as somehow illegitimate. This belief is expressed, as well as fueled, by both contradictory and complementary feelings. America's sense of superiority and entitlement, insecurity and paranoia, self-involvement and righteousness sustain its liberal nationalism and patriotism. The national interest is the obsessive, almost neurotic, hallmark of American foreign policy. Consequently, it has also come to regard the international interest, particularly embodied in multilateralism, as of no great concern. The American tendency has been to make multilateral discourse and practices serve its national interest.

The goal here is not to advocate a thorough reconsideration of American foreign policy, in which the international interest would become the primary concern. That is neither possible nor desirable. However, changes have to be introduced to temper the state-centric character of the United States' power projection. The sole-superpower status of America renders necessary the achievement of a better balance between national and international interests. American preponderance in the world makes it difficult to conduct a foreign policy first and foremost in the name of the U.S. national interest. Unlike the rather inconsequential international impact of a country at the low end of the distribution of power, the overwhelming international influence of the sole superpower is certain to affect other nations tremendously.[53] It is also likely to hurt them when it is principally guided by self-interest. Moreover, the primary attention given to its own national interest creates an imbalance that tends to empty multilateralism of its meaning and effectiveness. This endangers the interests of all states, including those of the United States.

The sheer amount of power that America enjoys allows it to believe that not only can it get away with adopting an à la carte approach to multilateralism in service to the international interest, but that in doing so it can also maximize its gains in international collaboration. That calculation is faulty because the United States, in its own way, is as much in need of multilateralism, of taking into account international interest, as other powers. Arguably, as a superpower, it is even more in need of multilateralism. To think otherwise is to misjudge how to make the most of U.S. power. A self-serving conception and discretionary use of multilateral mechanisms and obligations tends to discredit the system of international legitimacy that multilateralism seeks to provide. In this context, the United States deprives itself of one of the main instruments at its disposal to achieve what should be its principal goal: to generate a consensus based on its preponderance. It deprives itself of the possibility of making its preponderance part of a system of international justice and, thus, being considered legitimate by other countries; it deprives itself of having a foreign policy that is universally viewed as an expression and tool of international legitimacy.

The type of adjustment necessary to bring a better balance between national and international interests requires much moral and political courage. The extent of change that it implies also involves a visionary understanding of the international system and its evolution, if not a leap of faith. After all, the balance between national and international interests is anything but easy. The uncertainty at the core of the balance is deepened by the fact that the international distribution of power is inherently unstable. There is no historical determinism guaranteeing that the superpower of today will remain so tomorrow. If the United States is uncertain about payoffs on multilateral investments, why would it commit to an improbable future that could mean the demise of the current benefits that it gets out of being the sole superpower? The answer, of course, is that the status of the United States democratic superpower requires it.

Democratic values are extremely effective tools for establishing contemporary international legitimacy. Because they are based upon a sense of universality and equality, and because they coalesce around the peculiarly modern notion of progress—a betterment of people's condition—as one of their main goals, they are powerfully inspirational. By aiming to set individuals and countries on an equal footing, such values provide the substance—and, thus, the procedures—for imagining and implementing a structured international order in which the various actors involved can find an equal and effective place.[54] Nevertheless, for these values not to be a tool of neo-imperial political and cultural expansion, for them not to trigger violence from people feeling alienated and deceived, for them not to be divisive and a source of insecurity, they must be taken seriously. To take these values seriously presupposes ensuring that democratic values are neither underutilized nor instrumentalized, and it requires abiding by their progressive, inclusive character. This means encouraging the spread of those principles and mechanisms at the heart of the democratic creed, such as equality, without imposing a particular model for those values' inculcation.[55]

Although living up to democratic expectations at the international level is even more demanding than at the national level, America has to come to terms with the political and policy implications—and the responsibilities—brought about by being not only the sole superpower but also a *democratic* superpower. Not doing so will put the liberal structure of the international system, and the liberal values and ideas at its foundation, at risk of losing their claims to validity. Hence the necessity to ensure that calling upon democratic values in the international setting is not a disguise for universalizing an undemocratic hegemony.

Establishing a better balance between national and international interests and welcoming the foreign policy implications of being a democratic superpower relate to multilateralism in a constructive manner. This does not imply that America should give up its position of leadership and become a regular actor: Multilateralism does not work without leadership. Without leadership, the different perspectives that infuse multilateral collaboration are likely to cancel each other out and become a paralyzing factor. Multilateralism requires that a country, or a group of countries, points the direction for others to coalesce around a plan. From this perspective, the United States must mobilize its leadership potential in the international realm while acknowledging three elements.

First, international cooperation is not unidirectional. It cannot be called upon by the hegemon when viewed as useful and disregarded when considered inconvenient. Multilateral obligations must be upheld by all parties, and especially by the most powerful of them. Second, the United States must understand that leadership in multilateralism is not exercised without the consent of other countries; on the contrary, it builds upon consent. Although multilateralism does not exclude the resort to coercion and force in certain circumstances, it establishes the search for consent as an important way to regulate the international system. Third, for countries to join in multilateralism constructively means that the United States should not use its powers exclusively as bargaining chips and opportunities to advance its interests.

These requirements suggest that American preponderance should be used to favor an international system of reciprocity structured around rights that are universal and serve as the basis for the compatible plurality of views among and within nations. They suggest that the United States should live up to the expectations that its own democratic values and the most progressive aspects of its foreign policy, let alone political prudence, demand in order to satisfy any sort of global accountability.

For this to happen, U.S. foreign policy must overcome its parochialism, or what can be called "global provincialism," which is visible not only when its national interest is at stake but also when it is not at stake, as the story of the 1990s illustrates. The need for an internationalization of U.S. foreign policy calls for its political leaders to revisit their traditional positions on the role of America in the world. In this regard, despite differences between the foreign policy attitudes of Democrats and Republicans, they share a narrow conception of the U.S. national interest that is untenable in the contemporary international milieu.

Although willing to intellectually recognize the new complexities—the possibilities and constraints—of the post–Cold War era, Democrats tend to have difficulty coming up with a foreign policy grand strategy that can accommodate these new complexities. In addition, they have been, on the whole, reticent in advocating moral and political discipline and investing the moral and political capital that is needed at home to make the case for a more internationalist American foreign policy and to deliver it in zones of conflict. The tentative foreign policy of the Clinton administration in connection with the international interventions of the 1990s, in Bosnia and Rwanda in particular, serves as a case in point. The Democratic administration was eager to have Americans think that it was doing its best to end the humanitarian crises, but it was unwilling to put itself on the line by taking decisive action and extending a strong sense of international solidarity at the peak of the conflicts.

As for Republicans, they are wary of having a conception of an American national interest that admits an international interest into U.S. foreign policy in a significant way. This was the case throughout the 1990s, and it applies even more so to the 2000s. Although George W. Bush, at times with a tone slightly reminiscent of Ronald Reagan, speaks a great deal of the need to spread democracy, it is difficult to believe that he and his foreign policy team had the interest of Iraq and its people foremost in mind when the United States launched the war in March 2003.[56] Surely, the Republican attitude toward the world has its foreign policy virtues. Its singleness of purpose, essentially shaped by U.S. national interest, can make the deliberation and decision-making processes, and action, rather effective. However, a unidirectional and reactive approach to world order is perhaps most effective in aggravating dangerous challenges beyond America's shores rather than in attenuating them.

The prospects of the U.S. foreign policy establishment to change its perspective depends on two factors, one international and one domestic. The international factor resides in the capacity of U.S. allies to convey to America the need for change, both for its own sake and for that of the international order. The internal factor involves a less partisan and more conflict resolution–oriented training of policymakers in the areas of international affairs. The study and teaching of international relations in American universities, instead of being the celebration and legitimization of

American hegemony, could be the defining moment for an examination of and reflection on the international responsibilities of the United States as the world's democratic leader.

In that regard, perhaps America's greatest responsibility is acknowledging that it cannot manage all the world's humanitarian crises on its own. Nor should it, for it has partners in this burgeoning endeavor. International solidarity implies that America can rely on its transatlantic allies not only to share the burden of multilateral interventions, but also to make such multilateral responses more effective. Yet as long as American leadership is wedded to the realist paradigm, assessing the worthiness of international interventions according to narrowly defined national interests means that the prospects for the consolidation of international solidarity and the advancement of the international rule of law seem more and more remote.

But, again, perhaps this is looking at the wrong end of the problem. The fundamental choice in America's perspective on its role in the world as the lone superpower should not be cast in terms of liberal internationalism or the bald national interest of the realist paradigm. All foreign policies are based on national interests, just as the international order is largely nation-centric. However, national interests do indeed change, especially in light of new threats and challenges to the advancement of fundamental national interests, such as mere national survival in a hostile global environment. With such a reassessment of national interests comes a similar reassessment of modalities to manage the new threats and challenges in the service of advancing those interests.

What has come to be called "progressive" or "liberal" realism seeks to reframe U.S. national interests in the realist paradigm to account for these new threats and challenges.[57] Acknowledging the preponderance of national interests in the international realm, Robert Wright points to the need for such reframing:

> Progressive realism begins with a cardinal doctrine of traditional realism: the purpose of American foreign policy is to serve American interests. . . . But these days, serving American interests means abandoning another traditional belief of realists—that so long as foreign governments don't endanger American interests on the geopolitical chessboard, their domestic affairs don't concern us. In an age when Americans are threatened by overseas bioweapons labs and outbreaks of flu, by Chinese pollution that enters lungs in Oregon, by imploding African states that could turn into terrorist havens, by authoritarian Arab governments that push young men toward radicalism, the classic realist indifference to the interiors of nations is untenable.[58]

Such a reframing of national interests necessarily relies on international organizations to meet the new threats and challenges. In fact, the pre-scriptive dimension of such a reframed realist paradigm endorses the strengthening of multilateral bonds: "We need multilateral structures capable of decisively forceful intervention and nation building—ideally under the auspices of the United Nations, which has more global legiti-macy than other candidates. America should lead in building these struc-tures and thereafter contribute its share, but only its share. To some extent, the nurturing of international institutions and solid international law is simple thrift."[59]

America would be well advised to not lose sight of the basic consider-ations touched upon here. The ability to make American preponderance less a source of insecurity for the United States and the world depends to a great extent on keeping in mind these basic considerations when formulat-ing foreign policy and domestic policy that has international ramifications. In doing so, America's political leaders would display a global foreign policy commensurate to the country's nature, role, and responsibilities as a demo-cratic superpower.

Of course, conceiving, designing, and implementing a grand strategy along the lines of traditional foreign policy concerns is simpler. Addressing reality from a traditional point of view alone—that of the U.S. national interest—dispenses with the normative and logistical conundrums of bringing together disparate perspectives to work on international problems in a multilateral setting. Yet an American foreign-policy grand strategy, integrating a plurality of perspectives and interests at work globally, is the gateway to strengthening international solidarity and security in light of what will certainly be more crises across the globe.

However, one must concede that establishing the chances for a just and stable international order, of which the United States is largely the guarantor, are rather slim for two fundamental reasons. First, the foreign policy of the Bush administration since 2001 departs in practically every respect from the directions advocated here. Considering the centrality of the United States in the management of world order, such an agenda will continue to make it difficult in the short term to mitigate the tensions between the United Nations and the United States, if not among member states. Furthermore, it is indeed uncertain that the evolution of American foreign policy will introduce fundamental changes and provide reasons for optimism. After all, the Bush administration's foreign policy is not a "revo-lution" but rather, a radical version of enduring strains in American foreign policy and its conception of the country's place in the world.

The second fundamental reason not to expect such a transformation of American foreign policy along internationalist lines is the tendency of other UN member states to grudgingly defer to the demands of the hegemon; very few of them appear willing to invest much energy or capital to address the current shortcomings of multilateralism and the United Nations. There is hardly any serious desire to have the discussions on how to trigger change followed by real action to achieve a just and stable international order through multilateral collaboration. It seems that for most member states, including the harshest critics of the current international situation, getting by is a good enough option.

Afterword

MORE THAN TEN YEARS AFTER THE RWANDAN GENOCIDE, things do not seem to have improved much in terms of the willingness of the international community and its major powers to step into humanitarian crises. The situation in Darfur is terrible, with no end in sight for now. So far, more than 200,000 people have been killed and two million others displaced from their homes since fighting erupted in March 2003 between Sudanese government forces, allied militias, and rebel groups seeking greater autonomy. The United Nations also estimates that four million people now depend on humanitarian assistance.[1] Moreover, since the spring of 2006, the security situation in Darfur has been steadily deteriorating: All sides in the conflict are obtaining more weapons, and the number of armed opposition groups active in the region is multiplying. Heavy fighting continues unabated in the region's south and north. As for western Darfur, insecurity is also worsening and spilling over to Chad and the Central African Republic. In addition, targeted violence against humanitarian organizations is on the rise throughout the entire region, as is food insecurity.[2]

In November 2006, in Addis Ababa, the United Nations, the African Union (AU), and the government of Sudan held a summit to solidify the peace agreement Khartoum had entered into six months earlier. The representatives at the November summit agreed in principle on a three-phase plan to enhance the capacity of the African Union's Mission in Sudan to conduct effective peacekeeping through an increased UN role in the region, including a hybrid UN-AU force under UN command and control. But this agreement is likely to remain meaningless if it is not followed by action and improvement on the ground and if, beyond the immediate cessation of hostilities, it is not supported by a revived and all-inclusive peace process aimed at solving the root causes of the conflict.[3]

Writing on the May 2006 peace accord, *New York Times* columnist Nicholas Kristof noted that in order to stem the deterioration of the situation in Darfur and to avoid an expected 100,000 fatalities per month, the following measures would be needed:

> We need to amplify (though not reopen) the peace agreement to bring the [people of Darfur] in, and we need to ensure that its deadlines are met. We need a UN-led or French-led protection force in eastern Chad. We need to bolster the African Union force in Darfur immediately and push harder for Sudan to admit UN peacekeepers. We need a no-fly zone. We need to press Europeans to become more involved and to remind Arabs that the slaughter of several hundred thousand Muslims in Darfur is every bit as worthy of protest as cartoons of the prophet Mohammed. But most of all, we must put genocide squarely on the international agenda.[4]

In light of these needs, Kristof continued by expressing some measure of optimism, as he added, "One lesson of this story is that world leaders always prefer to ignore genocide, but when forced to face the horrors—as in Bosnia and Kosovo—they figure out ways of responding. The most acute need is not for policies but for political will."[5]

In those two sentences, Kristof captured the essence of the problem in Darfur and beyond the besieged Sudanese region: Addressing or ignoring emergent crises comes down to political will. But, in contrast to what Kristof seems to think, this does not necessarily leave room for much optimism.

As we have seen throughout this study, political will at the international level is anything but reliable. As political will continues to be informed by the demands of the national realm and the divide between "us" and "them," nation-states tend to favor their own interests over the rights of people beyond their borders. Unless there is a national interest at stake, or little cost and risk in engagement, there is reluctance among leading powers of the international community to act internationally.

If the more or less complacent attitude of the international community toward Darfur is not encouraging, the same complacency can be predicted for the future functioning of the UN Peacebuilding Commission. Slated to begin its activities in the second half of 2006, it was mandated to render peacemaking more encompassing. Its ambition is to coordinate, if not bring together, the actions of the different actors involved in peacebuilding, taking into account both prevention and postconflict management, within and beyond the UN system.[6] Yet despite the ambitious task, the commission has remarkably few resources at its disposal. Furthermore, its work, at least at the outset, is based on the assumption that it will address mainly those crises that are deemed solvable and are, therefore, potential success stories. From the perspective of resource allocation and public relations, such thinking makes perfect sense. At a time when the United Nations is, perhaps as much as during its low points of the 1990s, in need of proving its usefulness and ability to bring added value on the ground, generating success stories is a must. But what about the gravest crises? What about those other crises that are so deep and entrenched that the UN Peacebuilding Commission will avoid handling them for fear of failure? What about those situations where the level of tragedy and misery is too high to meet the sufficient threshold of a potential success? Does this mean that no attention, or only token action, will be dedicated to them?

The UN Peacebuilding Commission is a welcome element in the ongoing debate over the future of peacekeeping. Yet it is only one element among all the elements of the international community. What is missing in this seemingly bold innovation in the world organization is the role of the UN member states that will supposedly fulfill the Peacebuilding Commission's new approach to the multilateral handling of failed or failing states. In other words, the tentative commitment of member states, with their reluctance to allocate appropriate resources to support the international community when and where it decides to act multilaterally, and the dilemmas of solidarity beyond borders that we have seen at work throughout this study, have not lost one ounce of their actuality and relevance. Needless to say, this state of affairs exacts a price—a price that will be paid in the blood of the victims of future humanitarian tragedies around the world.

For powerful nation-states, the UN Peacebuilding Commission may be a convenient way to deflect authority and decision making away from them, but it does not absolve them of the moral or ethical imperative to sustain the international community—particularly the Western powers, whose democratic values have contributed so much to the normative bonds of that community.

States have no reason to rejoice from this situation, for this situation is at the same time an indictment of the international system and of the responsibility that they have in underwriting it. In the process, it is both the legitimacy of the international system and the states' own legitimacy that is undermined. In the process, also, states prevent themselves (the most powerful of them foremost) and the United Nations from being genuine providers of international security and solidarity.

To address the problems of international solidarity is a formidable challenge that amounts to a refusal to suffer from international anomie as a result of one's incapacity to see the "other," within and beyond borders, as an intrinsic part of the political self and the responsibility that necessarily accompanies that identity.

Chapter 6 argued that favoring the establishment of an international rule of law would address this challenge directly. Dovetailing international solidarity and international security—international solidarity no longer confined to the margins of international political theory—could be a win-win situation. By making the exercise of international solidarity more than simply a combination of doing the right thing (the ethical dimension) and taking political calculations, by making it a key aspect of an international public policy centered around the welfare of human beings within and beyond borders, justice and security could become mutually reinforcing.

Undoubtedly, this suggestion will appear naïve and utopian to many—all the more so considering that the Western developed countries, which have been historically committed to intertwining social solidarity and security policies domestically and which are among (although in a tentative way, as we have seen) the most active internationalist actors of the post–Cold War era, are increasingly moving away from "welfare state" approaches to domestic problems.[7] As Western countries endorse economic liberalism, their policy of choice is less and less to embed the political and legal dimensions of the rule of law in welfare policies meant to tame individual misfortune.[8] In such a milieu, how can a public-policy philosophy of order and justice that is in the process of being dismantled at the domestic level be promoted in the international realm?

Ultimately, it is very difficult to believe that the international realm will ever generate in the near future a "thickness" of solidarity similar to the one existing in the best-functioning advanced industrial (or postindustrial) democracies, or within regional agglomerations of them, as in the case of Europe. And so, the politics of traditional national interest is probably destined to continue to flourish and represent the animus for action in international affairs. Yet as the legitimacy constraints weighing on foreign policies become heavier, and as it becomes less and less manageable for the unilateral or exclusively self-interested international projection of power to make might right, the possibility and necessity of an international rule of law that informs a sense of international legitimacy are also becoming less and less avoidable. This reality puts the battle between particularist and universalist conceptions of ethics at the center of international affairs. And it shows that the outcome of the battle will determine not only the stability and legitimacy of international order as a whole but also that of its primary stakeholders.

Notes

INTRODUCTION

1. On rogue states in the context of U.S. foreign policy, see Robert S. Litwak, *Rogue States and U.S. Foreign Policy: Containment after the Cold War* (Washington, DC: Woodrow Wilson Center Press, 2000).

2. For an analysis of what constitutes a failed state and current surveys of failed states worldwide, see "The Failed States Index," conducted by *Foreign Policy* magazine and the Fund for Peace, available on the following Web sites: www.fundforpeace.org/programs/fsi/fsindex.php and http://www.foreignpolicy.com/story/cms.php?story_id=3098.

3. For a comprehensive account of conflicts in the twentieth century, see *Human Security Report 2005: War and Peace in the 21st Century*, ed. Andrew Mack and Zoe Nielsen (Vancouver: Human Security Center/University of British Columbia, 2005).

4. Lucien Poirier, *La Crise des Fondements* (Paris: Economica, 1994). For more on the link between national interest and geography, and therefore on geopolitics, see John Agnew, *Geopolitics: Re-visioning World Politics* (New York: Routledge, 1998).

5. On the apparent permanence of geopolitical divisions, see Yves Lacoste, *Géopolitique: La Longue Histoire d'Aujourd'hui* (Paris: Larousse, 2006). On "de-territorialization" in international politics, see John Gerard Ruggie, *Constructing the World Polity: Essays on International Institutionalization* (New York: Routledge, 1998), 172–97; David Held, Anthony McGrew, David Goldblattt, and Jonathan Perraton, *Global Transformations: Politics, Economics, and Culture* (Stanford, CA: Stanford University Press, 1999), 27–28. For a more philosophical, as well as speculative and radical, understanding of de-territorialization, see Gilles Deleuze and Félix Guattari, *A Thousand Plateaus: Capitalism and Schizophrenia*, trans. Brian Massumi (Minneapolis: University of Minnesota Press, 1987).

6. For legitimacy in general, see Jean-Marc Coicaud, *Legitimacy and Politics: A Contribution to the Study of Political Right and Political Responsibility*, trans. David Ames Curtis (New York: Cambridge University Press, 2002).

7. Any society that is not exclusively based on force, and that is mindful of its own people, embodies a sense of human rights—which can be different from a sense of individual rights. On this issue, see, for example, Daryush Shayegan, *Cultural Schizophrenia: Islamic Societies Confronting the West*, trans. John Howe (London: Saqi Books, 1992), 27–28. But what is quite specific to Western democratic culture, and therefore links

international solidarity to the idea of international democratic culture, is the idea that human rights are universal (i.e., that all human beings ought to have access to the same basic rights, whoever and wherever they are).

CHAPTER 1

1. United Nations Charter, Article 33.

2. Ibid., Article 34.

3. Ibid., Article 41.

4. Ibid., Articles 42, 43, 44, and 45 in particular.

5. On this issue in the context of the NATO intervention in Kosovo, see Albrecht Schnabel and Ramesh Thakur, "Kosovo, the Changing Contours of World Politics, and the Challenge of World Order," in *Kosovo and the Challenge of Humanitarian Intervention: Selective Indignation, Collective Action, and International Citizenship,* ed. Albrecht Schnabel and Ramesh Thakur (New York: United Nations University Press, 2000), 13.

6. Thomas M. Franck, *Nation Against Nation: What Happened to the UN Dream and What the U.S. Can Do About It* (New York: Oxford University Press, 1985), 168.

7. The UN operation in the Congo in the early 1960s ended up favoring one side against the other and degenerated into a conflict between the UN forces and the Katanga secessionists. Because this operation encompassed elements of peace enforcement policies, lessons could have been learned from it. Unfortunately, the lack of institutional memory and historical perspective from which the United Nations tends to suffer prevented the UN Secretariat from benefiting from the experience.

8. See the "Current Peacekeeping Operations" list on the Web site of the UN Department of Peacekeeping Operations, www.un.org/Depts/dpko/list/list.pdf.

9. The annual budgets for peace operations between 1991 and 2000 were the following: 1991, $0.4 billion; 1992, $1.4 billion; 1993, $3.8 billion; 1994, $3.5 billion; 1995, $3.1 billion; 1996–1997, $1.4 billion; 1997–1998, $1.3 billion; 1998–1999, $1 billion; 1999–2000, $1.7 billion; 2000–2001, $2.5 billion. See www.un.org/Depts/dpko/dpko/view.

10. Between 1991 and 2000, the United Nations' regular budget, based on obligatory contributions, did not surpass $13.7 billion: 1991, $1.1 billion; 1992, $1.2 billion; 1993, $1.2 billion; 1994, $1.3 billion; 1995, $1.3 billion; 1996, $1.3 billion; 1997, $1.3 billion; 1998, $1.3 billion; 1999, $1.3 billion; 2000, $1.2 billion; 2001, $1.2 billion. See www.un.org/news/facts/finance.

11. UNHCR's budget, almost entirely funded by direct and voluntary contributions from governments, nongovernmental organizations, and individuals, peaked in 1994. It exceeded $1.4 billion, primarily because of refugee emergencies in the former Yugoslavia and the Great Lakes Region of Africa. See www.unhcr.ch/fdrs/main.htm.

12. Michael E. Brown and Richard N. Rosecrance, eds., *The Costs of Conflict: Prevention and Cure in the Global Arena.* Report of the Carnegie Commission on Preventing Deadly Conflict (Lanham, MD: Rowman & Littlefield, 1999).

13. Mike Blakey, "Somalia," in ibid, 101–102.

14. Mike Blakey, "Haiti," ibid, 102.

15. Andrea Kathryn Talentino, "Bosnia," in ibid, 42. These are not the only costs that were borne by NATO in the context of the Bosnian conflict. NATO originally became involved in the Bosnian war in support of the United Nations. The tasks implied financial costs, as did the NATO-led Stabilization Force (SFOR) that succeeded IFOR at the end of 1996.

16. *SIPRI Yearbook 2000: Armaments, Disarmament, and International Security* (New York: Oxford University Press, 2000), 32.

17. "Funding for both operations and personnel had to be boosted dramatically in order to meet the requirements of the mission [in East Timor]. It is estimated that an additional Australian $4 billion [US$2.1 billion] will be required to fund the Timor deployment, including raising additional infantry and other operational units." Australian Defense Secretary Allan Hawke, "Money Matters" (address to the Royal United Services Institute of Victoria for Defense Studies, April 27, 2000), www.defence.gov.au/media/2000/270400.doc, p. 3.

18. Figure found in Blakey, "Haiti," 105.

19. Talentino, "Bosnia," 43–44.

20. Ibid.

21. This was especially the case for the United Kingdom and France in Bosnia. France suffered fifty-three fatalities between 1992 and 1995 in the context of UNPROFOR. These relatively high numbers have much to do with peacekeeping rules of engagement, which stipulate that peacekeepers are entitled to use force only to protect their lives. From this derives the fact that peacekeeping forces tend to be equipped with relatively light military materiel. This was the case for the United Nations Protection Force in Bosnia (UNPROFOR). At the time of its deployment in June 1992, UNPROFOR had military, police, and civilian components and was charged with opening Sarajevo's airport for humanitarian purposes, demilitarizing selected areas, and protecting residents. This mandate was difficult and dangerous to fulfill within regular peacekeeping rules of engagement—hence, in part, the level of casualties. The force retained the same mandate (without a change in engagement criteria) until December 1995. See the "Fatalities" page on the United Nations Peacekeeping Operations' Web site, www.un.org/Depts/dpko/fatalities.

22. Up to January 30, 2006. See www.un.org/Depts/dpko/fatalities/StatsByYear.htm.

23. Blakey, "Somalia," 82.

24. Figures in Talentino, "Bosnia," 40–42.

25. www.nato.int/kosovo/history.htm.

26. David Carment and Albrecht Schnabel, "Conflict Prevention: Taking Stock," in *Conflict Prevention: Path to Peace or Grand Illusion?* ed. David Carment and Albrecht Schnabel (New York: United Nations University Press, 2002).

27. Boutros Boutros-Ghali, *An Agenda for Peace*, 2d ed. (New York: United Nations, 1995).

28. Operation Uphold Democracy began in September 1994 with the deployment of the U.S.-led Multinational Force. The operation officially ended on March 31, 1995, when it was replaced by the United Nations Mission in Haiti (UNMIH). However, a large contingent of U.S. troops (USFORHAITI) participated in UNMIH until 1996, and the U.S. forces commander was also the commander of the UN forces.

29. David Cortright and George A. Lopez, *The Sanctions Decade: Assessing UN Strategies in the 1990s* (Boulder, CO: Lynne Rienner, 2000), 1–2 and passim. See also Larry Minear, David Cortright, Julia Wagler, George A. Lopez, and Thomas Weiss, *Toward More Humane and Effective Sanctions Management: Enhancing the Capacity of the United Nations System*. Occasional Paper, no. 31 (Providence, RI: Brown University/Thomas J. Watson Jr. Institute for International Studies, 1998), 3–6. During the 1990s, member states also imposed unilateral, bilateral, or regional economic sanctions more than three dozen times.

30. The sanctions against Iraq were instituted in the context of the Gulf War and its aftermath. They encompassed comprehensive trade sanctions (UN Security Council Resolution 661, adopted on August 6, 1990), air embargo (Resolution 670 of September 25, 1990), the maintenance of a full trade embargo pending Iraqi fulfillment of established conditions (Resolution 687 of April 3, 1991), the initial authorization of oil-for-food arrangements (Resolution 712 of September 19, 1991), and subsequent authorization of oil-for-food arrangements (Resolution 986 of April 14, 1995). The sanctions against Libya (Resolution 748 of March 31, 1992; Resolution 883 of November 11, 1993; and Resolution 1192 of August 27, 1998), Sudan (Resolution 1054 of April 26, 1996; and Resolution 1070, adopted on August 16, 1996), and Afghanistan (Resolution 1267 of October 15, 1999) addressed terrorism issues.

31. The UN Observer Group in Central America (ONUCA), active in 1989–1990, is part of this context. In the Esquipulas II Agreement, signed in 1987, Honduras, Nicaragua, Guatemala, Costa Rica, and El Salvador committed themselves to a number of tasks, including working toward national reconciliation, ceasing hostilities, democratization, ending the states of emergency, and holding free and fair elections. ONUCA, established pursuant to UN Security Council Resolution 644, adopted on November 7, 1989, was asked to conduct onsite verification of the security tasks contained in the Esquipulas II Agreement.

32. Boutros-Ghali, *An Agenda for Peace*, 6.

33. *Report on Allied Contributions to the Common Defense: A Report to the United States Congress by the Secretary of Defense* (Washington, DC: Office of the Secretary of Defense, 1995), Annexes 5, 15, and 16, www.defenselink.mil/pubs/allied.html.

34. An example of this was the allocation of far fewer troops than the UN secretary-general had recommended for the protection of the safe areas in Bosnia and their greatly delayed deployment. In the first of several reports on the implementation of the concept of safe areas, the secretary-general noted on June 14, 1993, that in order to ensure full respect for safe areas, the force commander of UNPROFOR estimated that an additional troop requirement of approximately 34,000 would be necessary to obtain deterrence through strength. He went on to note that it would be possible to start implementing the defense of the safe areas under a light option, envisaging a minimal troop reinforcement of around 7,600, with the understanding that this latter option could not, in itself, completely guarantee the defense of the safe areas. In the end, however, the Security Council authorized only the light option of 7,600 additional troops, the last of whom arrived in the theater a year later, in the middle of 1994. See *Report of the Secretary-General Pursuant to General Assembly Resolution 53/35. The Fall of Srebrenica*, UN Doc. A/54/549, pp. 27 and 41–42. Although this does not imply that more troops on the ground would have necessarily made a major difference for the outcome of the operations (especially in the context of the confusion of the mandates that prevailed in a number of peacekeeping operations involved in peace-enforcement activities), they would have helped.

35. *SIPRI Yearbook 2000*, 260.

36. See "Federal Budget Outlays for National Defense Functions: 1980 to 1999," in *Statistical Abstract of the United States: 1999* (Washington, DC: Bureau of the Census, 1999), 368.

37. Figures for peacekeeping operations include contributions toward UN peacekeeping assessments during 1994 but do not include voluntary contributions by countries in support of UN Security Council resolutions. Defense spending data reflect an agreed-upon definition of total defense spending adopted by NATO. For further information, see

Report on Allied Contributions to the Common Defense, "Selected Country Responsibility Sharing Indicators and Contributions" (table in the 1995 edition) and Table E-12 in the 1999 edition.

38. GDP measures economic activity and is composed of spending in four areas: consumption, investment, government purchases, and net exports. Thus, the measure allows for comparison of relative importance over time. In the United States, government spending (which includes defense spending) represents about 17 percent of GDP.

39. On these questions, see Daniel Druckman and Paul C. Stern, "Evaluating Peacekeeping Missions," *Mershon International Studies Review* 41 (1997): 151–65; Paul F. Diehl, "Forks in the Road: Theoretical and Policy Concerns for 21st Century Peacekeeping," *Global Society* 14, no. 3 (2000): 337–60. Refer also to Stephen John Stedman, *Implementing Peace Agreements in Civil Wars: Lessons and Recommendations for Policymakers.* Policy Paper Series on Peace Implementation (New York: International Peace Academy, May 2001), 7–8 and 15. For a more comprehensive view on the issues Stedman tackles, see Stephen John Stedman, Donald Rothchild, and Elizabeth M. Cousens, eds., *Ending Civil Wars: The Implementation of Peace Agreements* (Boulder, CO: Lynne Rienner, 2002).

40. Complex humanitarian emergencies are human-made crises and natural disasters that require multilayered international action by a wide range of military, political, and civilian actors. See the conference summary "Taking It to the Next Level: Civilian-Military Cooperation in Complex Emergencies" (Washington, DC: United States Institute of Peace, August 31, 2000), www.usip.org/virtualdiplomacy/publications/reports/nextlevel.html.

41. On the difficulties associated with using mandates as a baseline for the evaluation of peace operations, see Stedman, Rothchild, and Cousens, eds., *Ending Civil Wars,* 45–47.

42. For an overview of the UN Security Council resolutions in the 1990s regarding peace operations, see www.un.org/documents/scres.htm.

43. The Security Council issues public statements in the form of resolutions to state its position and the course of action it endorses. This gives Security Council policies a public character that echoes the normative and political demands of collective security. It is designed to help fulfill accountability and transparency requirements. It conveys the idea that Security Council initiatives are taken in the name of and in conformity with the ideals—both in terms of substance and decision-making processes—of the United Nations. These elements are important to satisfy the Security Council's quest for legitimacy before the United Nations and the world at large.

44. In the UN system, the economic reconstruction of war-torn societies is primarily the responsibility of the economic and financial agencies.

45. This assessment of peace operations echoes more or less that of Stedman, *Implementing Peace Agreements in Civil Wars,* 12–13. For an alternative approach to the evaluation of peace operations, see James Dobbins, Seth G. Jones, Keith Crane, Andrew Rathmell, Brett Steele, Richard Teltschik, and Anga Timilsina, *The UN's Role in Nation-Building: From the Congo to Iraq* (Santa Monica, CA: RAND Corporation, 2005). See also Roland Paris, *At War's End: Building Peace after Civil Conflict* (New York: Cambridge University Press, 2004), Michael W. Doyle and Nicholas Sambanis, *Making War and Building Peace: United Nations Peace Operations* (Princeton, NJ: Princeton University Press, 2006).

46. See UN Security Council Resolution 983 (March 31, 1995) for the creation of UNPREDEP.

47. Henryk J. Sokalski, *An Ounce of Prevention: Macedonia and the UN Experience in Preventive Diplomacy* (Washington, DC: United States Institute of Peace Press, 2003).

48. The new Macedonian government produced by the parliamentary elections of November 1998 recognized Taiwan (which had pledged $1.5 billion in economic assistance), leading China to veto the extension of UNPREDEP in February 2000. The Macedonian government must have known that recognizing Taiwan would trigger a negative Chinese reaction, which may have been its strategy all along, as it seemed to favor the end of UN involvement in Macedonia and its replacement by a NATO presence.

49. See UN Security Council Resolution 693 (May 1991), which establishes ONUSAL and the list of its responsibilities.

50. Susan D. Bergerman, "Building the Peace by Mandating Reform: United Nations-Mediated Human Rights Agreements in El Salvador and Guatemala," *Latin American Perspectives* 27, no. 3 (2000): 63–87.

51. See Robert C. Orr, "Building Peace in El Salvador," in *Peacebuilding as Politics: Cultivating Peace in Fragile Societies,* ed. Elizabeth M. Cousens and Chetan Kumar, with Karin Wermester (Boulder, CO: Lynne Rienner, 2001).

52. UN Security Council Resolution 797 (December 16, 1992) established ONUMOZ.

53. Demobilization of the two sides' armed forces was very slow to begin, but it was ultimately successful. However, very few of the soldiers' weapons were collected or destroyed. Disarmament in Mozambique as a national priority was never addressed seriously.

54. For a detailed evaluation of the UN peacekeeping operation in Mozambique, see Richard Synge, *Mozambique: UN Peacekeeping in Action 1992–1994* (Washington, DC: United States Institute of Peace Press, 1997), for example, pp. 10–11 and 165–67. It should be added that today, despite rapid economic growth in recent years, Mozambique remains one of the world's poorest countries. Opponents of the government also argue that it has favored the southern provinces, where the ruling Frelimo party's support has traditionally been the strongest.

55. UN Security Council Resolution 1094 (January 1997).

56. For more on MINUGUA, see, for instance, Bergerman, "Building the Peace by Mandating Reform."

57. For an overall description and evaluation of the United Nations' involvement in Haiti between 1990 and 1997, see David Malone, *Decision-Making in the UN Security Council: The Case of Haiti, 1990–1997* (New York: Oxford University Press, 1998).

58. UN Security Council Resolution 1141 (November 28, 1997) established the United Nations Civilian Police Mission in Haiti (MIPONUH) and called for a professional, self-sustaining, fully functioning national police; the consolidation of democracy; and the revitalization of Haiti's system of justice. See also the *Report of the Secretary-General on the United Nations Civilian Police in Haiti*, UN Doc. S/2000/150 (February 25, 2000).

59. Acting on the recommendation of the UN secretary-general, the Security Council adopted Resolution 1542 (April 30, 2004), establishing MINUSTAH for an initial period of six months. Authority was transferred from the MIF on June 1, 2004. It has been extended since (and was still active in the summer of 2006).

60. In November 2004, the International Crisis Group concluded that "Haiti is drifting towards anarchy." See International Crisis Group, *A New Chance for Haiti?* Latin America/Caribbean Report, no. 10 (Freetown/Brussels: ICG, September 2, 2003).

61. For a relatively recent assessment of the situation in Sierra Leone, see International Crisis Group, *Sierra Leone: The State of Security and Governance* (Freetown/Brussels: ICG, September 2, 2003).

62. See UN Security Council Resolutions 1289 (February 7, 2000) and 1299 (May 19, 2000). See also International Crisis Group, *Sierra Leone After Elections: Politics as Usual?* Africa Reports, no. 49 (Freetown/Brussels: International Crisis Group, July 12, 2002).

63. For its establishment, see "Letter Dated 6 March 2002 from the Secretary-General Addressed to the President of the Security Council," UN Doc. S/2002/246 (March 8, 2002), Appendix II. For its current progress and status, see "Letter Dated 26 February 2004 from the Secretary-General Addressed to the President of the Security Council," UN Doc. S/2004/182 (March 10, 2004).

64. The report presented a comprehensive understanding of the country's past and the many lessons that it holds for the politically and economically healthy future of Sierra Leone. See the Sierra Leone Truth and Reconciliation Commission's Final Report, October 27, 2004, www.trcsierraleone.org/drwebsite/publish/index.shtml.

65. On October 22, 1999, the Security Council authorized deployment of a new and significantly larger peacekeeping operation; UNOMSIL was replaced by UNAMSIL. See UN Security Council Resolution 1270 (October 22, 1999).

66. On March 30, 2004, the Security Council announced that UNAMSIL would retain a residual presence in Sierra Leone for an initial period of six months commencing January 1, 2005. See UN Security Council Resolution 1537 (March 30, 2004). See also "Transcript of Press Briefing by UNAMSIL SRSG Ambassador Daudi Ngelautwa Mwakawago," United Nations Mission in Sierra Leone, July 27, 2004. The last UN peacekeepers withdrew in December 2005, leaving full responsibility for security to domestic forces, but a new civilian UN office remains to support the government. Mounting tensions related to planned 2007 elections, deteriorating political and economic conditions in Guinea, and the tenuous security situation in neighboring Liberia may present challenges to continuing progress in Sierra Leone's stability.

67. Article 3 of the agreement signed in New York on May 5, 1999, between Indonesia and Portugal, under the auspices of the United Nations, stated that Indonesia would be responsible for maintaining peace and security in East Timor. Considering the depressing track record of the Indonesian military in East Timor, as well as the links between the Indonesian army and the predominantly pro-Jakarta paramilitary groups, whose acts of violence geared up in December 1998 and only increased after that, it was a dangerous course to take. For a historical perspective on the links between the Indonesian army and the militias, see Geoffrey C. Gunn, *East Timor and the United Nations: The Case for Intervention* (Lawrenceville, NJ: Red Sea Press, 1997), 10–12 and 51–55. See also George J. Aditjondro, "Ninjas, Nanggalas, Monuments, and Mossad Manuals: An Anthropology in Indonesian State Terror in East Timor," in *Death Squad: The Anthropology of State Terror,* ed. Jeffrey A. Sluka (Philadelphia: University of Pennsylvania Press, 2000).

68. It is true that because it was not a peace operation per se, UNAMET had no mandate to stop the violence, and Indonesia was in principle responsible for providing security; see UN Security Council Resolutions 1246 (June 11, 1999) and 1262 (August 27, 1999). The main task of UNAMET was to oversee the referendum. Nevertheless, there were enough signs that the situation was getting out of control to justify at least putting more pressure on the Indonesian government to stop the violence. In the end, however, the United Nations alone cannot be held responsible for its passivity. The Security Council refused to authorize the United Nations to have the kind of presence necessary to maintain the peace and to insist that Indonesian forces withdraw prior to the referendum. Furthermore, considering its strong links with Indonesia, the United States, both within the Security Council and directly vis-à-vis Indonesia, could have exercised pressure on Jakarta to help to prevent or stop the violence. See Stephen Zunes, "East Timor's Tragedy and Triumph," *Peace Review* 12, no. 2 (June 2000).

69. UN Security Council Resolution 1272 (October 25, 1999) lists the following elements in the mandate of UNTAET: to provide security and maintain law and order throughout the territory of East Timor; to establish an effective administration; to assist in the development of civil and social services; to ensure the coordination and delivery of humanitarian assistance, rehabilitation, and development assistance; to support capacity building for self-government; and to assist in the establishment of conditions for sustainable development.

70. Local factors could also facilitate a favorable outcome in the long run. The immediate geopolitical environment of East Timor is likely to be rather benign in the future. Chances are that Indonesia will no longer try to further undermine the political evolution of East Timor. Besides, unlike in the Balkans, where a legacy of victimization mentality tends to be an obstacle to reconciliation, the spirituality and faith of the East Timorese and their sense of social solidarity should help.

71. On May 20, 2002, a United Nations Mission of Support in East Timor was established for an initial period of twelve months. The mandate was to provide assistance to the judicial system and to the core administrative, political, and security structures of the country, as well as to support the maintenance of peace and stability. See UN Security Council Resolution 1410 (May 17, 2002). For more in-depth analysis, see Special Representative of the Secretary-General for Timor-Leste Sukehiro Hasegawa, "The Role of the United Nations in Peace-Building in Timor Leste: The Consolidation of Peace" (paper presented at the "Kyoto Meeting on Threats, Challenges and Change," Kyoto, July 6–7, 2004), www.unagencies.east-timor.org/Speeches/SRSGKyotoMeetingSpeech 6July04.pdf.

72. Also, in January 2005 the UN secretary-general established a commission of experts to analyze the transitional justice mechanisms put in place in Dili and Jakarta to handle crimes against humanity and other serious crimes committed in East Timor between 1975 and 1999 and to make recommendations regarding possible future actions. See "Summary of the Report of the Secretary-General of the Commission of Experts to Review the Prosecution of Serious Violations of Human Rights in Timor-Leste (East Timor) in 1999," UN Doc. S/2005/458 (July 15, 2005).

73. Michael W. Doyle, "Peacebuilding in Cambodia: Legitimacy and Power," in Cousens and Kumar, eds., *Peacebuilding as Politics*, 99–101.

74. See International Crisis Group, *Cambodia: The Elusive Peace Dividend*. Asia Report, no. 8 (Phnom Penh/Brussels: ICG, August 11, 2000); United Nations Development Program, *Reform for What? Reflections on Public Administration Reform* (Phnom Penh: UNDP, June 2002).

75. On May 14, 2003, the UN General Assembly adopted by consensus Resolution 10135, containing the draft agreement between the world body and Cambodia concerning the prosecution—under Cambodian law—of crimes committed during the period of Democratic Kampuchea. See "Human Rights Questions: Including Alternative Approaches for Improving the Effective Enjoyment of Human Rights and Fundamental Freedoms," *Report of the Third Committee, General Assembly*, UN Doc. A/57/806 (May 6,

2003); and "Secretary-General Replies to Cambodian Prime Minister's Letter on Trial of Khmer Rouge Leaders," United Nations Press Release, SG/SM/8341, January 20, 2002.

76. On the negotiations at Dayton and the Dayton Accords, see Jean-Marc Coicaud, "La Communauté Internationale et l'Accord de Dayton," *Le Trimestre du Monde*, Spring 1996. The United Nations had relatively little responsibility in the implementation of the Dayton Peace Accords. The implementation tasks fell principally to the Office of the High Representative (OHR), the NATO-led force, the Organization for Security and Cooperation in Europe (OSCE), and local actors. On the implementation of the Dayton Accords and the entire spectrum of peacebuilding activities conducted in subsequent years by various actors, see Elizabeth M. Cousens, "Building Peace in Bosnia," in Cousens and Kumar, eds., *Peacebuilding as Politics*.

77. See UN Security Council Resolution 1035 (December 21, 1995). In addition, the Dayton Accords gave the United Nations High Commissioner for Refugees (UNHCR) the responsibility of encouraging the return of refugees to their prewar place of residence. This was one of the keys to the successful implementation of the accords. Unfortunately, it has happened only to a very small extent. Moreover, it seems that a significant number of refugees only return to claim their properties in order to sell them at distressed prices, preventing them from starting new lives elsewhere.

78. International Crisis Group, *Bosnia's Stalled Police Reform: No Progress, No EU.* Europe Report, no. 164 (Sarajevo/Brussels: ICG, September 6, 2005).

79. The ad hoc International Criminal Tribunal for the Former Yugoslavia is another aspect of the ambiguous results of the UN involvement in Bosnia-Herzegovina. The track record of the tribunal is perhaps not as bad as the one for Rwanda: In early 2006, 85 cases had been completed, while 132 accused had appeared in proceedings before the tribunal, www.un.org/icty/glance-e/index.htm. In comparison, as of March 2005, the Rwanda tribunal had handed down seventeen judgments involving twenty-three accused. Twenty of them were convicted and three acquitted, www.ictr.org. But the various problems crippling it do not speak in its favor. The time that it takes for the tribunals to deliver a verdict is only one of the many problems—something that is well exemplified in the death of Slobodan Milosevic in March 2006, prior to the conclusion of his trial. For a critical evaluation of ad hoc international tribunals, see Ralph Zacklin, "The Failings of Ad Hoc International Tribunals," *Journal of International Criminal Justice* 2 (2004): 541–545; and Dominic Raab, "Evaluating the ICTY and Its Completion Strategy: Efforts to Achieve Accountability for War Crimes and Their Tribunals," *Journal of International Criminal Justice* 3 (2005): 82–102. For a general assessment on transitional justice, refer to the report of the UN Secretary-General, *The Rule of Law and Transitional Justice in Conflict and Post-Conflict Societies*, UN Doc. S/2004/616 (August 23, 2004).

80. For a good evaluation of the United Nations' involvement in Kosovo, see International Crisis Group, *A Kosovo Roadmap (II): Internal Benchmarks* (Pristina/Brussels: ICG, March 1, 2002).

81. www.un.org/Docs.scres/1999/99sc1244.htm.

82. See International Crisis Group, *A Kosovo Roadmap (II)*.

83. For a twofold account of the Kosovo Assembly elections, see "Elections 2004: A Major Milestone of Progress," *Focus Kosovo*, September–October 2004; and Daniel Williams, "Serbs Boycott Kosovo Elections," *Washington Post*, October 23, 2004.

84. On this issue, see, for example, International Crisis Group, "Testimony by Valery Percival before the U.S. Commission on Security and Cooperation in Europe (Helsinki Commission) on Ethnic Harmony in Kosovo," June 19, 2002. On the anti-Serb riots of

March 2004, see International Crisis Group, *Collapse in Kosovo* (Pristina/Belgrade/Brussels: ICG, April 22, 2004), i.

85. United Nations, "Letter Dated 7 October 2005 from the Secretary-General Addressed to the President of the Security Council," UN Doc. S/2005/635 (October 7, 2005).

86. Kosovo's "final status" talks were launched in February 2006; see International Crisis Group, *Kosovo: The Challenge of Transition.* Europe Report, no. 170 (Pristina/Belgrade/Brussels: ICG, February 17, 2006); and Nicholas Wood, "Kosovo Leaders Confer in Vienna, but Little Progress Is Seen," *New York Times,* July 25, 2006.

87. For a discussion on the number of casualties during the 1992–95 armed conflicts in Bosnia, see Ewa Tabeau and Jakub Bijak, "War-related Deaths in the 1992–1995 Armed Conflicts in Bosnia and Herzegovina: A Critique of Previous Estimates and Recent Results," *European Journal of Population* 21, no. 2–3 (June 2005).

88. David Rohde, *Endgame: The Betrayal and Fall of Srebrenica* (New York: Farrar Strauss & Giroux, 1997); and David Rieff, *Slaughterhouse: Bosnia and the Failure of the West* (New York: Touchstone Books, 1996).

89. See, for instance, Blakey, "Somalia," 82; and International Crisis Group, *Somalia: Countering Terrorism in a Failed State* (Nairobi/Brussels: ICG, May 23, 2002).

90. International Crisis Group, *Biting the Somalia Bullet.* Africa Report, no. 79 (Nairobi/Brussels: International Crisis Group, May 4, 2004).

91. Ibid. By June 2006, Islamist militias had gained control over the capital and large parts of central and southern Somalia, which caused the African Union to urge the international community to address the growing humanitarian problems.

92. With an annual budget of $118 million, the original strength of UNAVEM II was 350 military observers, 126 police observers, 87 international and 155 local civilian staff, and 400 electoral observers. See Dennis C. Jett, *Why Peacekeeping Fails* (New York: St. Martin's, 1999), 81–82.

93. With the Lusaka Agreement, signed in November 1994, the Angolan parties called for the supervision, control, and general verification of the reestablished cease-fire to be the responsibility of the United Nations acting in the framework of its new mandate with the participation of the government and UNITA. On February 8, 1995, the Security Council authorized the establishment of UNAVEM III, with a maximum deployment of 7,000 military personnel in addition to 350 military observers and 260 police observers. See ibid., 85.

94. Available on the UN Department of Peacekeeping Operations' "Best Practices" Web site, www.un.org/Depts/dpko/lessons/rwanda.htm.

CHAPTER 2

1. In addition, paragraph 2 of Article 12, in the UN Charter's Chapter IV, dedicated to the General Assembly, indicates the information role of the secretary-general vis-à-vis the General Assembly.

2. UN Charter, Article 99.

3. UN Charter, Article 100. For a critical and quite accurate picture of UN personnel problems regarding impartiality and objectivity, see Maurice Bertrand, *The United Nations: Past, Present, and Future* (The Hague: Kluwer Law International, 1997), 89–92.

4. UN Charter, Article 4.

5. UN Charter, Articles 5 and 6.

6. UN Charter, Article 25: "The Members of the United Nations agree to accept and carry out the decisions of the Security Council in accordance with the present Charter."

7. UN Charter, Article 24.

8. UN Charter, Article 34.

9. See UN Charter, Chapter VI, Article 33.

10. For the power of recommendation given to the UN Security Council, see UN Charter, Articles 36, 37, and 38.

11. See UN Charter, Articles 41 and 42.

12. See, in particular, UN Charter, Article 43.

13. See UN Charter, Article 52.

14. See UN Charter, Article 53.

15. See UN Charter, Article 97.

16. On U Thant as UN secretary-general, see, for example, Stanley Meisler, *United Nations: The First Fifty Years* (New York: Atlantic Monthly Press, 1995), 153–68, particularly p. 156.

17. The permanent members of the Security Council, like any other member states, perform their functions in the Security Council by keeping an eye on their interests. The selective attention given by the Security Council to international crises—each permanent member being, for instance, eager to leave off the Security Council agenda issues close to its immediate sphere of influence or interest—is a telling illustration of this situation. It also indicates the serious limitations of collective security as monitored by the Security Council.

18. United Nations, "Letter Dated November 29, 1992 from the Secretary-General Addressed to the President of the Security Council," UN Doc. S/24868 (November 30, 1992), 6.

19. This mandate is mentioned in ibid., and endorsed by UN Security Council Resolution 794 (December 3, 1992), paragraph 7.

20. "The progress of UNITAF forces thus far means that measures may now be taken to prepare for the transition to UNOSOM forces under United Nations command." United Nations, *Report Dated January 16, 1993, by the United States of America, Pursuant to Security Council Resolution 794 (1992)*, UN Doc. S/25126 (January 19, 1993), 3.

21. "In spite of the many positive aspects of the presence of UNITAF forces, the risk to relief workers remains exceedingly high. Theft, looting and extortion continue to plague relief efforts, albeit on a lesser scale. . . . Insecurity has also adversely affected the planning of future relief operations. . . ." United Nations, *The Situation in Somalia: Progress Report of the Secretary-General*, UN Doc. S/25168 (January 26, 1993), 8.

22. See United Nations, *Further Report of the Secretary-General Submitted in Pursuance of Paragraphs 18 and 19 of Resolution 794 (1992)*, UN Doc. S/25354 (March 3, 1993), 5–6.

23. UN Security Council Resolution 814 (March 26, 1993).

24. The delay reflected the UN secretary-general's attempt to secure a strong American commitment in terms of financial, political, and military support before finally accepting UN responsibility for the mission. John Hirsch and Robert Oakley comment that the "U.S.-UN dialogue on Resolution 814 resembled bargaining in a bazaar. In the end, the United States provided more support than had been planned and the Secretary-General agreed that the UN should take over from the U.S." John L. Hirsch and Robert B. Oakley,

Somalia and Operation Restore Hope: Reflections on Peacemaking and Peacekeeping (Washington, DC: United States Institute of Peace Press, 1995), 111.

25. United Nations, *Report of the Secretary-General Submitted in Pursuance of Paragraphs 18 and 19 of Security Council Resolution 794 (1992), Proposing that UNITAF Extends Its Operation to the Whole Somalia and Disarm the Factions before Handing Over Operational Responsibility to a New United Nations Peacekeeping Operation*, UN Doc. S/24992 (December 19, 1992), paragraphs 22, 23, 24, and 29. Incidentally, Boutros-Ghali quickly ended the practice of his predecessor, Javier Pérez de Cuéllar, of circulating drafts of his reports to the permanent members of the Security Council to make sure they had no objections before submitting the final report to the Security Council. In fact, he used his reports to the Security Council as a way to outline policy options and, at times, to let them know what he favored.

26. United Nations, "Letter Dated 19 January 1993 from the Permanent Representative of the United States of America to the United Nations Addressed to the President of the Security Council," UN Doc. S/25126 (January 19, 1993), 2–3.

27. "On other occasions, segments of the Somali population have attempted to interfere with UNITAF forces. When no other recourse was possible, UNITAF forces engaged in action against those elements. As it also became necessary to accomplish its mission, UNITAF forces have either convinced those Somalis holding heavy weapons to isolate them in specified areas or have taken action to seize such weapons." United Nations, *Report Dated January 16, 1993, by the United States of America, Pursuant to Security Council Resolution 794 (1992)*, 3. The description provided in this report appears quite self-serving, as it does not fit most information available on the issue. See, for instance, the fact that American officials told the Somali warlords that they could keep their weapons if they moved the arms out of Mogadishu or into their respective cantonments. On this issue, see Walter Clarke and Jeffrey Herbst, "Somalia and the Future of Humanitarian Intervention," *Foreign Affairs*, March/April 1996. See also Terrence Lyons and Ahmed I. Samatar, *Somalia: State Collapse, Multilateral Intervention, and Strategies for Political Reconstruction*. Brookings Occasional Papers (Washington, DC: The Brookings Institution, 1995), 41–42.

28. The UN secretary-general stated in his letter dated November 29, 1992, "The purpose of each of the three options involving the possible use of force would be to ensure, on a lasting basis, that the current violence against the international relief effort was brought to an end. To achieve this, it would be necessary for at least the heavy weapons of the organized factions to be neutralized and brought under international control and for the irregular forces and gangs to be disarmed." Furthermore, by specifically targeting heavy weapons, Boutros-Ghali, aware of the fact that Somalia has long been a society in which it is normal for individuals to bear arms, did not assign UNITAF what would have probably been an impossible task: going after small arms.

29. This should not come as a surprise considering that had there been any question of a protracted American commitment involving casualties, it is clear that President Bush would not have launched an intervention that was designed to end his presidency with a glittering humanitarian success. On the issue of casualties, see also Lawrence Eagleburger trying to justify, on December 6, 1992, the administration's differing responses to Somalia and Bosnia: "But the fact of the matter is that a thousand people are starving to death every day, and that it is not going to get better if we don't do something about it, and it is in an area where we can affect events. There are other parts of the world where things are equally tragic, but where the cost of trying to change things would be monumental. In my view,

Bosnia is one of those." Eagleburger is quoted in Adam Roberts, "Humanitarian War: Military Intervention and Human Right," *International Affairs* 69, no. 3 (1993): 442.

30. See the text of UN Security Council Resolution 814 (1993).

31. UN Security Council Resolution 837 (1993), paragraph 5.

32. Paragraph 13 of UN Security Council Resolution 794 (1992) "requests the Secretary-General and the Member States acting under paragraph 10 to establish appropriate mechanisms for coordination between the United Nations and their military force." Paragraph 15 "invites the Secretary-General to attach a small Operation liaison staff to the field headquarters of the unified command." Paragraph 18 "requests the Secretary-General and, as appropriate, the States concerned to report to the Council on a regular basis, the first such report to be made no later than fifteen days after the adoption of the present resolution, on the implementation of the present resolution and the attainment of the objective of establishing a secure environment so as to enable the Council to make the necessary decision for a prompt transition to continued peacekeeping operations."

33. United Nations, *Further Report of the Secretary-General Submitted in Pursuance of Paragraphs 18 and 19 of Resolution 794 (1992),* paragraph 78.

34. Ibid., paragraph 88.

35. One has to admit that such reluctance is largely justified, considering how ill equipped—in terms of human, political, and institutional resources—the United Nations is to perform, with a sense of responsibility and accountability embedded in them, military command functions.

36. See Hirsch and Oakley, *Somalia and Operation Restore Hope,* 118–19.

37. On August 8, 1993, while on a routine patrol in South Mogadishu, four U.S. soldiers serving with UNOSOM II were killed when their vehicle was destroyed by a command-detonated device.

38. See Clarke and Herbst, "Somalia and the Future of Humanitarian Intervention."

39. Close to 700 Somalis were killed in the course of the Aidid hunt. On October 3, 1993, in the sixteen-hour fight that led to the death of eighteen U.S. Army Rangers, five hundred Somalis were killed. See Nicholas J. Wheeler, *Saving Strangers: Humanitarian Intervention in International Society* (New York: Oxford University Press, 2000), 195–98.

40. As late as May 30, 1995, in a report to the Security Council, Secretary-General Boutros-Ghali had the need to recall that in May 1992 he did not think that the conditions existed on the ground to establish a peacekeeping mission, and indicated that since then not much had changed. See United Nations, *Report of the Secretary-General Pursuant to Security Council Resolutions 982 (1995) and 987 (1995).* UN Doc. S/1995/444 (May 30, 1995), paragraphs 17 and 68.

41. The secretary-general even went as far as saying that Bosnia risked being "a kind of Vietnam for the United Nations." Boutros-Ghali, quoted in Harvey Morris, "UN Chief Gives Warning of a Vietnam in Yugoslavia," *The Independent* (London), August 3, 1992, 1.

42. "[T]he credibility of the United Nations is of utmost importance and must be safe guarded at all times. Few things damage it more than to give United Nations peacekeepers tasks that cannot be accomplished in prevailing circumstances. And the damage is not only to the peacekeeping. Loss of United Nations credibility there will affect the Organization's endeavors for development, for the environment, for human rights and for every other important objective . . . ." United Nations, *Report of the Secretary-General Pursuant to Security Council Resolutions 982 (1995) and 987 (1995),* paragraph 82. This proved to be right: The debacle of the UN engagement in Bosnia contributed in no small measure to the sidelining of the world body; see also Boutros Boutros-Ghali, *Unvanquished: A U.S.-UN Saga* (New York: Random House, 1999), 248. Consequently, the United Nations was largely held back from participating in the Dayton negotiations in November 1995. For more details on this point, see Richard Holbrooke, *To End a War* (New York: Random House, 1999), 201–2. In the second half of the 1990s, most of the UN activities in Bosnia were scaled down.

43. This is not the sole cause of the fall of Srebrenica and Zepa in July 1995. The shortcomings of the safe-areas regime have to be taken into account as well. Successful implementation rested on the consent and the cooperation of the parties, which was by and large lacking; authority for the use of force did not go beyond the right to self-defense, which was probably insufficient; and airpower as a deterrent was limited by the constraints hampering its use. See, for example, United Nations, *Report of the Secretary-General Pursuant to Security Council Resolutions 982 (1995) and 987 (1995),* paragraphs 40 and 41.

44. On this issue, see, for example, Thomas G. Weiss, "Collective Spinelessness: UN Actions in the Former Yugoslavia," in *The World and Yugoslavia's Wars,* ed. Richard H. Ullman (New York: Council on Foreign Relations, 1996), 73–74.

45. The United Kingdom had a more ambiguous position; it did not rule out the use of selective air strikes. See James Gow, *Triumph of the Lack of Will: International Diplomacy and the Yugoslav War* (New York: Columbia University Press, 1997), 180.

46. See U.S. Department of Defense, "Background Briefing on Bosnia," April 22, 1994, Washington, DC.

47. On this point, see the troubling lack of explanation for the absence of air strikes in defense of Srebrenica in the report of Secretary-General Kofi Annan on the fall of Srebrenica. The report gives reasons why launching air strikes was a tricky decision. However, it remains silent on why in this precise instance, when air strikes were clearly warranted, as he notes himself, nothing happened. Refer in particular to paragraphs 480, 481, 482, and 483 of United Nations, *Report of the Secretary-General Pursuant to General Assembly Resolution 53/35: The Fall of Srebrenica.* UN Doc. A/54/549 (November 15, 1999).

48. See "Peace Agreement between the Government of the Republic of Rwanda and the Rwandese Patriotic Front," August 3, 1993, Arusha, Tanzania, www.incore.ulst.ac.uk/cds/agreements/pdf/rwan1.pdf.

49. Ibid. See in particular Articles 53–72 in the section "Protocol of Agreement between the Government of the Republic of Rwanda and the Rwandese Patriotic Front on the Integration of the Armed Forces of the Two Parties," and Articles 36–40 in the section "Protocol of Agreement between the Government of the Republic of Rwanda and the Rwandese Patriotic Front on the Repatriation of Rwandese Refugees and the Resettlement of Displaced Persons."

50. See United Nations, *Report of the Secretary-General on Rwanda.* UN Doc. S/26488 (September 24, 1993), especially paragraphs 21, 22, and 25: "21. . . . The principal functions of the Mission could be grouped in four categories: (a) to assist in ensuring the security of the city of Kigali, (b) to monitor the cease-fire agreement, including establishment of an expanded DMZ and demobilization procedures, (c) to continue to monitor the security situation during the final period of the transitional Government's mandate leading up to the elections, and (d) to assist with mine-clearance, including training and mine-awareness programs. . . . 22. . . . In addition, the Mission would be called upon to provide security of Rwandese refugees and displaced persons. . . . 25. . . . [T]he mission would monitor and verify the securing of weapons and the movements of all forces from both parties in the Kigali sector through the use of infantry and military observers." By September 1993, the UN Secretariat had realized, following the Somalia case, that there was great reluctance on the part of the key member states to deploy troops in the whole territory of the country where the intervention was taking place.

51. In the approval of the 1994 budget, the U.S. Congress had cancelled a proposed peacekeeping contingency fund that was intended to allow the United States to contribute emergency start-up funds for peace operations.

52. UN Security Council Resolution 872 (1993), paragraph 3, alinea (a).

53. Ibid., paragraph 3, alinea (f).

54. Ibid., pp. 82 and 85–86.

55. For details on this issue, see, for instance, Linda R. Melvern, *A People Betrayed: The Role of the West in Rwanda's Genocide* (London: Zed Books, 2000), 53–55. For a good overview of the historical background of the genocide in Rwanda, see also Gérard Prunier, *The Rwanda Crisis: History of a Genocide,* 2d ed. (New York: Columbia University Press, 1999).

56. Roméo Dallaire (with Major Brent Beardsley), *Shake Hands with the Devil: The Failure of Humanity in Rwanda* (Toronto: Random House Canada, 2003), particularly chapters 7 and 8.

57. On this issue, see, for example, Michael N. Barnett, "The Politics of Indifference at the United Nations and Genocide in Rwanda and Bosnia," in *This Time We Knew: Western Responses to Genocide in Bosnia,* ed. Thomas Cushman and Stjepan G. Mestrovic (New York: New York University Press, 1996), particularly p. 129. See also Michael N. Barnett, *Eyewitness to a Genocide: The United Nations and Rwanda* (Ithaca, NY: Cornell University Press, 2002).

58. See Melvern, *A People Betrayed,* 92, 99, and 101; and Dallaire, *Shake Hands with the Devil,* 145–47. See also Linda Melvern, *Conspiracy to Murder: The Rwandan Genocide* (New York: Verso, 2004); and Mahmood Mamdani, *When Victims Become Killers: Colonialism, Nativism, and the Genocide in Rwanda* (Princeton, NJ: Princeton University Press, 2001).

59. In an April 8 cable to UN headquarters in New York, Dallaire started formulating concrete proposals for the reinforcement of UNAMIR, which, he felt, could stop the killing. Some observers have doubted the validity of Dallaire's judgment about reinforcements and claimed that his estimate was problematic, given the determination of the extremists. But, three years after the genocide, a report to the Carnegie Commission pointed to a consensus that a force with air support, logistics, and communications would have prevented the slaughter of half a million people. The window of opportunity was April 7–21, while the political leaders responsible for the violence were still susceptible to international influence. This would have forestalled expansion of the genocide to the south; it was still relatively contained at this point. An intervention probably could have altered the political calculations of the extremists as to whether they could get away with the carnage. A larger force was needed after April 21 because by then the genocide had spread. The text of Dallaire's cable is given in full in *Commission d'enquête parlementaire concernant les événements du Rwanda: Report,* Belgian Senate, December 6, 1997, pp. 508–15, under publication legislatif no 1-611/7. See also Scott R. Feil, *Preventing Genocide: How the Early Use of Force Might Have Succeeded in Rwanda.* A Report to the Carnegie Commission on Preventing Deadly Conflict, Foreword by Roméo Dallaire (New York: Carnegie Corporation of New York, 1998), 26–27.

60. See paragraphs 3, 6, and 20 of United Nations, "Special Report of the Secretary-General on the United Nations Assistance Mission for Rwanda," UN Doc. S/1994/470 (April 20, 1994). Paragraph 20 is particularly telling: "Ultimately, it is only the parties who signed the Arusha Agreement, namely the Government of Rwanda (or its successor) and RPF, who must bear responsibility for deciding whether their country and people find peace or continue to suffer violence." The complexity of the situation and the lack of clear information on what was happening on the ground in the early days of the genocide should not be entirely dismissed by critics of the United Nations. This point is worth making, not to discharge the United Nations of its responsibilities, but to stress the critical importance for institutional actors to be as well informed as possible. Taking action also depends upon evidence, upon information as comprehensive and verifiable as possible. Needless to say, not all regions of the world benefit equally when it comes to information and intelligence data, and Africa is probably one of the areas that suffers the most from this inequality.

61. See United Nations, *Report of the Independent Inquiry into the Actions of the United Nations during the 1994 Genocide in Rwanda.* UN Doc. S/1999/1257 (December 15, 1999).

62. Dallaire's request to UN headquarters for an intelligence-gathering capability had been denied in January, leaving him practically helpless in the field. As such, he could collect only sketchy information about the looming tragedy. See Roméo Dallaire, "Military Aspects," in *A UN Rapid Deployment Brigade,* ed. Dick A. Leurdijl (The Hague: Netherlands Institute of International Relations, 1995).

63. See Barnett, *Eyewitness to a Genocide,* 88 and 161.

64. For an indictment of the role of France and the United States in not being able to stop the genocide, each in its own way, see Philip Gourevitch, *We Wish to Inform You That Tomorrow We Will Be Killed With Our Families: Stories from Rwanda* (New York: Farrar, Straus, and Giroux, 1998), for instance, pp. 143 and 150–51. France had been a supporter of the Hutu regime and its president, Juvénal Habyarimana, contributing to its reticence in not actively trying to stem the genocide. In addition, French suspicion generated by the growing influence of the United States in Africa in the 1990s, and the fact that the Rwanda Patriotic Army, led by Tutsis and based in Uganda, was Anglophone, played a role in France's reluctance to prevent the tragedy. For a French point of view on the role of France at the time of the Rwandan genocide, see Hubert Védrine, *Les mondes de François Mitterrand: À L'Élysée 1981–1995* (Paris: Fayard, 1996), 696–705. See also Gérard Prunier, *The Rwanda Crisis: History of a Genocide* (London: Hurst, 2002), 99–107.

65. For details on this issue, see Melvern, *A People Betrayed,* particularly chapters 11, 13, 14, and 15.

66. In the first days of the genocide, Belgium, France, and Italy sent troops to Rwanda to rescue expatriates. On April 9, Dallaire received a cable from Iqbal Riza, assistant secretary-general in the Department of Peacekeeping Operations, to tell him to cooperate with the evacuation. "You should make every effort not to compromise your impartiality and to act beyond your mandate," he was warned. "But you may exercise your discretion should this be essential for the evacuation of foreign nationals." In other words, only in the rescue of expatriates could Dallaire take risks. "This should not, repeat not, extend to participation in possible combat except in self-defense." Quoted in Melvern, *A People Betrayed,* 141. Furthermore, the mission was not authorized to rescue native UN personnel. Consequently, many of them were slaughtered.

67. See Presidential Decision Directive 25 (PDD 25), "Clinton Administration Policy on Reforming Multilateral Peace Operations," U.S. Department of State/Bureau of International Organizational Affairs, Washington, DC, February 22, 1996.

68. The secretary-general had approached the Organization of African Unity without success. Although a number of African countries were willing to contribute troops, they wanted equipment for their troops and to have the costs underwritten by the United Nations, which was not possible. See Melvern, *A People Betrayed*, 192 and 198.

69. United Nations, *Report of the Secretary-General on the Situation in Rwanda.* UN Doc. S/1994/565 (May 13, 1994).

70. Given the state of UN finances at the time and previous failed attempts to find alternative solutions to Western troop contributions, help for Rwanda quite obviously depended on Western states. Yet no permanent member of the Security Council volunteered to provide troops. As a result, no equipped troops were available for Rwanda. Furthermore, even if there had been troops, there was no airlift. Nor was there an agreed plan for what they would do when they got there. Colin Keating, the permanent representative of New Zealand, which was at the time a nonpermanent member of the Security Council, concluded, "[I]n reality the expansion is a fiction," quoted in Melvern, *A People Betrayed*, 198.

71. Any secretary-general who is eager to make a difference is faced with the ultimate diplomatic challenge: He lacks the two classical components and assets of traditional diplomacy: support by a nation and a sense of national interest. The conduct of traditional diplomacy is based upon and facilitated by the existence of national backing. The more powerful the backing, the more the diplomat enjoys an upper hand in negotiations. The sense of national interest is another critical tool for the conduct of traditional diplomacy. It provides key policy guidelines for diplomatic activity, outlining what is negotiable and what is not. These two elements are critical in structuring the bargaining power of the diplomat. Neither of them is available to the UN secretary-general. He is largely on his own, as the UN constituency is still more to be invented than to be called upon. Fragmented as it has been up until now, the UN constituency does not offer much international power backing and global interest to rely on. Consequently, human and moral qualities of inclusiveness are essential political qualities for the job of secretary-general.

72. Taking note of this state of affairs is, of course, not denying permanent members the right to have different views from one another, nor overlooking the positive aspects attached to a certain amount of discrepancies in their positions.

73. When the Security Council came to vote on the resolution to authorize the United States and its allies to use military force to drive Iraq out of Kuwait, China abstained. Later on, although it repeatedly asked Iraq to implement the Security Council resolutions on weapons inspection strictly, comprehensively, and completely and went along with the consensus on this issue, Beijing made it clear that it opposed using force even if Iraq refused to comply.

74. At the global level, China tends to interpret the balance of power in constitutional terms, as a system of checks and balances. In East Asia, China is obviously less vocal on the benefits of the balance of power, because it is itself a regional hegemon.

75. China vetoed the Security Council resolution to send military observers to Guatemala on January 10, 1997, because at the time the Guatemalan government was supporting Taiwanese representation at the United Nations. Similarly, the Chinese veto of the extension of UNPREDEP resulted from Macedonia's diplomatic recognition of Taiwan in January 1999 in exchange for $1.5 billion in aid.

76. China abstained on the following Security Council resolutions: 757 (May 30, 1992), tightening economic sanctions on the Federal Republic of Yugoslavia; 770 (August 13, 1992), authorizing the use of force to protect UN convoys; 776 (September 14, 1992), enlarging UNPROFOR's mandate pursuant to Resolution 770; 781 (October 9, 1992), banning under Chapter VII flights over Bosnia; 787 (November 16, 1992), prohibiting the transshipment of petroleum products through Serbia; 816 (March 31, 1993), authorizing all necessary measures to enforce the no-fly zone; 820 (April 18, 1993), further tightening sanctions and enhancing enforcement measures; and 942 (September 23, 1994), reinforcing and extending the measures imposed on Bosnian Serbs.

77. China abstained as well on UN Security Council Resolution 955 (November 8, 1994), recommending the establishment of the International Criminal Tribunal for Rwanda and the arrest of those responsible for the genocide. It considered the matter outside the jurisdiction of the Security Council.

78. A. J. R. Groom and Paul Taylor, "The United Nations System and the Kosovo Crisis," in Schnabel and Thakur, eds., *Kosovo and the Challenge of Humanitarian Intervention*, 296–99 and 302.

79. Quoted in M. Taylor Fravel, "China's Attitude toward UN Peacekeeping Operations since 1989," *Asian Survey* 11 (November 1996).

80. This led Russia on various occasions to launch its own brand of "peacekeeping operations" to address conflicts in the region. On this issue, see Lena Jonson and Clive Archer, "Russia and Peacekeeping in Eurasia," in *Peacekeeping and the Role of Russia in Eurasia,* ed. Lena Jonson and Clive Archer (Boulder, CO: Westview, 1996), 3–29.

81. The collapse of the Russian economy gave added importance to Western financial aid and may have served as a disincentive for Russia to speak up against Western policies.

82. Gow, *Triumph of the Lack of Will,* for instance, 184–201; and Mike Bowker, *Russian Foreign Policy and the End of the Cold War* (Burlington, Vt.: Dartmouth Publishing Company, 1997), 231–42.

83. The peace plan drafted by UN special envoy and former U.S. secretary of state Cyrus Vance, and European Commission representative and former British foreign minister Lord David Owen, would have divided Bosnia-Herzegovina into ten semiautonomous regions. The Contact Group was formed in April 1994, with five members—the United States, Russia, the United Kingdom, France, and Germany—to streamline the decision-making process regarding the search for a political solution to the conflict.

84. In 1993, Boris Yeltsin needed to appear tough and to support his Serb "brothers" or risk losing the support of Russian conservatives. See Peter Pringle, "UN Tightens Screw on Bosnia Serbs," *The Independent* (London), April 19, 1993, 10.

85. Julia Preston, "Russia Casts Veto in 1st Split on Bosnia," *Washington Post*, December 3, 1994, A22. If NATO had asked for UN approval of air strikes in Kosovo in March 1999 through a resolution, Russia would have used its veto against NATO. Russia was adamantly opposed to the use of force in Kosovo, as indicated by the "Appeal by the Federation Council of the Federal Assembly to the Parliaments of all Countries, the Inter-Parliamentary Union, the Parliamentary Assembly of the Council of Europe, the Parliamentary Assembly of the Organization for Security and Cooperation in Europe, and the Inter-Parliamentary Assembly of the State Members of the Commonwealth of Independent States," UN Doc. A/53/886, S/1999/352 (March 27, 1999). In fact, Moscow sponsored, without success, a Security Council resolution on March 26 1999, to condemn the use of force. Consequently, the United States was eager to avoid a vote in the Security Council.

86. Christopher S. Wren, "Russia Fails in UN to Bar Raids on Serbs," *New York Times,* September 13, 1995, A11.

87. It abstained on Security Council Resolution 820 (April 17, 1993), concerning the peace plan for Bosnia and the strengthening of the measures imposed by the earlier resolutions on the situation in the former Yugoslavia; Security Council Resolution 970 (January 12, 1995), dealing with the closure of the international border between Yugoslavia and Bosnia and Herzegovina with respect to all goods except for essential humanitarian needs; Security Council Resolutions 988 (April 21, 1995) and 1003 (July 5, 1995), asking for further extension of the partial suspension of sanctions against Yugoslavia; and Security Council Resolution 1022 (November 22, 1995), on suspension of measures imposed by or reaffirmed in Security Council resolutions concerning the situation in the former Yugoslavia. Later on, Russia also abstained on Security Council Resolution 1305 (June 21, 2000), on the continuation of the multinational Stabilization Force (SFOR) and the extension of the mandate of the UN Mission in Bosnia and Herzegovina (UNMIBH). The resolution envisioned the possibility of the use of force to carry out its mission; see paragraphs 6, 10, and 12 of the resolution.

88. The Russian abstention on Kosovo in May 1999 was in protest of continued NATO bombing. Shortly after the bombing of the Chinese embassy in Belgrade, both Russia and China felt that no further resolutions could be discussed on Kosovo until the bombing had stopped.

89. The United States effectively destroyed the Vance-Owen Plan through allegations that it favored the Bosnian Serbs, rewarded aggression, and condoned ethnic cleansing. Ironically, the Dayton Accords in November 1995 accepted the idea of an ethnically defined Serbian territory that would run contiguously from eastern Bosnia across the north and into the northwestern part of the country. The principles of resisting ethnic cleansing and Serbian territorial contiguity had been conceded. Having refused to attempt implementation of the Vance-Owen Plan on these grounds in 1993, the United States was prepared in 1995 to oversee and contribute significantly to a deal that was probably worse regarding the principles at stake. See Gow, *Triumph of the Lack of Will,* 313.

90. The same would happen in the context of the war against Iraq in the winter of 2002–03, with UN Security Council Resolution 1441. For more on this issue, see Michael Byers, "Agreeing to Disagree: Security Council Resolution 1441 and Intentional Ambiguity," *Global Governance: A Review of Multilateralism and International Organizations* 10, no. 2 (April–June 2004). See also Jean-Marc Coicaud, with Hélène Gandois and Lysette Rutgers, "Explaining France's Opposition to the War Against Iraq," in *The Iraq Crisis and World Order,* ed. Ramesh Thakur and Waheguru Pal Singh Sidhu (New York: United Nations University Press, 2006).

91. Because progress in this direction was hampered by financial constraints, one solution that was adopted was for member states (mainly developed countries) to loan personnel to the departments in charge of peace operations issues (in particular, the UN Department of Peacekeeping Operations, or DPKO) at no financial cost to the United Nations. The gratis personnel were mainly military personnel who could help monitor operational matters on the ground, thus complementing the work of DPKO desk officers. Developing countries were not enthusiastic about the use of these gratis personnel, believing they gave too much power to the developed countries. In time they successfully lobbied through the General Assembly to strictly limit the use of such personnel. See UN General Assembly Resolution 51/243 (September 15, 1997); and United Nations, *Report of the Secretary-General: Phasing Out the Use of Gratis Personnel in the Secretariat.* UN Doc.

A/52/710 (December 8, 1997). For more actions, see UN General Assembly Resolution 54/264 (July 21, 2000); United Nations, *Report of the Secretary-General: Gratis Personnel Provided by Governments and Other Entities.* UN Doc. A/C.5/55/13 (October 17, 2000); and United Nations, *Report of the Secretary-General: Gratis Personnel Provided by Governments and Other Entities.* UN Doc. A/57/721 (February 3, 2003).

92. Initially the Situation Room was set up to monitor the Unified Task Force (UNITAF) and UNOSOM II in Somalia. The Situation Room was renamed the Situation Center in November 1993. For more information on the strengthening of the Department of Peacekeeping Operations, see, for example, Oliver Ramsbotham and Tom Woodhouse, *Encyclopedia of International Peacekeeping Operations* (Santa Barbara, CA: ABC-CLIO, 1999), 255–56.

93. Information provided by the United Nations Department of Peacekeeping Operations.

94. On this question, see, for example, the remarks of Marrack Goulding, *Peacemonger* (London: John Murray, 2002), 43.

95. The current under secretary-general for peacekeeping operations, Jean-Marie Guéhenno, appointed in October 2000, made a special effort to address this problem. Field experience was made more or less a requirement for being hired in a professional capacity in the headquarters of the UN Department of Peacekeeping Operations. Those already employed at headquarters are encouraged to spend a period of time in the field.

96. On the issue of bureaucratic universalism in the context of international organizations, see Michael N. Barnett and Martha Finnemore, "The Politics, Power, and Pathologies of International Organizations," *International Organization* 53, no. 4 (Autumn 1999): 721. See also Michael Barnett and Martha Finnemore, *Rules for the World: International Organizations in Global Politics* (Ithaca, NY: Cornell University Press, 2004).

97. Mohamed Sahnoun, who was the Special Representative of the UN Secretary-General in Somalia between March and October 1992, was probably at the time the one official in the United Nations most sensitive to the need for this type of approach. See Mohamed Sahnoun, *Somalia: The Missed Opportunity* (Washington, DC: United Institute States Institute of Peace Press, 1997).

98. See United Nations, *Report of the Secretary-General Pursuant to General Assembly Resolution 53/53: The Fall of Srebrenica,* for example, 108–11. For more on the shortcomings of UN leadership, see Jean-Marc Coicaud, "International Organizations as a Profession: Professional Mobility and Power Distribution," in *The International Mobility of Talent: Types, Causes, and Development Impact,* ed. Andrés Solimano (New York: Oxford University Press, in press).

99. On indifference and bureaucracy, see Michael Herzfeld, *The Social Production of Indifference: Exploring the Symbolic Roots of Western Bureaucracy* (Chicago: University of Chicago Press, 1992).

100. See Ingrid A. Lehman, *Peacekeeping and Public Information: Caught in the Crossfire* (London: Frank Cass, 1999), for example, 1–5.

101. There has been an improvement of the communication system inside the United Nations, including between headquarters and the field, since 1997, namely with the implementation of the e-mail system. The communication between headquarters and the field is likely to improve further with the use of wireless communication systems to facilitate communications between headquarters and peacekeeping operations deployed in remote areas that lack a communications infrastructure.

102. For instance, between 1993 and 2000, the United Nations' involvement in Haiti went by the acronyms of UNMIH, UNSMIH, UNTMIH, and MIPONUH. In Croatia, from 1995 onward, the United Nations' involvement took the acronyms of UNCRO (UN Confidence Restoration Operation), UNTAES (UN Transitional Authority in Eastern Slavonia, Banjara, and Western Sirmium), UNPSG (UN Civilian Police Support Group), and UNMOP (UN Mission of Observers in Prevlaka).

103. See the description of the UNPROFOR chain of command in Institute for National Strategic Studies, *Command Arrangements for Peace Operations* (Washington, DC: National Defense University Press, May 1995).

104. See Marrack Goulding, Foreword, in Lehman, *Peacekeeping and Public Information,* xii.

105. Figures provided by the UN Web Services Section, News and Media Division, Department of Public Information.

106. See Warren P. Strobel, *Late-Breaking Foreign Policy: The News Media's Influence on Peace Operations* (Washington, DC: United States Institute of Peace Press, 1997).

107. The effectiveness of Bretton Woods institutions depended as much on their technical expertise as on the fact that they proposed economic remedies that echoed the prevalent Western economic ideology. Now that such neoliberal prescriptions have come under severe criticism, it is their ability to prevent financial crises and promote development—their effectiveness, if not legitimacy—that is questioned. See Joseph Stiglitz, *Globalization and its Discontents* (New York: Penguin Books, 2002).

CHAPTER 3

1. See Poirier, *La Crise des Fondements*, 111–13.

2. John Gerard Ruggie, "Multilateralism: The Anatomy of an Institution," *International Organization* 46, no. 3 (Summer 1992): 568. Defining multilateralism might seem relatively easy, until one considers what exactly constitutes a multilateral institution: The distinction between multilateral *institutions* and multilateral*ism* is often overlooked. Ruggie provides some clues about the nebulous distinction in terms of the regional normative dimension: "[T]he multilateral form should not be equated with universal geographical scope; the attributes of multilateralism characterize relations within specific collectivities that may and often do fall short of the whole universe of nations." For more, see idem, *Constructing the World Polity: Essays on International Institutionalization* (New York: Routledge, 2002), 102–130.

3. See Martha Finnemore and Kathryn Sikkink, "International Norm Dynamics and Political Change," *International Organization* 52, no. 4 (Autumn 1998).

4. Even though the only Article 5 mission invoked in NATO's history has been the defense of the United States (with flights of AWACS aircraft along the eastern seaboard) after the September 11, 2001, attacks on U.S. territory.

5. At NATO's April 1999 Washington Summit, the member states approved the organization's second "New" Strategic Concept of the post–Cold War era. According to the concept, and in contrast to the Cold War period, member states' military capabilities were now meant to be maintained for two purposes: collective defense in accordance with the North Atlantic Treaty's Article 5 and non–Article 5 crisis response operations. For more on this, see Allen G. Sens, "Living in a Renovated NATO," *Canadian Military Journal* 1, no. 4 (Winter 2000–01): 79–86.

6. John S. Duffield, "Transatlantic Relations after the Cold War: Theory, Evidence and the Future," *International Studies Perspectives* 2, no. 1 (February 2001): 109.

7. For an excellent survey of NATO's post–Cold War redefinition of its principal missions and tasks, see David S. Yost, *NATO Transformed: The Alliance's New Roles in International Security* (Washington, DC: U.S. Institute of Peace Press, 1998); and Robert McCalla, "NATO's Persistence after the Cold War," *International Organization* 50, no. 3 (Summer 1996).

8. For more about the "New World Order," see Eric A. Miller and Steve A. Yetic, "The New World Order in Theory and Practice: The Bush Administration's Worldview in Transition," *Presidential Studies Quarterly* 31, no. 1 (March 2001).

9. UN General Assembly Resolution 2625 (1971), 121–24.

10. For a detailed analysis of each of these international principles, see Antonio Cassese, *International Law in a Divided World*, rev. ed. (Oxford, UK: Clarendon Press, 1994), 129–57. Also, on the nonexhaustive character of this list and the status of international principles, see Michel Virally, *Le Droit International en Devenir: Essais écrits au Fil des Ans* (Geneva: Presses Universitaires de France, 1990), 206–12.

11. For a slightly different perspective on international principles, see Hedley Bull, *The Anarchical Society: A Study of Order in World Politics*, rev. ed. (New York: Columbia University Press, 1995), 65–68.

12. For a constructivist understanding, see, for example, Emanuel Adler, *Communitarian International Relations: The Epistemic Foundations of International Relations* (New York: Routledge, 2005), especially part 2, pp. 29–115.

13. For an overview of the relationship between law and legitimacy at the international level, see Thomas M. Franck, *The Power of Legitimacy among Nations* (New York: Oxford University Press, 1990).

14. On sovereignty and its interpretations, see Philip Allott, *Eunomia: New Order for a New World* (New York: Oxford University Press, 1990), 246–49.

15. On this issue in general terms and how it can be used to create a pluralist yet coherent normative international order, see Mireille Delmas-Marty, *Pour un Droit Commun* (Paris: Editions du Seuil, 1994); and Mireille Delmas-Marty, *Les Forces Imaginantes du Droit (II): Le Pluralisme Ordonné* (Paris: Editions du Seuil, 2006).

16. See Allen Buchanan, *Justice, Legitimacy, and Self-Determination: Moral Foundations for International Law* (New York: Oxford University Press, 2004). See also Robert O. Keohane and J. L. Holzgrefe, eds., *Humanitarian Intervention: Ethical, Legal, and Political Dilemmas* (New York: Cambridge University Press, 2003).

17. On the interaction between power and value ideals and their impact on change in the international community, see, for example, Alexander Wendt, *Social Theory of International Politics* (New York: Cambridge University Press, 2001).

18. In another context, see Kathryn Sikkink, *Mixed Signals: U.S. Human Rights Policy and Latin America* (Ithaca, NY: Cornell University Press, 2004).

19. A classic example is the influence of the American and French revolutions on the evolution of international legitimacy in modern times; see Mlada Bukovansky, *Legitimacy and Power Politics: The American and French Revolutions in International Political Culture* (Princeton, NJ: Princeton University Press, 2002). For an analysis of the historical evolution and dynamics of legitimacy at the international level, see Ian Clark, *Legitimacy in International Society* (New York: Oxford University Press, 2005).

20. For an excellent summary of collective security designs and NATO's assumption of collective security tasks in the immediate post–Cold War era, see Yost, *NATO Transformed.*

21. Ibid., 12.

22. Loc. cit., emphasis added.

23. The classic sociological treatises on solidarity are Émile Durkheim, *The Division of Labor in Society,* trans. W. D. Halls (New York: Free Press, 1997); and Ferdinand Tönnies, *Community and Society,* trans. and ed. Charles P. Loomis (Mineola, NY: Dover, 2002). For more on the notion of solidarity, its history, and application at the national and international levels, see Serge Paugam, ed., *Repenser la Solidarité* (Paris: Presses Universitaires de France, 2007).

24. See, for example, Louis Henkin, *The Age of Rights* (New York: Columbia University Press, 1990); and Mary Ann Glendon, *A World Made New: Eleanor Roosevelt and the Universal Declaration of Human Rights* (New York: Random House, 2001). For a critical assessment of U.S. contributions to the debates and drafting of the Universal Declaration of Human Rights, see Carol Anderson, *Eyes Off the Prize: The United Nations and the African-American Struggle for Human Rights, 1944–1955* (New York: Cambridge University Press, 2003).

25. See James Gow, *Triumph of the Lack of Will: International Diplomacy and the Yugoslav War* (New York: Columbia University Press, 1997), 255–59 and 261–62.

26. Ivo H. Daalder, *Getting to Dayton: The Making of America's Bosnia Policy* (Washington, DC: Brookings Institution Press, 2000), 180. On the connection between the evolving domestic democratic culture in the United States and the American defense of democratic rights at the international level, see also Thomas M. Franck, *The Empowered Self: Law and Society in the Age of Individualism* (New York: Oxford University Press, 1999), 45–46.

27. On these questions, see Georg Simmel, *Conflict and the Web of Group-Affiliations,* trans. Kurt H. Wolff and Reinhard Bendix (New York: The Free Press, 1964).

28. See Durkheim, *The Division of Labor in Society,* and Tönnies, *Community and Society.*

29. The movement toward a wide and profound sense of the realization of justice, fueled by democratic values and rights, is one of the defining "vectors" of modernity at the national and international levels, but such a movement did not happen without a struggle. Despite the declarations of principles, the beneficiaries of democratic universalism and equality initially formed an exclusive club, and it has been around the boundaries of inclusion and exclusion that the battles for political, economic, and social justice have focused throughout the evolution of modern democratic culture. On this question, see Andrew Linklater, *The Transformations of Political Community: Ethical Foundations of the Post-Westphalian Era* (Columbia, SC: University of South Carolina Press, 1998), 117–18. Also, the battles on where and how to draw the line between inclusion and exclusion in the key areas and roles of society, in connection with the expectations viewed as legitimate by excluded peoples (the evaluation of the just or unjust character of a situation), revolve around the need to accord more weight to the perspective of the excluded individual than to that of the privileged one. Being on the wrong side of the fence gives greater credence and validity to justice claims. On this issue, see John Rawls's second principle of justice in his *Justice as Fairness: A Restatement,* ed. Erin Kelly (Cambridge, MA: Harvard University Press, 2001), 42–43.

30. Competitive commercial and political interests have shaped international law in critical ways. For an account of the links between international legal arguments and justifications; commercial and political interests associated with European expansion overseas; and forms of colonization, including conquests and settlements, see Richard Tuck, *The Rights of War and Peace: Political Thought and the International Order from Grotius to Kant* (New York: Oxford University Press, 1999), 16–50, 78–108, and 166–96. See also Martti Koskenniemi, *The Gentle Civilizer of Nations: The Rise and Fall of International Law, 1870–1960* (New York: Cambridge University Press, 2002), especially chapters 1 and 2.

31. Anthony Anghie, *Imperialism, Sovereignty, and the Making of International Law* (New York: Cambridge University Press, 2005).

32. The seriousness of this issue has been a constant concern in the study of modernity. Anglo-American scholars have been particularly apt in identifying mechanisms of rational choice that ensure the cohabitation of self-interest and social cooperation; see Jane J. Mansbridge, "The Rise and Fall of Self-Interest in the Explanation of Political Life," in *Beyond Self-Interest,* ed. Jane J. Mansbridge (Chicago: University of Chicago Press, 1990), 3–22. European analysts have tended to explore a sense of community that is able to reconcile the autonomous agent and the social being by insisting on the role of shared culture and history, and of the reciprocity of rights and duties.

33. Although much of the scholarly literature on modern democratic culture focuses on its atomization, it remains shaped by forms of kinship. Its decisive contribution to the organization of collective life in connection with the attribution and distribution of goods (be they political, economic, social, or intellectual) based on talent and merit (hence the importance of access to education for a fair competition for goods) does not eliminate the remnants of kinship's influence, in which, for instance, familial social relations prove to be, in one way or another, a crucial determinant.

34. See, for example, Thomas M. Franck, "Legitimacy and the Democratic Entitlement," in *Democratic Governance and International Law,* ed. Gregory H. Fox and Brad R. Roth (New York: Cambridge University Press, 2000), 25–41.

35. Human rights conventions create legal obligations, and their ratification by member states leads political institutions, in principle, to guarantee their respect; see Paul Reuter, *Introduction to the Law of Treaties* (London: Pinter, 1989), 73–78; and Anthony Aust, *Modern Treaty Law and Practice* (New York: Cambridge University Press, 2000), 75–99.

36. The yearly assessment of national human rights situations by the United Nations Commission on Human Rights is barely a breach of the wall of *domaine réservé,* under which states have been historically tempted to shelter internal atrocities from international scrutiny.

37. See W. Michael Reisman, "Sovereignty and Human Rights in Contemporary International Law," in Fox and Roth, eds., *Democratic Governance and International Law,* 240–58.

38. On this issue, see William A. Schabas, *Genocide in International Law* (New York: Cambridge University Press, 2000), 545–46: "Perhaps the greatest unresolved question in the Convention is the meaning of the enigmatic word 'prevent.' The title of the Convention indicates that its scope involves prevention of the crime and, in article I, State parties undertake to prevent genocide. Aside from article VIII, which entitles State parties to apply to the relevant organs of the United Nations for the prevention of genocide, the Convention has little specific to say on the question. The obligation to prevent genocide is a blank sheet awaiting the inscriptions of State practice and case law. A conservative interpretation of the provision requires States only to enact appropriate legislation and to take other measures to ensure that genocide does not occur. A more progressive view requires States to take action not just within their own borders but outside them, activity that may go as far as the use of force in order to prevent the crime being committed. The debate of this is unresolved, and is likely to remain so, at least until the next episode of genocide, if there is no insistence that the subject be clarified."

39. See Allott, *Eunomia*, 248–50.

40. On the rule of law in general, see Brian Z. Tamanaha, *On the Rule of Law: History, Politics, Theory* (New York: Cambridge University Press, 2004).

41. Compliance with legal rules is rather low at the international level. On this issue and the debates that it has engendered on the nature of international law, see Franck, *The Power of Legitimacy among Nations*, 29.

42. Article 2 (7) stipulates "Nothing contained in the present Charter shall authorize the United Nations to intervene in matters which are essentially within the domestic jurisdiction of any state or shall require the Members to submit such matters to settlement under the present Charter; but this principle shall not prejudice the application of enforcement measures under Chapter VII." Article 39 of Chapter VII stipulates "The Security Council shall determine the existence of any threat to the peace, breach of the peace, or act of aggression, and shall make recommendations, or decide what measures shall be taken in accordance with Articles 41 and 42, to maintain or restore international peace and security." See also Simon Chesterman, *Just War or Just Peace? Humanitarian Intervention and International Law* (New York: Oxford University Press, 2001), 127–60. Rather than welcome the stretch as a sign of normative progress, Chesterman cautions against it (p. 161). See as well the review of the book by Nicholas J. Wheeler in *International Affairs* 77, no. 3 (July 2001).

43. On deliberation in general and the dilemmas that it can create, see, for example, *The Ethics of Aristotle: The Nicomachean Ethics*, trans. J. A. K. Thomson; ed. Hugh Tredennich (London: Penguin, 2004).

44. Between 1946 and 1989, the Security Council met 2,903 times and adopted 646 resolutions. Between 1990 and 1999, it met 1,183 times and adopted 638 resolutions (an average of 64 per year). In its first forty-four years, twenty-four resolutions cited or used the terms of Chapter VII. The total number of Chapter VII resolutions passed in the 1990s was 139 (1990: 11; 1991: 13; 1992: 10; 1994: 24; 1995: 21; 1996: 9; 1997: 15; 1998: 22; 1999: 14). See Chesterman, *Just War or Just Peace?* (p. 121).

45. On the role of the Security Council as an instrument of legitimacy, see, for example, Ian Hurd, *After Anarchy: Legitimacy and Power in the United Nations Security Council* (Princeton, NJ: Princeton University Press, 2007).

46. On this issue, see Michael Walzer, *Just and Unjust Wars: A Moral Argument with Historical Illustrations* (New York: Basic Books, 1977), for instance, pp. 120–24 and 231–32.

47. The total cost of the UN peace operations in Africa between 1991 and 2000 was $5.3 billion. For the same period in the Balkans, the cost to the international community, including UN peace operations and the NATO interventions, amounted to $30.1 billion ($6.1 billion and $24 billion, respectively); see the page on the UN Department of Peacekeeping Operations entitled "United Nations Peacekeeping Operations," www.un.org/ Depts/DPKO/missions; and *SIPRI Yearbook 2000: Armaments, Disarmament, and International Security* (New York: Oxford University Press, 2000). The source for NATO figures 1997–98 through 1999–2000 is International Institute for Strategic Studies, *The*

Military Balance (New York: Oxford University Press, various years). In the last few years, the problem of selective engagement has only deepened, with developed countries less and less willing to get involved in peace operations short of their immediate interests; see Jean-Marie Guéhenno, "Opérations de Maintien de la Paix: La Nouvelle Donne," *Le Monde* (Paris), December 17, 2002. In this article, Guéhenno notes that there were more NATO troops deployed in the Balkans in December 2000 than there were UN troops at work in the rest of the world, and that out of the 34,000 UN troops deployed worldwide, fewer than 4,000 came from the European Union and no more than a few dozen from the United States—a problem in subsequent years. See also Secretary-General Kofi Annan, "Remarks on UN Peacekeeping Operations to the Security Council," Press Release SG/SM/9311/SC/8096/PKO/107, New York: United Nations, May 17, 2004.

48. See Michael Walzer, "Kosovo," *Dissent*, Summer 1999.

49. This shift was not easy for an international community that was used to dealing with heads of states, legitimate or de facto. The focus of the international community on the "Belgrade-centric" diplomatic negotiations in the Balkans (to the detriment of the other capitals of former Yugoslavia), illustrates this difficulty. On this issue in the Rwandan context, see Samantha Power, "Bystanders to Genocide," *The Atlantic Monthly*, September 2001, 7.

50. Michael Ignatieff, *Virtual War: Kosovo and Beyond* (New York: Metropolitan Books, 2000); and Ivo H. Daalder and Michael E. O'Hanlon, *Winning Ugly: NATO's War to Save Kosovo* (Washington, DC: Brookings Institution Press, 2001).

51. At a general level, peace operations in the 1990s (as in any other period) were not about winning a war and defeating an enemy per se. Thus there were no conventional military laurels to be expected, and, in this regard, there is a striking difference between the way soldiers who die in the line of duty for the nation are celebrated, even in an era of waning patriotism, and the way those who die for internationalist causes in the UN context tend to be perceived. Consider the example of the United States: While the sacrifices of soldiers killed for the defense of the United States are remembered with gratitude and pride, there is some public bitterness, if not a sense of waste, when an American soldier dies within the framework of a UN operation. Moreover, for the intervening powers and their military forces, limited use of force in the context of peacemaking in the 1990s represented the worst of two worlds, the world of peacekeeping and the world of war. Unlike interpositional peacekeeping, which implies no traditional military glory and honor but little risk of casualties, and unlike war, which involves high risk of casualties but military glory and honor, limited use of force in the setting of peacemaking entailed high risk of casualties and hardly any prospect of military rewards.

52. See, for example, Wesley K. Clark, *Waging Modern War: Bosnia, Kosovo, and the Future of Combat* (New York: Public Affairs, 2001), 293–321.

53. Advanced technology certainly provides a crucial operational advantage in wartime, but its use would not be valued so much if it did not fit well with casualty aversion; see, for example, Edward N. Luttwak on the "post-heroic" war in "Give War a Chance," *Foreign Affairs*, July–August 1999: 40–41. And what is true of warfare conducted in the name of national interest is even truer for humanitarian crises: "For most of the six weeks of air and missile strikes, fear of casualties has limited the exposure of pilots to Yugoslavia's anti-aircraft batteries and surface-to-air missiles. As a result, most of NATO's 3,300 strike missions have been conducted from high altitudes, typically more than 15,000 feet," in Eric Schmitt and Steven Lee Myers, "NATO Planes Flying Lower, Increasing Risk of Being Hit," *New York Times*, May 4, 1999. See also David E. Sanger, "America Finds It

Lonely at the Top," *New York Times*, July 18, 1999; Ignatieff, *Virtual War*; O'Hanlon, *Winning Ugly*; and Eliot Cohen, "The Mystique of U.S. Air Power," *Foreign Affairs*, January–February 1994: "Air power is an unusually seductive form of military strength, in part because, like modern courtship, it appears to offer gratification without commitment" (p. 109).

54. For more on international law and nationalism, see, for instance, Nathaniel Berman, "The International Law of Nationalism: Group Identity and Legal History," in *International Law and the Rise of Nations: The State System and the Challenge of Ethnic Groups*, ed. Robert J. Beck and Thomas Ambrosio (Washington, DC: CQ Press, 2001).

55. See Mahmood Mamdani, *When Victims Become Killers: Colonialism, Nativism, and the Genocide in Rwanda* (Princeton, NJ: Princeton University Press, 2001).

CHAPTER 4

1. Coral Bell, "East Timor, Canberra, and Washington: A Case Study in Crisis Management," *Australian Journal of International Affairs* 54, no. 2 (2000).

2. See Henry Kissinger, *Diplomacy* (New York: Simon & Schuster, 1994), 46.

3. On Wilson's ideas, see Hidemi Suganami, *The Domestic Analogy and World Order Proposals* (New York: Cambridge University Press, 1989), 86–89.

4. See Inis L. Claude, Jr., *Swords Into Plowshares: The Problems and Progress of International Organization* (New York: McGraw-Hill, 1984), 61.

5. Roosevelt's commitment to internationalism was the product of a long development. When World War II elevated Roosevelt to a position of world importance, he had no consistent history of either isolationism or internationalism. Although he had defended the League of Nations' Covenant in the 1920 campaign, he became the first Democratic candidate to explicitly repudiate the League in 1932: It was Roosevelt's presidential campaign platform that recovery must be based on independent domestic action rather than world arrangements (such as the future Bretton Woods institutions). In the mid-1930s, he was in no mood to try to reshape the predominant isolationist and pacifist sentiment of the United States; in 1935, although he was opposed to its mandatory embargo provision, he signed the isolationist Neutrality Act. Roosevelt's first sign of a swing toward collective security came on October 5, 1937, when he proposed to "quarantine" aggressor nations and asserted that "there is no escape" for the United States from international anarchy and instability "through isolation or neutrality." From then on, while echoing the reluctance of the American people to go to war, he gradually made clear that the United States could no longer avoid involvement; see Richard Hofstadter, *The American Political Tradition and the Men Who Made It* (New York: Vintage Books, 1976), 444–56.

6. See Gabriel Kolko, *Confronting the Third World: United States Foreign Policy, 1945–1980* (New York: Pantheon Books, 1988).

7. Address by President George H. W. Bush to the United Nations General Assembly, September 2, 1992, *Weekly Compilation of Presidential Documents* 28, no. 39 (1992), 1697.

8. See David Halberstam, *War in a Time of Peace: Bush, Clinton, and the Generals* (New York: Scribner, 2001), especially chapter 1.

9. For instance, while the Bush administration had sought the support of the Kurds in northern Iraq and that of the Shiite Muslims in the south just before and during the war, it did not want to back up their claims for more autonomy, if not independence, once the war was won. The most it was willing to do was to decide, with France and Britain, that it did not need UN approval to impose a no-fly zone in northern Iraq to prevent Saddam Hussein from airlifting in troops to suppress the Kurds and, later, a similar zone in the south to protect the Shiite Muslims; see Lawrence Freedman and Efraim Karsh, *The Gulf Conflict, 1990–1991: Diplomacy and War in the New World Order* (Princeton, NJ: Princeton University Press, 1993), 410–27. Another example is Somalia: President George H. W. Bush saw only moral benefits in intervening in a country where clan leaders were warring with each other and destroying society by contributing to the starvation of the population. Moreover, the risks involved in intervening in Somalia seemed minimal, which made the U.S. involvement possible.

10. For more on the cast of characters of the foreign policy team of the first Clinton administration, see William G. Hyland, *Clinton's World: Remaking American Foreign Policy* (Westport, CT: Praeger, 1999), 18–20.

11. On the notion of how Clinton embraced democracy's enlargement, see Douglas Brinkley, "Democratic Enlargement: The Clinton Doctrine," *Foreign Policy*, Spring 1997; and Anthony Lake, "From Containment to Enlargement" (remarks at Johns Hopkins University, School of Advanced International Studies, Washington, DC, September 21, 1993).

12. For a detailed description of the draft, see Ivo H. Daalder, "Knowing When to Say No: The Development of U.S. Policy for Peacekeeping," in *UN Peacekeeping, American Politics, and the Uncivil Wars of the 1990s*, ed. William J. Durch (New York: St Martin's, 1996), 44–48.

13. For a comprehensive analysis of PDD 25, see, for example, Michael G. MacKinnon, *The Evolution of U.S. Peacekeeping Policy under Clinton: A Fairweather Friend?* (London: Frank Cass, 2000), 26–30.

14. The White House, Presidential Decision Directive 25, Executive Summary, "The Clinton Administration's Policy on Reforming Multilateral Peace Operations," May 1994, Washington, DC, www.whitehouse.gov/WH/EOP/NSC/html/documents/NSC Doc1.html.

15. Ibid.

16. For more on the Clinton administration's reversal of foreign policy in relation to the United Nations and humanitarian crisis, see John F. Harris, *The Survivor: Bill Clinton in the White House* (New York: Random House, 2005), 120–28.

17. John Dumbrell, *American Foreign Policy: Carter to Clinton* (New York: St. Martin's, 1997), 183.

18. Hyland, *Clinton's World*, 138.

19. See Steven Kull and I. M. Destler, *Misreading the Public: The Myth of New Isolationism* (Washington, DC: Brookings Institution Press, 1999).

20. See John Hart Ely, *War and Responsibility: Constitutional Lessons of Vietnam and Its Aftermath* (Princeton, NJ: Princeton University Press, 1993), 3–4.

21. Alexis de Tocqueville reasoned in the 1840s that "[if] the Union's existence were constantly menaced, and if its great interests were continually interwoven with those of other powerful nations, one would see the prestige of the executive growing, because of what was expected from it and of what it did"; *Democracy in America*, vol. 1 (New York: Anchor, 1969), 126.

22. Michael Lind, "Civil War by Other Means," *Foreign Affairs*, September/October 1999, 140.

23. Jeremy D. Rosner, *The New Tug-of-War: Congress, the Executive Branch, and National Security* (Washington, DC: Carnegie Endowment for International Peace, 1995), 66.

24. The U.S. Congress neither explicitly approved nor blocked the air strikes, and it appropriated funds for the air campaign and the U.S. peacekeeping deployment in Kosovo after the fact; see Steven Woerel and Julie Kim, *Kosovo and U.S. Policy* (Washington, DC: Congressional Research Service, June 22, 2001), 15.

25. See Rosner, *The New Tug-of-War*, 77–82.

26. James M. Lindsay and Ivo H. Daalder, "How to Revitalize a Dysfunctional Department," *Foreign Service Journal*, March 2001.

27. See James M. Lindsay, "Cowards, Beliefs, and Structures: Congress and the Use of Force," in *The Use of Force after the Cold War*, ed. H. W. Brands (College Station, TX: A&M University Press, 2000), 144–48.

28. United Nations, *Report of the Panel on United Nations Peace Operations* (the "Brahimi Report"), UN Doc. A/55/305–S/200/809 (August 21, 2000), 46.

29. See, for example, "Congress Folds State Department Authorization into Omnibus Spending Bill," *Congressional Quarterly* 14, no. 3 (1999).

30. For more on the congressional debates on this issue, see Nina M. Serafino, *Peacekeeping: Issues of U.S. Military Involvement* (Washington, DC: Congressional Research Service, June 6, 2001).

31. Eric Victor Larson, *Ends and Means in the Democratic Conversation: Understanding the Role of Casualties in Support for U.S. Military Operations* (Santa Monica, CA: RAND Corporation, 1996), 284–88.

32. See Ole R. Holsti, "A Widening Gap between the U.S. Military and Civilian Society? Some Evidence, 1976–1996," *International Security* 23, no. 3 (Winter 1999): 11.

33. Ibid.

34. On the Republican side, for instance, Georgia's Newt Gingrich was a rising political figure in the House of Representatives and might have posed as a defense hawk in 1992, but he had chosen not to serve in Vietnam, accepting instead a number of educational deferments. Mississippi Senator Trent Lott, a soaring luminary of the Southern wing of the GOP, had been able to come up with deferments for family reasons. Vice President Dan Quayle served in the Indiana National Guard and yet managed to hold a hawkish view of the war. Dick Cheney, then the secretary of defense, had not served in Vietnam, although he had been the right age to go; when asked about it, he casually said that he had "other priorities in the sixties than military service" (quoted in Halberstam, *War in a Time of Peace*, 110). Moreover, the eldest son of George H. W. Bush, George W. Bush, who would himself be elected president in 2000, had also avoided going to Vietnam, serving instead in a Texas Air National Guard unit.

35. "I particularly condemn the way our political leaders supplied the manpower for that war. The policies—determining who would be drafted and who would be deferred, who would serve and who would escape, who would die and who would live—were an antidemocratic disgrace. I can never forgive a leadership that said, in effect: these young men—poorer, less educated, less privileged—are expendable (someone described them as 'economic cannon fodder'), but the rest are too good to risk. I am angry that so many of the sons of the powerful and well placed and so many professional athletes (who were probably healthier than any of us) managed to wrangle slots in Reserve and National Guard units. Of the many tragedies of Vietnam, this raw class discrimination strikes me as the most damaging to the ideal that all Americans are created equal and owe equal allegiance to their country"; Colin L. Powell, with Joseph Persico, *My American Journey* (New York: Random House, 1995), 148.

36. A large margin of military officers is still very much opposed to gays and lesbians serving openly in the U.S. armed forces; see Peter D. Feaver and Richard H. Kohn, "The Gap: Soldiers, Civilians and their Mutual Misunderstanding," *The National Interest*, Fall 2000.

37. For an evaluation of the transformation of the American military in the aftermath of the Cold War, see Andrew J. Bacevich, *American Empire: The Realities and Consequences of U.S. Diplomacy* (Cambridge, MA: Harvard University Press, 2002), 130–40.

38. Jeffrey D. Brake, *Quadrennial Defense Review (QDR): Background, Process and Issues* (Washington, DC: Congressional Research Service, January 8, 2001).

39. Smaller-scale contingency operations were defined as those that "encompass the full range of joint military operations beyond peacetime engagement but short of major theater warfare: show-of-force operations, interventions, limited strikes, noncombatant evacuation operations, no-fly-zone enforcement, peace enforcement, maritime sanctions enforcement, counter-terrorism operations, peacekeeping, humanitarian assistance and disaster relief"; U.S. Department of Defense, *Quadrennial Defense Review*, section 3.

40. The White House, The Clinton Administration's Policy on Managing Complex Contingency Operations, Presidential Decision Directive, May 1997, http://clinton4 .nara.gov/WH/EOP/NSC/html/documents/NSCDoc2.html.

41. See Bruce W. Jentleson, *Coercive Prevention: Normative, Political, and Policy Dilemmas*. Peaceworks, no. 35 (Washington, DC: United States Institute of Peace, October 2000), 31. Later on, the *Quadrennial Defense Review* continued to make two theaters of operation in overlapping time frames a priority. It recognized the need "for smaller-scale contingency operations in peacetime, preferably in concert with allies and friends." However, it said nothing beyond this. *Quadrennial Defense Review Report* (Washington, DC: Department of Defense, September 30, 2001), 21, www.defenselink .mil/pubs/qdr2001.pdf. This confirmed that Operations Other than War (OOTW), which include peace operations and multilateral engagements of various sorts, remained very low on the U.S. armed forces' agenda. Whatever major changes would occur in the future in the appraisal of U.S. military strategy, they would continue to have little to do with the possible peace operations implications of the post–Cold War era international transformations.

42. See, for instance, the *National Military Strategy* endorsed in February 1995 by then-chairman of the Joint Chiefs of Staff, Gen. John M. Shalikashvili, www.fas.org/man/ docs/nms_feb95.htm.

43. The Pentagon hosted a very small peace operations office under the name of Contingency Operations Office, amounting to fewer than five professionals. Another illustration of the lack of importance ascribed to peace operations issues is the fact that the United States Peacekeeping Institute at the U.S. War College at Carlisle Barracks, Pennsylvania, did not have much capacity or prestige, let alone political clout, within the armed forces. (As the only center in the U.S. military dedicated to building knowledge of peace operations, the Peacekeeping Institute was created in July 1993 to guide the Army's thinking on how to conduct peacekeeping, to analyze the strengths and weaknesses of specific missions, and to promote Army exchanges with international organizations involved in peace operations.)

44. In the midst of the civil war in Lebanon in the early 1980s, U.S. Marines were deployed in Beirut as part of a Multinational Force of peacekeeping troops. As they came to be considered a partisan faction in the war, they came under attack. In October 1983, close to three hundred Marines perished in a suicide bombing attack on their barracks.

45. In a speech that he delivered in November 1984, then-Secretary of Defense Casper Weinberger outlined six major tests that should be applied when military force was being considered as a policy option. They are (1) vital interests must be at stake; (2) overwhelming force should be used so as to ensure victory; (3) objectives, both political and military, must be clear; (4) proper resources must be made available, and if the situation on the ground changes, the force structure must be adapted; (5) before troops are deployed, there must be bipartisan support from Congress and from the American people; and (6) the use of armed force should be the last resort. See MacKinnon, *The Evolution of U.S. Peacekeeping Policy Under Clinton*, 14.

46. When Weinberger drafted his six tests in 1984, Powell was his military adviser at the Pentagon and viewed by some as one of the doctrine's authors. On this issue, see the account in Powell, *My American Journey*, 302–3.

47. See ibid, 576–77: "My constant, unwelcome message at all meetings on Bosnia was simply that we should not commit military forces until we had a clear political objective. . . . The debate exploded at one session when Madeleine Albright, our ambassador to the UN, asked in frustration, 'What's the point of having this superb military that you're always talking about if we can't use it?' I thought I would have an aneurysm. American GIs were not toy soldiers to be moved around on some sort of global game board. I patiently explained that we had used our armed forces more than two dozen times in the preceding three years for war, peacekeeping, disaster relief, and humanitarian assistance. But in every one of those cases we had had a clear goal and had matched our military commitment to the goal. As a result, we had been successful in every case. I told Ambassador Albright that the U.S. military would carry any mission it was handed, but my advice would always be that the tough political goals had to be set first. Then we would accomplish the mission." For Powell's thoughts on nation building (and Somalia), see ibid., 578: "The UN approved a resolution shifting the mission from feeding the hungry to 'nation building,' the phrase I had first heard when I went into Vietnam. From what I have observed of history, the will to build a nation originates from within its people, not from the outside. . . . Nation building might have an inspirational ring, but it struck me as a way to get bogged down in Somalia, not get out." Incidentally, it is Powell who authorized in late August 1993 the deployment of the Army Rangers and Delta Force troops who would run into a fierce firefight in Mogadishu in October; see his views on the matter in ibid., 583–89.

48. A reluctance that in December 2005 took a drastic turn as the United States managed to rally the largest contributors to the UN budget to install a budget cap, tying the UN budget to reform and, more specifically, to management improvements. After six months, the cap was released, but with continued dissatisfaction and U.S. reluctance to contribute to the UN budget unless certain changes were made to the organization. For a detailed outline of member states' commitment in terms of contribution to the UN regular budget, see United Nations, "Assessment of Member States' Advances to the Working Capital Fund for the Biennium 2006–2007 and Contributions to the United Nations Regular Budget for 2006," UN Doc. ST/ADM/SER.B/668 (December 27, 2005).

49. See the vivid description of the events of October 3, 1993, in Mogadishu in Mark Bowden, *Black Hawk Down: A Story of Modern War* (New York: Signet, 2001).

50. The Clinton administration tried to address the disparity between the U.S. military and police tasks—particularly by enhancing U.S. capabilities to recruit, train, and deploy American police officers—in Presidential Decision Directive 71 (PDD 71):

Strengthening Criminal Justice Systems in Support of Peace Operations, www.state.gov/www/global/narcotics_law/pdd_71/white_paper.html. See also U.S. Institute of Peace, *American Civilian Police in UN Peace Operations: Lessons Learned and Ideas for the Future.* Special Report, no. 71 (Washington, DC: U.S. Institute of Peace, July 6, 2001), www.usip.org/pubs/specialreports/sr71.html#top.

51. For more information on the evolving relationship between humanitarian and military actors in peacekeeping operations, see Victoria Wheeler and Adele Harmer, *Resetting the Rules of Engagement: Trends and Issues in Military-Humanitarian Relations.* Humanitarian Policy Group Research Report, no. 21 (London: Overseas Development Institute, March 2006), especially chapter 4, "The Military and Civilian Protection: Developing Roles and Capacities." See also Roxanne D. V. Sismanidis, *Police Functions in Peace Operations: Report from a Workshop Organized by the United States Institute of Peace.* Peaceworks, no. 14 (Washington, DC: U.S. Institute of Peace, April 1997).

52. For more information on the adaptation of the U.S. military to the needs of peacekeeping operations in the post–Cold War era, see, for example, Colonel J. Michael Hardesty and Jason D. Ellis, *Training for Peace Operations: The U.S. Army Adapts to the Post–Cold War World.* Peaceworks, no. 12 (Washington, DC: U.S. Institute of Peace, February 1997); or Donald G. Rose, "Peace Operations and Change in the U.S. Military," *Defense and Security Analysis* 17, no. 2 (August 1, 2001).

53. Some services were more willing than others to envision the possibility of casualties. That was the case of the Marines. But the Army was especially adamant on the question, an attitude that was particularly important because it was assumed that ground forces were essential to the outcome of massive military engagements.

54. See Eliot A. Cohen, "Why the Gap Matters," *The National Interest,* Fall 2000. See also James Dao, "Ads Now Seek Recruits for 'An Army of One,'" *New York Times,* January 10, 2001. The subject of the article was a television advertisement that aired in the United States in January 2001, entitled "An Army of One." Trying to counter what Army officials saw as the widespread perception among young men and women that soldiers were faceless, nameless cogs in an impersonal military machine, the ad was intended to appeal to the individualism and independence of youth.

55. Chris Hables Gray, *Postmodern War: The New Politics of Conflict* (New York: Guilford Press, 1997), 212–27. This, however, begs the question of whether there is much military honor in a combat in which the armament disparity is such between the adversaries that one side can kill more or less at will while risking hardly anything in the process.

56. In Operation Desert Storm, casualty aversion accounted for the fact that, before the administration hawks were able make the war option prevail, Powell was willing to wait for months to see if economic sanctions against Iraq would work. See Michael R. Gordon and General Bernard E. Trainor, *The General's War: The Inside Story of the Conflict in the Gulf* (New York: Little, Brown, 1995), 130–31 and 149.

57. Although the idealism and progressivism of the U.S. military establishment should not be overlooked, it is, on the whole, less likely to buy into the internationalism favored by the Democrats than into the kind of interventionism found in one prominent wing of the Republican Party. It tends to echo the Republican vision of projection of U.S. power, inclined to take action internationally, unilaterally, or, if needed, in the context of an international coalition, primarily for reasons of national interest and security. See Michael C. Desh, *Civilian Control of the Military: The Changing Security Environment* (Baltimore: Johns Hopkins University Press, 1999), 29–33.

58. The lack of loyalty that the Clinton administration seemed to display vis-à-vis military leaders inclined to go along with its views confirmed the military's suspicion. In this respect, the inability of the White House to look after Wesley Clark in the aftermath of the Kosovo campaign did not cast Clinton in a favorable light. The detachment with which the Clinton team reacted to the suggestion—made by the less activist part of the military establishment that wanted to force Clark into retirement—that Clark should be replaced by General Joseph Ralston, vice chairman of the Joint Chiefs of Staff, as Supreme Allied Commander, Europe did not look good. The administration's inability to look after Clark's interests only confirmed its lack of commitment and loyalty, values that the military reveres most. The qualities that made Clinton a skillful politician—particularly his ability to convey different views to different constituencies, to be everything to everybody—were also attributes that led the military to distrust him. His talent for ambiguity, his preference for spinning reality over reality itself, led them to view him as a master of deception more than anything else.

59. In the aftermath of the Cold War, the U.S. defense budget exceeded overwhelmingly those of the largest military spenders around the world. The U.S. defense budget for 2000 was $280.6 billion, accounting for 37 percent of total world military expenditures. It took the combined annual defense budgets of the eleven largest military spenders around the world to get close ($291.6 billion) to what the United States spends yearly on defense (in US$ billions): Russia ($43.9), France ($40.4), Japan ($37.8), United Kingdom ($36.3), Germany ($33.0), Italy ($23.8), China ($23.0), Saudi Arabia ($19.1), Brazil ($14.9), Turkey ($10.5), and Israel ($8.9). See *SIPRI Yearbook 2001: Armaments, Disarmament, and International Security* (New York: Oxford University Press, 2001), 277–82. The War on Terror and the war in Iraq, combined with Hurricanes Katrina and Rita, further increased U.S. military spending. By 2005, the United States was responsible for 48 percent of total world military expenditures, distantly followed by the United Kingdom, France, Japan, and China, with 4–5 percent each. The next five states are Germany (3 percent), Italy (3 percent), Saudi Arabia (3 percent), Russia (2 percent), and India (2 percent). See Peter Stålenheim, Damien Fruchart, Wuyi Omitoogun, and Catalina Perdomo, "Military expenditure," in *SIPRI Yearbook 2006: Armaments, Disarmament, and International Security* (New York: Oxford University Press, 2006).

60. As the various U.S. government Web sites related to peace operations indicate, the wealth of studies generated in the past ten years by the executive branch (the National Security Council in particular), the legislative branch (Congress and the various committees and subcommittees dealing directly or indirectly with peace operations), and the various military branches is without comparison in other countries. Neither in the United Kingdom and France nor in the Nordic countries and Canada (which have been committed to peace operations throughout the 1990s) has the level of examination of peace operations been as thorough as in the United States. This level of expertise often makes American decision makers and diplomats better equipped to address peace operations issues. The same disparity exists at the academic, think tank, research center, and NGO levels (on NGOs, see, for instance, the Academic Council on the United Nations System, which is mainly a North American organization, or the United Nations Association of the United States of America). As a result, although UN studies are less prestigious than traditional security studies in U.S. academia, the American academic production on UN and peace operations issues still tends to be better than elsewhere.

61. In *The Limits of Humanitarian Intervention: Genocide in Rwanda* (Washington, DC: Brookings Institution Press, 2001), Alan Kuperman indicates that the core agencies of the federal government (the State Department, Pentagon, National Security Council, and Central Intelligence Agency) either failed to absorb the information available on the unfolding killing, or explicitly rejected it as unreliable until further evidence emerged on or after April 20 (see pp. 36–37). On May 20, 1994, at a time when ample evidence had become available on the mass killings that had been going on for weeks, an action memorandum from the State Department, destined for the secretary of state, was asking "whether (1) to authorize Department officials to state publicly that 'acts of genocide have occurred' in Rwanda and (2) to authorize U.S. delegations to international meetings to agree to resolutions and other instruments that refer to 'acts of genocide' in Rwanda, state that 'genocide has occurred' there or contain other comparable formulations." Action memorandum (Document 14) from Assistant Secretary of State for African Affairs George E. Moose; Assistant Secretary of State for Democracy, Human Rights, and Labor John Shattuck; Assistant Secretary of State for International Organization Affairs Douglas J. Bennet; and Legal Adviser Conrad K. Harper, through Under Secretary of State for Political Affairs Peter Tarnoff and Under Secretary of State for Global Affairs Tim Wirth, to Secretary of State Warren Christopher, "Has Genocide Occurred in Rwanda?" (May 21, 1994). Unclassified, http://128.164.127.251/~sarchiv/NSAEBB/NSAEBB53/index2.html.

62. Linda R. Melvern, *A People Betrayed: The Role of the West in Rwanda's Genocide* (London: Zed Books, 2000), 198–99.

63. The fact that France pushed for getting involved was not a satisfactory substitute for an engagement of the international community as a whole. France's poor track record in Rwanda, the timing of the French deployment, when most of the genocide had already taken place, and the modalities of its intervention raised more doubts and suspicions than it brought solutions. It was a problematic replacement for what would have been a genuine concern and attempt, if not to prevent, at least to minimize the amount of killing.

64. Samantha Power, *A Problem from Hell: America and the Age of Genocide* (New York: Basic Books, 2002), 382–83.

65. See the reflections of Anthony Lake on this issue in Samantha Power, "Bystanders to Genocide," *The Atlantic Monthly*, September 2001, p. 7: "I was obsessed with Haiti and Bosnia during that period, so Rwanda was, in William Shawcross's words, a 'sideshow,' but not even a sideshow, a no-show." Power adds, "during the entire three months of the genocide, Clinton never assembled his top policy advisers to discuss the killings. Anthony Lake likewise never gathered the 'principals,' the cabinet-level members of the foreign policy team. Rwanda was never thought to warrant its own top-level meeting. When the subject came up, it did so along with, and subordinate to, discussions of Somalia, Haiti, and Bosnia. Whereas these crises involved U.S. personnel and stirred some public interest, Rwanda generated no sense of urgency and could be safely avoided by Clinton at no political cost."

66. Wayne Bert, *The Reluctant Superpower: United States' Policy in Bosnia, 1991–95* (New York: St. Martin's, 1997), 189–219; Ivo H. Daalder, *Getting to Dayton: The Making of America's Bosnia Policy* (Washington, DC: Brookings Institution Press, 2000), 162–66. See also David Owen, *Balkan Odyssey* (New York: Harcourt Brace and Company, 1995), 401–2.

67. James Gow, *Triumph of the Lack of Will: International Diplomacy and the Yugoslav War* (New York: Columbia University Press, 1997), 313–15.

68. President Clinton's national security adviser during his second term, Samuel ("Sandy") Berger, did not have a foreign policy background. As a successful trade lawyer,

Berger was a decided asset for Clinton's free-trade policies, but he probably lacked the forward-looking strategic road map that is necessary for a global power in a time of transition. See Halberstam, *War in a Time of Peace*, for example, 404–9 and 424.

CHAPTER 5

1. Ivo H. Daalder and James M. Lindsay, *America Unbound: The Bush Revolution in Foreign Policy* (Washington, DC: Brookings Institution Press, 2003).

2. For a good definition of grand strategy, see Charles A. Kupchan, *The End of the American Era: U.S. Foreign Policy and the Geopolitics of the Twenty-First Century* (New York: Alfred A. Knopf, 2002), 26–27.

3. *The National Security Strategy of the United States of America* (Washington, DC: The White House, 2002), Section I, "Overview of America's International Strategy," 1–2.

4. See *A National Security Strategy of Engagement and Enlargement* (Washington, DC: The White House, February 1995), i; *A National Security Strategy of Engagement and Enlargement* (Washington, DC: The White House, February 1996), 2; *A National Security Strategy for the New Century* (Washington, DC: The White House, May 1997), 2; *A National Security Strategy for a New Century* (Washington, DC: The White House, October 1998), iii; *A National Security Strategy for a New Century* (Washington, DC: The White House, December 1999), 3; *A National Security Strategy for a Global Age* (Washington, DC: The White House, December 2000), Section I, "Fundamentals of the Strategy."

5. See *National Security Strategy of the United States* (Washington, DC: The White House, August 1991), 3–5.

6. On the cautious optimism of the George H. W. Bush administration's foreign policy, see, for instance, *National Security Strategy of the United States* (Washington, DC: The White House, 1991), Section 1, "The Foundations of National Strategy: Interests and Goals, New Era." On Clinton's cautious foreign policy optimism, see, for example, *A National Security Strategy of Engagement and Enlargement* (1995), i and iii; *A National Security Strategy for a New Century* (1997), preface; *A National Security Strategy for a New Century* (1998), 1; *A National Security Strategy for a New Century* (1999), 4–5.

7. See John Lewis Gaddis, "A Grand Strategy of Transformation," *Foreign Policy*, November–December 2002, 50–51; and Stefan Alper and Jonathan Clarke, *American Alone: The Neo-Conservatives and the Global Order* (New York: Cambridge University Press, 2004), 142.

8. *The National Security Strategy of the United States of America* (2002).

9. Alper and Clarke, *America Alone*, 3.

10. On this point, see, for example, David C. Hendrickson, "America's Dangerous Quest for Absolute Security," *World Policy Journal* 19, no. 3 (Fall 2002).

11. G. John Ikenberry, "America's Imperial Ambition," *Foreign Affairs*, September/October 2002; and David E. Sanger, "Bush to Outline Doctrine of Striking Foes First," *New York Times*, September 20, 2002.

12. *The National Security Strategy of the United States of America* (2002), 25. In addition, see Secretary of Defense Donald H. Rumsfeld, "Transforming the Military," *Foreign Affairs*, May/June 2002: "The mission must determine the coalition, the coalition must not determine the mission, or else the mission will be dumbed down to the lowest common denominator."

13. The preface of the 2002 report states that "(c)oalitions of the willing can augment these permanent institutions." Yet one could argue that coalitions of the willing contribute more to the weakening of multilateral institutions rather than to their strengthening.

14. Ibid., 30: "We will take the actions necessary to ensure that our efforts to meet our global security commitments and protect Americans are not impaired by the potential for investigations, inquiry, or prosecutions by the International Criminal Court (ICC), whose jurisdiction does not extend to Americans and which we do not accept. We will work together with other nations to avoid complications in our military operations and cooperation, through such mechanisms as multilateral and bilateral agreements that will protect U.S. nationals from the ICC." Note that President Clinton's signing of the Rome Statute of the International Criminal Court on December 31, 2000, was far from an unequivocal endorsement of the court. On this issue, see Eric P. Schwartz, "The United States and the International Criminal Court: The Case for 'Dexterous Multilateralism,'" *Chicago Journal of International Law* 4, no. 1 (Spring 2003).

15. See *A National Security Strategy of Engagement and Enlargement* (1995), 7. See also *A National Security Strategy of Engagement and Enlargement* (1996), 4.

16. *The National Security Strategy of the United States of America* (2002), 31.

17. On the other hand, assessing that Russia was not in a strong position and thus not a threat, the Clinton administration did not hesitate to push for the enlargement of NATO in the second half of the 1990s.

18. Richard A. Clarke, *Against All Enemies: Inside America's War on Terror* (New York: The Free Press, 2004), 90–93.

19. Ibid., preface. See also the quote from the September 17, 2002, White House press release on p. 15, specifically: "We cannot let our enemies strike first," www.whitehouse. gov/nsc/nss/2002/nssintro.html.

20. *The National Security Strategy of the United States of America* (2002), 15.

21. See Presidential Statement, The White House, Office of the Press Secretary, October 31, 1998, www.library.cornell.edu/colldev/mideast/libera.htm.

22. *The National Security Strategy of the United States of America* (2002), Section V, "Prevent Our Enemies from Threatening Us, Our Allies, and Our Friends with Weapons of Mass Destruction."

23. Ibid., 1.

24. See *A National Security Strategy of Engagement and Enlargement* (1995), 16–17; *A National Security Strategy of Engagement and Enlargement* (1996), 17 and 27–28; *A National Security Strategy for a New Century* (1998), 20–21. See also *A National Security Strategy for a Global Age* (2000).

25. *The National Security Strategy of the United Sates of America* (2002), 11: "Africa's great size and diversity requires a security strategy that focuses on bilateral engagement and builds coalitions of the willing. . . . [C]ordination with European allies and international institutions is essential for constructive conflict mediation and successful peace operations."

26. *A National Security Strategy of Engagement and Enlargement* (1995), 12–13. See also *A National Security Strategy of Engagement and Enlargement* (1996), 22–24; *A National Security Strategy for a New Century* (1997), 12; *A National Security Strategy for a New Century* (1999), 24–25.

27. *The National Security Strategy of the United Sates of America* (2002), 7.

28. Ibid., 21–22: "Results of aid are typically measured in dollars spent by donors, not in the rate of growth and poverty reduction achieved by recipients. These are the indicators of a failed strategy. . . . We forged a new consensus at the UN Conference on Financing for Development in Monterrey that the objectives of assistance—and the strategies to achieve those objectives—must change. . . . We propose a 50 percent increase in the core development assistance given by the United States. While continuing our present programs, including humanitarian assistance based on need alone, these billions of new dollars will form a new Millennium Challenge Account for projects in countries whose government rule justly, invest in their people, and encourage economic freedom." See also 31: "Our diplomats serve at the front line of complex negotiations, civil wars, and other humanitarian catastrophes. As humanitarian relief requirements are better understood, we must also be able to help build police forces, court systems, and legal codes, local and provincial government institutions, and electoral systems. Effective international cooperation is needed to accomplish these goals, backed by American readiness to play our part."

29. Ibid., 1.

30. Ibid., 3.

31. Ibid., 10: "In Africa, promise and opportunity sit side by side with disease, war, and desperate poverty. This threatens both a core value of the United States—preserving human dignity—and our strategic priority—combating global terror. . . . Together with our European allies, we must help strengthen Africa's fragile states, help build indigenous capability to secure porous borders, and help build up the law enforcement and intelligence infrastructure to deny havens for terrorists. An ever more lethal environment exists in Africa as local civil wars spread beyond borders to create regional war zones. Forming coalitions of the willing and cooperative security arrangements are key to confronting these emerging transnational threats."

32. For more recent statements on the U.S. security strategy, see *The National Defense Strategy of the United States of America* (Washington, DC: Department of Defense, March 2005), www.dami.army.pentagon.mil/offices/dami-zyg/National%20 Defense%20Strategy%20Mar05-U.pdf; and *Quadrennial Defense Review Report* (Washington, DC: Department of Defense, February 6, 2006), www.comw.org/qdr/ qdr/2006.pdf.

33. Condoleezza Rice, "Promoting the National Interest," *Foreign Affairs,* January/ February 2000, 53–54.

34. Condoleezza Rice, transcript of an interview on *The Charlie Rose Show*, Public Broadcasting Service/WNET, New York, October 12, 2000, 4 and 18–19.

35. For example, in 1997 Clinton refused to sign an international treaty banning land mines that had won the support of 123 nations. Among the other holdouts were countries like Afghanistan, Iraq, Libya, China, Russia, and North Korea. In 1998, the Clinton administration signed the Kyoto Protocol on global warming but then demurred on implementation.

36. On the missile defense issue, see Bill Keller, "Missile Defense: The Untold Story," *New York Times*, December 29, 2001.

37. Quoted in Thom Shanker, "White House Says the U.S. Is Not a Loner, Just Choosy," *New York Times*, July 31, 2001. A few months earlier, Richard Haass went as far as to call on Americans to "reconceive their global role, from one of a traditional nation-state to an imperial power," in "Imperial America" (paper presented at the Atlanta Conference, November 11, 2000), www.brook.edu/views/articles/haass/2000imperial. htm.

38. Lawrence F. Kaplan and William Kristol, *The War over Iraq: Saddam's Tyranny and America's Mission* (San Francisco: Encounter Books, 2003), 64. Kaplan and Kristol are quick to mention that internationalism is not the monopoly of liberalism. They recognize that the "distinctly American internationalism" that they identify with concurs with certain tenets of realism (above all, the view of the international environment as a fundamentally dangerous place). They argue that their attachment to American exceptionalism and its use as a model for the rest of the world sets them apart from traditional realists. But their preference for American power over international organizations and their view that America's mission—going far beyond the role of global policeman—is to shape the world along values of liberal democracy also sets them apart from liberal internationalists.

39. UN Security Council Resolution 1373 (2001).

40. See UN Security Council Resolution 1386 (2001).

41. Following the UN-brokered Bonn Agreement of early December 2001, UNAMA gave the United Nations special responsibilities in the areas of national reconciliation, human rights, rule of law, the role of women, and humanitarian affairs; see UN Security Council Resolution 1401 (2002).

42. Victoria K. Holt, *Peace and Stability in Afghanistan: U.S. Goals Challenged by Security Gap.* Henry L. Stimson Center Peace Operations, Factsheet Series (June 2002), 5, www.stimson.org/fopo/pdf/AfghanSecurityGapfactsheet_063102.pdf; and William J. Durch, *Peace and Stability Operations in Afghanistan: Requirements and Force Options* (Washington, DC: Henry L. Stimson Center, June 28, 2003), 17, www.stimson.org/fopo/pdf/afghansecurityoptions070103.pdf.

43. For more on the reluctance of the Bush administration to invest much in Afghanistan's future, see Seymour M. Hersh, *Chain of Command: The Road from 9/11 to Abu Ghraib* (New York: HarperCollins, 2004), chapter 3. As a result, the international community's failure to extend a strong security umbrella beyond Kabul was perpetuating, in the spring of 2004, the economic and political power of regional commanders. On this issue, see International Crisis Group, *Elections and Security in Afghanistan* (Kabul/Brussels: ICG, March 30, 2004).

44. George W. Bush, *The President's State of the Union Address* (Washington, DC: The White House, January 29, 2002), www.whitehouse.gov/news/releases/2002/01/2002012 9-11.html. See also David Frum, *The Right Man: The Surprise Presidency of George W. Bush (An Inside Account)* (New York: Random House, 2003), chapters 10 and 12.

45. Bob Woodward, *Plan of Attack* (New York: Simon & Schuster, 2004), 111–12.

46. On the neoconservatives and their influence on Bush's foreign policy, see, for example, "The Shadow Men," *The Economist* (April 26–May 2, 2003), 27–29. See also Halper and Clarke, *American Alone*, chapter 4, for example.

47. See the "The Secret Downing Street Memo" from Matthew Rycroft, reporting on the findings of "C," the head of British Intelligence, from a summer 2002 visit with his U.S. counterpart in Washington, DC. The memo shows that despite public claims that the Bush administration would go to war in Iraq only as a "last resort," it had decided by mid-2002 to wage that war no matter what: "The Secret Downing Street Memo," *Sunday Times* (London), May 1, 2005.

48. On the role played by Vice President Cheney in making the case for war, see, for instance, David Barstow, William J. Broad, and Jeff Gerth, "Skewed Intelligence Data in March to War in Iraq," *New York Times,* October 3, 2004.

49. On Colin Powell and his views on multilateralism, see, for instance, Bill Keller, "The World According to Powell," *The New York Times Magazine*, November 25, 2001.

See also Paul Reynolds, "Bush Turns Tables on Critics," *BBC News*/World Edition, September 16, 2002, http://news.bbc.co.uk/2/hi/middle_east/2261307.stm. On George W. Bush and his relationship with the various political forces in his administration, see Bill Keller, "Reagan's Son," *The New York Times Magazine*, January 26, 2003.

50. "My nation will work with the UN Security Council to meet our common challenge. If Iraq's regime defies us again, the world must move deliberately, decisively, to hold Iraq to account. We will work with the UN Security Council for the necessary resolutions. But the purposes of the United States should not be doubted. The Security Council resolutions will be enforced—the just demands of peace and security will be met—or action will be unavoidable. And a regime that has lost its legitimacy will also lose its power," in The White House, "Remarks by the President in Address to the United Nations General Assembly, New York, September 12, 2002," www.whitehouse.govnews/releases/2002/09/print/2002912-1.html.

51. UN Security Council Resolution 1441 (2002), para. 13.

52. In their various briefings to the Security Council (on January 9, 2003, reporting on the Iraqi arms declaration; on January 27, 2003, in their sixty-day update of the UN Monitoring, Verification and Inspection Commission's (UNMOVIC) activities since its return to Iraq; and on February 14 and March 7, 2003), Hans Blix, UNMOVIC executive chairman, and Mohamed ElBaradei, IAEA director-general, indicated that, based on the information collected, the existence of weapons of mass destruction in Iraq was not proved. See also Glen Rangqala, Nathaniel Hurd, and Alistair Millar, "A Case for Concern, Not a Case for War," in *The Iraq War Reader: History, Documents, Opinions*, ed. Micah L. Sifry and Christopher Cerf (New York: Touchstone, 2003), 457–63; and Hans Blix, *Disarming Iraq* (New York: Pantheon Books, 2004).

53. On January 9, 2003, reporting on Iraq's arms declaration; on January 27, in their sixty-day update on UNMOVIC's activities since its return to Iraq; and on February 14 and March 7, 2003. See also Blix, *Disarming Iraq*, 176–78: and Rangwala, Hurd, and Millar, "A Case for Concern, Not a Case for War," in Sifry and Cerf, eds., *The Iraq War Reader*, 457–63.

54. From Hans Blix's statement of February 14, 2003, quoted in Blix, *Disarming Iraq*, 177.

55. Powell ended up being isolated within the Republican administration and in the United Nations, unable to secure Security Council backing. At the height of the confrontation between the United States and the United Kingdom, on the one hand, and France and Germany, on the other, Powell appeared as upset with Defense Secretary Rumsfeld and his tendency to antagonize positions as he was with France and Germany; see Steven R. Weisman, "Powell at New Turning Point in His Evolution on Iraq War," *New York Times*, March 14, 2003. See also Bill Keller, "Why Colin Powell Should Go," *New York Times*, March 22, 2003.

56. Pierre Hassner, "Definitions, Doctrines and Divergences," *The National Interest*, Fall 2002, 33.

57. On U.S.-European relations in the first months of Bush's presidency, see, for example, Ivo H. Daalder, "Are the United States and Europe Heading for Divorce?" *International Affairs* 77, no. 3 (July 2001): 553–67.

58. See Thierry Tardy, "France and the U.S.: The Inevitable Clash?" *International Journal*, Winter 2003–04.

59. Wherever and whenever its interests are at stake and its power permits, France does not shy away from acting against the principles that it commends in the UN context.

France's poor track record in West Africa is one of many examples of French realism, of the limits of its internationalism and solidarity. The minor place left to human rights issues in French foreign policy as a whole is another one.

60. On UN sanctions against Iraq in general, see, for instance, Meghan L. O'Sullivan, *Iraq: Time for a Modified Approach*. Policy Brief, no. 71 (Washington, DC: Brookings Institution, February 2001). For the French position on sanctions, see, for example, *Les Propositions Françaises pour l'Iraq*, August 25, 1999, www.diplomatie.gouv.fr/actual/dossiers/iraq/index.html, or *Intervention Publique du Représentant Permanent de la France aux Nations Unies*, New York, June 26, 2001, www.diplomatie.gouv.fr/actual/dossiers/iraq2/iraq260601.html.

61. Dominique Moïsi, "Iraq," in *Transatlantic Tension: The United States, Europe, and Problem Countries,* ed. Richard N. Haass (Washington, DC: Brookings Institution Press, 1999); Georges Corm, *Le Proche-Orient éclaté – II: Mirages de Paix et Blocages Identitaires 1990–1996* (Paris: Editions la Découverte, 1997), 35 and 55, for example. See also Jean-Pierre Chevènement, *Le Vert et le Noir: Intégrisme, Pétrole, Dollars* (Paris: Grasset, 1995). On January 29, 1991, Chevènement, minister of national defense at the time in the Socialist government, offered his resignation to mark his opposition to the war in Iraq.

62. See, for example, the interview of the French minister of foreign affairs, Hubert Védrine, with *Al Hayat*, August 1, 2000, www.diplomatie.gouv.fr/actual/dossiers/iraq2/vedrinealhayat.html.

63. On the history of sanctions and their effect in Iraq, see, for example, David Rieff, "Were Sanctions Right?" *New York Times*, July 27, 2003.

64. Because of its increasing reliance on nuclear power in its energy profile ever since the OPEC oil shocks in the 1970s, French dependence on Iraqi oil has never been critical. In fact, in the early 2000s (2000–2003), French oil imports from all OPEC countries averaged only about one-third of total gross imports of 2.275 million barrels per day. OPEC–Persian Gulf countries supplied almost 20 percent of total gross imports, with Saudi Arabia leading at 10.4 percent of total gross imports; the comparable figure for Iraq during the early 2000s averaged 2.83 percent. See U.S. Department of Energy/Energy Information Administration, *International Petroleum Monthly*, February 2007, Table 4.13 ("France—Petroleum [Oil] Imports, 1991–2005 [Million Barrels per Day]). See also Jacques Beltran, *French Policy toward Iraq.* U.S.-France Analysis Series (Washington, DC: Brookings Institution, September 2002). The contracts obtained by France through the UN Oil-for-Food Program starting in the second half of the 1990s were another aspect of French economic interests in Iraq; for an analysis of the Oil-for-Food Program, see, for instance, *Independent Inquiry Committee into the United Nations Oil-for-Food Program, Interim Report* (New York, February 3, 2005), especially part II, chapter 2. Certainly, oil-for-food contracts went largely to France for a while, but in this area, too, French interests should not be overstated. In 2001, France ranked eleventh in terms of such contracts, behind Egypt, Jordan, Syria, the United Arab Emirates, Turkey, Russia, China, and India. The potentially lucrative oil concessions that would have been granted to French companies had sanctions been lifted were another reason for France's desire to proceed carefully with Saddam Hussein's regime. A final concern was the debt of some $5 billion accumulated by Baghdad over the years. The fact that the Bush administration did not say what position it would adopt after the war on some of these issues (for instance, whether or not the Iraqi debts would be honored and whether or not France (and Russia) would be allowed to participate in the reconstruction of Iraq) did not encourage Paris to share the enthusiasm of the United States and the United Kingdom for war.

65. France has been a longtime advocate of the existence of a Palestinian state alongside Israel.

66. There are four reasons for this. First, France does not see itself as particularly targeted. Second, France's foreign policy is not about trying to achieve absolute security against external threats, because France does not view absolute security (the total absence of external threat) as either achievable or desirable. This attitude could be called insecurity tolerance. Third, France does not believe that a foreign policy of military intervention is essential to ending terrorism. It is more inclined to think that the answer is to address the root causes of terrorism. Fourth, France is wary of giving the Arab masses the impression that the West is adopting policies of force. In its view, such policies are likely to add fuel to their sense of historical humiliation. Moreover, the fact that Arab populations resent most of their local political leaders does not mean that they are eager to embrace foreign troops.

67. See, for example, Stephen F. Szabo, *Parting Ways: The Crisis in German–American Relations* (Washington, DC: Brookings Institution Press, 2004), 67–74. For more information on the French perspective, see Marc Perelman, "How the French Fight Terror," *Foreign Policy,* online version, January 2006, www.foreignpolicy.com/story/cms.php?story_id=3353.

68. To a certain extent, the French government was worried as well by the fact that an intervention in Iraq, particularly if it led to widespread Arab civilian deaths, could have spillover effects in France. It could provoke unrest among France's 4 to 6 million Muslim population (nearly 10 percent of France's population) and be exploited by fundamentalists. France did not want to give the Muslim world the impression that the West is opposed to Islam; see Stanley Hoffmann, "Out of Iraq," *New York Review of Books*, October 21, 2004. It wanted to project an alternative vision of the West to the Arab and Muslim populations in the Middle East, but also in Europe.

69. See the remarks of the French ambassador to the United Nations, Jean-David Levitte, following the adoption of UN Security Council Resolution 1441 (2002); UN Doc. S/PV.4644 (November 8, 2002), 5.

70. For an interesting analysis of the debate surrounding the interpretation of UN Security Council Resolution 1441, see Michael Byers, "Agreeing to Disagree: Security Council Resolution 1441 and Intentional Ambiguity," *Global Governance: A Review of Multilateralism and International Organizations* 10, no. 2 (April–June 2004).

71. Paragraph 13 of UN Security Council Resolution 1441 mentions only that "the Council has repeatedly warned Iraq that it will face serious consequences as a result of its continued violations of its obligations."

72. See, in particular, the statement of the U.S. Permanent Representative to the United Nations, John Negroponte, on November 8, 2002: "As we have said on numerous occasions to Council members, this resolution contains no 'hidden triggers' and no 'automaticity' with respect to the use of force. If there is a further Iraqi breach, reported to the Council by UNMOVIC, the IAEA, or a Member State, the matter will return to the Council for discussions as required in paragraph 12," in UN Doc. S/PV.4644, p. 3.

73. Ibid. Negroponte again: "The resolution makes clear that any Iraqi failure to comply is unacceptable and that Iraq must be disarmed. And, one way or another, Iraq will be disarmed. If the Security Council fails to act decisively in the event of further Iraqi violations, this resolution does not constrain any Member State from acting to defend itself against the threat posed by Iraq or to enforce relevant United Nations resolutions and protect world peace and security."

74. For the attitude of the Bush administration, see Bob Woodward, *Plan of Attack* (New York: Simon & Schuster, 2004); and Stefan Halper and Jonathan Clarke, *America Alone*, 2004, chapter 4, for example. For the United Kingdom, see John Kampfner, *Blair's Wars* (London: Free Press, 2004).

75. Kampfner, *Blair's Wars*, 157.

76. See Tony Blair's statement on Iraq following the adoption of UN Security Council Resolution 1441: "I may find this regime abhorrent. Any normal person would. But the survival of it is in his hands. Conflict is not inevitable. Disarmament is." See also Peter Stothard, *Thirty Days: A Month at the Heart of Blair's War* (New York: HarperCollins, 2003), 141: "If Saddam had disarmed and remained in place, Tony Blair would not have been 'comfortable' at all."

77. Nicholas J. Wheeler, "Liberal Interventionism versus International Law: Blair's Wars over Kosovo and Iraq" (paper presented to the 2003 Foreign Policy School at the University of Otago, Dunedin, New Zealand, June 2003).

78. Ibid.

79. Pew Global Attitudes Project, *America's Image Further Erodes, Europeans Want Weaker Ties, But Post-War Iraq Will Be Better Off, Most Say: A Nine-Country Survey* (Washington, DC: Pew Research Center for the People and the Press, March 18, 2003), 1.

80. For a unified position by Spain, Portugal, Italy, the United Kingdom, the Czech Republic, Hungary, Poland, and Denmark, see "Europe and America Must Stand United," Jose Maria Aznar, Jose-Manuel Durao Barroso, Silvio Berlusconi, Tony Blair, Vaclav Havel, Peter Medgyessy, Leszek Miller, and Anders Fogh Rasmussen, *Wall Street Journal Europe*, January 20, 2003.

81. See Steven Schiffers, "U.S. Names 'Coalition of the Willing,'" *BBC News*, March 18, 2003, http://news.bbc.co.uk/1/hi/world/americas/2862343.stm; and Dan Balz and Mike Allen, "U.S. Names 30 Countries Supporting War Effort," *Washington Post*, March 19, 2003, A01. It should be noted that in most of the countries making up the "coalition of the willing," the majority of the populations did not support the endeavor; see the summary of the Gallup International Iraq Poll 2003, www.gallup-international.com/content Files/survey.asp?id=10.

82. The number is subject to continuous revision. In February 2005, it had shrunk to twenty-six countries. See Web site for the Multinational Force Iraq: www.mnf-iraq.com; and Robin Wright and Josh White, "U.S. Moves to Preserve Iraq Coalition," *Washington Post*, February 25, 2005, A1. As of March 1, 2006, the multinational force was made up of twenty-seven countries: Albania, Armenia, Australia, Azerbaijan, Bosnia-Herzegovina, Czech Republic, Denmark, El Salvador, Estonia, Georgia, Italy, Japan, Kazakhstan, Latvia, Lithuania, Macedonia, Moldova, Mongolia, Netherlands, Poland, Portugal, Romania, Slovakia, Republic of Korea, Ukraine, United Kingdom, and the United States; see www.mnf-iraq.com/coalitionpartners.htm. For the preparation of the military campaign against Iraq and the occupation itself, see Michael R. Gordon and General Bernard E. Trainor, *Cobra II: The Inside Story of the Invasion and Occupation of Iraq* (New York: Pantheon Books, 2006).

83. UN Security Council Resolution 1483 (2003) requested the secretary-general to appoint a Special Representative for Iraq, with the responsibilities of coordinating humanitarian and reconstruction assistance by UN agencies and between UN agencies and nongovernmental organizations. Sergio Vieira de Mello took his position on June 2. On August 14, 2003, the Security Council adopted Resolution 1500, establishing the United

Nations Assistance Mission for Iraq (UNAMI), designed to support the work of the secretary-general and the special representative.

84. Michael E. O'Hanlon and Adriana Lins de Albuquerque, *Iraq Index: Tracking Variables of Reconstruction and Security in Post-Saddam Iraq* (Washington, DC: Brookings Institution, October 4, 2004), 15, www.brookings.edu/iraqindex. For the sites of the September 2004 attacks on coalition forces, see Howard Fineman, Richard Wolffe, and Tamara Lipper, "90 Minutes Later, a New Race," *Newsweek,* October 11, 2004.

85. Michael E. O'Hanlon and Nina Kamp, *Iraq Index: Tracking Variables of Reconstruction and Security in Post-Saddam Iraq* (Washington, DC: Brookings Institution, March 2, 2006), 22, www.brookings.edu/fp/saban/iraq/index.pdf. The same document gives the following additional information (p. 18): Insurgent attacks in 2004, 26,496; in 2005, 34,131. Car bombs in 2004, 420; in 2005, 873. Suicide car bombs in 2004, 133; in 2005, 411. Roadside bombs in 2004 5,607; in 2005, 10,953.

86. Ibid., 12.

87. Dexter Filkins, "One by One, Iraqi Cities Become No-Go-Zones," *New York Times,* September 5, 2004.

88. For the sites of the September attacks on coalition forces, see Fineman, Wolffe, and Lipper, "90 Minutes Later, a New Race," 28.

89. O'Hanlon and Kamp, *Iraq Index*, 18.

90. Ibid., 19.

91. Michael E. O'Hanlon and Andrew Kamons, *Iraq Index: Tracking Variables of Reconstruction and Security in Post-Saddam Iraq* (Washington, DC: Brookings Institution, June 29, 2006), 18.

92. The United States had around 150,000 troops in Iraq; Britain, 12,000. Of the other countries helping, only Poland, Spain, Ukraine, and the Netherlands were contributing more than 1,000 troops each. The rest of the contingent was made up of a few hundred Danes and Italians, along with an assortment of Macedonians, Latvians, Nicaraguans, Azerbaijanis, and troops from other countries not known for the professionalism of their forces; see Peter Ford, "Stretched in Iraq, U.S. May Return to UN," *Christian Science Monitor,* July 18, 2003. In comparison, during Operation Desert Storm, eight nations deployed more than 10,000 troops.

93. By September 2004, it was estimated that the United States had 138,000 troops in Iraq; the United Kingdom, 8,300; South Korea, 3,600; Poland, 3,000; Italy, 2,800; Ukraine, 1,600; the Netherlands, 1,300, and all the others, fewer than 1,000 each; see O'Hanlon and Lins de Albuquerque, *Iraq Index*, 13–14; and Hanlon and Kamp, *Iraq Index*, 20–21.

94. Jonathan Weisman, "Iraq Cost Could Mount to $100 Billion," *Washington Post,* July 13, 2003. See also Marina S. Ottaway, "One Country, Two Plans," *Foreign Policy,* July/August 2003, 58.

95. Linda Bilmes and Joseph Stiglitz, *The Economic Costs of the Iraq War: An Appraisal Three Years after the Beginning of the Conflict.* NBER Working Paper Series, no. 12054 (Cambridge, MA: National Bureau of Economic Research, February 2006).

96. See O'Hanlon and Lins de Albuquerque, *Iraq Index*, 3.

97. O'Hanlon and Kamp, *Iraq Index*, 4.

98. "U.S. Death Toll in Iraq Hits 2,500," *BBC News,* June 15, 2006, http://news.bbc.co.uk/go/pr/fr/-/1/hi/world/americas/5084068.stm; and O'Hanlon and Kamons, *Iraq Index*, 4.

99. Between 3,211 and 4,757 Iraqi civilians were killed as a result of acts of war between May 2003 and the end of September 2004; O'Hanlon and Lins de Albuquerque, *Iraq Index*, 7. An October 2004 survey published in the British medical journal *The Lancet* gave very different figures: "Making conservative assumptions, we think that about 100,000 excess deaths, or more have happened since the 2003 invasion of Iraq. Violence accounted for most of the excess deaths and air strikes from coalition forces accounted for most violent deaths," Les Roberts, Riyadh Lafta, Richard Garfield, Jamal Khudhairi, and Gilbert Burnham, "Mortality Before and After the 2003 Invasion of Iraq: Cluster Sample Survey," *The Lancet*, no. 364 (November 20, 2004): 1857. On the survey itself, see the article "Counting the Casualties," *The Economist*, November 4, 2004. The high numbers were confirmed in June 2006 when the United Nations published for the first time combined statistics from the Iraqi Ministry of Health and Baghdad's main morgue. According to the monthly *Human Rights Report* of the UN Assistance Mission for Iraq for May 1–June 30, 2006, civilian deaths in Iraq had been steadily increasing since the previous year at least, and, in the first six months of 2006, the death toll had jumped from 1,778 in January to 3,149—a 77 percent increase. For June 2006, this meant that more than 100 civilians per day were killed.

100. The figure is mentioned in International Crisis Group, *Reconstructing Iraq* (Amman/Baghdad/Brussels: ICG, September 2, 2004), 2.

101. *Interim Strategy Note of the World Bank Group for Iraq* (Washington, DC: World Bank, January 14, 2004), 8.

102. See International Crisis Group, *Reconstructing Iraq*, 2. The ICG report also contains an interesting evaluation of the U.S. reconstruction strategy, or lack thereof, in Iraq.

103. Curt Tarnoff, *Iraq: Recent Developments in Reconstruction Assistance*. CRS Report to Congress (Washington, DC: Congressional Research Service, January 4, 2006); Carlos Pascual and Michael E. O'Hanlon, "Iraq: A Boost for Reconstruction," *Baltimore Sun*, July 2, 2006.

104. For these figures, see O'Hanlon and Lins de Albuquerque, *Iraq Index*, 21.

105. See as well ibid., 33. More positively, the members of the Paris Club, which includes France and Germany, agreed on November 21, 2004, to a reduction of 80 percent of the public external debt owed to them by Iraq. A bilateral agreement was signed between France and Iraq on December 21, 2005, implementing the 2004 agreement, amounting to a cancellation of $5.2 billion in debt.

106. European Community, *Reconstructing Iraq: State of Play and Implementation to Date*, November 2005, http://ec.europa.eu/comm/external_relations/iraq/doc/assist_2005.pdf.

107. European Commission, Iraq Assistance Program 2006/E/2006/470-C(2006)864, March 28, 2006, http://ec.europa.eu/comm/external_relations/iraq/doc/assist_2006.pdf.

108. European Community, *Reconstructing Iraq*, pp. 24–26.

109. Throughout 2004, France and Germany continued to be adamant against deploying their troops in Iraq, even within a NATO framework; see Jackie Calmes, "Chirac Reaffirms No Wider Role for NATO in Iraq; Bush, Blair Are Rebuffed in Spite of Their Victory a Day Earlier at the UN," *Wall Street Journal*, June 10, 2004; and Richard Bernstein and Mark Landler, "German Leader to Oppose Sending NATO Troops to Iraq," *New York Times*, May 21, 2004. The deterioration of the security situation in Iraq and throughout the region in 2005, and even more so in 2006, only reinforced the European leaders' opinions.

110. John Hamre, Frederick Barton, Bathsheba Crocker, Johanna Mendelson-Forman, and Robert C. Orr, *Iraq's Postconflict Reconstruction: A Field Review and Recommendations* (Washington, DC: Center for Strategic and International Studies, July 17, 2003), 3.

111. Graham Day and Christopher Freeman, "Policekeeping is the Key: Rebuilding the Internal Security Architecture of Postwar Iraq," *International Affairs* 79, no. 2 (March 2003): 299–313.

112. For an assessment of the difficulties encountered by the U.S. occupation in Iraq, see Anthony Shadid, *Night Draws Near: Iraq's People in the Shadow of America's War* (New York: Henry Holt, 2005).

113. See UN Security Council Resolution 1546 (2004).

114. For an overall assessment of U.S. involvement in Iraq, see Ricks, *Fiasco*.

115. For the Iraqi opinion on the occupation force, see O'Hanlon and Lins de Albuquerque, *Iraq Index*, 38. For world public opinion on the United States, see, for example, Pew Global Attitudes Project, *A Year after the Iraq War, Mistrust of America in Europe Ever Higher, Muslim Anger Persists: A Nine-Country Survey* (Washington, DC: Pew Research Center for the People and the Press, March 16, 2004).

116. G. John Ikenberry and Charles A. Kupchan have a nice way of summarizing the opinion of the Bush foreign policy team on legitimacy at the international level: "The Bush team believes that to be overly concerned with the opinion of other states is a dangerous sign of weakness. Simply put, legitimacy is for wimps," in "Liberal Realism: The Foundations of a Democratic Foreign Policy," *The National Interest*, Fall 2004.

117. www.9-11commission.gov/hearings/hearing12/staff_statement_15.pdf. See also *The 9/11 Commission Report: Final Report of the National Commission on Terrorist Attacks Upon the United States. Authorized Edition* (New York: W.W. Norton, 2004), especially chapters 11 and 12.

118. See Central Intelligence Agency, *Comprehensive Report of the Special Advisor to the Director of Central Intelligence on Iraq's Weapons of Mass Destruction* (Washington, DC, September 30, 2004), www.cia.gov/reports/iraq_wmd_2004/index.html.

119. See the January 25, 2002, memorandum from White House Counsel Alberto Gonzales to President Bush on the application of the Geneva Convention on prisoners of war to the conflict with al Qaeda and the Taliban. In the memorandum, Gonzales argues that the War on Terror "renders obsolete Geneva's strict limitations on questioning of enemy prisoners"; a copy of the memorandum can be found on the Web site of the Center for American Progress, www.americanprogress.org/site/pp.asp?c=biJRJ8OVF&b=246536. See also "Shameful Revelations Will Haunt Bush," *The Economist*, June 18, 2004; Center for Economic and Social Rights, *Beyond Torture: U.S. Violations of Occupation Law in Iraq* (Brooklyn, N.Y.: CESR, June 2004), www.cesr.org/beyondtorture.htm; Hersh, *Chain of Command*, chapter 1; and Karen J. Greenberg and Joshua L. Drate, eds., *The Torture Papers: The Road to Abu Ghraib* (New York: Cambridge University Press, 2005).

120. Christian Reus-Smit, *American Power and World Order* (Cambridge, MA: Polity Press, 2004), 55–67.

121. For a critical assessment of Bush's foreign policy, see Philippe Sands, *Lawless World: America and the Making and Breaking of Global Rules* (New York: Penguin Books, 2005).

122. See, in particular, a World Public Opinion.org poll, "What the Iraqi Public Wants," indicating that as of January 31, 2006, a majority of Iraqis, despite the hardship suffered from the U.S.-British invasion, believed that ousting Saddam Hussein was worth it: overall, 77 percent; Kurds, 91 percent; Shiites, 98 percent; and Sunnis, 13 percent

(p. 38). In the same poll, an overwhelming majority also favors the Iraqi government's endorsement of a timeline for U.S. withdrawal: overall, 87 percent; Kurds, 64 percent; Shiites, 90 percent; and Sunnis, 94 percent (p. 37). Also, to the question "What is your overall support for attacks?" the answers showing support are the following: attacks on United States–led forces, 47 percent support; attacks on Iraqi government security forces, 7 percent support; attacks on Iraqi civilians, 1 percent support (p. 39). See O'Hanlon and Kamp, *Iraq Index*.

123. Thomas M. Franck, "The Role of International Law and the United Nations After Iraq," American Society of International Law, Washington DC, April 2, 2004.

124. Francis Fukuyama, "The Neoconservative Moment," *The National Interest*, Summer 2004.

125. See Wikipedia, s.v. Iraqi legislative election, December 2005, http://en.wikipedia.org/wiki/Iraqi_legislative_election,_December_2005#United_Iraqi_Alliance_.28.23555.29, and relevant information on the Web site of the Independent Electoral Commission of Iraq, www.ieciraq.org.

126. Michael Slackman, "Chaos in Iraq Sends Shock Waves Across Middle East and Elevates Iran's Influence," *New York Times*, February 27, 2006. For more information about the tensions and the outbreak of violence on July 9, 2006, see International Crisis Group, *Iraq's Muqtada Al-Sadr: Spoiler or Stabiliser?* Middle East Report, no. 55 (Brussels: International Crisis Group, July 11, 2006).

CHAPTER 6

1. See United Nations, *Comprehensive Report on Lessons Learned from United Nations Assistance Mission for Rwanda (UNAMIR), October 1993–1996*, Lessons Learned Unit, Department of Peacekeeping Operations, 12/1996, www.un.org/Depts/dpko/dpko/lessons/rwanda.htm; idem, *Comprehensive Report on Lessons Learned from United Nations Operations in Somalia (UNOSOM), April 1992–March 1995*, Lessons Learned Unit, Department of Peacekeeping Operations, 3/1995, www.un.org/Depts/dpko/lessons/; idem, *Comprehensive Report on Lessons Learned from United Nations Transition Authority in Eastern Slavonia (UNTAES)*, Lessons Learned Unit, Department of Peacekeeping Operations, 7/1998, http://pbpu.unlb.org/pbpu/library/UNTAES.pdf; and idem, *Multidisciplinary Peacekeeping: Lessons from Recent Experience*, Department of Peacekeeping Operations, www.un.org/Depts/dpko/lessons/handbuk/htm.

2. United Nations, *Report of the Independent Inquiry into the Actions of the United Nations during the 1994 Genocide in Rwanda, December 15, 1999*; and idem, *Report of the Secretary-General Pursuant to General Assembly Resolution 53/35* (1999). For interesting insights on Kofi Annan's attitude vis-à-vis these reports, see James Traub, *The Best Intentions: Kofi Annan and the UN in the Era of American World Power* (New York: Farrar, Straus, and Giroux, 2006), 111–15.

3. See United Nations, *Report of the Panel on United Nations Peace Operations*.

4. One of the boldest recommendations of the Brahimi Report stated that the Security Council should not formally adopt resolutions related to peace operations until there is assurance that member states will provide the appropriate means to implement them: "(b) The Security Council should leave in draft form resolutions authorizing missions with sizeable troop levels until such time as the Secretary-General has firm commitments of troops and other critical mission support elements, including peacebuilding

elements, from Member States," ibid., Annex III, Summary of Recommendations, para. 4, p. 54.

5. See David Harland, "The Brahimi Report: Challenges to Implementation" (remarks at the International Peace Academy seminar on "Cooperation in Peace Operations: The United Nations and Europe," Vienna, July 4, 2003).

6. See United Nations, *Report of the Secretary-General on the Implementation of the Report of the Panel on United Nations Peace Operations*, UN Doc. A/55/502 (October 20, 2000); idem, *Resource Requirements for Implementation of the Report of the Panel on United Nations Peace Operations: Report of the Secretary-General*, UN Doc. A/55/507 (October 27, 2000); idem, *Resource Requirements for Implementation of the Report of the Panel on United Nations Peace Operations: Report of the Secretary-General, Addendum*, UN Doc. A/55/507/add.1 (October 27, 2000).

7. See Harland, "The Brahimi Report."

8. For the politics of apology in general, see Jean-Marc Coicaud and Jibecke Jönsson, "Elements of a Road Map for the Politics of Apology," in *The Age of Apology: The West Confronts Its Past*, ed. Mark Gibney, Rhoda Howard-Hassmann, Jean-Marc Coicaud, and Niklaus Steiner (Philadelphia: University of Pennsylvania Press, 2007).

9. For a good summary of the variants of realism in international relations theory, see Chris Brown, *Understanding International Relations*, 2d ed. (New York: Palgrave, 2001), 44–48.

10. The internationalism of the 1990s did not especially indulge the most radical of them, the cosmopolitans and the three views that they advanced: *individualism* (with human beings viewed as the ultimate units of concern), *universality* (with the status of "ultimate unit of concern" attached equally to every human being), and *generality* (with human beings as ultimate units of concern for everyone, and not only for their compatriots, fellow religionists, or so forth); see Thomas W. Pogge, "Cosmopolitanism and Sovereignty," *Ethics* 103, no. 1 (October 1992): 48–75. On cosmopolitanism and critical theory writers, see also Brown, *Understanding International Relations*, 59–60.

11. This also meant that the power and influence that countries enjoyed internationally continued to derive from their home base. The stronger this home base was and the more it loomed internationally, the more weight a country had at the global level. The influence of powerful countries (most of the time "calling the shots") on international organizations served as a good illustration of this reality.

12. See "Pays-Bas: Le gouvernement chute sur Srebrenica. Kok a admis la coresponsibilité de son pays dans le massacre," *Libération*, April 17, 2002, 14.

13. Although U.S. power was unparalleled in the 1990s, justifying as a result the use of the term *unipolarity* to describe the new international landscape, it is probably more accurate to speak of *quasi-unipolarity*. Other major poles of power continued to exist and even grew stronger in the aftermath of the Cold War—the European Union and China in particular. Samuel P. Huntington suggests the coinage *uni-multipolar* to describe this state of affairs, in "The Lonely Superpower," *Foreign Affairs*, March/April 1999. See also Coral Bell, "American Ascendancy—and the Pretense of Concert," *The National Interest*, Fall 1999.

14. In December 2004, the U.S. Congress mandated the establishment of a bipartisan Task Force on the United Nations within the United States Institute of Peace. The task force was to report to Congress within six months of its establishment with conclusions and recommendations on how to make the United Nations more effective from the perspective of American interests and international responsibilities. See *American Interests and*

UN Reform: Report of the Task Force on the United Nations (Washington, DC: United States Peace Institute of Peace, 2005); and *The Imperative for Action: An Update of the Report of the Task Force on American Interests and UN Reform* (Washington, DC: United States Institute of Peace, 2005).

15. For figures from the respective fiscal years, see: www.gpoaccess.gov/usbudget/fy03/pdf/bud12.pdf; www.gpoaccess.gov/usbudget/fy04/pdf/budget/defense.pdf; www.white house.gov/omb/budget/fy2005/defense.html; http://origin.www.gpoaccess.gov/usbudget/fy06/browse.html; and http://origin.www.gpoaccess.gov/usbudget/fy07/browse.html.

16. For figures from the respective fiscal years, see www.fas.org/asmp/profiles/aid/fy2001_pko.htm; www.fas.org/asmp/profiles/aid/fy2002-intro.pdf; www.state.gov/documents/organization/17237.pdf; and www.fas.org/asmp/profiles/aid/aidindex.htm; www.state.gov/s/d/rm/rls/iab/2007/html/60200.htm.

17. Stephen Holmes and Cass R. Sunstein, *The Cost of Rights: Why Liberty Depends on Taxes* (New York: W.W. Norton, 2000).

18. See Tamanaha, *On the Rule of Law*.

19. The "functionalist" approach to international organizations' management of intra- and international conflict emphasizes the welfare state's policy expertise and technical solutions to the creation and distribution of public goods. In his classic summary of functionalism in the creation and evolution of the repertoire of problem-solving skills in international organizations, Inis Claude observes that functionalism "represents the application of the welfare state philosophy to the international sphere, emphasizing the responsibility of international agencies for rendering services rather than merely enforcing controls, and for extending their concern into areas hitherto falling within the private entrepreneurial domain of the national state" (p. 387); see Inis L. Claude, Jr., *Swords Into Plowshares: The Problems and Progress of International Organization,* 4th ed. (New York: McGraw-Hill, 1984), chapter 17. See also the comparison of David Mitrany's functionalist approach (most notably in his *A Working Peace System*) and those of Ernst B. Haas and James P. Sewell in Robert E. Riggs and I. Jostein Mykletun, *Beyond Functionalism: Attitudes toward International Organization in Norway and the United States* (Minneapolis: University of Minnesota Press, 1979).

20. See the recommendations of Jürgen Habermas on the establishment of a "world domestic policy" in his *The Postnational Constellation: Political Essays,* trans. Max Pensky (Cambridge, MA: MIT Press, 2001). Habermas argues that "a prospect for a world domestic policy without a world government [is possible]—provided that two problems can be clarified. The first problem is more fundamental; the second is empirical. (a) How can we envision the democratic legitimation of decisions beyond the schema of the nation-state? And (b), what are the conditions for a transformed self-understanding of global actors in which states and supranational regimes begin to see themselves as members of a community, who have no choice but to consider one another's interests mutually, and to perceive general interests?" (p. 110). See also Delmas-Marty, *Les Forces Imaginantes du Droit (II)*, 167 ; and Martti Koskenniemi, "Global Governance and Public International Law," February 9, 2004, www.helsinki.fi/eci/Publications/MFrankfurt.pdf.

21. See Inge Kaul, Isabelle Grunberg, and Marc A. Stern, eds., *Global Public Goods: International Cooperation in the 21st Century* (New York: Oxford University Press, 1999); Inge Kaul, Pedro Conceição, Kattel Le Goulven, and Ronald U. Mendoza, eds., *Providing Global Public Goods: Managing Globalization* (New York: Oxford University Press, 2003); and Inge Kaul and Pedro Conceição, eds., *The New Public Finance: Responding to Global Challenges* (New York: Oxford University Press, 2006). See also Thomas M. Franck,

Fairness in International Law and Institutions (New York: Oxford University Press, 1998); and Thomas Pogge, *World Poverty and Human Rights: Cosmopolitan Responsibilities and Reforms* (Cambridge, MA: Polity Press, 2002). On "human security," see, for example, the special issue of *Security Dialogue* 35, no. 3 (September 2004); and Andrew Mack, *The Human Security Report 2005: War and Peace in the 21st Century* (New York: Oxford University Press, 2006).

22. Robert O. Keohane, *The Contingent Legitimacy of Multilateralism.* GARNET Working Paper, no. 09/06 (September 2006), www.garnet-eu.org/fileadmin/documents/working_papers/0906.pdf. On a broader level, see the reforms of international institutions that Joseph E. Stiglitz advocates in *Making Globalization Work* (New York: W. W. Norton, 2006).

23. Keohane, *The Contingent Legitimacy of Multilateralism, 22.*

24. Ibid., 17.

25. See also the idea of a "Concert of Democracies" alluded to in the final report of the Princeton Project on National Security, in G. John Ikenberry and Anne-Marie Slaughter, *Forging a World of Liberty under the Law: U.S. National Security in the 21st Century* (Princeton, NJ: Woodrow Wilson School of Public and International Affairs, Princeton University, September 27, 2006).

26. For more on this, see Jean-Marc Coicaud, "Quest for International Solidarity: Benefits of Justice versus the Trappings of Paranoia," in *Globalization and Environmental Challenges: Reconceptualizing Security in the 21st Century,* ed. Hans Günter Brauch et al. (New York: Springer-Verlag, 2007).

27. Pierre Hassner, "La Revanche des Passions," *Commentaire,* Summer 2005.

28. On "tranquility of spirit" in the perspective of "secured security" by acknowledging the rights of all, see Montesquieu, *The Spirit of the Laws,* trans. Anne M. Cohler, Basia C. Miller, and Harold Stone (New York: Cambridge University Press, 1989), 157.

29. Jean Jacques Rousseau, *The Social Contract, or Principles of Political Right,* trans. Maurice Cranston (New York: Penguin Books, 1968), Book I, chapter 3.

30. See, for example, Ruth W. Grant and Robert O. Keohane, "Accountability and Abuses of Power in World Politics," *American Political Science Review* 99, no. 1 (February 2005).

31. Moreover, it is a proactive dimension that has the potential of being more or less permanent, because the pervasive nature of terrorism (the danger that it is meant to counter) calls for vigilance and being ready to intervene on a constant basis.

32. See Allen Buchanan, *Justice, Legitimacy, and Self-Determination: Moral Foundations for International Law* (New York: Oxford University Press, 2004), 321.

33. See also the five basic criteria of legitimacy for the use of force in general (either for reasons based on national interest or on our common humanity) identified by Gareth Evans, in "When is it Right to Fight?" *Survival* 46, no. 3 (Autumn 2004): 75: seriousness of threat; proper purpose; last resort; proportional means; balance of consequences. See also United Nations, *A More Secure World: Our Shared Responsibility.* Report of the High-Level Panel on Threats, Challenges, and Change (New York: United Nations, December 2004), 65–67, paras. 199–209. The 2005 World Summit Outcome, UN Doc. A/RES/60/1 (October 24, 2005) recognizes, under the notion of "the responsibility of protect" (also in *A More Secure World,* p. 66, para. 203), the need for the international community to be more active in preventing genocide. This entails the possibility of taking collective action in accordance with the UN Charter, including Chapter VII (p. 30, paras. 138 and 139). The recognition of the responsibility to protect is a progressive interpretation of the need to prevent genocide mentioned in the Genocide Convention. As such, it can be viewed as normative and political progress. But it is in no way a guarantee that the next time genocide occurs, the international community will take action to stop it.

34. See United Nations, *Report of the Panel on United Nations Peace Operations*; idem, *Implementation of the Report of the Panel on United Nations Peace Operations*; idem., *Report of the Advisory Committee on Administrative and Budgetary Questions*, UN Doc. A/55/676 (December 8, 2000); and idem., Remarks of Jean-Marie Guéhenno, Under Secretary-General for Peacekeeping Operations, to the Fourth Committee of the General Assembly, October 25, 2004.

35. William J. Durch and Victoria K. Holt, *The Brahimi Report and the Future of UN Peace Operations* (Washington, DC: Henry L. Stimson Center, March 9, 2004), table 4, part 1, www.stimson.org/fopo.

36. See United Nations, Remarks of Jean-Marie Guéhenno (2004).

37. United Nations, Remarks of Jean-Marie Guéhenno, Under Secretary-General for Peacekeeping Operations, to the Fourth Committee of the General Assembly, October 20, 2005.

38. Remarks of Jean-Marie Guéhenno (2004).

39. Ibid.

40. Ibid.

41. Ibid.

42. United Nations, Remarks of Jean-Marie Guéhenno, Under Secretary-General for Peacekeeping Operations, to the Fourth Committee of the General Assembly, October 19, 2006.

43. For these figures, see the UN Web site page on "Who Works at the United Nations?" chapter 6 of "Questions and Answers, Images and Reality," www.un.org/geninfo/ir/index.asp?id=160.

44. In 2005, the regular budget of the UN Secretariat was some $1.9 billion for UN activities, staff, and basic infrastructure, excluding peacekeeping operations, which have a separate budget. According to 2005 estimates, the UN system spends some $15 billion a year, taking into account the United Nations, UN peacekeeping operations, the programs and funds, and the specialized agencies, but excluding the World Bank, the International Monetary Fund (IMF), and the International Fund for Agricultural Development (IFAD). Just over half of this amount comes from voluntary contributions from the member states; the rest is from mandatory assessments on those states. The United Nations and its agencies, funds, and programs—mainly, the UN Development Program, the World Food Program, the UN Children's Fund, and the UN Population Fund—spent some $10 billion a year on operational activities for development, mostly for economic, social, and humanitarian programs to help the world's poorest countries. In addition, the World Bank, the IMF, and IFAD provide billions more dollars annually in loans that help to eradicate poverty, foster development, and stabilize the world economy. To gain perspective on UN expenditures, these numbers can be compared with the equivalent spending of governments and other bodies. The administrative budget of the European Community for 2004 amounts to €5.73 billion (approximately $7.3 billion); the annual budget of the New York City of Board of Education (excluding pensions and debt-servicing costs) amounts to some $12.4 billion. The World Health Organization, which has reduced or eliminated the incidence of a number of diseases worldwide, has an annual budget of $440 million—less than the cost of a luxury liner (more than $450 million for Holland America Line's *Grand Princess*) or the new baseball stadium to be built in Washington, DC

Metropolitan Tokyo's Fire Department has an annual budget of 237.5 billion yen (approximately $2.2 billion). Time Warner, the media conglomerate, spent nearly $3.3 billion on advertising in 2004. Bonuses paid out on Wall Street for 2005 rose to a high of $21.5 billion. Also, world military expenditures—some $1 trillion plus per year—would pay for the entire UN system for more than sixty-seven years. For these figures, see "Is the United Nations Good Value for the Money?" in the UN Web site page on "Questions and Answers, Images and Reality," chapter 5, www.un.org/geninfo/ir/index.asp?id=150.

45. For more on these issues, see Coicaud, "International Organizations as a Profession."

46. The latest effort of UN human resources reform is spelled out in United Nations, *Investing in the United Nations: For a Stronger Organization Worldwide. Report of the Secretary-General*, UN Doc. A/60/692 (March 7, 2006).

47. On the UN Peacebuilding Commission, see UN General Assembly Resolution 60/180, UN Doc. A/RES/60/180 (December 30, 2005).

48. EUMS operations include Operation CONCORDIA, with 350 soldiers deployed in the Former Yugoslav Republic of Macedonia in 2003; Operation ARTEMIS (autonomously led by the European Union), with 1,800 soldiers in the Democratic Republic of Congo in 2003; and Operation ALTHEA, with 7,000 soldiers in Bosnia-Herzegovina in 2004. For more information about the European Security and Defence Policy, see www.consilium.europa.eu/cms3_fo/showPage.asp?id=261&lang=EN&mode=g.

49. On Europe and the European Union, multilateralism, and the United Nations, see *The Enlarging European Union at the United Nations: Making Multilateralism Matter* (Luxembourg: Office for Official Publications of the European Communities, 2004); Espen Barth Eide, ed., *Global Europe. Report 1: "Effective Multilateralism": Europe, Regional Security, and a Revitalized UN* (London: Foreign Policy Centre, 2004); and Joachim Krause, "Multilateralism: Behind European Views," *The Washington Quarterly*, Spring 2004.

50. For interesting insights on Chinese foreign policy today, see James Traub, "The World According to China," *New York Times*, September 3, 2006.

51. See Colum Lynch, "China Filling Void Left by West in UN Peacekeeping," *Washington Post*, November 24, 2006. See also "Chinese Foreign Policy: A Quintet, Anyone?" *The Economist*, January 11, 2007.

52. For more on NGOs and the United Nations, see Jean-Marc Coicaud, "INGOs as Collective Mobilization of Transnational Solidarity: Implications for Human Rights Work at the United Nations," in *Ethics in Action: The Ethical Challenges of International Human Rights Nongovernmental Organizations*, ed. Daniel A. Bell and Jean-Marc Coicaud (New York: Cambridge University Press, 2007).

53. Building alliances among nations of secondary importance can change this state of affairs and give them noteworthy international power. This is what happened in the 1960s and 1970s when developing countries formed coalitions within the United Nations, leading the United States largely to desert the world organization until the late 1980s.

54. On the link between substance and procedure in democratic values, see Charles Taylor, "Le Juste et le Bien," trans. P. Constantineau, *Revue de Métaphysique et de Morale* 1 (January–March 1988).

55. For more on this, see, for example, the preface (particularly the second section) to the Japanese edition of Jean-Marc Coicaud, *Legitimacy and Politics: A Contribution to the Study of Political Right and Political Responsibility* (Tokyo: Fujiwara Shoten, 2000).

56. At the time of writing, it remains difficult to draw any definitive conclusions about the consequences of the Iraqi War in the Middle East. Also, it remains to be seen what parallels can be drawn between the influence that Reagan might have had on the unification and, hence, democratization of Europe and the influence of the George W. Bush administration in the Middle East.

57. See, for example, Charles A. Kupchan and G. John Ikenberry, "Liberal Realism: The Foundations of a Democratic Foreign Policy," *The National Interest,* Fall 2004; Robert Wright, "An American Foreign Policy that Both Realists and Idealists Should Fall in Love With," *New York Times,* July 16, 2006; and Joseph Nye, "Progressive Realism," *The Bangkok Post,* August 25, 2006. See also G. John Ikenberry, *After Victory: Institutions, Strategic Restraint, and the Rebuilding of Order after Major Wars* (Princeton, NJ: Princeton University Press, 2001).

58. Wright, "An American Foreign Policy."

59. Ibid.

AFTERWORD

1. See *UN News,* December 20, 2006.

2. For an analysis of the Darfur crisis, see, for example, Alex de Waal, ed., *War in Darfur and the Search for Peace* (Cambridge, MA: Harvard University Press, 2007).

3. This analysis is based on the insights of Isabelle Balot, whom I thank for sharing her knowledge on Darfur with me.

4. Nicholas D. Kristof, "When Genocide Worsens," *New York Times,* July 9, 2006.

5. Ibid.

6. The Peacebuilding Commission is meant to marshal resources at the disposal of the international community to advise and propose integrated strategies for postconflict recovery, focusing attention on reconstruction, institution building, and sustainable development in countries emerging from conflict. The commission will bring together the United Nations' broad capacities and experience in conflict prevention, mediation, peacekeeping, respect for human rights, the rule of law, humanitarian assistance, reconstruction, and long-term development. Specifically, the commission will propose integrated strategies for postconflict peacebuilding and recovery; help to ensure predictable financing for early recovery activities and sustained financial investment over the medium to longer term; extend the period of attention by the international community to postconflict recovery; and develop best practices on issues that require extensive collaboration among political, military, humanitarian, and development actors. See the UN Web page on the commission: www.un.org/peace/peacebuilding.

7. Robert Castel, *From Manual Workers to Wage Laborers: Transformation of the Social Question,* trans. Richard Boyd (Somerset, NJ: Transaction Publishers, 2002).

8. Zygmunt Bauman, *Wasted Lives: Modernity and Its Outcasts* (Cambridge, MA: Polity Press, 2005), for example, 51–53.

Index

H

Haass, Richard
  Bush administration's "à la carte" multilateralism, 149
Habyarimana, Juvénal, President (Rwanda), 49, 50
Haiti. *See also* MINUSTAH peacekeeping mission; United Nations Civilian Police
    Mission in Haiti
  cost of U.S. intervention in, 17
  mixed impact of peace operations, 26–27, 216 n60
  Operation Uphold Democracy, 20, 213 n28
  UN sanctions against, 20
  U.S.-led Multinational Force success, 26
Hammarskjöld, Secretary-General Dag
  preventive diplomacy and, 19
Human resources committed to peace operations, 17–18
Humanitarian aid. *See* International humanitarian interventions
Hun Sen
  role in Cambodia, 28–29
Hungary
  support for the Iraq war, 159
Hutu people. *See* Rwanda

I

ICC. *See* International Criminal Court
IFOR. *See* Implementation Force
Ikenberry, G. John
  legitimacy at the international level, 255 n116
Implementation Force
  cost of IFOR activities in Bosnia, 17, 212 n15
  number of troops committed to, 18
  use of force and, 20
India/Pakistan
  interpositional peacekeeping mission, 15
Indonesia
  East Timor's independence and, 28, 217 n67
INTERFET. *See* International Force for East Timor
International Covenant on Civil and Political Rights
  Western powers' support for, 88
International Covenant on Economic, Social, and Cultural Rights
  Soviet Bloc and developing countries' support for, 88
International Criminal Court
  Bush administration rejection of, 142
  United States' reservations about, 84
International Criminal Tribunal for the Former Yugoslavia
  indictment of Serbian war criminals, 20, 29
  track record of, 219 n79

About the Author

Jean-Marc Coicaud heads the United Nations University (UNU) Office at the United Nations in New York, prior to which he was senior academic officer in the UNU Peace and Governance Program at the university's headquarters in Tokyo. He also served in the executive office of UN secretary-general Boutros Boutros-Ghali as a member of the speechwriting team. A former fellow in Harvard University's Department of Philosophy, the Center for International Affairs, and Harvard Law School; the United States Institute of Peace in Washington, D.C.; and New York University's School of Law, Coicaud has held appointments with the French Ministry of Foreign Affairs, the European Parliament (Financial Committee), the University of Paris-I Sorbonne, and the École Normale Supérieure in Paris. His previous published works include *Power in Transition: The Peaceful Change of International Order,* coauthored with Charles A. Kupchan, Emanuel Adler, and Yuen Foong Khong (United Nations University Press, 2001); *Legitimacy and Politics: A Contribution to the Study of Political Right and Political Responsibility* (Cambridge University Press, 2002); and *Ethics in Action: The Ethical Challenges of International Human Rights Nongovernmental Organizations,* coedited with Daniel A. Bell (Cambridge University Press, 2007). He was educated at the Sorbonne, the Institut d'Études Politiques (Paris), and Harvard University. He holds doctoral degrees in political science/ law and philosophy.

JENNINGS RANDOLPH PROGRAM
FOR INTERNATIONAL PEACE

This book is a fine example of the work produced by senior fellows in the Jennings Randolph fellowship program of the United States Institute of Peace. As part of the statute establishing the Institute, Congress envisioned a program that would appoint "scholars and leaders of peace from the United States and abroad to pursue scholarly inquiry and other appropriate forms of communication on international peace and conflict resolution." The program was named after Senator Jennings Randolph of West Virginia, whose efforts over four decades helped to establish the Institute.

Since 1987, the Jennings Randolph Program has played a key role in the Institute's effort to build a national center of research, dialogue, and education on critical problems of conflict and peace. Nearly 200 senior fellows from some thirty nations have carried out projects on the sources and nature of violent international conflict and the ways such conflict can be peacefully managed or resolved. Fellows come from a wide variety of academic and other professional backgrounds. They conduct research at the Institute and participate in the Institute's outreach activities to policy makers, the academic community, and the American public.

Each year approximately fifteen senior fellows are in residence at the Institute. Fellowship recipients are selected by the Institute's board of directors in a competitive process. For further information on the program, or to receive an application form, please contact the program staff at (202) 457-1700, or visit our Web site at www.usip.org.

Steven Heydemann, Ph.D.
Associate Vice President

ABOUT THE INSTITUTE

The United States Institute of Peace is an independent, nonpartisan, national institution established and funded by Congress. Its goals are to help prevent and resolve violent conflicts, promote post-conflict stability and development, and increase peacebuilding capacity, tools, and intellectual capital worldwide. The Institute does this by empowering others with knowledge, skills, and resources, as well as by directly engaging in peacebuilding efforts around the globe.

Chairman of the Board: J. Robinson West

Vice Chairman: María Otero

President: Richard H. Solomon

Executive Vice President: Patricia Powers Thomson

Vice President: Charles E. Nelson

Board of Directors

J. Robinson West (Chair), Chairman, PFC Energy, Washington, D.C.
María Otero (Vice Chairman), President, ACCION International, Boston, Mass.
Holly J. Burkhalter, Vice President, Government Affairs, International Justice Mission, Washington, D.C.
Anne H. Cahn, Former Scholar in Residence, American University, Washington, D.C.
Chester A. Crocker, James R. Schlesinger Professor of Strategic Studies, School of Foreign Service, Georgetown University, Washington, D.C.
Laurie S. Fulton, Partner, Williams and Connolly, Washington, D.C.
Charles Horner, Senior Fellow, Hudson Institute, Washington, D.C.
Kathleen Martinez, Executive Director, World Institute on Disability, Oakland, CA
George E. Moose, Adjunct Professor of Practice, The George Washington University, Washington, D.C.
Jeremy A. Rabkin, Professor of Law, George Mason University, Fairfax, Va.
Ron Silver, Actor, Producer, Director, Primparous Productions, Inc., New York, NY
Judy Van Rest, Executive Vice President, International Republican Institute, Washington, D.C.

Members ex officio

Robert M. Gates, Secretary of Defense
Condoleezza Rice, Secretary of State
Richard H. Solomon, President, United States Institute of Peace (nonvoting)
Frances C. Wilson, Lieutenant General, U.S. Marine Corps; President, National Defense University

BEYOND THE NATIONAL INTEREST:
THE FUTURE OF UN PEACEKEEPING AND
MULTILATERALISM IN AN ERA OF U.S. PRIMACY

This book was set in the typeface Adobe Garamond Pro; the display type is Trajan Bold. Cover design by Hasten Design Studio, Washington, D.C. Interior design, page makeup, copyediting, and proofreading by EEI Communications, Inc., Alexandria, Virginia. Production supervised by Marie Marr Jackson. Peter Pavilionis was the book's editor.